MY SISTER,
MY BROTHER

MY SISTER, MY BROTHER

Womanist and XODUS God-Talk

Karen Baker-Fletcher
Garth KASIMU Baker-Fletcher

Wipf and Stock Publishers
EUGENE, OREGON

Wipf and Stock Publishers
199 West 8th Avenue, Suite 3
Eugene, Oregon 97401

My Sister, My Brother
Womanist and Xodus God-Talk
By Baker-Fletcher, Karen
©1997 Baker-Fletcher, Karen
ISBN: 1-57910-999-3
Publication date: June, 2002
Previously published by Orbis Books, 1997.

Dedicated to the ones on whose shoulders we stand:
Henry and Ella Mitchell
and to our youngest child of three:
Desiree Aisha Dawn Baker-Fletcher

Contents

Acknowledgments xi

Introduction 1
   The Womanist Context   3
   The XODUS Context   7
   Methodology   15

Part I
G O D

1. **God as Spirit: Womanist Perspectives on God** 25
   God as Strength of Life   29
   God as Empowering Spirit   30
   To Image the Unseen   35
   God as Unnameable in Womanist Literature   37
   Loving the Spirit   38

2. **GOD on the Streetz:**
   XODUS Intuitions of the Divine 43
   GOD Is Love   51
   GOD on the Streetz and in Rap   54
   XODUS Moral Philosophy   56
   GOD as ONE and Also OTHER   61
   GOD Is ABLE   61

3. **Dialogue on GOD** 64

Part II
C H R I S T

4. **Immanuel: Womanist Reflections on Jesus**
   as Dust and Spirit 73
   Womanism and the Prc 🔺 *n of Atonement Theory*   75
   Crucifixion and Resurrection Reenvisioned   77

Jesus and the Least of These   81
A Creation-Centered Christology   85
Creation as the Least of These   88
Jesus as the Greatest of the Ancestors   89
Immanuel: God Feeling with Us   91

5. **The Scandal of GOD with a Body:**
   XODUS Perspectives on Jesus **94**
   Creation-Centered Christology in XODUS   99
   XODUS Cross   104
   Jesus the Rider on a White Horse   106

6. **Dialogue on CHRIST** **110**

Part III
HUMANITY

7. **Only "Human" Nature: XODUS Anthropology** **119**
   Construction: "Twenty Million Black People in Prison"   121
   Criminalization   126
   Awakening   128
   Liberation   131
   Resistance as Liberation   138

8. **Womanhood: It's a Way of Being Human** **143**
   Womanist Powers (Virtues)   148
   Gifts of Power for Survival and Wholeness
   *   in Black Women's Narratives*   150
   Reflections   159

9. **Dialogue on HUMANITY** **164**

Part IV
GENERATIONS

10. **Unto All Generations: Mothers, Other Mothers,**
    and Honoring the Ancestors **173**
    Biological Motherhood   173
    Other Mothers (and Fathers)   176
    Generational Activity and the Womb of Life   178
    Remembering Who We Are and Whose We Are   180
    Ancestry   186
    Honorable Choices and Rainbows   189

11. **Unto the Fathers' Fathers: XODUS Generations** 192
   BABA-Hood   195
   BABA-HOOD and Black Churches   199
   BABA Values in XODUS   203
   Virtue and Character   205
   For the Fathers and the Generations   211

12. **Dialogue on GENERATIONS** 216

Part V
CHURCH

13. **SPIRIT-Church: Justice-Making Virtuous Energy
    in XODUS Community** 225
   Prayer, Praise, and Powerlessness   227
   SPIRIT   229
   The Liberating SPIRIT's Ole Ship of ZION   231
   GOD's Colony and FAMILY on Earth   233
   The "MARKS"   236

14. **"Having Church": A Womanist Perspective** 243
   Denominational Churches: Liberating or Oppressive?   247
   The Generations and the Church   251
   Church as the Living Body of Christ   252

15. **Dialogue on CHURCH** 258

Part VI
LAST THINGS

16. **Future Now!: XODUS Eschatology** 269
   Reversals   274
   XODUS Basepoints for Eschatological Transformation   277

17. **Dust to Dust, Spirit to Spirit:
    A Womanist Eschatology** 283
   Heaven and Earth   284
   Living into Eternity   288
   The Fullness of Time, the End of Time   291
   Dust to Dust, Spirit to Spirit   292

18. **The "Shout"** 299

Index 301

Acknowledgments

To write a book is never an individual achievement but is ever the accomplishment of a group of supportive contributors. We would like to give honor to those professors who had so much to do with the formation of our theological and ethical imaginations at Harvard Divinity School, particularly our mentor and friend Preston Williams, Houghton Professor of Theology and Contemporary Change; Harvey Cox, Victor S. Thomas Professor of Divinity; Richard R. Niebuhr, Hollis Professor of Divinity; Gordon Kaufman, Mallinckrodt Jr. Professor of Divinity Emeritus; and Margaret Miles, Professor of Historical Theology and now Dean of Graduate Theological Union, Berkeley, California. We appreciate the ongoing interest in our work shown by James Cone, Charles A. Briggs Professor of Systematic Theology at Union Seminary, New York, and Peter Paris, Elmer G. Homrighausen Professor of Social Ethics at Princeton Theological Seminary. Thanks to our colleagues at Claremont School of Theology, particularly Dean Marjorie Suchocki, David Griffin, Dan Rhoades, Karen Jo Torjesen, John Cobb, Jr., and Cornish Rogers. Cornish was instrumental in helping Kasimu travel to South Africa in the summer of 1995 for a study tour, particularly in eliciting grant monies from the Board of Global Ministries of the United Methodist Church. Bonita Ramsey, Director of the Office for Black Student Affairs at Claremont, as well as Sidney Lemelle and Agnes Jackson create an atmosphere of rigorous Black discourse at the Claremont Graduate School and Colleges.

The women faculty at Claremont invited Karen to speak with Rosemary Radford Ruether on ecowomanism and ecofeminism for the Bennet-Morton Lectures of April 1995. Many thanks for that opportunity to initiate a systematic discussion on womanist theology and environmental justice. The Pomona Valley Chapter of Delta Sigma Theta Sorority, Inc., is an organization of brilliant, resourceful women who are supportive and inspiring.

Most importantly, we are grateful for those numerous spiritual experiences we have relied on from our church backgrounds. We gladly cite saints from around the nation, including Barnes United Methodist

Church and Faith United Christian (D.O.C.) of Indianapolis, Indiana; Antioch Baptist Church of Cleveland, Ohio; Massachusetts Avenue Baptist Church and St. Paul A.M.E. in Cambridge, Massachusetts; South Hills Presbyterian and Primm A.M.E. in Pomona, California; First New Christian Fellowship Baptist of South Los Angeles and Grace U.M.C. in Pasadena. All these followers of Jesus Christ have struggled with us as we have sought to name and define our faith as living, relevant, and meaningful.

Students of Karen's Womanist Theology and Ethics course at CST, Spring 1996; Bessie Collins, who proofread the text and engaged in critical conversation; Reverends Kerry Allison, Sylvester Warsaw, Norman Johnson (Pastor of First New Christian Fellowship Baptist Church of South Los Angeles), Gail Davis Culp (Associate Pastor of Holy Trinity A.M.E. Long Beach, California), Ricky Porter (Pastor of South Hills Presbyterian, Pomona, California), Marvin McMickle (Pastor of Antioch Baptist Church, Cleveland, Ohio) — all have been partners in the construction of our theo-ethics.

Our colleagues and friends continue to inspire our journey. These include Katie Cannon, Emilie Townes, Cheryl Kirk-Duggan, C. S'thembile West, Dwight Hopkins, Theodore Walker, Jr., Victor Anderson, Lee Butler, Anthony Pinn, Cornel West, and Michael Eric Dyson.

Alexis Dotson and Wanda Howard were "Auntie" and "Big Sister" to our children during the writing of this book. They also provided some recreational walks and refreshing conversations about issues in the community. With great sadness we lost Wanda to the mountains that she loved so much in October 1996. Her earthy spirit and fierce love of freedom contributed much.

To our children, Kristen Adwin Joelle, Kenneth Ikenna Taylor, and Desiree Aisha Dawn, we thank GOD every day for you because your very existence is a reminder of true love.

Finally, we would like to thank Erica Foreman, godmother of Desiree, for helping us organize our lives! She and her husband, Kenneth, children, Kenny and Britnee, are family away from home, without whom this book could not have been written.

Introduction

THIS BOOK is an affirmation of mutual respect and uplift between an African American woman and an African American man. In tones strong and urgent it declares a positive message in the midst of our social devaluation. Yet how can we as Black women and men affirm our love in a land which presses us down and spits us out? We need to look at the issues which sometimes render our love ineffectual and mute. What are these issues in the Black community today? The media gives us one set of representations. If we relied upon the media, we would be led to believe that every Black man in America is an admitted wife-beater and potential Bigger Thomas. The power of these negative portrayals was most recently iconized in the frenzy over the O. J. Simpson murder trial. The fallout after he was acquitted demonstrated that putting a Black face on domestic abuse is considered newsworthy. Media images of Black women are mixed but equally problematic: Black women are always suspect even when in high political office as evidenced in rumors of Joycelyn Elder's support of the legalization of narcotics and her motherhood of a son convicted of drug possession. Lani Guinier, respected law professor and legal scholar, was not even allowed the professional courtesy of defending her controversial views on the reallocation of voting rights by the "moderate" Democratic president who had nominated her for attorney general. And the entire nation fixed its fascinated attention on the Clarence Thomas/Anita Hill hearings.

In the midst of media-driven controversies, particularly regarding cases like the Thomas/Hill hearings or the Mike Tyson/Desiree Washington legal suits, Black women and Black men have divided views on gender issues. Through exaggeration of such division and the iconization of particular successful Black males and females into demonized, universalized symbolic figures of fallenness and failure, the media generates a spiral of controversy. This spiral is akin to a social tornado which sucks into its vortex both pertinent facts of our multiple situations and distortions of our humanity. Our energies dissipated and enervated by reactionary postures, it is impossible for us to name our own realities, issues, and concerns before they become media fodder. Such spirals have a Machiavellian

1

effect, supporting our suspicions that there exists an intentional strategy of "Divide and Conquer" practiced by White institutions of sociopolitical and economic power.

This book seeks to move "beyond the veil" created by the maelstrom of racialized iconography that feeds sociopolitical and economic disinheritance. How do we move beyond this force that seems to obsess, oppress, possess, and depress us? It seems that only powerful rituals of exorcism can rid us of these demons. Before we can celebrate our life together, our struggles, our disagreements, and the many creative ways that African American women and men have found to overcome adversity between us, we must rid ourselves of the "voices" of those who do not understand our ongoing struggle.

Sadly, some of those "voices" are not only from outside hegemonic sources, but arise from within. Products of dreams deferred, economic opportunities denied, and misguided applications of patriarchal power, these "voices" are destructive of love and generate division. Threatening to annihilate our future, these inner voices deny wholeness and communion as thoroughly as do the external forces. They produce division not only in the Black secular community but in the church as well. Moreover, women are divided among themselves about Black women's responsibility to uphold and uplift Black men at all costs in the name of protecting the Black community and family. The virtuous Black woman is she who "stands by her man" come hell or high water. Those who publicly resist patriarchal abuses of power in the Black community all too often are considered suspect, disloyal, sell-outs, and are cast as castrating money-grubbers. This is part of the story and part of the reality among Black folk today. Yet, it is not the entire story. What of those who envision a new reality for male/female relationships? We are affirming the internal community of aunts and uncles, cousins and friends, brothers and sisters, all of whom are beloved however whole or fragmented they may be.

This book is a Creative Space where systematic theology dances with ethics, the two intertwining and flowing into each other. The concerns of an academic systematic theology are to clarify, elaborate, and exemplify an understanding of God that is appropriate, credible, and morally adequate.[1] The task of an academic exercise in ethics is to provide a rational accounting of various theories of morality, human agency, good and bad, and the process of decision making. Such understandings separate theology and ethics as having fundamentally divergent tasks — theology being concerned with the things of God, ethics taking as its aim to provide a "science" of morality. Womanist ethics describes any appropriate, credible, and morally adequate theology and ethics arising from Black experiences as addressing persons, according to Katie Cannon, "with their backs up against the 'Wall' (of Life), holding it up for the young to pass by unscathed."[2] Such a view presses academic theology and ethics out of their depth, but makes it possible for African American religious folk to see the tasks of theology and ethics as both fundamentally united and necessarily inseparable. Some of our philosophical colleagues have noted that the kind of pragmatic imperative Cannon articulates is precisely why it is existentially "difficult" for Black students to study the precise abstractions of Higher Thought — as couched in philosophy, of course! We laugh, wondering if they realize how thoroughly deluded they are in valorizing any field that cannot conceive of putting the practical tasks, flesh-and-blood pain, and ongoing struggle to maintain a sturdy sense of human dignity together with the keen insights, clearsightedness, and intellectual vigor of a relevant theoretical construct. Any articulation of womanist or XODUS God-talk must hold theology and ethics together, with just as much determination and zeal as is necessary to hold back the crumbling "Wall" of despair.

The Womanist Context

Since the terms "womanist," and "XODUS" may not be familiar, it is important to clearly state what we take these terms to mean and to describe the contexts from which they emerge. When Alice Walker coined the term "womanist" in 1983, a number of Black women religious scholars and clergy quickly accepted and built on the term as one that best described their own interests and concerns. Womanist theology is based in part on Walker's definition of "womanist," which emphasizes a love for Black women's history and culture. Most simply, Walker explains, a womanist is "a black feminist or feminist of color." The term "womanist" comes from the Black cultural understanding of "womanish," which is the opposite of "girlish," frivolous, irresponsible, lacking of seriousness.[3] It means acting grown up, serious, and in charge. Womanist theology and ethics draws extensively on Black women's culture, religion, and experience, particularly as it is found in narrative. Narrative includes all kinds of texts, from historical documents to fiction, poetry, and song. Each of these resources represents a variety of African American women's voices. During the last decade, womanist theologians and ethicists have dusted off forgotten and neglected texts, recovered the memories of living Black women in the aural-oral tradition, lifted theological and ethical themes from such cultural resources, and are in the continual process of analyzing, critiquing, and building on those themes that meet contemporary needs and concerns.

Walker does not define what she means by "women's culture" in her definition of "womanism." One can gather from the corpus of her writings that she has in mind Black women's particular forms of creativity in language, writing, relationships, religious and political understandings, moral values, and articles of beauty that Black women have created for everyday use from flower gardens to quilts to blues and literature. She suggests such an understanding in her essay "In Search of Our Mothers' Gardens," in which she speaks of her appreciation for her mother's "love for beauty" and "respect for strength."[4] This love for beauty and respect for strength is evident in Walker's description of her mother, praised by people who came from three counties to be given cuttings from her flowers "because whatever rocky soil she landed on, she turned into a garden. A garden so brilliant with colors, so original in its design, so magnificent with life and creativity, that . . . perfect strangers and imperfect strangers . . . ask to stand or walk among my mother's art." Walker further describes her mother as one "who literally covered the holes in our walls with sunflowers."[5] She was one who had the power to make a way out of no way, a woman of vision. For Christian womanists like Delores Williams and myself, the source of that vision is "a God of Seeing" who empowers the dispossessed with vision and a "creative spark" to make a way out of no way. This "creative spark," I would say, makes possible the creation of positive, life-affirming Black and women's cultures even in the midst of dominant, oppressive cultural strategies in the larger society. While larger southern culture, and American culture in general, deemed that Black women, children, and men were fit only for shacks with holes in them, women like Walker's mother moved and acted out of cultural norms that were resistant to dominant cultural expectations.

By surrounding her family with beauty in the midst of poverty, Walker asserts, her mothers and grandmothers, "more often than not anonymously, handed on the creative spark, the seed of the flower they themselves never hoped to see."[6] Walker's words suggest that culture and spirit are within each other. The creative spark she refers to is spiritual and concrete. It is empowering and sustaining in ways that are palpable. Within Black women's culture there is enormous creativity that is usually passed on by women whose names are never recorded in history books or museums.

One might say that Walker's mother overcame the conditions created by the power of negative, evil, and oppressive systems of racist, sexist, and classist injustice in Euro-American culture (especially in the South) by the strength of her own creative power. Walker is not clear about the source of this creative power in her essay "In Search of Our Mothers' Gardens." However, in her definition of "womanist," Walker emphasizes that a womanist "*Loves* the Spirit." Both Walker, who would not describe herself as Christian, and Christian womanists find loving the Spirit to be an important aspect of Black women's culture. This love is not separate from love of self, folk, or the music, dance, and food in women's culture. Nor is it separate from love of nature and the cosmos (the moon) or one's own body (the roundness of Black women's hips, for example). Love of creation, Spirit, and Black women's culture are deeply intertwined and interrelated. These are all qualities of God that I derive from the works of various Black women and womanist writers.

It is important not to ignore Walker's inclusion of all women of color, and not only Black women, in her definition of "womanist." Such inclusion indicates to me that Black womanists must be open to and in solidarity with cultural perspectives of other women of color. While the vast majority of those who call themselves womanist are of African descent, theologians like Rita Nakashima Brock, who is Asian, Native American, and Hispanic, has called herself womanist. African scholars like Mercy Amba Oduyoye as well as Caribbean women are increasingly engaged in women's studies from their own cultural perspectives as well as cross-culturally. Hispanic and Latin American feminist theologians, such as Ada María Isasi-Díaz, employ the term *mujerista* to refer to their distinctive understanding of feminist theological issues. *Mujerista* means "womanist" in Spanish. There is at once a sense of solidarity with other women of color and of self-naming in the use of the term *mujerista*. Although I focus on the relationship between theology and culture from a Black Christian womanist perspective in this book, I find it important to acknowledge that there are other voices with distinctive perspectives to offer in women's dialogues.

From slavery, to the Reconstruction period, through Jim Crow, and during the post-Civil-Rights anti-affirmative action era, the social historical context for Black women in America is one in which racism, sexism, and classism have been daily evils to confront. Moreover, as Alice Walker points out in her lengthy definition of "womanism," a womanist as a Black feminist or feminist of color affirms women's culture and other women regardless of sexual preference. A womanist, then, is not heterosexist.

Another "ism" that has historically assaulted women of color and the Black community as a whole is environmental racism. This issue emerges in Walker's corpus of writings and is a womanist concern. A woman-

hetero sexism — different social relationships in which one sex is denigrated by the other, a denial of rights or privileges on the basis of their sex.

ist, because she faces jeopardies of racism, sexism, classism, heterosexism, and environmental racism, has been required to develop survival, liberationist, and resistance ethics. Such ethics have been necessary in contexts that are dehumanizing to Black women and the Black community as a whole.

In addition to the universal evils of illness and death, Black women in America have relentlessly struggled against the particular evils of racism, sexism, and classism. While White women daily struggle against the evil of sexism, and classism in the case of those who are not affluent, they are in a position of privilege in regard to their race. While Black men daily struggle against the particular evils of racism and, disproportionately with regard to Whites, classism, they are in a position of privilege in the matter of gender. While Whites and Blacks, male and female, wrestle with the evils of heterosexism and environmental abuse in varying degrees and hold these in common, what makes Black women's oppression distinctive is that such evils are — *always* — combined with the evils of sexism *and* racism. Classism, environmental racism, and heterosexism for Black women, then, take on a particularly *thick* character. While the Black middle class has expanded to around 33 percent, Black women still make less than Black men; 66 percent of the population is working poor or unemployed poor, and Black women are disproportionately poor in relation to White Americans and African American men.

Moreover, just as the land of their African and Native American ancestors has been raped of its peoples, so Black women have been physically raped and bodily exploited for the satisfaction and economic gain of their oppressors. Just as the land from which Africans were stolen has been raped of gold and diamonds, so have Black slave women been raped of the dignity of owning their own bodies, choosing whether or not to bear children and with whom. Black women in America were used as surrogates to nurse the children of their masters and as broodsows to breed new slaves. After slavery, working Black women — especially in domestic and menial work — have had to resist abusive advances by their male bosses. Black women today are disproportionately affected by sexual harassment in the work place. Black women live disproportionately in poor urban and rural areas where hazardous waste sites, incinerators, and industry are located. They are more likely to work in polluted, unhealthy work environments.

While it is difficult for Black heterosexual women to find employment to support themselves and a family, it is even more difficult for Black bisexual and lesbian women to find or retain employment. Such women face exacerbated levels of hostility from their employers and sometimes are sexually harassed *because their supervisors know or suspect that they are gay.* Whether the church is scripturally confident about salvation for gays, bisexuals, and lesbians, it is nevertheless called to decry social, economic, and physical abuse wherever it exists. We act idolatrously, as pseudo-gods, when we determine that we, not God, will judge *which* human beings are worthy of compassion and care.

Finally, because we are both earth and spirit, we are called to be not only good stewards of one another but also good stewards of the earth, working with God to sustain it and resisting destructive acts against it. Our present context is not only one of xenophobia that creates isms against one group or another daily, but also one in which we risk losing the planet we depend on for daily physical bread because of abusive habits, negligence, the greed of an economic industrial elite, and the militaristic angst of nuclear-weapon-holding nations and terrorists.

The evils of sexism, racism, classism, heterosexism, and environmental abuse have required an ethics of resistance. They have also resulted in an ethics of survival and liberation. Black women in America are able to celebrate resistance and survival despite a lack of equal opportunity. Moreover, there have been celebratory moments of liberation — the Emancipation Proclamation, increased educational and economic opportunity during Reconstruction, the establishment of Black colleges for women and men, Brown vs. Board of Education, the Voting Rights Act of 1964, the Civil Rights Act of 1965, gains in desegregation. Each liberating event presses home our equality in spirit *and* body, ontologically and existentially. The context out of which womanists construct theology and ethics is a complex context of struggle and celebration, evil and goodness, abuse and survival, bondage and liberation, illness and health, sorrow and hope. This is the context in which those who are Black and female in one body define what it means to be human in relation to God and work toward the survival, liberation, and wholeness of entire communities *male and female.*

The XODUS Context

"XODUS" is a term which arose in KASIMU's mind as a creative way of naming the various liberative responses — in second-generation Black male theology — to the crisis in African American hope and vision in the early 1990s. The most spectacular example of the increasing frustration and disillusionment with the deferred promises and cancelled policies of the Civil Rights era that many of the poorest of African Americans are experiencing was the conflagration in April 1992 in Los Angeles, which followed the acquittal verdict of four "Anglo" policemen for beating African American male Rodney King. Under the shrewd counsel of their lawyers the policemen turned the infamous video-taped beating of Rodney King into what was called a "justifiable use of force," subdividing the gruesome fifty-one second beating scene by "explaining" the reason for each stroke of their batons. The "justifiable use" strategy convinced the all-White jurors of Simi Valley. The explosive reaction to this verdict is still variously described by Angelenos as "rebellion," "outcry," "revolution," "wake-up call," and "riot." A studied analysis of "the Event" (my own naming) infers that it was all of the above. Initially it began as the angry rebellious/revolutionary outcry of predominantly young African American males, which was projected in the arresting counter-symbol of young Black men beating Euro-American truck driver Reginald Denny.

This image of "Black violence" became the media-promoted "take" on the entire four-day Event. However the Rebellion which surged out onto the streets on April 29, 1992, was multiracial. The poor of all colors, particularly Latinos, as well as some Koreans and Euro-Americans, were the ones who chanted the phrase "No Justice, No Peace!" The night of burning was followed by days of looting and pillage, yet most of those arrested for this period of the Event were Latino (some 51 percent), while the media continued to portray the Event as "Black rage" about the verdict. A synergy of justifiable rage and crass opportunism conspired with the inaction of Chief of Police Daryl Gates to keep the Event unfolding over a period of four days. Images of entire sections of the city in flames caught the attention of the entire world, but such images do not adequately portray the gutted terrain of lost opportunity and imprisoned economics which afflicted most of the poor who participated in the Event.

XODUS is a way of naming the necessary theological, ethical, political, and economic analysis and constructive alternatives which second-generation Black theology must address. To the issue of racial justice, which James Cone, J. Deotis Roberts, Gayraud Wilmore, and others so aptly addressed in the first generation, XODUS theologians must now address the interlocking issues of gender discrimination (sexism), class privilege (classism), and homophobia (heterosexism), as well as some of the lesser recognized forms of oppression in the dominant society, such as discrimination against the aged (age-ism) and revulsion toward the physically challenged and infirm (able-ism). Initial work on these issues has already been done by first-generation Black male theologians. Our work — especially that of Dwight Hopkins, Josiah Young, Will Coleman, Anthony Pinn, George Cummings, Jon Michael Spencer, Elias

Farajaje-Jones, Theodore Walker, Darryl Trimeuw, Cornel West, and KASIMU — is to "stand on their shoulders" and reach a little further than they could. XODUS, therefore, is not a radical break from the past but, in the best of African traditions which honor and respect the elders, sees itself as building on the work of those who have gone before us. Black feminists and womanist scholars such as Katie Cannon, Delores Williams, Jacquelyn Grant, Cheryl Townsend Gilkes, bell hooks, Patricia Hill Collins, Cheryl Sanders, Renee Hill, Kelly Brown Douglas, Toinette Eugene, and Karen Baker-Fletcher are active dialogue partners to the constructive energies of XODUS creativity. All of us were raised as "Children of the Dream"[7] of Martin Luther King *and* as heirs to the legacy of uncompromising militant Blackness as espoused by Malcolm X and the Black Power movement.

The "X" of XODUS reminds us of that "lost-found" legacy of West African ancestry remembered by Malcolm X and others of the Nation of Islam. Not only are we Martin's Dream Children, we are also an X People who no longer "remember" our ancient kinship names. As Dream Children we seek a place and Space BIG enough for our Blackness, Roundness, S/spirit, food, music, struggle, and the funkiness of our African selves in all their variety. As X People we gather in a Circle of Love and recount the Ancient Stories which have been neglected and dis-remembered. As Dream Children and X People African Americans of the late twentieth century into the twenty-first century stand on the brink of an important transition. Is our future that of complete and utter assimilation into Euro-Americanness, or are we to stand firm as a distinct "Black" culture in the midst of the "White" United States of America? Are we really "Americans," or are we, as Malcolm X said so long ago, Africans who happen to be in America?

The XODUS theological answer to these questions can be summarized in the works of several authors.

• *XODUS theology and ethics insists that the contributions of Martin Luther King, Jr., and Malcolm X (El Hajj Malik El-Shabazz was his last Name) must be brought together.* Cone's *Martin & Malcolm & America* insists that the next step for Black theology must be to find a way of holding these two legacies together. Cone lifts up Malcolm's fiery militant and prophetic rhetoric as the greatest safeguard against the genocide of our culture and bodies. Cone embraces Martin's prophetic vision of the moment of destiny for America, as well as his multicultural inclusiveness as a complementary tradition which ought not to be lost.[8] Dwight Hopkins's research indicates that both Malcolm and Martin criticized the lack of economic opportunities and access afflicting Black Americans and leaned toward a socialist recasting of the economy.[9] Both were pan-African, deepening their struggles here in the USA by extensive international African contacts.

• *XODUS theology and ethics resonates with liberation theology.* Such a statement does not preclude attention to the personal, individual, or psychological, but places concern for these matters within a contextual framework of social analysis. In my own work *XODUS: An African American Male Journey* I use a great deal of space demonstrating the ties between media portrayals and society's stereotypes and expectations, on the one hand, and the actual psychospiritual health of African Americans, on the other, insisting that it is precisely in the area of inner transformation that social frameworks and space are created.[10] Further, XODUS liberation does not confine the term "liberation" to political or economic policies or timetables, but insists that traditional Christian understandings of "salvation" and "atonement" would benefit from a more concrete "this-worldly" interpretation which presses toward greater political action. Finally, along with womanists, XODUS theology and ethics insists that liberation ought to be for the *entire* community. Thus it looks closely at the ways in which relationships between men and men, women and men, women and women, parents and children, and children with each other can be strengthened.

• *XODUS theology and ethics moves beyond liberation to Reconstruction.* As the "New South Africa" struggles to find ways to rebuild, heal, and reconstruct aspects of Black South Africa's economic, psychological, and spiritual structures, so XODUS theology and ethics sees its task as envisioning the reconstruction of a people. African Americans live in a confusing miasma of postliberal political ideology in which even the most unmasked forms of racialized rhetoric are deemed "acceptable" in the public sphere of the USA. So-called "conservatives" revel in casting African Americans as pariahs who must learn how to "do for yourself" and stop asking for "hand-outs." We live in a post-Freedom-Struggle, post-Civil-Rights era which has no patience or interest in hearing about "Black problems." We have gained *legal* and *civil* rights, but those victories of an earlier generation are thrown in our faces in the most uncivil and vitriolic form of racialized rhetoric! The effect on our self-image, self-respect, and confidence has been devastating. After those few gains won in the civil rights battles to gain access to the Industrial Age, its factories and assembly-line disappeared in the wake of the high-tech Information Age. After experiencing a kind of "Second Reconstruction" of gains in legal and civil rights, we have suffered the indignity of being humiliated by the demise of the industrial era's economy because so many of our folk were heavily invested and trained in industrial skills. Now, forced to work in the lowest-paying service sector jobs, many young men, in particular, have opted for the high-risk possibility of large sums of cash by selling illegal drugs. The drug culture has replaced the honorable "Mom and Pop" entrepreneurship of the Jim Crow era, and all African Americans are paying a tremendous price because of the attendant violence. Various theories of "White conspiracy" concerning the influx of drugs into Black communities point to the objective reality that Blacks use 17 percent of the drugs in the USA but comprise 55 percent of those arrested and 74 percent of those sentenced![11] In light of these statistics and the fact that one of every three young Black males between the ages of eleven and twenty-five is involved with the criminal justice system (either in jail, on parole, or awaiting trial), we see the virtual decimation of future Black manhood already becoming a reality. At the same time Black women and Latinas comprise 77 percent of the most recently reported cases of HIV/AIDS. Such a people require a reconstructed view of themselves, one sturdy enough to withstand the dire consequences of politically institutionalized neglect and malevolence.

• *XODUS theology and ethics practices genuine "family values."* In our time the phrase "family values" has become a political football passed back and forth between the two poles of "conservative traditional values" and "progressive politics." In the African American community "family values" is not a slogan of political competition for votes but rather often makes the difference between those who survive and those who do not. Since family was the first victim of the rupturing experience of enslavement for Africans, nurturing kinship ties remains one of the most important loyalties of African American Folk. First-generation Black theologian J. Deotis Roberts presciently wrote about "family values" in 1980 in his volume *Roots of a Black Future: Family and Church.*[12] A more controversial treatment of family ushers forth in Theodore Walker's *Empower the People.*[13] Walker's call for early marriages and early sex education demonstrates his willingness to engage in issues critical to this formative Space for nourishing Black life and resonates with XODUS energy.

• *XODUS theology and ethics is church-based and church-nurtured.* The wellspring and source of Black Theology was in the conversation of Black Christian males between their Black church experience and their critical appropriation of the European-American-dominated academic theological milieu. This intellectual and theological conversation has been rich and multivalent, but it has also left behind most Black church pastors and members. Perhaps those of us who write Black theology are trying to speak to two different kinds of audiences in a language which is not comprehensible or acceptable to either! Nevertheless XODUS theology, as a second-generation Black male theology, arises from the experience of GOD, Christ, and SPIRIT in various Black churches, as did the first-generation theology. Bridging the gap between the academy's interest in a philosophically sophisticated theology (a form of *didache*) and the church's need for proclamation (*kerygma*), XODUS theo-ethics places itself in the mediating position — teaching both audiences about each other. Why do we do this? It is necessary that the intellectual life and the spiritual life be brought together. Despite frequent references in Black preaching to the lack of SPIRIT in the "cemetery" (the often repeated humorous term for "seminary"), XODUS theo-ethics pushes itself to remain true to its SPIRIT-based church roots. As a seminary professor I can attest to the power of Black preaching as a gift not just to our own churches, but also to the Universal Church.

• *XODUS theology and ethics is "Streets"-aware.* For those on XODUS JOURNEY the Streets are a SPACE of enormous pain and power. Such painful power cannot be passed over for more traditionally accepted resources. So, flying in the face of what would be considered "normal" theology, XODUS turns to the streets in order to be "real."

• *XODUS theology and ethics is pan-African.* One of the best examples of intentionally self-conscious pan-Africanity is in the work of Josiah Young.[14] While there are various definitions of "pan-African," I specifically want to *differentiate* a pan-African perspective from an "Afrocentric" approach. A *pan-African theology and ethics is African-appreciative* — willing to tease out and analyze all cultural, psychological, and normative patterns of a practice and concept that owe something to various African cultures and traditions, *but is not ideologically African-centered.* XODUS thinking values things African. To express such ideas publicly usually produces a barrage of questions which imply that by valuing Africa and African ideas I mean to devalue other cultures, particularly the European and Euro-American. I have tremendous respect for the accomplishments and legacy of achievements in all cultures. One cannot help but stand in awe of the magnificent dynasties of China, the legacy of spiritual warriors in Japan, the technological genius of various European nations, and so forth.

Nevertheless, we live in a world where European and Euro-American historical accomplishments are still deemed "classic" and "basic," allowing ignorance and misconceptions about Native cultures that flourished for a millennium on this "American" soil and disdain for Africa to go unchallenged. Africa becomes nothing more than a geographical locale where "we" got "our" slaves, even though NOW "we" are too "Enlightened" to believe in slavery anymore. Africa is not presented as the place where one of the longest (some say *the longest*) civilizations flourished for thirty-five hundred years, the ancient Egyptians who called themselves "Kamites" or "Black Ones." Africa is not presented as a place where Timbuktu existed as one of the greatest centers of academic learning for over eight centuries. The accomplishments of great Angolan warrior-queen Nzinga are never mentioned, nor are the civilizations of Mali, Songhay, or the Yoruba at Ife, even though most African Americans could trace some of their ancestral lineage to such places if the means for such tracing had not been erased.

XODUS ethics necessarily insists that until such a time as these things are taught with the achievements of other eminent cultures, Africans living in places like the USA have the moral duty and obligation to be *African-appreciative*. Africans are now scattered throughout the globe. Their contributions have richly mixed with those of Europe, South America, and North America in particular. The pan-African perspective of XODUS theo-ethics insists that *one ought to lift up the inherent diversity, hybridity, and complexity of African presence rather than press toward the identification of an ever elusive, purported "authentic" African "essence" that appears to be one of the fundamental presuppositions of Afrocentric scholars.*[15] Thus, to be pan-African is to be *appreciative of African presence in all of its rich particularity*, seeking a complex and diversified conceptuality of Blackness or "Africanity" grounded in examples taken from a variety of different African peoples throughout the globe. Pan-African analysis stresses:

1. historiographic retrieval of various African contributions to cultures and civilizations, such as those of Egypt, Cush, Ghana, Songhay, Mali, and the USA;

2. critical contemporary reinterpretation of ancient traditions which insists upon the importance of valuing those aspects of a historic culture appropriate to our contemporary context and Christian values; and

3. casting a wide net of examples, looking for the "particulars" of African cultures before attempting tentative generalizations in order to avoid simplistic idealizations of "Africa" or a romanticized uncritical appropriation of anachronistic attitudes of an ancient time.

• *XODUS theology and ethics is Nature-Grounded and SPIRIT-filled.* Ecological consciousness is not a "White thing," but a human thing. Traditional autochthonous (earth-grounded) cultures throughout the world have always honored the SPIRIT-filled Power and Awe that comes from communing with the ALL that surrounds us. Currently throughout the pan-African Diaspora Afrikan[16] persons are arising to the challenge of saving the earth from human abusive practices. In Zimbabwe ZIRRCON (Zimbabwean Institute of Religious Research and Ecological Conservation) has been organizing an ecumenical group of over one hundred African Independent churches for the explicit purpose of waging a *chimurenga* (war of liberation) for the planet. In Zimbabwe efforts are being made at reforestation of millions of the deforested acres and delivering the earth by *clothing the land* with trees (*kufukidza nyika*).[17]

Efforts to bring Black churches in the United States into the "green army" have met with varying levels of success, dependent on whether the environmental group leading the cause has shown sufficient understanding of the interrelationship between racist policies and ecological abuse. Greenpeace has one of its primary bases in a poor Black neighborhood in Washington, D.C., and has helped local people to fight against toxic levels of lead. XODUS theology and ethics sees the necessity of re-Connecting human beings with the Earth. To speak of re-Connection is to recognize that the onslaught of modern technology also brought a wake of technicized instrumentalized logic which reduced the Earth to its objective "function" as a site for exploiting "natural resources." This mentality has spread over the face of the globe. It afflicts the moral and spiritual imagination of every continent and nation. XODUS African Americans join persons throughout the globe, and particularly other Afrikans, as we all struggle together to become EARTHKEEPERS[18] rather than earth-exploiters.

To value the Earth and all of Her creatures is an essential task of being HUMAN, according to Genesis 1:28, and so XODUS reflection points out that as we are "earth creatures" (*ha adam* in Hebrew) taken from the earth (*ha adamah*), so we must treat the ground as Sacred GROUND. From the Sacred GROUND GOD has formed and fashioned us, and we are made of the same materials as the trees, rocks, eagles, bears, and the soil under our feet. As we have emerged from COMMON GROUND, so we *are* COMMON GROUND.

• *XODUS theology and ethics creates Psycho-Spiritual SPACE through the use of Visualized Written Rhetoric.* There is not enough linguistic breathing space within the traditional confines of traditional academicism for the flesh-and-blood terrors, joys, and frustrations of being "Black" in a "White"-dominated cosmos. Throughout our sojourn in the so-called "New World" Africans have taken the language of the masters/mistresses and reshaped it into something meaningful to our experience. We have elongated the sounds of words to provide a sonic painting of the meaning of the words. So "long" became "lo-o-o-ong" and "hot" was transmuted into a staccato shout — "HOT!!!" So doing we Africanized English, painting words into the world of meaning, as is true for several West African cultures. The flat, dull, monochromatic, and unmodulated drone of traditional academic "description" is at odds with the en-fleshing, vitalist linguistic style which is still present in African American speech patterns.

XODUS theology and ethics insists that such vivifying practices have more to offer the academy than the academy has to offer them. Therefore the rhetoric of XODUS shifts, CAPITALIZES WORDS it deems important, Disrupts using **boldface** and *italics* in *"inconvenient" places,* all in the attempt to actually *VISUALIZE* the language. Such disruptive patterns are not random, but designed with the intent to bring to the *WRITTEN WORD,* something of the salty, tangy, pungent urgency and expressiveness which *is* BLACK ENGLISH, or, as it is referred to in the Afrikan-centered Community of scholars — EBONICS. Staying true to an Ebonic sense of the flow and rhythm of the language is a hermeneutical demonstration of the underlying liberative intent of XODUS analysis — to free Afrikans of their unconscious assimilation of monochromatic Euro-ness. If we cannot *WRITE* in a fashion that actually *expresses* our deepest longings, desires, and reflections, we perpetuate and unconsciously condone the centuries-long modulation of our Afrikan-ness into something deemed more "acceptable" to European "standards."

Methodology

Dialogical. Our methodology is similar to what Gordon Kaufman and David Tracy refer to as theological conversation. Will Coleman refers to it as tribal talk. It involves the talking out of theological and ethical ideas in a dialogical process. We take seriously the notion that theology is God-talk. God-talk is a dialogical encounter. Here, it is dialogical in a literal sense because we are two voices — one womanist and one XODUS. The purpose of writing this book is not to come to full agreement on various theological issues. Rather our purpose is to engage in dialogue in an appreciative and critical manner to reveal both similarities and differences in Black male and Black female God-talk. We are *only two voices,* bringing our distinctive perspectives as a womanist and a Black male theologian. We hope that more womanist and Black male theologians will engage in this kind of dialogue in the future. Such dialogue is important because it values the ongoing process of theological reflection. It neither pits ideas against one another, nor gives token nods to each other. Genuine engagement is necessary for real theological and ethical change to take place in the academy, church, and community. This book is an exercise in dialogical theology and ethics.

Each chapter includes two perspectives on theological doctrine and theological ethics. A womanist and an XODUS angle of vision are presented in full. Following the two presentations are our responses to each other's theological and ethical constructions. We have chosen this format so that the reader is required to fully listen to and become familiar with each perspective in order to ascertain some of the similarities and differences in our thought. This also requires that we, the conversationalists, listen to one another in full before determining where our thought is similar and where differences arise. Since our intent is not to blend or blur our ideas, our conclusions will discuss a range of ideas presented. The objective is not to come to any comfortable resting place or caesura in the restlessness of theological process. Our goal is to leave signposts marking the direction we discern our theological and ethical ideas are moving.

Inductive. Inductive logic is a way of reasoning that starts with particular facts, building them toward a general conclusion. Unlike deduction, which begins with a general proposition or principle and proceeds with demonstrations of the particular, induction privileges the ability of particular experiences to create a more complete understanding when they are brought together. Womanist theology and ethics begins with the facticity of Black women's daily lives. It quilts these particular experiences into a pattern of conclusions about the general situation of Black women. XODUS theology and ethics privileges the raw experiences of Black men speaking for themselves, not being spoken about by others. Both womanist and XODUS thinking insist upon the ability of the microscopic data of real lives to make an impact on the macroscopic conclusions which an argument seeks to achieve.

Diunital. Womanist theologians and ethicists have long proclaimed the importance of moving beyond the strictures of either/or means of logic to a both/and method of thinking. H. Richard Niebuhr employs a similar method in his well-known work *Christ and Culture*. Theophus Smith, African American cultural anthropologist and philosopher, has identified the *both/and* approach as a uniquely African retention in African American culture. Citing philosopher Vernon Dixon, Smith names this approach "diunital."

Diunital thinking involves appreciating the tensions of difference. It affirms the facticity of contrasts, opposites, and apparently conflicting coexistence. For example, much moral truth in life is neither purely innocent nor purely evil, but rather is a frustrating combination of both. A question that arises in response to this kind of thinking is: So, what? Does that mean anything goes? That is not the purpose of diunital thinking; it is rather to clarify the complexity of genuine moral dilemmas. For example, no one who participated in the April 1992 Uprising/Riot/Rebellion of Los Angeles can claim innocence in the face of their justifiable rage at an unjust verdict. Neither can the legal system be exonerated from taking responsibility for its participation in creating the conditions whereby feelings of deferred justice and dispensability of people of color and the poor could boil into such a massive outpouring of rage.

The purpose of diunital reasoning is not to blur the lines between good and evil, but, to the contrary, it clarifies the complexity of moral experience and reclaims those goods which have been falsely labeled evil by oppressive forces. Womanists seek to rename and reclaim female *and* male, Black *and* White, rich *and* poor as ontologically, existentially, and aesthetically good in a patriarchal, Western culture in which female- ness, Blackness, and the poor have been cast as evil. XODUS thought seeks to reclaim ancient Kemetic moral notions of Blackness as spiritu- ally positive. Doing so does not negate White people. XODUS thought further insists on African peoples throughout the world finding their own socioeconomic and political determination, but does so within the global affirmation of multiculturalism. Womanist thought likewise seeks a positive reclamation of color within the affirmation of multiracial and multicultural reality.

In both XODUS and womanist thought, neither Blacks nor Whites, women nor men, rich nor poor are purely good or evil. Each is fully human. Each is capable of participating in human existence both as op- pressor and oppressed. This means that while Black women and White women are both on the receiving end of sexist acts, White women can be racist and Black women who are middle class can be classist. While poor White men and poor Black men are both victims of classism, White men can be racist and Black men can be sexist. On the positive end, such diunital thinking moves beyond the problems of sin and evil to consider the positive moral values in the cultures of women and men, Blacks and Whites, rich and poor. It moves beyond the problems of sin and evil to look for solutions. To this effect, it examines the liberating, saving, heal- ing faith doctrines and moral powers of dispossessed peoples, particularly those of Black men and women.

Diunital thinking is ontological and axiological, that is, it moves throughout the realms of both be-ing and do-ing. We cannot confine it to the realm of Be-ing alone or to the realm of Act-ing alone. Rather, because our characters consist of both moral excellences and spiritual torpor (Calvin's term for that aspect of our spiritual self which is asleep, dulled, and unenlightened), we are capable of both good and evil decisions. In XODUS the diunitality of moral life is to develop greater awareness and facility in living in harmony with the GOOD which is GOD, while simultaneously achieving a more chastened power over those weaknesses, faults, and rebellious ways which enervate and undermine our virtues. In ancient Kemetic thought this moral aim, to develop greater harmony with the cosmos and greater powers of virtues and self-control, culminated in gaining the high title of *geru ma'at* ("one who is self-mastered"). Christian Scripture refers to this same process as developing the "fruits of the Spirit" in Galatians 5:20–24.

In womanist thought, who human beings are cannot be separated from what they do. Beingness is inextricably interrelated with acts. Anna Julia Cooper refers to such a diunital mode of thinking in her essay "The Gain from a Belief," in which she emphasizes *faith that works* in contrast to skeptical philosophical systems. Such an emphasis points to faith as more than a state of be-ing. Faith is evidenced in action. Jacquelyn Grant in her womanist Christology refuses to separate the "person of Christ" from the "work of Christ." In womanist thought one discerns that Jesus is the Christ by what he does. In this sense, womanist thought is in keeping with the book of Mark, where Jesus' identity is revealed through appellative acts.[19] During slavery, one refrain of a popular spiritual proclaimed that "everyone talkin' 'bout heaven ain't goin' there," *Claiming* to *be* Christian did not mean you *were* Christian if you did not *act* Christian. The song indicates that slaves were valuing the consistency of moral acts in relation to *claims* of belief as the plumbline of true faith. Slaves insisted on the inseparability of moral actions and claims to ontological goodness. Such a hermeneutic of suspicion is still in effect today. KASIMU refers to this hermeneutic as *iconoclasm.*

Iconoclastic. XODUS and womanist theology and ethics are iconoclastic — they are idol-identifying and idol-smashing enterprises. One of our most influential professors was womanist ethicist Katie Geneva Cannon during our graduate school sojourn at Harvard in the 1980s. She embodied iconoclastic methodology. Her style of teaching was rooted as much in "down-home" southern Black women's cultural traditions as in academic traditions. Well-versed in classical and modern ethical "canons," these were always intentionally interpreted through "Katie's Canon." Her "Canon" is not an individual possession, but a canon of Black women's writings and oral traditions that reveal moral agency, virtues, and values. From her comes the insight that the task of a liberative ethics is threefold:

1. *debunk* to undermine oppressive foundations and assumptions which bind hopes, smash dreams, and keep the poor locked out;

2. *demystify* to cast off the illusions, obfuscating language, and faulty logics that legitimate systems of oppression; and

3. *disentangle* the webs of lies, distortions, manipulations, and perversions of truth which pass for social norms and values. Disentangling's second task is to tease out and lift up strands of hope and the dreams of the dispossessed from the morass of silencing in order for the narratives, lives, and traditions of survival-in-the-midst of oppression to finally be heard publicly.

Social-Historical. Womanist and XODUS theology and ethics are contextual. The starting point is social-historical experience, as evidenced in written and oral sources by Black women and men, from the modern period to our postmodern present. Both perspectives presuppose that theology and ethics move from a particular body of experiential knowledge to universal claims and understandings about the God-human relationship. They are both particular and universal, continuing in the diunital process of reasoning described above.

Out of the sociohistorical contexts and experiences of pan-African women and men there is a complex dynamic of oppression, reaction, occasional eruptions of freedom, and an ongoing praxis of psychospiritual character building. African experiences in the Americas cannot be reduced to a shallow victimology or a dialectic of accommodation and resistance, nor can it be trumpeted as a stream of temporary "victories" in the midst of tyranny. It is a complex interactive dynamic in which the historical fact of oppression cannot be understood unless one also factors in the melody of eruptive victorious resistance and the counter-melody of occasional repressive backlashes by dominant populations. This complex interactive dynamic is a strange "music," dissonant and atonal even though there are moments of sweet melody and glorious harmony.

The praxis of psychospiritual character building is something passed on from one generation to the next. In recent years many of the best African retentions (such as the Ashanti proverb "It takes a whole village to raise a child"), practiced and learned for generations as part of the embedded reality of being "Black," have been neglected and discarded in the rush to join the European American middle-class mainstream. Those precious "village ways" by which every adult not only *felt responsible* for all of the children, but *acted responsibly* have been lost in a mad rush for American "success."

Are we condemning the values and norms of the United States of America? Not completely, because we are as much *American as we* are still *African*. Rather, we write in keeping with the positive longing within many contemporary circles for persons to gain a genuinely *multicultural* consciousness. Womanist and XODUS theological-ethical creativity pushes against the tide of uncritical conformity to both European American-influenced "middle-class" values *and* against romanticized visions of a "glorious" African past which can never have much relevance for overlapping crises threatening Black folk today. Our dialogue will seek to systematically plumb the theological and ethical resources available to those who love themselves and God . . . *regardless*. With a firm faith in the possibilities of two heads being more wholistic and inclusive than one, we put our minds and spirits together in the service of God's Reign on Earth.

Notes

1. These are the three desiderata of former colleague Clark Williamson of Christian Theological Seminary, Indianapolis.

2. This is one of Katie Cannon's favorite images of African American traditional mores. She repeats it in various forms whenever she lectures.

3. Alice Walker, *In Search of Our Mothers' Gardens* (New York: Harcourt, Brace, Jovanovich, 1983), xi–xii.

4. Ibid., 231–43.

5. Ibid.

6. Ibid., 240.

7. This is a phrase which Karen Baker-Fletcher uses frequently to describe those of us whose childhood encompassed the promising, hope-filled, yet harsh period of early integration from 1955 to 1975.

8. James H. Cone, *Martin & Malcolm & America* (Maryknoll, N.Y.: Orbis Books, 1991), 315–18.

9. Dwight Hopkins, *Shoes That Fit Our Feet: Sources for a Constructive Black Theology* (Maryknoll, N.Y.: Orbis Books, 1993), 195–97.

10. Garth KASIMU Baker-Fletcher, *XODUS: An African American Male Journey* (Minneapolis: Fortress, 1995).

11. These statistics were taken from a 1995 survey at Harvard University.

12. J. Deotis Roberts, *Roots of a Black Future: Family and Church* (Philadelphia: Westminster, 1980).

13. Theodore Walker, *Empower the People* (Maryknoll, N.Y.: Orbis Books, 1992).

14. Josiah Young, *Black and African Theologies* (Maryknoll, N.Y.: Orbis Books, 1986), and *A Pan-African Theology* (Trenton, N.J.: Africa World Press, 1992).

15. One cannot read the important conceptual works of Molefi Kete Asante without recognizing that he presumes to identify a *simple, nonhybrid, and non-*

complex Africanity which is held in common throughout all noncoopted, resistant, and "African-aware" Africans in the Diaspora. Study of various African cultures and practices has convinced me that while there may be some "typical" practices shared commonly by various African peoples (e.g., a great appreciation for the centrality of music as an expressive cultural mode), it is difficult to isolate and speak *definitively* of a *singular identity known as "Africanity."* See Molefi Kete Asante, *The Afrocentric Idea* (Philadelphia: Temple University Press, 1987); *Afrocentricity* (Trenton, N.J.: Africa World Press, 1988); and *African Culture: The Rhythms of Unity,* ed. Kariamu Welsh Asante (Trenton, N.J.: Africa World Press, 1990).

16. The spelling "Afrikan" has recently been adopted by various authors like Haki Madhubuti and Na'im Akbar as a way of describing the reality of an African Diaspora — the global disbursement of various African peoples.

17. M. L. Daneel, "African Independent Churches Face the Challenge of Environmental Ethics," in *Ecotheology: Voices from the South and North,* ed. David G. Hallman (Maryknoll. N.Y.: Orbis Books, 1994), 248–57.

18. This is a term borrowed from the AAEC (Association of African Earthkeeping Churches); see ibid., 249ff.

19. Richard R. Niebuhr, lectures on symbolizations of Christ, class notes, Harvard University, 1989.

Part I

GOD

One _____

God as Spirit

Womanist Perspectives on God

> *The Lord is my light and my salvation.*
> *The Lord is my light and my salvation.*
> *The Lord is my light and my salvation.*
> *Whom shall I fear?*
>
> *Whom shall I fear?*
> *Whom shall I fear?*
> *The Lord is the strength of my life.*
> *Whom shall I fear?*
>
> — "The Lord Is My Light and My Salvation,"
> a spiritual popular in Black churches

NANA PEAZANT, an elder who remembers the ways of old Africans in Julie Dash's film *Daughters of the Dust*, comments at a family farewell gathering, "We've taken old Gods and given them new names."[1] Womanist theologians have described God as a God of liberation, a God of survival, and a God of resistance against evil. Delores Williams, building on the language of traditional Black church cultures, has carefully demonstrated that for Black women God "makes a way out of no way."[2] Jacquelyn Grant, building on other aspects of Black women's experience and the work of James Cone and feminist liberation theologians, has suggested that God is a God of liberation and survival who is concerned with the well-being and survival of men *and* women.[3]

There are many names for God in Black women's culture that emerge from a diversity of experiences of the nature of God; taken together these provide a deep, rich spiritual heritage. But what is striking is the theme of finding God as Spirit within. The poet Ntozake Shange, author of *for colored girls who have considered suicide when the rainbow is enuf,* is known for the last section of her famous choreopoem, which asserts, "I found God in myself and I loved her fiercely."[4] Shange's poem, while

25

initially striking and jarring to many, is in keeping with Black women's
Christian and other spiritual traditions. It simply reminds all that God
is the strength of life. This strength and life is with and within Black
women and all of creation.

Many Black women in churches will argue that it "sounds funny" to
call God "she." Many women find Shange's emphasis on finding God in
oneself and loving *her* fiercely a stumbling block. We are not accustomed
to thinking of ourselves as being created in God's image, really, which
means we have difficulty imaging God as female. But if we are to love
our God with all our heart, mind, strength, and soul, and our neighbors
as ourselves, it is impossible to love God or neighbor if we do not love
ourselves. If we take the first account of the creation of human being
in the book of Genesis, we find the creation of Adamah, which means
simply "earth creature." "Male and female" God "created *them*," asserts
Genesis 1:27–29.

If we, male and female, are created in God's image, then it is possible to image God as male and female. This happens occasionally in
certain prayers and songs in traditional Black worship where God is "my
mother, my father, my brother, and my sister." There is something within
Black culture that recognizes the wholistic nature of God, which identifies with humanity in its fullness as male *and* female. Such recognition
resonates with the first creation account of humanity in Genesis. Such
understanding must be lifted up without shame. To be ashamed of it is
to be ashamed of the fullness of God and of women created in the likeness of God. If that likeness of God is within us, in each gender, surely
we can find God in ourselves, realizing empowerment and our full potential as we learn to love God and ourselves. Such love is the first order
of business before we can go on to love others, beginning with our own
daughters *and* sons to whom we pass on the unholy, unsacred habit of
low self-esteem if we do not love ourselves. We cannot claim to love life
as a whole without loving our own lives.

Lucie Campbell's "Something within Me" is a fine traditional hymn
sung in Black churches that reminds singers and listeners alike of the
power of God as Spirit within the souls of those who walk in faith with
a God in whose likeness they are created. "There is something within
I cannot explain," the hymn goes.[5] Shange's "I found God in myself
and I loved her fiercely" is a contemporary way of describing the spiritual experience of finding something within that reveals "the rainbow
is enough." Her choreopoem goes beyond Christian understandings of
spirituality to speak in broad terms. However, it is a poem that both
Christian women and Black women of other faiths can relate to. For

Christian Black women, the rainbow has long been a symbol of God's covenant with humankind and with creation. For Shange the rainbow similarly symbolizes a covenant with life rather than a contract with death. Colored girls do not have to consider suicide when the rainbow is enough. We are called away from choices in our lives that are ultimately self-destructive and called to a covenant with the source of life itself. In the early twentieth century Anna Cooper referred to this as "a Singing Something" that can be traced back to the Creator. Even in the face of the evil of sociopolitical domination it rises up and cannot be squelched. For Cooper humankind is not only created in the physical image of God but echoes something of God's voice, word, and speech. This suggests a prophetic element in human nature. She saw such prophetic speech in various social movements around the world — in India and Russia, for example, as well as in the French Revolution and Haiti's revolt against French slavery and colonial rule.[6] This is yet another way of talking about God as empowering Spirit or the Strength of Life which moves people and enables them to engage in courageous acts.

Favored hymns among Black Christian women refer to *feeling* God, Jesus, the Spirit *within the heart*. God is embodied in humankind in Black Christian women's concepts of God. Moreover, if we look beyond Christian Black women to womanist author Alice Walker, God is not only within the human heart but within all of creation. God is perpetually present, always immanent. Even as God transcends particular human situations God is present in our everyday lives, and infinite possibilities for healing and wholeness are in our midst. For womanists God is neither simply that ultimate ground of being by which we are grasped in moments of mystical experience nor some ultimate point of reference whom we come to understand primarily by reason. It is in our human bodies, souls, and minds in our everyday lives that we *experience and reason* about the sacred. Such experience and thought empowers humankind to *practice* survival, healing, and liberation in the midst of oppression, injustice, and the multitudinous vicissitudes of life.

As the descendants of a people who know what it means to belong to the life-giving source of the universe, African Americans have a long tradition of faith in a God of empowerment. We may have many names for God. We may not always agree on who God is or how to describe God. Indeed, what an ambitious task it is to name the unnameable. For this reason, in the Hebrew tradition God is simply called *Ha Shem*, which means "The Name." This name is a name above, beneath, beyond, and within all the great names we can conceive of for God — the very source of our lives and of our power to name. What we know best about this unnameable, unseen God are the ways in which God has functioned, acted, and moved in our various communities, histories, and individual lives to provide empowerment for personal and social transformation.

Within Christianity, let alone across the spectrum of organized religions and nonorganized spirituality, God has *many* names. Yet God is unnameable. That is a necessary paradox with which we wrestle. It is not so problematic if we realize that God's unnameability does not mean that we should discontinue to name God according to our experiential, traditional, and biblical understandings of God. Rather, God's unnameability means that we must always remind ourselves that while certain namings of God have great meaning for us, none of these names can fully define or contain God.

On another note, that which we traditionally call God in Black Western culture has to do with belief and practice in day-to-day life situations. It is something one carries within always and is not limited to a place one visits Sunday mornings and weekday evenings. Shug Avery suggests in Alice Walker's *The Color Purple* that people bring God to church with them. I would add that when people bring God with them to church, it is possible to find God in church. Moreover, if God is everywhere, one can find God in church even when no one else is there — whether that God is found within oneself or appears to be revealed from who knows where in the midst of prayer. Ultimately, however, faith in God must emerge from something deeper and more ancient than denominational churches — fallible human institutions. One must be grounded in the source which the churches claim to represent, the divine ground of all creation, of all that is and all that will be — God Godself.

Christian churches and the God-talk that emerges from them are sources of both liberation and oppression for women. While there are more women in church leadership positions previously confined to men, many women continue to be outsiders in terms of leadership in the very churches, synagogues, and mosques that they hold together as subordinate insiders. Such subordination cannot end until God-talk becomes more inclusive of women's experience of God and their naming of that experience. The challenge for womanist theologians, both Christian and across a diversity of religions, is to consider the type of God-talk that leads to true liberation and wholeness for entire communities, male and female. Why is it important to consider womanist God-talk and God-imagery? It is important for the well-being of self, family, community, and religious institutions. But who or what are we talking about when we talk about God? Are we speaking of an old man in the sky, the Spirit, a heavenly dove, winds of inspiration, a comforter, a friend, a brother, a sister, a mother? Where is God? Moreover, how do we know that it is really God that we are talking about when we claim to talk about God?

God as Strength of Life

While there are many names for God among African American women, there is a common strand that appears. There is a tendency to image God as empowering, sustaining, life-giving, strengthening, delivering bodies and souls from the miry pits of death whether such death is imposed from outside by oppressive forces or from within by self-destructive, suicidal tendencies. Psalm 27 speaks of soteriological hope in God as the strength of life who sustains not only one's self, but the universe. In the end, it is this God that will prevail. For womanists God as a God of light, strength, and salvation has to do with the daily moment by moment business of living. God as God of light, strength, and salvation may be seen as empowering Spirit. God as Spirit provides light for envisioning survival and liberating resources, strength to carry out visions, and salvation through the transformation of life as it is to life as it should be. The reign of God's strength for life is an ever-present reality. The *life* referred to by the spiritual quoted at the beginning of this chapter is key. That God is the strength of one's life indicates God's presence in human history. Not only is God present, but God's presence has a specific quality to it. God has a saving, strengthening presence in human life and, one might add in keeping with the Psalms' frequent references to the earth, the life of all creation. This also has eschatological ramifications, since God as the strength of life is not only in and with creation, but transcends it. God as the strength of life is the power of life. Given such power, whom should one fear? Ultimately, that which threatens life is limited in contrast to the very strength of life. That which is the very strength of life transforms fear into faith, salvation, and hope.

Salvation involves the transformation of society and all creation from what it is to what it ought to be according to God's vision for the world. As Psalm 27 and the spiritual "The Lord Is My Light and My Salvation" indicate, such transformation does not necessarily mean that evildoers are always transformed. But rather, regardless of the presence of evil in human existence, believers are transformed by the empowering strength of God so that they no longer live in fear. One then has the capacity for the kind of womanist audacity and courage that Alice Walker refers to in her definition of "womanist."[7] Given such courage, there is hope not only for personal transformation in the life of the believer but for social transformation as believers press on with the strength of God for the improvement of society.

For womanists and for Black women historically hope and salvation have not been a matter of interpreting what it means to "be grasped by the ultimate ground of being" as if God were outside the self. Rather, theological reflection involves interpreting what it means to experience connection with God as Spirit within creation — in sky, trees, water, land, birds, family, friends, humanity, one's own self and body — and gaining wisdom from such experience to practice harmonious living with that which is on the side of life. Nineteenth-century evangelist Zilpha Elaw, for example, describes her sanctification experience as one in which she seems to hear God rustling in the tops of the mulberry trees and feels herself moving beyond the trees to find herself caught up in the disk of the sun. Whether in body or out of body, she does not know. She experiences herself as part of the cosmos and transcending it at the same time, her spirit merging with the Holy Spirit in nature.[8] The narrative of Sojourner Truth and a multiplicity of slave narratives refer to finding God in hush arbors, out in the wilderness.[9]

The task for a womanist theology of survival, liberation, and wholeness is to address the brokenness of all of creation in a wholistic manner, ministering to body, mind, spirit, and the material world. An adequate theology is one that remembers God who is the strength of *all* life, who keeps humankind in harmony with the sacred in our everyday work, and works for the healing and wholeness of creation. There is a tendency to forget that there is something greater than our individual selves or communities within the very midst of us that can transform fear into hope, ignorance into the light of wisdom and knowledge, weakness into strength, and brokenness into salvation.

God as Empowering Spirit

The spiritual quoted above, "The Lord Is My Light and My Salvation," derived from Psalm 27, is a popular one in contemporary Black churches. Womanist hope is found in that which is greater and stronger than any evil. Such hope transcends fear, creating visions of promise and resources for survival, for resistance against evil, for liberation, and for healing. "The Lord" refers to God, which from a womanist perspective is Spirit. For womanists, "God is Spirit and those who worship God worship God in spirit and in truth" (John 3:24). God as Spirit is the light, salvation, and strength of one's life. With such inner spiritual affirmation, suste-

nance, and empowerment one need not fear the vicissitudes of life or
those who bear ill will against one's self, family, and community.

Psalm 27 is a first testament text, written hundreds of years prior to
the life of Jesus. In traditional Black churches where this song is popular,
however, "Lord" refers to God and Jesus. Among many Black Christian women, there is a tendency to conflate God (Creator), Jesus, and
Holy Spirit during the ordinary, everyday eloquent prayers in homes,
churches, and gatherings. Sharp lines are not always drawn between the
three persons of the Trinity. God is Spirit. Jesus is Spirit and human.
The Spirit is the all-encompassing, inclusive force in which God/Creator,
Jesus, and all of creation are inextricably enwombed. Igbo African theologian Okechukwu Ogbannaya has explained that from an Igbo perspective
the nature of God most fundamentally is Spirit. Spirit, he explains, is like
the amniotic fluids — the waters of the womb — that encompass a child
before it is born, and accompany it, flowing out with it as it makes its way
into the world as we know it. It surrounds the child and forms the first
environment out of which it is born. Among the Igbo, the third person
of the Trinity is referred to not simply as the Holy Spirit, as in Western
tradition, but as Holy Mother. In this worldview, Jesus has a mother *and*
a father, as does all that lives. Without the Holy Mother (Spirit), life and
creativity could not exist.[10]

Jesus is the human embodiment of Spirit. "Lord" in the spiritual
quoted above may refer to God, Jesus, the Spirit, or all three. Since
God and Jesus for Black women are experienced as Spirit, the song likely
refers to the entire Trinity or community of God. While the reference
to "Lord" is somewhat problematic in an era when we question hierarchical models of reality, what is significant is the faith in a Spirit of
light, salvation, and strength. These appellations for God/Jesus are sung
in mantra-like repetition.

Spirit is the source of strength and courage. *God is the strength of life.*
Moreover, God is the *light of salvation.* Light provides visibility in the
dimmest of circumstances. God as light of salvation, then, enables vision
to see resources for healing, wholeness, and sustenance. Delores Williams
has argued that for Black women God is primarily a God of survival, who
makes a way out of no way and provides vision for survival resources.[11]
God as the *light of salvation*, one might say, functions in this way. Sojourner Truth described herself as being led by the witness within her
to free her children and others from the prisons of slavery and sexism.
She believed God to be "an all-powerful, all-pervading spirit." So strong
a believer in God as Spirit was Sojourner Truth that she developed her
own hermeneutics by which she interpreted Scripture. She believed that

"the spirit of truth spoke in those records, but that the recorders of those truths had intermingled with them ideas and suppositions of their own."[12] For this reason, she came to conclusions such as: human beings need a sabbath, but God does not, because God is a spirit:

> God does not stop to rest, for he is a spirit, and cannot tire; he cannot want for light, for he hath all light in himself. And if "God is all in all," and "worketh all in all," as I have heard them read, then it is impossible he should rest at all; for if he did, every other thing would stop and rest too; the waters would not flow, and the fishes could not swim; and all motion must cease.[13]

For Sojourner Truth, God was a spirit. God did not need light, because God was the source of light, having light within Godself. Such light, one might suggest, is not only the light of vision but the light of knowledge. It involves knowledge and wisdom about how to generate more strength and abundance of life. God does not rest but is in dynamic motion. To envision God as a *spirit* for Sojourner suggests that God is not static, is not an object, but is the continuous *Movement of Life Itself.* Whereas Sojourner Truth described God as "a spirit," I would refer to God as "Spirit." Sojourner's language may have been influenced in part by the notion of God as unmoved mover that is embedded in the worldview of Newtonian physics. In today's Einsteinian nuclear world we understand life as being made up of a multiplicity of continuously moving, dynamic quanta of energy-matter. Not even rocks are truly static but are made of quanta of energy particles, moving at a slower pace than other parts of creation we perceive to be in motion. I understand God as the source of such energy, dynamism, and movement. On the other hand Truth's concept of God may have been influenced by her mother's African understanding of a world inhabited by many spirits. For me, God *is* Spirit, that which is the source of all spirits and creates dynamic relations in a spirited universe. This God is the strength of all life. The heart of Sojourner Truth's symbolization of God as a spirit, motion, light informs my womanist concept of God along with Walker's postmodern symbolization of God as Spirit.

In order to properly understand what it means for Black women and men to envision God as the *strength of life*, it is necessary to understand this metaphor in relation to Black women's social-historical context. Womanist theology is contextual theology. It considers the revelation of God in the lives of Black folk historically and in the present, particularly in the lives of ordinary women of African descent. It may take the form of a Christian theology, Islamic theology, or nonorganized religion and spirituality. Womanist theology asks, "Who has God been in the lives of Black women historically and today?"

While women and men evidence the power of creation within our bodies and participate in God's creative activity, the stuff out of which we are made, its cycles, development, and organization are not really of our own making. We think we have so many answers, but where the power of life really comes from remains a mystery. Even when modern technology enters in to create babies through in vitro fertilization it is dependent on that which already exists, previously created by the mysterious source and strength of life itself. Technology and our own acts function at best as secondary sources in the creative process. There is something greater than ourselves that surrounds us, embraces us, encompasses us, gives us life, and interconnects us within a web of creation and creative activity that is beyond our understanding. It precedes us and survives us.

In traditional Black churches, women rejoice in being touched by or moved by the Spirit. God is beseeched in opening prayer to send the Holy Spirit to bless the service, the pastor, the speaker, the congregation. A good church service is one where we can really feel "the Spirit." The Spirit is a healing, reviving source of positive power that gives new insight, courage, endurance, and meaning in the midst of the trials and tribulations of life. Through being touched by the Spirit, Black women proclaim that God provides vision for new resources of survival and liberation.[14] In Christian Scriptures, the Spirit is described as searching everything, even the depths of God.[15] Delores Williams suggests that the God-content of womanist theology draws on a theology of "spirit" which is informed by Black women's political action and is represented by a diversity of voices. Williams and other womanists find Walker's appeal to love "the Spirit" authentic to Black women's respect for the work of the Spirit in the everyday lives of ordinary women and men. Williams puts it this way:

> Walker's mention of the black womanist's love of the spirit is a true reflection of the great respect Afro-American women have always shown for the presence and work of the spirit. In the black church, women (and men) often judge the effectiveness of the worship service not on the scholarly content of the sermon nor on the ritual nor on orderly process. Rather, worship has been effective if "the spirit was high," i.e., if the spirit was actively and obviously present in a balanced blend of prayer, of cadenced word (the sermon), and of syncopated music ministering to the pain of the people. The importance of this emphasis upon the spirit is that it allows Christian

womanist theologians, in their use of the Bible, to identify and reflect upon those biblical stories in which poor oppressed women had
a special encounter with divine emissaries of God, like the spirit.[16]

For me, Spirit is a synonym for God, because God is Spirit. It is
our sharing in God as Spirit that makes us in God's likeness. God is
the source and ground of all spirits, be they angels, saints, the human
spirit, or ancestors. Genesis 1 reads: "Then God said, 'Let us make
humankind in our image, according to our likeness...'" "Our likeness,"
as Okechukwu Ogbannaya observes, suggests a communitarian image of
God. The Trinity is a community and a model of the relational activity of
God. Not only are we, *humankind*, created in God's image as individuals
but in community. This requires both communal *and* individual responsibility. We do not participate adequately in the community of God if we
do not love God and neighbor.

There is so much love of the Spirit in traditional Black churches and
Pentecostal churches generally, however, that caution to "discern the spirits" is advice well-given. Sometimes people confuse their own desires, the
desires of other people, or the person of the pastor or choir for the Spirit.
Sometimes women claim the Spirit has instructed them to remain in
abusive relationships. Sometimes the pastor or deacon who is so deeply
moved by "the Spirit" during church service returns home to beat his
wife. More Christians are learning to ask whether this is really the will of
God. The problem of discernment is serious. The word "Spirit" is part of
our God-talk. It is a symbol of God that refers to the true or actual God
beyond all of our words, limited interpretations of our experience, and
finite understanding. That which we designate by the term "Spirit" often
has nothing to do with God who is the power and strength of goodness,
justice, healing, and wholeness. How do we discern when a religious experience is truly an experience of the Spirit and a revelation of God?
Who is God? What is the Spirit? How do we know when revelation has
truly occurred? How do we know when we've read God's message to us
correctly? How clear is our vision? Do we have a darkened eye that needs
to be restored?

Emilie Townes gives very careful criteria for discerning the presence of
Spirit from the perspective of womanist spirituality. She emphasizes that
womanist spirituality "adds its voice to any spirituality that is based on
hope and refuses to accept the narrowness and death-dealing of today and
only grips prospects for tomorrow." She explains that womanist spirituality joins love with justice — the notion that each of us has worth and that
we owe one another respect. She indicates that we evidence the activity

of the Spirit when we not only minister to others by preaching, teaching, and living love, but when we allow justice to hold us accountable to the demands of love:

> Knowing the Spirit is to use both heart and head. It is to lean into God's word as both salvation and challenge. It is to allow ourselves to experience and live out of the experience of being wrapped in God's love and peace. It is to witness out of the hope we grow into with the Spirit. It is to love God with our minds through a rigorous and relentless pursuit of grasping, however imperfectly, God's unfolding revelation in our lives through our ever-expanding understanding of the nature of the universe. It is in our struggles to live into our witness that we find God waiting for us and also prodding us into wholeness as individuals, as a people, as a church.[17]

Knowing the Spirit is more than a passive, emotive experience. It involves *head and heart, reason and feeling*. Moreover, it involves struggle *and* living out the experience of being wrapped in God's peace. This is not an individualistic activity but a communal one that requires sharing to be authentic. While God as Spirit may ultimately be unnameable and unseen, we name and see God daily in small ways by giving witness to the palpable Spirit of God who touches humankind and all of creation through our own daily acts of struggle for justice, love, peace, and respect of others. Knowing the Spirit involves tough thinking and tender feeling. These are the ethical ramifications of living in the Spirit. We are required to discern the truth of our participation in systemic societal injustice, to name systemic societal injustice, and to challenge the powers that be to transform dehumanizing, necrophilic (death-loving) socioeconomic practices into systems that value the worth of all humanity and creation. We are required to engage our minds in rigorous socioeconomic analysis. At the same time, we are called by God as Spirit to move beyond analysis to practically deal with the spiritual and emotional needs of one another. Womanist spirituality engages spiritual and material requirements as interrelated, dynamic aspects of human nature. We evidence the Spirit not only in seemingly transcendent moments of spiritual ecstasy, but in our daily practice.

To Image the Unseen

God as empowering Spirit is not only ultimately unnameable but is also unseen in any ultimate sense. At the same time God's presence is visible and palpable in the way it moves and acts in history, in our everyday lives, and in our most memorable moments. As Jacquelyn Grant suggests in her Christology, God is evident in the bodies, faces, thoughts, and actions of ordinary Black women — in "the least of these."[18] No man or woman has seen God, who is Spirit, but we can see the path of God's hand as God moves trouble out of the way. We feel God beneath us, upholding body and soul, when it seems there is nothing to walk on but we do not fall. Those in trouble across the ages have announced the wonder of seeing the path God's light makes when it seems darkness surrounds them. They have put their faith in the unseen, unnameable God within who provides resources for survival, makes the wounded whole, liberates the oppressed, and redeems the goodness of creation. Assurance of the presence of such divine power comes in the midst of walking in the belief that God's loving presence is real even when it appears that the bottom has fallen out and there is nothing to walk on, only an abyss.

In African cosmologies God is not only present in the least of these in a humanocentric sense, but God — the sacred — is present in all of creation. There is nowhere that God is not. Even in Christian Scriptures, for those who may wonder about God's presence in the midst of evil, there is the saying that "even in the depths of hell, there am I." And yet, no one has seen God, according to Christian Scriptures — certainly not in any complete or final sense. The book of Exodus reminds Christians that when Moses asked to see God's full glory so as to see God face to face, God shielded Moses' face so that he would not be destroyed by the power of that glory. So powerful is God's glory, according to the writers of Exodus, that God removed this shield to reveal only the hindmost parts of that glory, God's back.[19] Sifting through the rich imagery of Exodus, I find that the image or metaphor of God's back refers to Moses' incomplete vision of God's glory. So in the midst of all our experience and talk about God's revelation, we are reminded that our knowledge of God is incomplete. Similarly the Pauline writer of 1 Corinthians cautions that "now we see in a mirror, dimly." The cautionary words of contemporary theologians who emphasize God's relativizing activity, which reminds us that our knowledge is partial and incomplete, have a biblical basis and are in keeping with Christian tradition. Admitting that our knowledge of God is not a finished product but limited in scope is the first step toward nonidolatrous imaging of God. It reminds us that imaging God is the most humble, finite of tasks.

God as Unnameable in Womanist Literature

One of the foundational resources in womanist narrative for God as ultimately unnameable is Alice Walker's *The Color Purple*. When Walker published *The Color Purple*, it was received as a controversial novel for a number of reasons. Most obvious and best known is that it was openly critical of sexism, incest, and domestic violence on the part of Black men in relation to Black women. While Walker's purpose in writing the novel was to demonstrate a movement from spiritual sickness on the part of Celie and Albert, who were in an abusive marriage, to a condition of healing and wholeness — salvation if you will — there were many people in the Black community who argued that the introduction of an abusive Black male fed too easily into media stereotypes of Black men in America.[20] Many failed to recognize the character development central to the progression of the narrative, which ends with events of redemption and salvation for both Mister (who becomes Albert) and Celie. The point I want to make here, however, moves beyond the rehashed and frequently debated issue of the portrayal of Black men to discuss the image of God Walker presents through the character Shug Avery.

For Shug, God is in creation. She explains that her first connection to God was a tree, a rock, or a flower, then later people. Transformed from feeling like a motherless child, which she was, to courageous survivor, she exclaims that if someone cuts a branch from a tree she feels that her own arm bleeds.[21] God is not only within her but in nature and the entire cosmos. Moreover, God is not male — an old White man in the sky with a long white beard and gray eyes. God is beyond gender altogether. Admonishing Celie that she needs to "get man off her eyeball," Shug calls God "It." "It" likes to be loved and admired. Christians, in discussing this reference to God as "It" often express discomfort and a sense of dis-ease, explaining that it seems to depersonalize God. This nonimagistic naming of God has a startling effect on the reader or hearer.

Referring to God as "It" transcends all names and images for God, including gendered ones. Much of the discomfort surrounding Shug's reference to God as "It" arises not simply because of a perceived depersonalization of God, but because Shug degenders God. The sacred is neither God nor Goddess. God is not a superman or a superwoman in the sky, created in our own perfected, idealized images. Rather, we are created in God's likeness and God is Spirit. For me, degendering God and referring to God with such an amorphous image as "It" is radically iconoclastic because it breaks all images of God. It is a reminder that no image adequately contains God. God is more than we have seen or can ever imagine. Referring to God as "It" is a reminder that God is Spirit. In human history, Spirit is not seen. Rather, Spirit is experienced through movement. It may be evidenced in beauty, but it is more than beauty. It is the power of beauty. It may be evidenced in abundant life, but it is more than abundant life; it is the *Power of Life* or *Life Itself.* To be created in God's likeness is to embody and reflect the Spirit. For Christians, this is biblically illustrated in Genesis, in which life is created by the very breath and speech of God.[22] Not only does naming God "It" imply that God transcends gender; it suggests that, while God is present and evident in all of creation, there is not one image or metaphor that can contain God. That is, there is no one image of God that fully portrays God. God in creation is unseen in any complete sense. We humans have limited, finite powers of vision and naming. And yet, when we *touch our own spirit,* we find ourselves connected with Spirit-Itself and experience abundant life. To be disconnected from one's own spirit is to be disconnected from all that is. Likewise, to be disconnected from God is to be disconnected from self and others. God as Spirit, while unnameable and unseen, is also very present.

Loving the Spirit

Psalm 100 begins: "Shout for joy to the Lord, all the earth." All the earth is portrayed as embodying the capacity to rejoice and to praise God. This refers to humankind and, one could say, to the rest of creation. Those who are familiar with earthquakes know that even the rocks of the earth give rise to a grand announcement of the life within them. They shift, rumble, and groan. The earth, which we are a part of, moves, giving rise to awe and terror among us humans and giving testimony to the mystery that underlies their creation and very presence. We who have been gifted by God with the beauty of voice, of song, and of Spirit, we with all the rest of creation, are called to sing praises to that which has created us with the rest of creation. But who is this God and what is this God's name? How do we praise one who is unnameable, yet who has so many names given by so many worshipers?

Psalm 100 instructs hearers to give thanks to God and to praise God's *name.* What does that mean? In Exodus Moses is said to have received a mysterious revelation regarding the name of God: YHWH (Yahweh). In the Christian tradition this is often translated simply as "I am that I am." In Hebrew the name "Yahweh" means being. This name for God transcends not only all names, images, and metaphors for God, but it transcends all nouns. As Paul Tillich emphasized in his systematic theology, God is not an object among other objects. God is Being-Itself.

Likewise, Shug's understanding of God as "It" in *The Color Purple* refers to divine movement, agency, and relationality in creation. One cannot read her words superficially. "It" is not understood as an object. "It" refers to creative activity in the universe. "It" is vital, empowering, loving, creative movement within the cosmos. Her understanding of God is not static. "It" is a referent to God as verb, not so much to God as Be-ing — which is the kind of emphasis we see in Tillich and early Mary Daly — but to God as Spirit. God as Spirit within creation is dynamic, powerful, and empowering. It is the ineffable source and power of all that is, within all that is and will be. Moreover, "It" as a referent for this dynamic spiritual power within all of creation is not impersonal at all. It likes to be loved, Shug explains. It loves admiration most of all and gets upset if we do not notice the color purple in a field. "It" — this unnameable power and source of all life — is deeply relational, deeply personal, deeply connected with all that is. But relational loving is not limited to male or female or to human beings at all.

Alice Walker emphasizes that womanists *love* the Spirit. Perhaps we best praise God by demonstrating loving relationship with life in its diversity. By admiring Spirit within all of creation, we learn to live more wisely and with better hope for assuring more abundant life both for ourselves and the planet. Moreover, the well-being and wholeness of each generation requires acts of healing and wholeness by communities of women and men. To engage in such acts is to embody God as empowering Spirit. God as empowering Spirit is the source of the courage and audaciousness that Walker describes as a hallmark of womanist moral agency. To work for the healing and wholeness of community is to act in harmony with God, who as the strength of life is the source of healing and wholeness.

Ultimately, Spirit and creation are beyond our control. Earthquakes come because the earth is living. Hurricanes roar as wind and water whip into furious play. Tornadoes whirl, destroying beloved homes. The sturdiest of structures fall in the midst of mud slides, sometimes because we have cut trees and built where we should not have. Sometimes we suffer because we interfere with nature's complex, subtle systems of survival. Sometimes we suffer even when we are respectful of the earth, because it has its own movement independent of our desires. Reversing destructive habits so that future generations have greater promise of clean air, water, and earth frees us from nihilistic patterns in human culture. It does not, however, free us from the power of nature to live its own life, which from a human vantage point can be nurturing *and* destructive.

God does not always answer prayers the way we would like. Sometimes our prayers are not answered because we have asked unwisely. Sometimes our prayers are not answered for mysterious reasons. We often suffer for no reason other than that it seems to be part of being human. Struggle is part of life, just as peace is also part of life. No one fully knows the mind of nature, despite the best efforts of scientific technology. No one completely understands the mind of God although we have a multiplicity of scriptural and historical narratives that portray certain experiences of God. But we can work to better understand what it means to live in loving relationship with one another, God, and creation.

To live in harmony with Spirit and creation does not mean existence will be idyllic. It means, rather, that we can live with greater dignity and with respect for life in all its forms. In the midst of the freedom of nature and the freedom of Spirit, womanists seek respect for life and work for survival in a world of change, love, and risk. Humankind will continue to require wisdom and faith for survival in the midst of the freedom with which Spirit empowers all life. We require a more cosmocentric theology that truly places God at the center of the universe and not just at the center of humankind. It is necessary to consider how to more fully participate in the creative activity of God, Spirit, who is the strength of *all* life, not just our own.

Notes

1. Julie Dash, *Daughters of the Dust: The Making of an African American Woman's Film* (New York: The New Press, 1992), 158–59.

2. Delores Williams, *Sisters in the Wilderness: The Challenge of Womanist God-Talk* (Maryknoll, N.Y.: Orbis Books, 1993), 6.

3. Jacquelyn Grant, *White Women's Christ and Black Women's Jesus* (Atlanta: Scholars Press, 1989), 1–7, 195–222, and "Black Theology and the Black Woman," in James Cone and Gayraud Wilmore, eds., *Black Theology: A Documentary History, 1966–1979* (Maryknoll, N.Y.: Orbis Books, 1979), 418–33. See also Jacquelyn Grant, "Subjectification as a Requirement for Christological Construction," in Susan Brooks Thistlethwaite and Mary Potter Engel, eds., *Lift Every Voice* (New York: Harper & Row, 1990), 201–14.

4. Ntozake Shange, *for colored girls who have considered suicide when the rainbow is enuf* (New York: Macmillan, 1975, 1976, 1977), 63.

5. See Jualynne Dodson and Cheryl Townsend Gilkes, "Something Within," in Rosemary Ruether and Rosemary Keller, eds., *Women and Religion in America*, vol. 3 (New York: Harper and Row, 1986), 81–84, 93–94.

6. Karen Baker-Fletcher, *A Singing Something: Womanist Reflections on Anna Julia Cooper* (New York: Crossroad, 1994), 27–85. See also Anna Julia Cooper, *A Voice from*

the South, ed. Mary Helen Washington, Schomburg Library of Nineteenth-Century Black Women Writers (1892; reprint, New York: Oxford University Press, 1988), 168, and Anna Julia Cooper, "Equality of Races and the Democratic Movement," privately printed pamphlet, Washington, D.C., 1945, 4–5.

7. Alice Walker, *In Search of Our Mothers' Gardens* (New York: Harcourt, Brace, Jovanovich, 1983), xi–xii.

8. William L. Andrews, ed., *Sisters of the Spirit* (Bloomington: Indiana University Press, 1986). See also Karen Baker-Fletcher, "Voice, Vision and Spirit: Black Preaching Women in Nineteenth-Century America," in Nantawan Boonprasat Lewis et al., eds., *Sisters Struggling in the Spirit* (Louisville: Women's Ministries Program Area, National Ministries Division, Presbyterian Church [U.S.A.], 1994), 31–42.

9. Margaret Washington, ed., *Narrative of Sojourner Truth* (New York: Vintage Classics, 1993), xxii–xxix, 43–55. This reprint of Olive Gilbert's 1850 *Narrative of Sojourner Truth* has an introduction that is attentive to both the African and New York Dutch foundations of Truth's spirituality, as well as informative appendices.

10. Okechukwu Ogbannaya, *On Communitarian Divinity: An African Interpretation of the Trinity* (New York: Paragon House, 1994), 12–31, 55–62, 72, 80–86, and class notes from lecture by Ogbannaya, "On Communitarian Divinity," for Garth and Karen Baker-Fletcher's course, "Pan African Theology and Moral Philosophy," Claremont School of Theology, Fall 1994, 12–31, 55–61.

11. See Williams, *Sisters in the Wilderness*, 15–59.

12. Washington, ed., *Narrative of Sojourner Truth*, 86–88.

13. Ibid., 86.

14. See Williams, *Sisters in the Wilderness*, for a discussion of God as that which gives women of color (sisters of Hagar) vision for survival resources.

15. See 1 Corinthians 2:9–13: "No eye has seen, nor ear heard, nor the human heart conceived, what God has prepared for those who love him [sic]; these things God has revealed to us through the Spirit; for the Spirit searches everything, even the depths of God.... no one comprehends what is truly God's except the Spirit of God."

16. Delores Williams, "Womanist Theology: Black Women's Voices," in Judith Plaskow and Carol Christ, eds., *Weaving the Visions* (New York: Harper & Row, 1989), 185–86.

17. Emilie Townes, *In a Blaze of Glory* (Nashville: Abingdon, 1995), 143–44.

18. Jacquelyn Grant, "Subjectification as a Requirement for Christological Construction," in Susan Thistlethwaite and Mary Potter Engel, eds., *Lift Every Voice* (New York: Harper & Row, 1990), 201–14.

19. See Exodus 33:7–22, where God is described as speaking to Moses through a pillar of cloud. While God speaks one on one with Moses, when Moses asks God to show God's glory, God responds, "You cannot see my face; for no one shall see me and live." God explains, "I will cover you with my hand until I have passed by; then I will take away my hand, and you shall see my back; but my face shall not be seen." Moses is not able to look upon the face of God. The book of Hebrews refers consistently to God as "unseen." Hebrews refers to Moses as persevering "as though he saw him who is invisible." Similarly, Noah is described as holding faith in God who was "as yet unseen" (Heb. 11:1–28). Biblical quotations are from *HarperCollins Study Bible, New Revised Standard Version* (New York: Harper Collins, 1993).

20. Alice Walker, "In the Closet of the Soul," in *Living By the Word: Selected Writings, 1973–1987* (San Diego: Harcourt Brace Jovanovich, 1988), 80.

21. Alice Walker, *The Color Purple* (New York: Harcourt Brace Jovanovich, 1982), 167.

22. See Genesis 2:5–23. God is described as forming *adam,* which means earth creature, out of the dust of the ground (*adamah*) and breathing into its nostrils the breath of life so that it becomes a living being. Woman is described as being created out of the rib of Adam in Genesis 2:18–23. Both men and women possess the breath of Adam or spirit of life. Eve means mother of life. Genesis 1 simply claims that God created "them male and female."

Two

GOD on the Streetz

XODUS Intuitions of the Divine

I N ORDER TO BEGIN the heady, risky, and dangerous work of conceiving Divinity worthy to be called that ultimate name "God," the work of an XODUS Traveler is to excavate historical treasures from African and Afrikan sources. Dr. Henry Mitchell's *Black Beliefs* explored the thesis that African American religiosity has explicit and implicit roots in various West African belief systems. His *Soul Theology* (co-written with Nicholas Cooper-Lewter) traversed the other tenable thesis — that Black beliefs and spirituality are somehow embedded in the culture of Black folk, Christian or not, faithful or faithless. Mitchell's two books help us to name Afrikan theological excavation as having at least two separate tasks: (1) to dig into the hidden, neglected, and often dis-regarded African retentions still resident in African American understandings of God and divinity in general, and (2) to tease out the culturally coded divine mores and traditions as they impact the "common man and woman" on the streets. XODUS theological excavation appreciates both aspects of this approach because so often it is easier to take a "research model" methodology and go to various nations in Africa, searching for one's "lost roots," without ever considering the ways in which Black people on the city streets and everyday byways of life utilize God-talk as a way of negotiating through the pains and joys of life.

Maulana Karenga has provided an exceptionally clear structural analysis of African religions in his chapter "Black Religion" in the textbook *African American Religious Studies.*[1] His approach to African religiosity notes that the creation myths and stories of the gods of African peoples are as rich, complex, and worthy of comparative and scientific respect as are the myths of monotheistic Western religions. Having established this, Karenga unfolds a five-point characterization of African traditional religions:

43

1. *A belief in one supreme God* named differently by the various tribes and nations. For example, the supreme Deity is called "Oludumare" by the Yoruba, "Nkulunkulu" by the Zulu, and "Amma" by the Dogon. This supreme Deity is "father" in most societies, but "mother" in "matriarchal societies such as the Ovambo in Namibia and the Nuba of Kenya." Karenga notes that Amma contains both "male and female characteristics, reflecting the Dogon concept of binary opposition as the motive force and structure of the universe."[2]

2. *A belief in an immanent and transcendent* God with whom daily human interaction takes place in the framework of "divinities who are seen as God's intermediaries and assistants." Karenga likens these "intermediaries" to the Christian relational conception of Deity with the angels serving as messengers of Jesus and God. He insists that Western deference to "monotheism" must be extended respectfully to African traditional religions as well.

3. *Stress on ancestor veneration.* Ancestors are not "worshiped" as God is, but they are "venerated" because they contributed greatly to life when they were alive, serve as guardians of family traditions and ethics, and, most importantly, are believed to be the most valuable intermediaries between humanity and God.

4. *Stress on the necessary balance between one's collective identity and responsibility as a member of society, on the one hand, and one's personal identity and responsibility, on the other.* He cites John Mbiti's famous African formulation of personhood (*contra* the solipsism of René Descartes): "I am because we are, and since we are, therefore I am." Karenga expands Mbiti's notion by noting that the Dinka nation resonates with this collective-personal ideal by stressing "the moral ideal of harmonious integration of self with the community in their word *cieng,* which means both *morality* and *living together.*"[3] An important aspect of this collective-personal identity and responsibility in Karenga's view is the *"profound respect for nature"* embedded in African traditional religious worldviews. He notes that "because humans live in a religious universe, everything that is has religious relevance." Thus the cosmos, Nature herself, is vibrant symbolic witness to "the power, beauty, and beneficence" life has gifted unto us.

5. *The importance of death and immortality.* Several views about death are expressed in Africa. One, death is not an "end" or completion of life, but is another stage or the next stage, "a beginning of another

form of existence." The aim humans ought to have for this next stage is to attain the status of ancestors or "spirits." Second, death is reflective of cosmic patterns such as the rising and setting of the sun and moon. Third, the transition of death is one leading to "personal and collective immortality." Thus persons are expected to "live" after death through "four media: (1) children; (2) other relatives; (3) rituals of remembrance; and (4) great works or significant deeds."[4] Those remaining are morally obligated to keep the memory of the name, deeds, and works of those passed on, lest they be considered "utterly dead," an accursed situation for Africans. Collectively the people live on in their descendants who, by their remembrance, give ancestors their form of immortality.

Karenga's depiction of African traditional religious worldviews may be sharpened and deepened by the particular understanding of God as explicated by E. Bolaji Idowu as cited in the pan-African research of Robert Hood. Idowu lists five particular aspects of belief in God common to Africans:

1. *God is real, concrete, and not philosophically abstract;*

2. *God is unique, incomparable, and absolutely supreme* among all deities and divinities, though not necessarily immutable;

3. *God is absolute lord of the universe* who keeps the universe going at all levels, even when delegating authority to the divinities or spirits, since only God can give breath to animals, plants, and humankind alike;

4. *God is one,* even though God is identified by different tribal names;

5. *God is just but also righteous,* as illustrated in the beliefs about the wrath of the supreme Deity, humanity incurring judgment, and the need to maintain a good relationship with God through the observation of traditions and taboos.[5]

At a national conference on Christianity, African culture, and development in South Africa that I attended in 1995, the ties between specifically *theological* understandings of the Divine and cultural moorings were investigated. Veteran African theologian Gabriel Setiloane explored connections between African indigenous religious views of Divinity and traditional Christian views. Countering the claim of African Anglican priest and professor W. Kuse that African traditional religion begins merely with "ancestors" whereas Christianity is founded on "God as the

ultimate beginning," Setiloane insisted that traditional African understandings of the ancestors is rooted ontologically and linguistically in
the realm of the Divine. In the Tswana language, for example, the word
for Divinity, *Modimo* (pronounced "Moo-DEE-moh"), and that for the
ancestors, *Badimo,* indicate that the literal translation of the word for ancestors means "the people of Modimo." While Kuse believed that African
traditional or indigenous religious practices ought to be moved toward
Christianity (the strategy of "Christianization"), Setiloane firmly stood
in the camp that African traditional religious practices and beliefs must
be thoroughly respected for their indelible spiritual imprint on Africans
who are Christian (the "Africanization" trajectory). Modimo, according
to Setiloane, *is* Divinity. Divinity cannot be circumscribed by personalized understandings such as "father" or "mother," but is to be understood
as *an Energy, Force, and Power* that suffuses and enthuses all that is.[6]
Specifically, Modimo *permeates* all things, and *spreads itself into all things.*
As the Energy/Force/Power of Divinity, Modimo is a natural phenomenon, not above or beyond nature (not "supernatural"), but is nevertheless
intangible and ineffable.

The moral qualities of Modimo, according to Setiloane, are related to
the dreams and visions human beings have about their ancestors. That is,
as the ancestors are present in the everyday ordinary vicissitudes of life,
and are *faithful* to their families, so Modimo is Faithful. Modimo is the
Energy of love and life which undergirds and seeps through our acts of
vibrant loving and living. It is Power operative in procreation, re-creation,
and all the forces of creation surging forward to affirm itself.

It becomes apparent in these listings of traditional African understandings of God that the unnameable God, the One hidden in life but
sought after as the "object" of theological discourse, cannot be understood with one image or name. As we saw in the previous chapter, written
by Karen, God has many names, even within the sometimes imperialis-
tic "Father-God" rhetoric of Christianity. The followers of Jesus, among
whom I walk, recognize that God has many names. Sometimes God is
"Father to the fatherless" when we ache inside for that male hand of love
and concern. Other times God is "Mother to the motherless," especially
during those times when it seems only a mother's touch and presence
could really meet our needs. It seems the height of dogmatic rigidity to
insist upon God's Father-ness as the only symbol appropriate to God's
Divinity. How could that which has created all of us, male and female,
be only a "Father"? It does not even make any earthly sense when we stop
to consider the information provided by the Creation which God has created all around us. When God for us is *only* Father, we oppress God and

ourselves. Why would the Un-Nameable consent to be confined to the narrow confines of one name? In Jewish tradition there is a proliferation of God-names. God is *Adonai* in spoken Hebrew, held so that the sacred tetragrammaton (which Christian scholars so easily call "Yahweh") is never spoken by any but the High Priest, and even he cannot utter such a Holy Name except one day a year after extensive ritual preparations! God is commonly called *Ha Shem*, or "The Name," but Hebrew biblical tradition complements God's divine fullness by noting that God is also "rock," "fortress," "mother eagle," "rock of help," and so on. XODUS theo-language seeks to learn from this Jewish theological humility as well as from the powerful imagery of womanist expressions of divinity. Before I turn to these I want to consider some of the moral implications of God's "Un-Nameability."

The most important ethical assurance to be gained by God's Un-Nameability is the preservation of God's "GODness." This precious quality of Divinity has been named "aseity" by the great theologians of yore. In my own XODUS explorations I try to delineate the distinction between our rigidly enculturated and dogmatized understandings of the Divine with the word "God" and the Divine itself, or "GOD." GOD cannot be "captured" or "controlled" by the utterance of a word. Ancient religious customs used to hold that every thing in the universe — including the "gods" — had a "secret" name which, if discovered, would allow the one who uttered it *power over* that person, creature, or even a god. It would be an abomination to think that one could control GOD by saying "Father," but sometimes it appears that way in the face of the severe reactions generated when one mildly suggests that GOD just might be understood as *more than* "Father." Many African American churches are so wedded to the God-Father language that even to suggest that GOD is more than Father is taken as an affront and attack on Christianity itself. It is time to crack open this hardened shell of dogmatism that parades as self-righteous adherence to Christ's Gospel since the Gospel of Jesus Christ is a message of GOD's "freedom news." If we should know the truth and be set free by it, then let us move forward, unafraid to explore what the Bible itself has already recorded about GOD's GOD-ness. Gratefully, it is time to demonstrate that GOD's GOD-ness ought never to be constrained by those "containment forces" within our human need for order and security known as "religious dogma."

If it seems that I am particularly critical of the church's "God," the perception is correct. So often it is in the church, even Black churches, that GOD is overlooked in favor of God — the controlled, oppressive/liberating Being in whose "Name" so much that is both good and bad has been committed. GOD is seeking to burst the boundaries imposed by the human-constructed God used by so many churches. It is this patriarchal God which Karen decries in chapter 1, the God which Black women have believed in and trusted, despite the manner in which this same God has been used as a sacralizing force for restraining women's rightful demands for redress of psychic, spiritual, and physical abuse. This abuse has occurred in church services with God represented as seemingly unconcerned about the pain of domestic violence, unjust relations between men and women, and the ongoing ways in which traditionally revered moral practices of self-sacrifice are deliberately manipulated to encourage abused women to "forgive" their abusers and return to the relationship! The time for overlooking the ways in which God has been used to bolster abusive practices is over. An XODUS excavation of GOD insists that now is the time to "sweep out the moneychangers" who stand as religious leaders in the Black church while providing a religious cloak for abusers to hide their horrors. Why should such a call even appear as *radical* if it were not addressing something that those who would be honest must concede? It is a tribute to the power and wondrous grace of GOD that Black women have found liberating/surviving/flourishing powers in which to *be*-come and to *be*-lieve within Black churches who promote God. The powers of GOD are stronger than the puny-yet-persistent God so often represented to us as "Savior" and "Lord" on Sunday mornings.

How do we recognize God? God is silent and unmoved by the suffering of women, the torture of children, the imprisonment of young Black males in the most technologically advanced civilization on the planet. God cannot muster the courage to speak critically to the wounds and brokenness of humanity because God is a tool of those who would dominate and control suffering peoples and the Earth itself. God is quite approachable, can be "caught" in any slick "Name-It-Claim-It" pseudo-Gospel preacher's exhortations, and is always revealed as the one who is concerned with individuals getting what they "want" and not inviting us to move beyond our self-enclosed desires. God is never satiated because "He" always "needs" more money. GOD, on the other hand, is the source and spring (what Jonathan Edwards called the "principium") of genuine *wealth and abundance* beyond the materialist imaginations of the promoters of God. Finally, God cannot respect and promote any innovative ministries which free us of dominating images of power and material "success" because "He" is the sacralizing ideal supporting the entire superstructure and infrastructure of materialistic, disrespectful, and dominating ministries.

Jesus preached the freedom news of GOD, the Mother who gathers Her children under Her wings like a mother hen does her chicks, protecting them from all hurt, harm, and danger (Matt. 27:37). GOD symbolized as the protective Mother Hen is rarely expressed, yet note how this notion of the Divine projects an image of comfort, warm security, and "blessed assurance." A mother hen is particularly attentive to her chicks, clucking over them, feeding them, seeing to their needs. Her entire attention is fixed on the care, nurture, and welfare of her children.

A very particular ethical understanding of Divine Love is exemplified in the Mother Hen imagery. Such Love is one which pays close attention to the minute details of life. It is an Attentive Love which springs from an attentive GOD who can count the hairs on our heads, number the grains of sand, "clothe the grass of the field" (Matt. 6:30), and array all the vast flora and fauna which delight our senses. Such Attentive Love is not something which ought to be overlooked, but it is overlooked because Black churches shy away from the femaleness of its imagery. Yet Afrikan Christians throughout the planet ought to affirm the freedom quality of the Mother Hen because without Her, it will be difficult for us to find the inner nurturing of spirit, will, and desire necessary for the generations-long struggle for socioeconomic and political freedoms. We pay a profound inner price if we reject Her, no matter what traditionalists may say.

Another freedom and salvation image of GOD may be found in Deuteronomy 32:11 — GOD as *Mother Eagle*. Aretha Franklin's father, the famous C. L. Franklin, made famous a very traditional African American sermon (whose origins hearken back to the "dim unknown" of slavery), "The Eagle Stirreth Her Nest." In the verse *God*'s activity toward humanity is compared to that of a mother eagle:

> ...like an eagle that stirs up its nest and hovers over its young; as it spreads its wings to catch them and carries them on its pinions. (NIV)

The NRSV version is slightly different, describing the activity of "catching" falling and unskilled young eagles:

> ...as it spreads its wings, takes them [the young] up, and bears them aloft on its pinions

The mother eagle raises up her eaglets by "stirring her nest" with Her wings, driving them out of their secure place into the dangerous unknown of the air. The young eaglets, in a free-fall caused by their lack of experience in flying, can nevertheless be reassured that mother eagle will be there to "catch them," or "bear them up." The mother eagle trains her children to fly this way, by the rough and tumble of trial and error until one day, as if by a combination of hidden instinct and budding strength, the young eaglets suddenly find a way to use their tiny little wings, and they begin to fly.

The Divine Love which the mother eagle exemplifies is of a different sort than that of the mother hen, because hers is a kind of liberating tough love necessary to enable the immature to grow into maturity. While the attentive love of the mother hen is necessary for the vulnerable, the weak, and the very young, the tough love of the mother eagle encourages those who think themselves unable to form the capabilities, skills, and strength required of being able. Yet such "Ableness" does not refer merely to being physically capable, even though the imagery of flying eaglets might suggest GOD's way of toughening our physical frames. The Tough Love of the Mother Eagle enables because it demands that those caught up in the comfortable "nesting places" of life be thrown out into the uncomfortable, insecure "open air" spaces where life in all of its freedom and danger takes place. Outside of the "nest" (the place where the Mother Hen's Attentive Love can become a narcotizing opiate) one either "flies" or "free-falls." There is no in-between.

The ethical implications of a Divine Love that "throws us out of our nesting places" is tremendously important for those who are physically "disabled," or, in a more appropriate naming, are physically challenged. As one who has suffered through numerous hip operations, hospitalizations, and times when I had to compel myself to reengage in the rough and tumble of life, even as the pain in my limbs seared me to the bone, I know the importance of Divine Tough Love. Tough Love does not require one to be "heroic" or a "whiner," but it places an ethical imperative upon us so that even in wheelchairs or with walking aids, talking devices or sight and sound aids, we *can* and *must* move on. Mother Eagle requires all of Her eaglets to fly in every possible way because if they cannot learn to fly, they will not be able to hunt for themselves and will eventually starve. In our sophisticated technological and "democratic" society, it is not likely that we (the physically challenged) will starve outright, but our self-respect, self-esteem, and right to the dignity of work and the pursuit of "happiness" must drive us to move out of the places where we are so often confined. We are not alone. Mother Eagle will not "drive us out" and allow us to be crushed in the inevitable "falls" that we must make as we learn to navigate through a world in which discrimination against those who are not visibly "able" are often mistreated and degraded as mentally incompetent, or as paying some terrible cosmic "price" for somebody's "sin." If we are so mistreated, imagine the magnitude of misunderstanding and maltreatment afforded those who are both physically and mentally challenged! Imagine the outrage we experience every day as we struggle to open doors that strain our muscles and prevent rather than enable access. Imagine the stares, shaking heads, and condescending glances as we struggle to navigate hallways and byways not intended for our use — whether the law says "handicap access" is an enforceable mandate or not. Mother Eagle hovers over us, attentive in Her own way, catching our exhausted spirits and flagging hearts when there is no one else present to hear our cries.

As Afrikan peoples fight the long fight of socioeconomic and political liberation, Mother Eagle hovers over us. A people who are still grappling with the uncertainties of a poorly executed "liberation" (as occurred in the USA in 1865 after the Civil War) recognize that it is tempting to retreat to an image of Divine consolation and care much like that of the Mother Hen and to remain safely tucked away, out of the burning glare of unfreedom. Everyone appreciates the detailed attention of Attentive Love, especially freedom fighters when we are discouraged. Freedom fighters, however, require a Tough Love as their spiritual sustenance. They require a Love which attends to the business of developing strength out of weakness, confidence out of despair, and hope from the seemingly bottomless pit of nihilism. Tough Love suits such a massive reconstructive task, and GOD, the Mother Eagle, does too.

As a theological ethicist, I cannot rest on this topic until I have explored the more standard interpretation of GOD as "Love" and its moral implications.

GOD Is Love

> Beloved let us love one another, because love is from God; everyone who loves is born of God and knows God. Whoever does not love does not know God because God is love... God is love, and those who abide in love abide in God, and God abides in them. (1 John 4:7–8, 16b)

Whenever I preached this passage as a pastor, I could always expect to gain at least one new convert! There is something inviting about such love, a love which has been poured out toward us human beings first, by GOD. For no earthly rhyme or reason the GOD of the universe has "loved us first," sending an "only Son" to die for us and become "the atoning sacrifice for our sins" (1 John 4:10b), that through the death and resurrection of GOD's Son, we might die to our sins and live in the reassurance of GOD's mighty love. Such is the standard "atonement-love doctrine" preached weekly in Christian churches throughout the world. Abiding in this sacrificial love of GOD as expressed through the death and resurrection of "His" Son Jesus is posited as the consummate experience and expression of a GODly life.

The strengths of this position are time-honored. When one conforms one's life to a model of love-as-atoning sacrifice, then the complications of prioritizing are greatly simplified. Life becomes one's individual sense of a calling by GOD. Life unfolds as a conflictual, strenuous, and yet not unmanageable series of testings, temptations, victories, and occasional failures to do GOD's "will." The important norm for such a life is *obedience to the will of GOD,* and the GOD adored and followed is regularly consulted for guidance. GOD's love, in such a view of love-as-atoning sacrifice, enables one to become "Christ-like" because of one's willingness to die to self and rise in Christ. There is galvanizing power in believing that even if one dies for a particular "cause," all things will be all right because it is a redeeming and atoning sacrifice, a sacrifice of love, freely given. Such a view of love conflates sacrificial acts, all such acts, with GOD's Christ-like love. The conflationary energy of such love enables one to *be Christ* in situations of conflict, trial, oppression, and even abuse.

It is precisely in the conflationary energies of love-as-atoning sacrifice that its greatest danger and weakness resides. Women who are abused by their spouses or lovers often justify staying in the abusive relationship with such sacrificial love rhetoric. Being "like Christ" or *imitating Christ* by sacrificing one's self for another is dangerous. Without a doubt, even when the "cause" one is willing to die for may be a good one (such as fighting racism as did so many during the Freedom Struggle of the mid-twentieth century), the end result is still physical death!

Martin Luther King's reformulation of GOD's love — Agape — as incorporating elements of justice, social power, hope, sacrifice, and a vision of the *telos* of community has great potential for a healthier view of GOD's love. Agape ought never to be considered only as sacrifice. Even 1 John 4:17–21 suggests that a "perfect love" or *completed love* is far richer than the sacrifice of one's self for a purported "greater good." 1 John 4:18 notes that such Agape casts away fear; the presence of fear indicates a consciousness of punishment and a cycle of retribution and violence. While King speaks along the lines of an individual's journey toward moral "perfection" and the final redemption of an afterlife, the implications for freeing one's self from the fear of punishment in society did not allude him. King often stated that because he had embraced the possibility of dying for his Agapic concern for racial justice, he had been given a boldness to stand before sheriffs, attack dogs, fire hoses, and violent mobs *without fear.* Such a statement is assuredly tied to sacrificial notions, but goes beyond them by noting that the goal is not a sacrifice of one's self, that sacrifice is not an end in and of itself. Rather, because he had faced the possibly fatal consequences of Agape as the energizing force undergirding nonviolent protest, he had been gifted with a *psychological freedom from fear which enabled him to stand up and protest with a supernaturally grounded boldness.* Any examination of King's life reveals a willingness to boldly seek ways for all peoples to get along with each other in justice. Yet King did not call such an accomplishment merely the victory of justice, but insisted that such moments of community across differences were a victory of GOD's Agape, an in-breaking of the Beloved Community.

King's Beloved Community, the *telos* ("end" or "goal") of Agapic nonviolent resistance, is the social incarnation of GOD's love spoken of in the following last verses of 1 John 4:

> Those who say, "I love God," and hate their brothers or sisters, are liars; for those who do not love a brother or sister whom they have seen, cannot love God whom they have not seen. The commandment we have from him is this: those who love God must love their brothers and sisters also. (1 John 4:20–21 NRSV)

These simple verses reveal something about the nature of GOD's Agape as necessarily embodying itself in a community of persons who relate to each other as "sister" and "brother." This Sister-Brother love *is* the Agape of GOD. We recognize this Agape because it is Sister-Brother love and not love of clan, creed, color, or any other particularity of difference used to exclude a "them" by creating an "us."

God's Agape incorporates power because, as Reinhold Niebuhr and Martin Luther King said, love without power is anemic, and power without love is tyranny. Powerless love leads to abuse and a loss of self-esteem. Loveless power leads to the violent manipulation of an ennobling rhetoric of "love" into the basest form of cruelty. Followers of Jesus on XODUS seek to rekindle the energizing force of love-justice-power which King called Agape. Such Agape is not a certain fixed quality. It is a fluid power which emerges from the inner nature of GOD and flows into all peoples. With it we can find ways to build community together. Without it we fall back on intellectual "ideas" which have no energizing force to transform us, help us to forgive each other, or enable us to move on together.

GOD on the Streetz and in Rap

At the beginning of the chapter I indicated that the "streetz" (as Rappers call and spell it) are a viable place for exploring God-talk. Believe it or not, one of the most creative sources for understanding the fundamental beliefs of ordinary folk living on the "streetz" is the audaciously controversial lyrical space of Rap music. Rappers are quite concerned about the DIVINE, particularly in terms of retribution for their misdeeds and what such misdeeds will cost them "on the other side." Among the Raptivists — Rap activists like Chuck D, Public Enemy, Sister Souljah, and Paris — we find various Christian, traditional African, and Moslem understandings of GOD emerging from almost every album.

Sister Souljah calls GOD "Justice!" She decries the weak-minded, sappy, sentimental "White" Jesus who forgives all sins. For her such an understanding of Divine Mercy (traditional christological language) eviscerates the majesty of God's "good name." Such an understanding of DIVINITY is hard-edged. It emerges with the rawness of hip-hop cadences, with an emphasis on bringing forward in the mixing of sounds and timbres a "funky" bass line moving in synch with a loud drumbeat. Sister Souljah utilizes the musical format of Rap to put forward a message of social activism. The theological center of her message is that the GOD who is "Justice!" will not forever remain silent in the face of racism, sexism, and the violence which permeates American life. She calls for African Americans to utilize their belief in GOD as a sure means for calling down the vengeance of the DIVINE on Euro-Americans for the "sins of the fathers." Such a view of GOD resonates with the more strident theological polemics of prophets like Amos and Jeremiah in the Hebrew Bible. Theirs was a rhetoric of purging away the sinful and polluting ways of the surrounding Canaanite peoples and their gods and returning to "the way of YHWH." Likewise Sister Souljah's lyrics place GOD as Justice! at the center of a prophetic purging of European American middle-class values, which she criticizes African Americans for wrongly embracing.

Other Raptivists like Chuck D and Paris refer to GOD in a specifically Moslem manner. Invoking the name of Allah, both spend a great deal of time criticizing the Europeanization of Jesus — "blue eyes and blond hair" — as depicted in the art work found in many churches, including Black churches. Like Sister Souljah, they decry the use of the message of Jesus to pacify the morally appropriate energies of oppressed Afrikans throughout the world, preventing them from rising up and wreaking vengeance. Paris, in particular, sees in Allah a "Black God" capable of speaking to and for the various Black peoples of the world. He understands Allah to be superior to all other understandings of the DIVINE.

While Paris, Chuck D, and Sister Souljah have elaborate themes concerning GOD in their Rap, other popular Rap groups like DRS (Dirty Rotten Scoundrels) and Arrested Development also incorporate a view of GOD. In the Rap song "Fishin 4 Religion," the writer, named "Speech," assaults a passive view of GOD, which he claims is often found in Black Baptist churches:

> The reason why I'm fishin 4 a new religion is my church makes me fall to sleep. They're praising a God that watches you weep. And doesn't do a damn thing about it. When they want change the Preacher says shout it. Does shoutin bring about change I doubt it. All shoutin does is make you lose your voice.[7]

For Speech a God who can stand idly by and watch the suffering of those praising Him/Her is intolerable. Such a God is not worth praising or believing in. Such a God is really not GOD, therefore Speech enjoins others to come along with him as he is "fishin 4 a new religion."

It is important in XODUS for us to recognize in such lyrics not a lack of faith or even a rebelliousness against GOD. Rather there is an insistence that one cannot claim to be following GOD when those ostensibly representing this GOD do so in images and language that point to a God unconcerned about the conditions of suffering and oppression. GOD must be concerned about these things for Speech. God ought not to be praised if "He" could stand by unconcerned.

The rest of "Fishin 4 Religion" extends the critique of pacifying faith, noting that preachers call for those suffering to pray not for change but for the ability to cope. To cope with suffering rather than nurture the revolutionary energies of "Change" is unacceptable to Speech.[8] What kind of GOD is Speech reaching out to describe? Is GOD the power of revolutionary Change? Perhaps. Interestingly enough, Speech never really specifies exactly who GOD is; rather he clarifies what GOD must not be. This way of approaching GOD, which in classical theological terms is called the *via negativa*, or way of negation, is never merely a methodology of nay-saying. A moral idea of GOD is present which suggests that GOD *ought to be concerned with those aspects of society which cause suffering and oppression*. Further, the *via negativa* theological approach entailed in "Fishin 4 Religion" suggests that *one can discern the true GOD from false representations by determining whether revolutionary social change is valued.* These two moral ideals of GODness point toward a view of the DIVINE which resonates closely with liberation theologies. Any examination of Black liberation theology, particularly the writings of James Cone, Gayraud Wilmore, and, in the second generation, Dwight Hopkins, reveals an underlying theological assumption that if GOD is truly GOD, then liberating activity of the oppressed is this GOD's first priority. Such a GOD is loyal to the oppressed and to the concept of social justice in which there is egalitarian distribution of a society's wealth and material goods.

Am I saying that the GOD we find on the streetz is really interested only in vengeful justice or revolutionary social change? Not completely. Mitchell and Cooper-Lewter's *Soul Theology* notes that the popular or streetz conceptions of GOD incorporate diverse affirmations of:

1. the providence of God,

2. the justice of God,

3. God's majesty and omnipotence,

4. God's omniscience,

5. God's goodness and creation,

6. God's grace, and finally

7. Divine justice as embodied by creating persons as unique in identity, equally regarded, a family, and capable of perseverance.[9]

In much of popular music we find corroboration of these findings. Sayings such as "what goes around comes around" imply a cultural awareness of the cosmic justice of God.[10] The currently popular hip-hop culture phrase "It's all good" reveals a providential confidence, however unspoken, that "somebody" or "something" will make "all things work together for the good of them who love GOD and walk according to GOD's purpose" (Rom. 8:28).

XODUS Moral Philosophy

One of the most important self-liberating acts of moving into XODUS for second-generation Black theologians is to affirm our ability to think in many ways about GOD and God. Dwight Hopkins has based much of his work on identifying liberating elements of various experiences of Black Americans throughout our sojourn here in the United States — from slavery into the contemporary period.[11] It is not necessary for us *always* to speak about our religious experiences, what we call by our faith "GOD," from the confines of church-authorized doctrine. Part of the challenge of XODUS thought to the Black churches will be in the way in which we remind our own faith communities of how they "look" from outside the circle of privileged spiritual access. If we permit ourselves to look at how the concept of "GOD," or the "ultimate," functions, from a variety of viewpoints, we may open a SPACE of discourse previously closed by strictures of faith. From my vantage point, opening up a philosophical discussion of GOD as a concept allows us to look with greater clarity on the moral possibilities of GOD-language in our concrete social life.

"GOD" is an ultimate concept. It is not amenable to the kinds of historical negotiations and quibbling about "what really happened..." that a particular documented "event" in chronological time can avail. For instance, we know that President John F. Kennedy was assassinated on November 22, 1963, in Dallas. This is a well-established historical fact, verifiable by a multiplicity of various sources in many languages. The debate begins about the scope of meaning surrounding the assassination, and either widens into various complex conspiracy theories, or narrows its focus to defending the "official" government version of the Warren Commission, which cited Lee Harvey Oswald as the sole assassin. The debate rages about the significance of Kennedy's presidency and often includes various levels of speculation about how long he might have lived even without having been assassinated since he was very ill with Graves' disease at the time of his death. GOD cannot be discussed in these same ways, however, because every "sacred event" attributed to the action of the DIVINE cannot be evaluated without a cultural-religious element of faith. The factor of "faith" injects a hermeneutic which affirms the active existence of some "thing" or some "Body" or some "Spirit" which is, if not nonempirical, then at least nonverifiable. We cannot directly observe GOD's behavior, but rather only what is attributed by faith to be GOD's actions.

Things become complicated even further when the observable actions of military groups conquering entire nations and peoples are attributed to the superior power and efficacy of their God. It *is* possible to verify that this or that particular nation's military forces won a battle on a certain day and year, in a certain place. Again, it is *not* possible to say, with any degree of verifiability, that GOD had anything to do with it, unless we attribute *everything* to GOD, including this particular event! It is disconcerting to realize, however, that most mass conversions to this or that religious understanding of GOD have pointed to some particular concrete historical event, which GOD is supposed to have arranged, foreordained, and sanctified on a cosmological scale.

We cannot make any discernment about whether there is a GOD or not unless we agree upon a set of ethical criteria concerning the moral character of GOD, or at least how belief in this ultimate concept *functions in people's behaviors and decision making*. Is GOD an arbitrary power, sometimes working wonders of good for humanity, but just as often striking us with a seeming "anger" which destroys life? Is GOD the absolute determiner of destiny, both on the global and collective level, and on the personal level? Is GOD a *reflection* of the vicissitudes and serendipity of human transient emotions, or is GOD an *unattainable ideal of emotional control, perfection, and greatness which we human beings ought to strive to imitate?* Is GOD finite and conditioned in some sense, or is GOD the Unconditioned, Infinite One? Is "GOD" One or Many, or Both in some sense? Each one of these interpretations of the Ultimate Concept we call "GOD" generates a set of sociomoral expectations and behaviors.

In an XODUS moral philosophy the theological concept of Agape can take the deontological character[12] of a moral imperative, that by which we must do all things and without which nothing else matters. Such a casting of Love is absolute, necessarily so, because one requires a firm foundation on which to build a pluriform community of many kinds of persons, classes, and interests. The energizing force of Agape can enable various Afrikans to truly become community with each other and sets no barriers to others' becoming part of that community. It is certainly more important as a basis upon which to build community than any "contract" *on* America[13] made by those wishing to conserve the riches of a particular social, ethnic, and privileged class.

Western historical practices of conquering the entire globe in the name of the "love of Christ" provide an ironic contradiction of its philosophical and theological ideals of love. A critical appraisal of the West's conception of God is fruitful for sorting out the dissonances between ideals and practices, a list of ironies started by the phrase, "God" is . . . :

- . . . *a loving yet often arbitrary power.* This irony is most noticeable after a natural disaster where the destructive arbitrary event is named "an act of God," on the one hand, and then church members "pray" to this same God for help, mercy, and relief from the effects of the disaster.

- . . . *a forgiving yet wrathful deity.* This tenet leads to a kind of spiritual schizophrenia, especially within contemporary evangelical Christianity. God is presented as forgiving of everyone, all the time,

IF one confesses one's sins and repents! The problem with this kind of forgiveness theology is that it does not extend to repeat criminals (often African American), "liberals," who are considered heretics or despised as "bleeding hearts," and various other "law-breakers" such as so-called "illegal immigrants" (brown-skinned Mexicans and black-skinned Haitians in particular).

- *. . . the absolute determiner of destiny yet loving to all.* Egalitarian theological ethics and contractarian social-political idealism often subverted actual concrete practices of many "Christians." Particularly in Arminian and Wesleyan-influenced Protestant churches (with which most African American churches share some spiritual heritage), there has been an emphasis on our choosing to follow GOD rather than on an inscrutable fatalist Deity who chooses us to be either eternally saved or eternally damned. Perhaps the most pernicious extension of this tenet is the way in which certain Darwinian-Spencerian scientific theories of "survival of the fittest" have been transferred into the sociopolitical realm of international strife. Throughout its history the United States has seen conquering the Native peoples of this continent as an aspect of its divine destiny, its "manifest destiny" of occupying one land from the Atlantic to the Pacific. The core theological tenet of this ironic doctrine revolved around a providential notion of a God who foreordains the events of human history so that some come up winners and others losers, while God's love still encompasses all.

- *. . . the unattainable ideal which all human life must strive to imitate.* This quality has enabled the People of the Christian Bible to look at all the ultimate symbols of Christian faith — God, Christ, Holy Spirit, and even church — as that toward which we ought to direct our aspirations. Thus God has functioned as an Ideal Telos, that which draws us toward an Ideal Future, be that future encompassed in the biblical expression "the Kingdom, or Reign, of God," or the Rauschenbusch-Royce-King version of the same — the Beloved Community.

- *. . . the one encompassing our many-ness.* This is the peculiarity of Jewish theism that Christianity inherited in a rather unusual way. The Deuteronomist's cry, "Hear, O Israel, the LORD our God is ONE!" otherwise known as "the Shema," has had a powerful galvanizing effect throughout history. For those suffering under the iron boot of oppression the cry that GOD is One always served as a reminder to those who would differentiate themselves as "children of a superior God" that GOD cannot be divided. GOD is ONE, and because GOD is Father (and in some of the subjugated discourses "Mother" as well) we human beings are inescapably related to each other. We all share a common Divine heritage. Ethically, of course, this spun into calls for greater social equality and denunciations of those who would claim to be the heirs of a "superior God" rather than GOD GODself. For those who either were born to social privilege and entitlements or wrested them from the nobility by dint of their tenacious and successful struggle to acquire sociopolitical, and often military, might, the ONE-ness of God has served as a convenient legitimation of their designs. God as One enables those who control economic distribution, social entitlements, and class privileges to look at those outside of their charmed circle as "children of a lesser god," perhaps even of the Devil! If one has all that the world offers, then God's Oneness appears as a shining "AMEN!" to all of the sordid crimes, passions, and injustices one has committed.

Lest it appear that I am unable to appreciate the unifying powers of the concept of DIVINE ONE-ness, let me note that cultures which have striven mightily to uphold the MANY-ness of GOD are by no means perfect embodiments of justice, peace, and harmony. The question concerning us is whether the Christian compromise between ONE-ness and MANY-ness in the doctrine of the Trinity successfully holds together the tensive power of unifying energies and dispersionary energies. A. Okechukwu Ogbannaya persuasively explores the notion that the Tertullian construct of a Triune GOD, GOD in Three Persons, was a product of the *communotheism* of African religions. His contention is that African *communotheism* — a community of DIVINE persons/beings, or *communitarian Divinity — enables a successful synthesis of ONE-ness with a concern for uplifting Community by sanctifying it in the symbol of GOD.* Family is so central to traditional African culture and spirituality, according to Ogbannaya, that only when GOD could be envisaged as a Family of Mother (Spirit), Father (GOD), and Son (Jesus Christ) could most African cultures begin to grasp this new religion of Christianity as something meaningful to their lives.[14]

Concern for galvanizing our communities to fight for their future as well as for learning to embrace the great diversity of subcultures within an Afrikan cosmos makes work on the Trinity very important to Christians who are on XODUS. The Trinity enables the ONE-ness of GOD to be preserved within a multi-faced community of DIVINE energies. Trinity, when understood as it was by many Africans in Tertullian's time as the Faith/Community of GOD, enables a conceptuality of DIVINITY to emerge that is very different from the Holy Boys Club of "Father-Son-Holy Ghost" intoned by most churches. This concept of the Holy Family/Divine Community has great potential for reforming patriarchal ideals of Male-headed households, since the Mother-Spirit "person" of GOD is central to the operation, welfare, and meaning of all the other members of that Community.

GOD as ONE and Also OTHER

Charles Long has written with typical eloquence and beauty about the *mysterium tremendum*, about the feeling of holy awe, dread, and wonder which engulfs persons when they sense that they are in the "presence" of GOD. Borrowing Rudolf Otto's famous category from *The Idea of the Holy*, Long brings this somewhat abstract understanding of religious experience into the pulsing heart of African American spirituality. Long's description of the otherness of the GOD of creation is deeply interwoven with his experience as a Black American living in a country unable to deeply encounter this *Otherness* because of its inability to accept and embrace the *otherness* of persons like African Americans.[15] The *OTHERness* of GOD for African Americans has served as a kind of transcendent Cosmic Law enabling slaves to say without remorse or regret that they "knew" "Massa" was burning in hell because of all of his cruel misdeeds in this life! The *OTHERness* of GOD sanctified a sense of dignity and an ability to withstand tremendous social humiliation because there was the "blessed assurance" that at the end of this side of life those who had been treated cruelly would be rewarded, and those who had been cruel would be punished. Such dignity ought never to be misunderstood as passivity or weak resignation. Rather, it was a theological recognition that the *OTHER* who is "above" stood watching our acts, judging our deeds, and was not going to be "silent" forever.

GOD Is ABLE

An important aspect of an XODUS musing on GOD is to consider the ways in which GOD is experienced by Black people. GOD is much more than a "good feeling" in a church service; GOD is that "Able" one who "makes a way out of no way."[16] Such phrases about GOD's ever-present and enabling qualities can be found throughout the oral "canon" of Black preaching, be it Christian, Islamic, or traditionally African. The

ABLE-ness of GOD rises as a challenge to humanity for both communion with DIVINITY and energetic moral action throughout humanity. Even if our body is physically challenged or our economic options have been limited by poor education, the ABLE GOD empowers us human beings to *re-cognize* ourselves as CAPABLE human beings. The mighty rhetorical flourishes of Black preachers enjoin believers of all faiths, every worship day, to remember and rejoice in GOD's ABLE-ness and our resulting CAPABLE-ness. Even in the Neo-Ausarian revival of ancient Egyptian religion which informs the work of Karenga and other radical African-centered scholars, GOD's ABILITY empowering human CAPABILITY is celebrated in proverbial phrases such as "To Know GOD, strive to grow in stature beyond all measure; conceive that there is nothing beyond thy capability."[17] It is this universality of apprehension concerning GOD's ABLE-ness that interests XODUS musings because XODUS aims at being an interfaith theological reflection even while it is situated, in my particular case, firmly in the traditions of following Jesus as Christ.

Notes

1. Gayraud Wilmore, ed., *African American Religious Studies: An Interdisciplinary Anthology* (Durham, N.C.: Duke University Press, 1989).
2. Ibid., 272.
3. Ibid., 273.
4. Ibid., 273–74.
5. Robert Hood, *Must God Remain Greek? Afro Cultures and God-Talk* (Minneapolis: Fortress, 1990), 140–41, quoting from E. Bolaji Idowu, *African Traditional Religions: A Definition* (London: SCM Press, 1973), 8, 47, 99.
6. Gabriel Setiloane in a seminar on African theology at the National Conference on Christianity, African Culture, and Development in Southern Africa, Telkom College, Olifantsfontein, August 11, 1995.
7. Arrested Development, "Fishin 4 Religion," in *3 years, 5 Months & 2 Days in the Life of...*, New York, Chyrsalis Records F4–21929.
8. Ibid.
9. Nicholas Cooper-Lewter and Henry Mitchell, *Soul Theology: The Heart of American Black Culture* (Nashville: Abingdon, 1986).
10. Ibid., 32.
11. See in particular Dwight Hopkins and George Cummings, eds., *Cut Loose Your Stammering Tongue* (Maryknoll, N.Y.: Orbis Books, 1991), and Dwight Hopkins, *Shoes That Fit Our Feet: Sources for a Constructive Black Theology* (Maryknoll, N.Y.: Orbis Books, 1993).
12. "Deontology" is moral argumentation based on strong emphases of duty, obligation, and principled positioning. Moral actions are to reflect the moral principles of the actor in deontology. It differs from "teleological" argumentation, which has the character of working toward a notion of "the good." In teleological argumentation moral actions aim toward a goal or end.

13. A reference to the Republican "Contract with America" of 1994 masterminded by Speaker of the House Newt Gingrich.

14. A. Okechukwu Ogbannaya, *On Communitarian Divinity: An African Interpretation of the Trinity* (New York: Paragon House, 1994).

15. Charles Long, *Significations: Signs, Symbols, and Images in the Interpretation of Religion* (Philadelphia: Fortress, 1986), 138–39.

16. A classic example of the sermonic theme "God is Able" may be found in Martin Luther King, Jr.'s sermon, "Our God Is Able," in *Strength to Love* (Minneapolis: Fortress, 1981), 107–14.

17. Taken from the Egyptian proverbs as compiled by Muata Aghaya Ashby, *Tent Tchass Egyptian Proverbs* (Miami: Cruzian Mystic Books, 1994), 38.

Three

Dialogue on GOD

Karen

Your discussion of female images of the divine builds on certain aspects of womanist and feminist God-talk. Feminists in particular have observed that there are female images of God in Hebrew and Christian Scriptures. The Mother Hen and Mother Eagle images are two symbolizations that biblical and reformist feminists point to, as well as images of God laboring in childbirth. I have some concerns, however, about the Mother Hen image in relation to cultural understandings of gender. Is it only God as mother who is nurturing? Are males less capable of nurturing than females? Are you interested in uncovering neglected biblical images of God as nurturing father?

KASIMU

The image of a nurturing male as father is one that is both overlooked and degraded. It is degraded by patriarchal culture, which controls God-language, twisting potentially nurturing scenes into displays of power. For example, it is much more likely that one will hear of God as the jealous and demanding Father of Abraham who almost sacrificed his son in order to pass God's "test" of faith than of God as the quiet-voiced father who spoke to the distraught and depressed prophet Elijah in a cave, or the forgiving father of the Prodigal Son parable. I remember hearing prayers about a "tender and loving Father" in Black churches, but reconceiving popular ideas about the *biblical Father* as tenderly nurturing will require much work.

Karen

While the Mother Hen can function positively as a nurturing image of God, the image of women as "hens" has also been used negatively in patriarchal culture. There are negative stereotypes of women as "old hens," of "hen-pecking," or of the *overprotective* "Mother Hen." In contrast, the image of God as Mother Eagle has not met with the same kind of negative stereotyping. The Mother Eagle image is less problematic, because the eagle is a symbol of power and transcendence in its ability to fly, bear aloft the weak, and deliver the suffering from evil. One could say that the eagle's symbolism of concreteness *and* transcendence, nurture *and* independence, compassion *and* strength makes the image of God as Mother Eagle an androgynous symbol. God as Mother Eagle shares the powers of God as Father. Is the Mother Eagle symbol more equalizing than the Mother Hen image? If so, is the Mother Hen image helpful? Or is it possible to reclaim the original power associated with the Mother Hen, a power which has been subjugated?

KASIMU

Personally I prefer the Tough Love of the Mother Eagle symbol to the Nurturing Love of the Mother Hen. Yet as a male trying to reconfigure traditionally nonnurturing understandings of both masculinity and fatherhood I believe that reappreciating the nurturing powers of GOD as Mother Hen may be quite beneficial to a societal transformation of attitudes which stereotypically feminize nurturing (and degrade it as "female"). If I really am *self*-critical, I must admit to finding less challenge in the reassuring power of the Mother Hen imagery. On the other hand, it is most assuredly true that GOD as Mother Eagle shares in the power dynamics traditionally associated *only* with "God the Father" and as such shares in a culturally defined "androgyny." Yet the Mother Hen challenges me as a man to embrace that aspect of the DIVINE which is purely nurturing, tender, and compassionate. The Mother Hen love of GOD *can* beckon us to strive toward becoming more nurturing and tender in much the same way that positive aspects of GOD as Father potentially empower women. In this way, traditional understandings of how fathers and mothers "ought to be" might be gradually dissolved — at least that is the aim of the XODUS proposal.

Karen

You talk about the "unnameable GOD who has many names." XODUS and womanist thought have something in common here. However, it appears that you privilege the image of God as "Able." In some sense I do that with God as "Strength of Life," which I see as related to other names for God, or "GOD" as you would say. How is "God as Able" related to the many other names of God that you present?

KASIMU

I have always been moved in worship services by gospel-song refrains which lift up the idea that "GOD is able...." This Able GOD empowers those who are rendered unable to cope with life — physically, spiritually, and mentally. Throughout the historic trajectory of African American Christian faith there is an embedded notion that "GOD makes frequent visits" to *us*, and thereby strengthens us to cope with whatever violence, subterfuge, and destruction that various forms of hatred can muster against us.[1] So I see the Able GOD as the One who *strengthens* and *empowers for life* in much the same way that you speak of the image of GOD as "Strength of Life." Historically, I believe that to understand GOD as the One who enables, strengthens, and makes us capable of surviving (sometimes even *transforming*) our sociopolitical and economic circumstances is an accurate primary naming of the Divine from an African American perspective.

I have a question for you in relationship to the various ways that you articulate the symbolism of GOD as "Strength of Life." Early on you refer to Ntozake Shange's famous dictum from *for colored girls who have considered suicide*," "I found God in myself and I loved her fiercely." How is the strength of life that is GOD related to the strength of loving oneself fiercely?

Karen

Actually, your discussions of God as Love and God as Able have compelled me to think about this question. That's why I am wondering whether it is adequate to privilege God as Strength of Life or God as Able without clearly balancing such symbolizations of God with the symbol of God as Love. There can be no life, ableness, or strength of life without love. While we are called to love God, self, and one another, our *ability* to love or the *strength* to love must come from that which is greater than ourselves — the source of all life and all loving action. I would build on the womanist concept of God as Spirit to emphasize that God as Strength of Life *and* God as Love are descriptive of two fundamental movements that describe the activity and being of God as Spirit.

This would make God as Spirit an overarching symbol of God, with other symbolizations, particularly Strength and Love, describing Spirit. Another symbolization that describes God as Spirit is God as Creativity.

KASIMU

If GOD as Spirit is an overarching symbol of GOD's GODness and you believe that Spirit is described particularly in the movements of love and life, then how do we deal with the moral ambiguity of the terms "life" and "love"? For instance, "life" in and of itself is morally ambiguous. Life both nurtures and destroys its creatures in an inexplicable cycle of birthing-moving, loving-conflict, and death-stasis. How is GOD as Spirit related to this moral ambiguity?

Karen

Your question is really asking how my concept of God — my theology — is related to ethics. In talking about God I am talking about the strength and source of Life in the most ideal, ultimate sense. And yet, if we turn to the material world and humanity, morality becomes very important, because we are not God. We are more limited than God. On the other hand, we can also put limits on God's strength moving through us because of our freedom to choose life-promoting or death-dealing acts. We are not ultimate or ideal. Moreover, we are born and we die; we produce and we destroy. We are capable of both loving and deadly acts. These are differences between humankind as creatures and God as infinite creating activity itself. At the same time, I would say that it is possible to have a positive view of death. Morally, death-dealing behavior is problematic and sinful. In terms of our creatureliness, however, death is a part of life, and we have to take seriously the meaning of death as part of our humanness. We all will die to life, as we know it now, but in keeping with African, Native American, and traditional Christian concepts of death, I would say that our lives continue in new and mysterious forms because we are held in God.

KASIMU

Let me put the question more sharply. Natural events like tornadoes, hurricanes, and drought afflict creation, destroying various forms of life —

plant, animal, and human. There is a kind of cruel capriciousness to life. Yet as a believer I can affirm your contention that GOD is the underlying source and strength of life. My question is one of theodicy, correlating the idea of a Good GOD with unjust, unfair, cruel, and capriciously destructive events in life. It is a theological as well as an ethical dilemma which sometimes challenges my faith! How can a Good GOD, the GOD who is the most perfect ideal of the GOOD, allow for the cruelties, afflictions, and sufferings rampant in life as we know it?

Karen

I appreciate this rephrasing of the question, because I have had to think about this a great deal, not only academically but out of Job-like questioning that emerges in the face of the vicissitudes of life. Like everyone, I have experienced a share of death, tragedy, and cruelty. In the end, I have not come to any answers, but to more questions and choices. Do I really want a controlling God who insists on a perfect world where people and other creatures never bump up against one another, often uncomfortably or even with toxic effects?

Or do I want God to continue allowing humankind freedom to make choices; do I want God to continue to allow nature to live the life it needs to live according to its own dynamics? For human beings, it is easy to suggest that God participates in evil, because God allows us to make cruel choices as well as loving ones and allows nature to live its life decentered from human desires. There is a tendency for humankind to see this as evil. At the same time, we want freedom to make our own choices, to choose our own religions, to choose how we will act. We want to have our cake and eat it too.

Is it really God we should question or ourselves? What does it mean to suggest that God should control those *other* bad, evil, people and forces of nature? Doesn't it mean that we want God to make the world the way *we* think it should be? Not only would that deprive humankind of freedom, but it would also absolve humankind of responsibility for self-discipline. We would be like computer programs that never break down. In the end, we would not even need relationship with God, because there would be no need for communication, for the freedom of asking questions. Moreover, it would absolve us of respect for aspects of creation that are not like us or compatible with human lifestyle concerns. If we ask God to make the world perfect *for* us, do we really want what we are asking for? Womanists deeply appreciate and seek freedom. I have come to accept life with risks rather than pray for life without freedom.

Notes

1. Based on quotation from James H. Cone, *God of the Oppressed* (Westport, Conn.: Seabury, 1975), 1.

Part II

CHRIST

Immanuel

Womanist Reflections on Jesus as Dust and Spirit

THE QUESTION of who Jesus Christ is for Black women and communities today is a much-discussed topic among Christian womanists. Alice Walker, who coined the term "womanist," provides a critical analysis of Christianity and constructive understandings of Jesus' suffering in relation to Black women's suffering. In *Possessing the Secret of Joy*, I find it striking that Walker's characters suggest a womanist understanding of Jesus. Olivia, introduced to most readers as Celie's daughter in *The Color Purple*, describes Woman as a sacrificial provider of life who loses her own life to give it to others much like Christ. The narrative describes Jesus as oppressed by those to whom he gives life, much as women are oppressed in patriarchal cultures.[1] The character Tashi-Evelyn-Mrs. Johnson, introduced as Adam's wife, Tashi, at the end of *The Color Purple*, suffers from complications of female circumcision and speaks of the connection she sees between women's suffering and Jesus' suffering. She explains that every time her minister husband, Adam, Celie's son, preached on the suffering of Jesus she grew agitated:

> I am a great lover of Jesus, and always have been. Still, I began to see how the constant focus on the suffering of Jesus alone excludes the suffering of others from one's view. . . . I knew I wanted my own suffering, the suffering of women and little girls, still cringing before the overpowering might and weapons of the torturers, to be the subject of a sermon. Was woman herself not the tree of life? And was she not crucified? Not in some age no one remembers, but right now, daily, in many lands on earth?[2]

Tashi-Evelyn-Mrs. Johnson explains that she begged Adam for one sermon on the circumcision of little girls, involving genital mutilation, and its connection to the crucifixion and suffering of Jesus. "He said the congregation would be embarrassed to discuss something so private and that, in any case, he would be ashamed to do so." Adam avoids the parallels his wife makes between Jesus and Woman as the crucified tree of life. She raises the kinds of christological questions that emerge out of women's experience of evil and suffering. But the church, with its patriarchal structure, is ill-prepared to handle questions regarding violence against women.

Not only does the discussion of female genital mutilation shock readers into new awareness about the types of gender issues the church and Christology could wrestle with, but Walker's images of Woman/Jesus as the *tree of life* suggest that there are images of the suffering of Jesus in nature beyond humanocentric ones. Womanist theologians, in their search for wholistic theological constructions, need to draw on women's experiences in relation to the total social, historical, cultural, and *natural* environments in which they live and work.

Although Walker identifies Western institutional Christianity as a historically oppressive force in the lives of women and men of color, she employs examples of Black Christian women to illustrate womanism, leaving room for a broad interpretation of the life of the Spirit. While Tashi-Evelyn-Mrs. Johnson, for example, is critical of Christianity and patriarchy, she does love Jesus. Harriet Tubman, to whom Walker alludes in her definition of "womanist," brought a vision of resistance and freedom to her interpretation of God's spiritual movement in her life and the lives of her people. Rebecca Cox Jackson, who she names in her earliest definition of "womanist," moved beyond male-centered understandings of God to envision God as mother. Walker's definition of "womanist" is not religious-specific. The fictional character Celie in *The Color Purple*, a novel which Walker describes as *theological*, finds God as Spirit in creation. God is present in all that lives. God is ever-present and visible in creation — in the color purple in a field. Shug's injunction about the necessity to get man off one's eyeball to see God moves beyond androcentrism *and* anthropocentrism.

Historically for Black Christian women, the embodiment of God as Spirit is evident in Jesus, who provides empowerment for resistance, survival, healing, and liberation in times of trouble. For some womanists, like Jacquelyn Grant and Kelly Brown Douglas, the biblical Jesus and Jesus in the historical lives of Black women has been a liberator. For others, like Delores Williams, Jesus has not been primarily a liberator, but has been one who assured salvation by a life of resistance and by the strategies he used to help others survive the death of identity. Whether liberation has come or not, Black women have historically depended on

Jesus in the midst of waiting on and working for liberation. Jesus has empowered them with vision for resources in the midst of bondage and scarcity, making a way out of no way, just as God's messenger did in the life of Hagar.

Christian womanists and Black women in general identify Jesus by his work in the synoptic Gospels — laying on hands to heal, sharing food and wine, empathizing with the woman with the issue of blood, loving widows and orphans, forgiving women condemned by society, passing on wisdom as a teacher, listening to Mary and Martha, weeping over and healing Lazarus, conquering death and evil in his historical life and beyond. To know Jesus for Black women has meant knowing that there are powers of healing, sustenance, and liberation in the universe. Christian Black women believe that Jesus Christ, who lives spiritually in and beyond time, continues to provide empowerment for their lives today. Moreover, humankind across race, class, and gender lines is called to embody the Spirit of Christ. Building on such previously established arguments and expressions of faith, I would argue that we must expand our understanding of the embodiment of Spirit to include the rest of creation. All that sustains and renews us physically, spiritually, and aesthetically embodies Spirit and is Christ-like in its salvific activity of sustenance and re-creation.

Womanism and the Problem of Atonement Theory

One of the liveliest conversations in womanist theology is on the meaning of the cross. Delores Williams questions traditional Christian emphasis on Jesus' atonement. For Williams what is most significant about Jesus is not his death on the cross but his life, which was a ministry to the poor and the outcast, those whose survival was in jeopardy. Jesus is concerned with the survival of all such people, including Black women. Williams finds the cross a problematic symbol for womanists because of its association with surrogacy and structures of domination. She emphasizes that a more adequate symbolization of Jesus for Black women points to Jesus' promise of healing, survival, and abundant quality of life as evident in his ministry to women. "There are quite enough Black women bearing the cross by rearing children alone, struggling on welfare, suffering through poverty, experiencing inadequate health care, domestic violence and various forms of sexism and racism,"[3] she argues. Jacquelyn Grant similarly points out that Black women, as the servants of servants, have already mastered endless lessons in suffering servanthood since at least the modern era.[4] This symbolization of Jesus Christ, she contends, has become a symbolization of bondage that imprisons him. Jesus' servant-hood is rendered painless by making him King of Kings. It imprisons Black women because it sacralizes the pain of their debased servanthood. Grant, however, goes on to symbolize the crucified Jesus as co-sufferer, as I discuss below.

Williams and Grant have something in common, even though they draw different conclusions about the atonement. They both reveal the connections between Black women's suffering and Jesus' suffering that are deeply etched in American religio-cultural consciousness. Their insights resonate with Tashi-Evelyn-Mrs. Johnson's observations of parallels be-tween Black women's suffering and the suffering of Jesus. Unlike the character from *Possessing the Secret of Joy*, however, Williams eschews the notion of more sermons on suffering, whether about women or about Jesus. But perhaps the two perspectives can work together. Like Wil-liams, the fictional Tashi-Evelyn-Mrs. Johnson identifies the torture and defilement of women as sin. She does not glorify women's suffering, al-though she would like a sermon on it. Like Williams she seeks public discourse on it for the purpose of criticizing torture as a great human and patriarchal evil. The task is not to focus on Jesus' life to the exclusion of his suffering but to examine both his life and his suffering in new ways that take into account women's understanding of evil, sin, and defile-ment. Williams's theology and Walker's theological narrative reinterpret the crucifixion of Jesus as human sins rather than as an act of God.

Williams, eschewing a Christology that glorifies the cross, argues that "the spirit of God in Jesus came to show humans *life* — to show redemp-tion through a perfect *ministerial* vision of right relations between body (individual and community), mind (of humans and of tradition), and spirit." Because the cross for Williams symbolizes the sin of defilement, to ask Black women to glorify Jesus' suffering on the cross renders their own exploitation sacred.[5] Such Christology encourages Black women to accept their suffering, often phrased by preachers as "bear the cross God has given you." It is not pastoral or empowering to encourage them to glorify the miry pits in which they struggle.

Protestant churches, Williams contends, tend to teach that "sinful humankind has been redeemed because Jesus died on the cross in the place of humans, thereby taking human sin upon himself."[6] In this sense, she argues, Jesus represents "the ultimate surrogate figure." Jesus "stands in the place of someone else: sinful humankind." The concrete effect is that churches implicitly sacralize surrogacy and the notion that imi-tating Christ means condoning Black women's exploitation as breeders and mammies. But, as Williams points out, the cross was *not* a glorious act of God. The cross is a symbol of human sinfulness. She emphasizes that Jesus' life and ministry committed to the well-being of others was testimony to the glorious power of God.

Crucifixion and Resurrection Reenvisioned

While I agree that atonement theory is problematic, we are still left with the historical reality of the cross. Undoubtedly this is why Williams contends that womanists must neither ignore nor glorify the cross. The theory of the atonement is an interpretation of the meaning of the cross. I propose that neither to ignore nor to glorify the cross means that it is necessary to rethink its actual meaning in history and its symbolic meaning today. In effect, this is what Williams does when she redefines the cross as a symbol of human sinfulness. She does not ignore the cross in her criticism of theories of substitution, ransom, and surrogacy. She reconstructs its meaning even as she deconstructs the rationalizations of abuse surrounding it.

It is vital for Christians to focus on the life and ministry of Jesus rather than his death because of the tendency to focus on the crucifixion in necrophilic ways. An emphasis on the ministerial life and sustaining vision of God as Spirit in Jesus points to a life-affirming promise of deliverance and salvation that deemphasizes sacrifice. On Sunday mornings, some of the most resounding shouts in traditional Black churches are to Jesus "my deliverer!" The testimonies that receive some of the most heartfelt responses witness to the healing, saving, delivering power of Jesus. While preachers may preach at length about the cross, it is Jesus' empowering activity that provides daily wholeness that moves believers to testify.

Most would agree with Williams that the spirit of God in Jesus came to show humans *life*. This particular interpretation of Jesus is consistent with the symbolization of Jesus in the book of John: who "came that they might have life and have it abundantly" (John 10:10). I find it important to reenvision the meaning of the crucifixion, but it is important to reconsider the resurrection as well. It is not only the historical Jesus that has given meaning for life to Christians, but the resurrected Jesus Christ of today. Jesus (God our deliverer) as Christ (anointed one) is eternally now and continues to work healing, deliverance, and salvation in the lives of Black women and the rest of creation. Sojourner Truth's sermon "When I Found Jesus," which she preached time and time again, testifies to belief in Jesus who is not only in history but transcends it. While the historical Jesus was crucified, the resurrected Jesus lives. While the historical Jesus is the prime exemplar of what it means to embody God, actually and symbolically, for Christians, the resurrected Jesus is embodied in the hearts of all believers. Jesus' resurrection is evident in the lives of those throughout history who have been empowered by his ministry of Spirit in the struggle to overcome evil and sin, which thwarts abundant life for the planet. While it is important to give more emphasis to Jesus' ministry of abundant life, is it also possible to seek life-affirming interpretations of the cross, interpretations that neither glorify nor ignore suffering? Williams implies there is room for such exploration and I find it important to pursue it. I refer to this both/and approach as a diunital approach to the problem of Christology. It gives attention to both the life and death of Jesus.

The cross, or tree, may be a symbol of both life and death. Black writers like W. E. B. Du Bois have drawn powerful connections between the tree of Jesus' crucifixion and the lynching trees of Black oppression. On Sunday mornings during the Easter season, voices rise to sing most plaintively, "Were you there when they crucified my Lord?...Were you there when they hung him from the tree?...Were you there when they laid him in the grave?...Oh, oh, sometimes it causes me to tremble, tremble, tremble." No one sings this hymn as mournfully as the older mothers in the church who well remember that time in America's history when Black men, women, and children were hung from trees because their color threatened their oppressors. There is a visceral identity Black Americans have with the cross because of the hangings of thousands of our people on trees. For this reason, I believe African Americans will continue to feel a deep psychic and physical connection to the image of crucifixion. The deaths of the crucified, the lynched, the bullet-ridden can never be forgotten. But ultimately it is their lives that we ought to remember. We must try to continue their struggle for justice and fulfillment. We must always ask, "What did their lives stand for?" Perhaps, Tashi-Evelyn-Mrs. Johnson's suggestion that Women and Jesus both can be symbolized as trees of life is helpful here. It helps us remember that while humankind in patriarchal cultures has defiled trees and people alike by making trees tools for executing freedom fighters and the dispossessed, trees are in truth symbols of life. Moreover, the lives of those lynched or crucified on trees are also sacred. Those who have struggled for justice are like a tree of life, which gives hope to the dispossessed.

Black women undoubtedly will endlessly debate the meaning of the cross. Since for some the cross is no longer a powerful symbol, one might ask why not emphasize the Ikhthus — the fish — which is an earlier Christian symbol for Jesus. The fish recalls Jesus' calling to his disciples to become "fishers of men" and women. Others will continue to find meaning in the cross. KASIMU's XODUS theology suggests that the cross is an ancient African symbol appropriated by Christians in a new way to refer to the death and resurrection of Jesus Christ. Why not explore the meaning of some of these earlier symbolizations which point to life and life-giving power? There are ways of understanding the cross that glorify God's vision of abundant life.

At the same time, one must consider a diversity of interpretations of the symbolism of Jesus Christ crucified in relation to the whole of his life, including the continuing power of that life *after the resurrection*. It is important to examine these questions critically. What might womanists propose to clergy, male and female, who have been shaped by the often cited scriptural injunction that to preach is "to preach Christ and him crucified?" (1 Cor. 2:2). Grant's persistent inclusion of the atonement in her Christology implies that from a womanist perspective this continues to be important for the life of Black churches as well as for Black women's personal spirituality. If one reads the Pauline author of 1 Corinthians 1 and 2 further, it is evident that the purpose of preaching "Christ crucified" is not to glorify crucifixion but to reveal human limitations and sinfulness in relation to the power of God to resurrect and overcome evil through the Holy Spirit. The cross is a symbol of our capacity to sin — to abuse others and in the process defile that which is sacred. The resurrection is a symbol of the Spirit's power to re-create.

The problem is not preaching "Christ crucified." The problem is *how* we preach Christ crucified. Do we preach it in such a way that it glorifies the sinfulness of human acts of torture and defilement of the sacred, which is sin, or in such a way that it glorifies *God?* To preach involves the theological task of interpreting the symbols of the Christian tradition. It is *how we interpret* the symbol of the cross that is problematic. When we glorify the human capacity to oppress others, we fail to glorify the power of God to give life and give it abundantly, to provide survival resources, and to liberate the oppressed.

Persecution and violence suffered by those who resist evil and injustice is the result of an *ethic of risk*. The assassination of a Martin King or the crucifixion of Jesus Christ is part of the risk involved in actively struggling for social justice. But such people daily resist the very power of systemic injustice that may crucify or assassinate them. Their will and desire for themselves and others is not death but life. In reading the writings of Dr. Martin Luther King, Jr., I have been impressed by his

ethic of risk. Building on the life and writings of Black thinkers who
have fought for freedom and justice in the United States, White feminist theologian Sharon Welch has derived a feminist ethic of risk from
Black culture. Her ethic of risk criticizes symbolizations of Christ that
see Jesus' suffering on the cross as a call to sacrifice for all who follow
Jesus. She rejects obsession with suffering as sacrifice, whether voluntary
or coerced.[7]

The notion of an ethic of risk suggests a viable alternative to the ethic
of sacrifice which often influences Sunday morning sermons. It is more
realistic and true to the strategies that have actually worked in forward-
ing healing, survival, and liberation for African American communities,
male and female. Rather than deny the reality of violence, an ethic of
risk suggests another angle of vision on the meaning of suffering. Jesus'
ministry of resistance against evil and his empowerment of others involved the real risks of political persecution, character assassination, and
even death. The cross must not be forgotten because such persecution
is a possible consequence of standing up for what is morally right. The
cross must not be glorified because it was a tool of oppression, much
like the automatic rifle that assassinated Martin Luther King, Jr., or like
the lynch-roped trees from which hung thousands of Black bodies in the
segregated South. They are symbols of humankind's capacity for violence.
More than that, they are symbols of the risk involved in standing up for
human rights and the rights of the planet.

What do we make, however, of the resurrection? If we reenvision the
cross as a symbol of humankind's capacity for the sin of defilement on
the one hand and a symbol of an ethic of risk on the other hand, do we
still find meaning in the biblical accounts of the resurrection? Do we see
the resurrection as a rationalization for humankind's capacity for defiling
the sacred? Or do we continue, as Christians traditionally have done, to
interpret the resurrection as God's power in Jesus to overcome death? I
would argue that while the cross is *not* a glorious act of God, the resurrection *is* a glorious act of God. Its purpose, however, is not to *excuse* or
glorify the problem of defilement. While biblically, Jesus is described as
forgiving his persecutors, he does not *excuse* their actions. The Lukan and
Matthean accounts of the resurrection, however, do represent resurrection
as an act that glorifies God. While the crucifixion points to human sinfulness, the resurrection points to the unquenchable fire of the everlasting
Spirit to create, "die," and create anew. Moreover, I would add that the
power to embody Spirit is innate within creation. Beyond the life and
ministry of the historical Jesus, Jesus' gift of embodying Spirit becomes
the gift of Spirit to humanity and all that lives today.

Jesus and the Least of These

The concept of "the least of these," drawn from Jesus' injunction in Matthew 25 to care for him by caring for the dispossessed, is a key theme in liberation theology's understanding of daily relational activity among humankind. The least of these are the poor. Today, the poor are predominantly people of color when we look at humankind globally. Jacquelyn Grant, who has developed a womanist liberation Christology within the interstices of Black and feminist liberation theology, fleshes out the meaning of "the least of these" beyond the iconography of men of color. Sexism is one of several forms of oppression, she admonishes, that binds not only humankind but Jesus Christ. But sexism must not be overlooked.

Describing Jesus as a tool for undergirding oppressive structures, she discusses the "troubles" of African American women by exploring three ways in which Jesus has been imprisoned: (1) the imprisonment of Jesus Christ by patriarchy; (2) the imprisonment of Jesus Christ by White supremacy; and (3) the imprisonment of Jesus Christ by the privileged class who romanticize Jesus' suffering servanthood, rendering him King of Kings and Servant of Servants, and thus exploiting true servants.[8] For Grant these are three sources of the troubles of African American women in relation to Christology that form the context from which the liberation efforts of Black women arise. Black women as the poorest of the poor globally are among the least of these today, Grant argues. Jesus is in the faces, work, and experience of such ordinary women. We are challenged, then, to move beyond the tendency to connect Christ's work with "male-ness." Rather than limit the experience of Christ to the historical Jesus, we must remain open for redemption through new means. Grant concludes that with openness, "we can even experience 'Christ in the form of our sister.' The historical Jesus was a man, but men do not have a monopoly upon Christ."[9]

Similarly, Kelly Brown Douglas suggests that Jesus today is seen in the lives of ordinary Black women. Building on such symbolism, she fleshes out this understanding to talk about iconography of Jesus in Black culture. It is not enough to take the position of Black liberation theology that Jesus is Black, if Jesus is still identified exclusively with maleness. Building on Cone's symbol theory that Jesus is Black because he identifies with the least of these and is on the side of the oppressed, she argues that Jesus today can be seen in the faces of Black women who work for freedom, survival, and wholeness. However, she seeks to move beyond Grant's explication by arguing that even this is not enough. Because the least of these includes people of color of both genders, it is necessary to consider "a diversity of icons or symbols."

For Brown Douglas this means that Jesus is embodied in a variety of Black women and men in history and culture. Therefore, "Christ can be seen in the face of a Sojourner Truth, a Harriet Tubman, or a Fannie Lou Hamer," as well as Black male liberators, all of whom struggled to help lead the entire Black community into survival and wholeness. A womanist portrayal of the Black Christ, she argues, avails itself of a diversity of living symbols and icons of Christ as a living Christ. This Christ is present in the Black community "wherever people are engaged" in struggle for a community's wholeness. Such symbolization challenges Black people to participate in the advancement of unity and freedom.[10]

Williams reinterprets the incarnation of God in the Christian tradition altogether. For Williams, the embodiment of God as Spirit in women is a historical, biblical event in the person of Mary. She argues that by removing sexist lenses, one can see that "though incarnation is traditionally associated with the self-disclosure of God in Jesus Christ, incarnation also involves self-disclosure in a woman: Mary."[11] The self-disclosure of the Spirit of God in Mary suggests that women have both female and male incarnations as exemplars of the embodiment of Spirit. I would add that it is important to consider that the blood Jesus shed is also Mary's blood. Jesus and Mary shared blood and Spirit. The connection between Mary and Jesus, their embodiment of Spirit, their sharing of flesh and blood sheds new light both on incarnation and the crucifixion. Male and female alike have the capacity to embody God. This affects how we interpret the ministries of Jesus and Mary and how we understand the ongoing process of incarnating Spirit.

While Black female symbolizations of incarnation may seem novel, a prototype of Jesus as Black woman can be found in the historical work of Anna Julia Cooper. Cooper, a nineteenth-century Black feminist church woman and educator, never explicitly said she saw Jesus as a Black woman. But through the power of parallel literary portraits of Jesus and "the Black woman" she implied as much in her book, *A Voice from the South* (1892). For Anna Cooper, just as Jesus is a vital element in the regeneration of civilization in a universal sense, so is the Black woman a vital element in the regeneration of a race. Jesus and the Black woman of the South each have muted, liberating messages. Society can and must hear this liberating message, bringing it out of suppression to full voice. Like the Black woman of the South, Jesus leads society onward to a fuller realization of ideals of freedom and equality. For Cooper, to be a Black Christian woman meant embodying the compassionate leadership of Jesus.[12]

If Black women can embody such Spirit, then they too are part of the community of the sacred. To treat Black women as outside of God's community, then, is a sin. If Jesus is indeed embodied in Black women, then sin against Black women is sin against God. Moreover, if all are created in the likeness of God, then perpetrators of abuse and oppression defile themselves more than anyone else. While it may appear that the oppressed are defiled and dehumanized, in truth their defilers are defiled and dehumanized.[13] It is the slaver, the slaveowner, the torturer who dehumanizes him or herself through hateful acts.

By considering Black women's incarnation of God as Spirit today, womanists rehumanize Black women, reclaiming their womanhood and full humanity with the rest of the human race, male and female, including every ethnicity. Both women and men are called to imitate Jesus' embodiment of Spirit by engaging in humane, humanizing activity. However, is rehumanization enough? While it is important for womanists to reclaim Black women's full humanity, how might one do so in a way that moves beyond both *androcentric and anthropocentric positions?*

Ecological abuse, I would argue, is one of many forms of imprisonment. Not only human bodies but the environments where poor people and people of color live and work have been exploited in North America and around the globe. The creation, which Jesus proclaimed would cry out if he were torn down, has been raped and imprisoned in the name of the progress of Christian civilization. Jesus and *all* of creation struggle toward dynamic, liberating relationship. Grant incisively observes that the experiences of African American women "reveal a process of mutual liberation: Jesus was liberating or redeeming African American women, as African American women were liberating or redeeming Jesus." Both suffered "triple bondage or imprisonment."[14] I would suggest that this relationship of mutuality includes the natural environments in which poor and working-class people of color live and strive to earn enough to feed, clothe, and shelter themselves and their families. Increasingly, Black Americans are no longer satisfied to simply have the jobs that manufacturing industries located in their neighborhoods have promised, but actually given to only a few. They desire jobs free from the cancers, respiratory illnesses, lead poisoning, and other illnesses industries inflict on the community's women, men, and children.

To date, womanist theology has focused primarily on human beings in its descriptions of the least of these. In the last ten years, however, Black women and men activists in the larger community have increasingly included environmental abuse in their protests and demonstrations for socioeconomic equity. There are hundreds of grassroots organizations led by communities of poor people of color that have emerged across the United States in the last decade. For womanist theology to complete its vision of wholistic theologies of liberation (and survival), the natural environment where poor and working people live, work, and look for physical sustenance needs to be addressed. Whereas in the 1960s and 1970s grassroots and mainstream Black activists focused on jobs and housing, today African American women and men are also demanding a healthy environment for themselves, their elders, and their children.[15] This reality needs to be reflected in womanist theology.

We must wonder if it is only Jesus' humanity that makes him significant. Is it not his createdness and his identification with the well-being and suffering of all of creation that makes Jesus' embodiment of God who is Spirit so meaningful? Jesus' flesh, like the flesh of humankind, was made up of the elements that form our planet, our entire biosphere — earth, water, wind, heat. Jesus identifies not only with the sufferings and joys of being human, but with the sufferings and joys of all creation. Womanists must move beyond humanocentric discussions of symbolizations of Christ in its understanding of community. In traditional African worldviews, such as the Muntu cosmology of Bantu cultures, the community includes plants, animals, earth, sky, sun, moon, stars, and planets as well as women and men. Humankind is not disconnected from creation. To act as if we are results in discord and disease.

While womanist inclusion of Black foremothers and forefathers as symbolizations of Jesus appeals to African traditions of venerating ancestors, womanists must more fully consider the sacredness of earth, which is also part of our African religio-cultural heritage. The earth, after all, nurtures and sustains communities. It is our oldest ancestor, the womb that gives birth to our flesh, renewing it daily. Without the life-sustaining fruits of the earth, there would be no hope of survival and, as a result, no hope for freedom or liberation. Without the life-sustaining warmth of the sun, the quenching power of rain, the oxygen the air provides, there would be no hope for the physical sustenance of the bodies that enflesh our spirits. The entire cosmos, then, is engaged in God's activity of providing resources for survival and wholeness. Not only do we see Jesus in the faces of Black women; we see Jesus in the face of the earth, in the face of the waters, in the faces of wind and sun and moon. One of the forms of captivity that keeps human beings enslaved, womanists must add, is environmental racism and the global problem of environmental justice.

A Creation-Centered Christology

Womanist theologians and ethicists have been careful to consider the multivalent meanings that Walker assigns to the term "womanist." Walker most simply defines a womanist as a "black feminist or feminist of color." She struggles for the freedom of her people and loves women's culture, dance, food, the moon, the Spirit, love, roundness, and herself regardless. However, while Christian womanists have been careful to write texts that are consistent with Walker's basic definition of womanism, the creation-centered aspect of Walker's spirituality warrants more attention. Her reference to the moon, for example is a reference to a cosmologically based worldview found in women's cultures. "We Have a Beautiful Mother" in *Her Blue Body Everything We Know* is a love poem to Mother Earth. Moreover, Walker's writings in *Living by the Word* contain several essays that suggest a creation-centered spirituality.

Walker's writings reveal that a womanist not only loves women's culture, the *Spirit*, and herself regardless, but she also loves *creation*. In *The Color Purple* Celie's salvation (healing and wholeness) is symbolized by her decision that it is time to "enter into Creation." The concept of God and spirituality Celie embraces is panentheistic. God is in creation — in the purple flowers of the field, in rocks, in trees, as well as in Black women's bodies. For Walker, not only is God embodied in people, but God is embodied in creation as well. Womanists must consider the implications of such a worldview for womanist Christology.

From a womanist perspective that is in keeping with Walker's understanding of Spirit, creation, and human being as dynamically interrelated, it is true that Black women are connected to nature, but so is everyone else — White men, Black men, other women and men of color, White women. Walker makes this explicit in her essay "Everything Is a Human Being." *Building on Native American worldviews of plants and animals as our relatives, she reconfigures the meaning of human being and family.* To call every being human still suggests an anthropocentric perspective, but perhaps this is only honest since human beings understand reality with human hearts and minds. While eco-womanists, like eco-feminists and other eco-theologians, may strive to move toward a less humanocentric perspective on God and creation, perhaps it is best to admit the limitations of our ability to do this completely or perfectly. What is most important is that we treat the earth as our kin or neighbor. The crux of Walker's argument is that we must treat all of creation as we would our nearest, dearest relative. Humankind is not separate from nature but is a part of it. To be part of creation is to belong to God who is Spirit.

Walker's writings suggest that for a theology to be authentically womanist it must be creation-centered *and* Spirit-centered. Walker's Spirit-centeredness is creation-centered.[16] By proposing a creation-centered spirituality, Walker builds on traditional African and Native American cosmologies. Such spirituality is also Spirit-centered, because one encounters Spirit in creation. Creation embodies Spirit. Native American cosmologies emphasize a dynamic, nondualistic relationship between human beings, Spirit, and the rest of creation. Likewise, traditional African cosmologies like African Muntu presuppose that creation is good. Such an understanding of the goodness of creation is evident in the *Confessions* of the great North African (Numidian) theologian St. Augustine. African cosmologies and positive understandings of creation in relation to God or Spirit are not new to the Christian tradition. For Christian womanists, to turn to a creation/Spirit-centered understanding of God and the world is in keeping with the Christian tradition.

If womanist theology is creation/Spirit-centered, what is the meaning of Jesus Christ? Does this mean womanist theology is not Christ-centered? Since not all womanists are Christian, womanist theology is not Christ-centered for all womanists. It certainly is not Christ-centered for Walker. Womanists belong to a diversity of traditional and nontraditional religions. To claim that all womanist theology is Christ-centered would be to universalize the perspective of church-based womanists. But Christian womanists find Christianity compatible with Walker's spirituality. Likewise, Walker finds inspiration in the lives and writings of women from a diversity of religious traditions, including Christianity. How is it that so many Christian womanists identify with Walker's creation/Spirit-centered worldview? While not all womanist spirituality is Christ-centered, and Walker definitely does not seek Christ-centeredness, creation/Spirit-centered theology is not antithetical to Christ-centeredness. If one understands Christ as creation/Spirit-centered, it is possible to be womanist and Christian. I understand Christ as the incarnation of Spirit in creation. Christ as fully human and fully God is the perfect manifestation of Spirit in creation working in harmony with itself, something most of humankind fails to do.

For Jesus Christ to be fully human is to be fully *dust*, because according to Genesis we humans are created from dust. Dust is a metaphor for our bodily and elemental connection to the earth. Dust includes within it water, sun, and air, which enhance the vitality of its bodiliness and ability to increase life abundantly. So dustiness refers to human connectedness with the rest of creation. Jesus as dust represents God, who is Spirit, as fully embodied in creation. Jesus fully represents such connection, while we strive not to forget it.

For Jesus Christ to be fully God is to be fully Spirit with all the knowledge and power of God. Just as we humans, according to Genesis, are empowered by the breath, or Spirit, of God, so also is Jesus empowered by Spirit. However, as the Nicene Creed states, Jesus is far more than empowered by Spirit. Jesus is fully God and fully human. I would say that not only is Jesus fully God and fully human, but since God is Spirit and humans are dust, *Jesus is fully Spirit and fully dust.* Jesus as God incarnate is Spirit embodied in dust. Jesus is God as dust. God as dust is Immanuel, God who is with us in our joys, our suffering, our bodiliness, our spiritual growth and struggles. Jesus reminds us of God's intimate love of creation, which is so deep that God, who is Spirit, chooses to be one with creation, transcending it, yet permeating it even as it moves out and beyond into all that is unknown to human being. God as Spirit is the lovingness in creation, which is the empowerment of life whose aim is balance (justice). Spirit is like the water which permeates the mass of our bodiliness. It is incarnate even in the dust of the earth and in human bodies. I draw the metaphor of dust from Genesis, traditional Southeast African religious traditions, and Julie Dash's work *Daughters of the Dust.*[17]

What makes the rest of us humans, who are also dust and Spirit, different from Jesus? While we human beings are created in the likeness of God, Jesus *is* God. While we have the Spirit of God breathed into us, Jesus, fully dust in sharing the bodiliness of humanity and creation, fully embodies Spirit with perfect knowledge, wisdom, and power, fully knowing the mind of God. The author of the book of John emphasizes Jesus as Logos — the Word that was with God at the beginning of creation. As the very word of God, Jesus who is like us humans — suffering and celebrating with the rest of humanity — is for Christians also something more than us. While Jesus rolls in the dust with us, so to speak, Jesus is fully unified with that power which is the source of our existence — the Word of God, which is present in Genesis.

God's incarnation in Jesus is significant not only because God is manifest fully and perfectly in a human, but because God is manifest fully and perfectly in a creature. That creature is part of the rest of creation. God, embodied in Jesus, joins perfectly and anew with the dust of the earth, reconciling the broken relationship with God and creation in which we humans have involved ourselves by engaging in evil. Jesus realizes harmony of creation and Spirit in the actions associated with his life and work. As Rosemary Ruether observes, Jesus' prayer — known by Christians as the Lord's Prayer — contains remnants of the Jewish Jubilee tradition, connecting heaven with the renewal of earth and its peoples: "Our Father, who art in heaven, hallowed be thy name. Thy kingdom come. Thy will be done on earth as it is in heaven."[18] Over time, she explains, we have lost the traditions that underlie the full meaning of this passage, which is more than interhuman in its covenant. Salvation involves healing and wholeness for the entire earth.

Creation as the Least of These

While Christians generally understand God's will for salvation on earth to involve healing and wholeness for human beings, we must extend our understanding to include healing and wholeness for the rest of creation. To usher in God's will on earth as in heaven requires that we treat the earth as if it were heaven. This means we must treat it with respect for its sacredness and ensure its health, beauty, and wholeness. If Jesus is on the side of the least of these, as Matthew 25 suggests and womanist liberation theologians emphasize, then this includes the earth. It too is hungry for nourishment. It too is increasingly impoverished. The Psalms of the first testament of the Bible make several references to the entire earth singing praises to God. Jesus builds on first testament Scripture, observing that "even the rocks will cry out." The earth itself is described as fallen because of humankind's corruption through concupiscent acts in Genesis. It too is in need of redemption and salvation. It too rejoices that there is power in the universe "to make the wounded whole." Human responsibility that reconciles humankind and creation with God does not require dominating the earth, as Christians have often misunderstood their task, but loving the earth as one's kindred and one's self. Such relationship moves more wholistically toward renewed, restored relationship with creation and God. Restoration of right relationship with God includes restoration of right relationship with the earth. Such restoration is redemptive because we move toward God's original intention of the harmonious interrelatedness of life.

Moreover, if Jesus' ministry was "to set the captives free" as the author of Luke 4 writes (quoting Isaiah 61), then what does that mean for the earth, since the earth is also captive? Anthropocentric readings extend Jesus' ministry to the poor, outcast, sick, and captive as an exclusive concern for women, men, and children. The synoptic Gospels, however, also portray Jesus as one who is in harmony with all aspects of nature. He doesn't fear the winds but has the power to speak to them and still them, quieting the waves of the ocean at the same time. He warns his disciples that whatever they curse will be cursed and whatever they bless will be blessed, demonstrating by cursing a fig tree into barrenness. This particular story seems cruel. Does it suggest a domination of nature? Or is it a warning about our responsibility for how we use our powers to create and destroy? Since the synoptic Gospels do not portray Jesus as one who curses elsewhere, his actions and words here would best be taken as a warning not to take powers of blessing and cursing lightly. As followers of Jesus we are called to be self-conscious and responsible about our words and actions in relation to creation whether tree, woman, man, or child.

Jesus as the Greatest of the Ancestors

Theologians like Kortright Davis and Josiah Young image Jesus as the greatest of the ancestors. Grounding their theology in African worldviews, they share with African and Afrikan theologians around the world an understanding of Jesus that is communal, familial, and social. Spiritually and historically, Jesus is a member of an entire community of wise ancestors — similar to saints in the Christian tradition. What makes Jesus distinctive is his perfect wisdom and embodiment of God, who is Spirit.

The significance of the ancestors and the responsibility to remember them is a theme in Morrison's novel *Beloved*. Toni Morrison's narrative suggests that the mysterious character Beloved is more than the ghost of Sethe's child, whose neck she cut with a handsaw to save her from slavery. Beloved's memory holds knowledge of the experiences of the ancestors, extending to the slave ships of the Middle Passage. She has a memory of African mothers who died during the trans-Atlantic slave trade. Beloved represents not only the ghost of Sethe's dead daughter but also ancestors from Sethe's slave and African history.[19] The dedication of the novel to "Sixty million and more" refers to the estimated number of Black Africans who never made it into slavery, but died as captives in Africa or on slave ships. Morrison explains that "one account describes the Congo as so clogged with bodies that the boat couldn't pass. That's a river broader than [the Hudson]."[20]

Beloved is a woman who "walked out of the water" and who remembers the brutality of slavery and the slave passage.[21] Similarly, in Julie Dash's film and screenplay *Daughters of the Dust*, the characters Nana Peazant, Eli, and Eulah ponder the myth of slaves who walked on the water back to Africa. There is a scene in Dash's film in which Eli walks on the water like his mythic ancestors — a symbol of the power to overcome bondage and enter freedom. Dash's narrative explains that according to some, the Ibo walked on the water back to Africa and freedom. According to others they drowned. In any case, their intention, whether we go with history or myth, was to find freedom and home on "the other side" of bondage. Beloved, in Morrison's novel, moves in reverse. She walks *out* of the water, representing the *return* of historical and mythic ancestors. Neither Dash nor Morrison nor the myths they draw on are Christocentric. The myth of walking on water is not peculiar to Christian narrative. The power to walk on water is present in pre-Christian and Christian narrative. Moreover, Jesus is like African ancestors in his power over death. Death fails to erase the power of his life. For humankind, he lives in communal memory.

The only way to erase those who have died unjustly is to erase memory, but not even memory can be erased permanently. The memories with which Morrison's characters wrestle are memories of bondage and violence. They finally gather together to exorcise the ghost of the past, deeply abused Beloved, who haunts Sethe and her family. But the novel's postlude suggests that the most haunting truths of Black experience exist always on the boundaries of communal memory and culture.[22] Morrison's work reminds us that we cannot erase histories we would like to forget. Memories have prophetic value. Although no chains or restraining devices like the ones Beloved refers to in her remembrance of the Middle Passage are preserved in the United States, in Brazil "they've kept *everything*," Morrison observes.[23] The past can be "disremembered" but never erased. Beloved "erupts into her separate parts" in the postlude to her exorcism, but she still exists on the margins of consciousness. The text criticizes her exile to these margins.

> Everybody knew what she was called, but nobody knew her name. Disremembered and unaccounted for, she cannot be lost because no one is looking for her, and even if she were, how can they call her if they don't know her name?... By and by all trace is gone, and what is forgotten is not only the footprints but the water too and what it is down there. The rest is weather. Not the breath of the disremembered and unaccounted for, but wind in the eaves.... Certainly no clamor for a kiss. Beloved.[24]

Beloved, a representation of African ancestors, is present in the midst of supposed absence. Like the bones of sixty million and more African ancestors who lie in the depths of the Atlantic Ocean, she is remembered by few. Explained as a coincidental change in weather, she is dismissed as "wind," which is also a metaphor for spirit. According to certain African cosmologies, the ancestors, which contemporary African Americans too often disremember, live on through "children, relatives, *rituals of re-*

membrance, and significant deeds."[25] Those ancestors whose names no one remembers attain the status of spirits. Though no one can recall their names, they remain part of the community. They are considered part of present, past, and future reality. Morrison's allusion to such a cosmology challenges readers to reconstruct their understanding of community.

One constant regarding Beloved's person is reference to her severed neck.[26] Beloved's severed neck recalls the "snake-haired" or dreadlocked African goddess Medusa, who was co-opted by the Greeks and beheaded.[27] Whoever Beloved is, Stamp Paid observes that she is a reminder that people "who die bad won't stay in the ground" — not "Jesus Christ Himself...."[28] Reflecting African pre-Christian and African American Christian worldviews, he suggests Jesus is one of many who will not stay buried because they have died violently. Jesus is one of millions of persecuted ancestors who live in the margins of everyday consciousness. Moving beyond Morrison's text, one might consider that the ground itself will not hold the blood of murder. Just as the earth cried out at Cain's slaying of Abel, so it continues to cry out across the centuries against injustice.

Christian womanists might argue that in the ancestral community of Moses, Zipporah, Jethro, Nat Turner, Harriet Tubman, and Sojourner Truth, Christ perfectly embodies the power of the God of Moses, "I Am," Being-Itself. Jesus Christ as greatest of the ancestors sustains community. Community includes the earth, which in some sense is our oldest living elder and our elemental ancestor. Jesus, who is *God as dust and spirit*, is organic to creation's physical and spiritual sustenance. Women as well as men are called to participate in this sustaining activity. In spite of our limitations, our finite understanding, and our struggle with violence, we are called to participate in such embodiment of Spirit.

Immanuel: God Feeling with Us

I began this chapter by quoting Tashi-Evelyn-Mrs. Johnson's criticism about separating Jesus' suffering from the suffering of others. Not only do we need to reconnect Jesus' suffering with the suffering of women, but with the entire earth. As a Christian womanist, I would say that Jesus, who is God as Dust and Spirit and Greatest of the Ancestors, reveals God with us, Immanuel. Jesus as Immanuel feels with us. Jesus not only sustains us but teaches us to feel anew the interconnectedness of life. Feeling such interconnectedness moves people out of prisons of individualism to relearn compassion, to experientially know and understand that injustice anywhere is a threat to justice everywhere, when one suffers all suffer, when one rejoices all rejoice. It *moves* believers to *act* for justice.

Process theologian Marjorie Suchocki emphasizes that God *feels* with creation. For me, Jesus' suffering with humanity has to do with feeling, which Suchocki describes as God's *relational* activity.[29] Jesus, as greatest ancestral exemplar of right relationship, heals broken relationship by teaching us to feel *with* one another. Such feeling is traditionally called love, mercy, compassion. Jesus' suffering is connected with women's suffering because Jesus *feels with women*. It is connected with the earth's suffering because Jesus *feels with the earth*. Truly following Immanuel empowers those who seek to participate in Spirit to feel injustice so that we can identify it and overcome it. We are empowered to feel goodness, joy, and right relationship so that we can move more fully toward it. The significance of Jesus' suffering with creation cannot be reduced to idolizing martyrdom. Rather, it has to do with spiritual fellow-feeling. To follow Jesus requires learning to feel distinctions between right and wrong so that we are drawn to participate in God's justice-making activity. Such feeling is not irrational. It is connected with reason. It relates heart with mind, spirit with reason. Spirit and Reason are One. For process theologians it refers to consciousness. This kind of feeling, which is different from feeling in the conventional sense, empowers human beings to work toward balancing the scales of justice to make for right relationship. It is a revelation of *Spirit*.

impt. point.

Notes

1. Alice Walker, *Possessing the Secret of Joy* (New York: Harcourt Brace Jovanovich, 1993), 227.

2. Ibid., 273–75.

3. Delores Williams, *Sisters in the Wilderness: The Challenge of Womanist God-Talk* (Maryknoll, N.Y.: Orbis Books, 1993), 169.

4. Jacquelyn Grant, "The Sin of Servanthood," in Emilie Townes, ed., *A Troubling in My Soul* (Maryknoll, N.Y.: Orbis Books, 1993), 199–218.

5. See Williams, *Sisters in the Wilderness*, 164–66.

6. Ibid.

7. Sharon Welch, *A Feminist Ethic of Risk* (Minneapolis: Fortress, 1990), 65–100.

8. Jacquelyn Grant, "Womanist Jesus and the Mutual Struggle for Liberation," in Randall C. Bailey and Jacquelyn Grant, eds., *The Recovery of Black Presence: An Interdisciplinary Exploration* (Nashville: Abingdon, 1995), 139.

9. Ibid., 39.

10. Kelly Brown Douglas, *The Black Christ* (Maryknoll, N.Y.: Orbis Books, 1994), 108–9.

11. Williams, *Sisters in the Wilderness*, 167–69.

12. See my book *A Singing Something: Womanist Reflections on Anna Julia Cooper* (New York: Crossroad, 1994), 68–74, for a fuller discussion of Anna Cooper's symbolizations of Jesus in relation to Black womanhood.

13. I am indebted to Bessie Collins, a Ph.D. student in my 1996 Womanist Theology and Ethics class, who argues that acts of defilement corrupt the defiler.

14. Grant, "Womanist Jesus and the Mutual Struggle for Liberation," 130–31.

15. See Robert D. Bullard, *Dumping in Dixie: Race, Class, and Environmental Quality* (Boulder, Colo.: Westview Press, 1990, 1994), 27–31 and 171.

16. The writings of Cheryl Townsend Gilkes, Delores Williams, Jacquelyn Grant, and Katie Cannon, for example, all give some attention to the concept of God as Spirit. James H. Evans in *We Have Been Believers* observes that "throughout the personal narratives and literary works of African American women the emphasis on the spiritual essence of God is a recurring theme. This motif is most poignantly expressed in Alice Walker's novel *The Color Purple....* There Shug affirms that God can be found only by 'them that search for it inside.'" While Evans and womanists are careful to observe the significance of Walker's work for a concept of the Spirit, the concept of creation in relation to Spirit in the same text deserves fuller exploration (see James Evans, *We Have Been Believers* [Minneapolis: Augsburg Fortress, 1992], 73).

17. See Julie Dash, *Daughters of the Dust: The Making of an African American Woman's Film* (New York: The New Press, 1992).

18. Rosemary Ruether, *Gaia and God: An Ecofeminist Theology of Earth Healing* (San Francisco: HarperCollins, 1992), 214–15.

19. Toni Morrison, *Beloved* (New York: Alfred K. Knopf, 1987), 210–17. See also Walter Clemons, "A Gravestone of Memories," *Newsweek* (September 28, 1987), 74–75.

20. Clemons, "A Gravestone of Memories," 74–75.

21. Morrison, *Beloved*, 50ff.

22. Ibid., 274–75.

23. Clemons, "A Gravestone of Memories," 74–75.

24. Morrison, *Beloved*, 274–75.

25. Maulana Karenga, "Black Religion," *African-American Religious Studies*, ed. Gayraud Wilmore (Durham and London: Duke University Press, 1989), 274.

26. Morrison, *Beloved*, 132, 211–15, 261, 264–67.

27. See Norma Lorre Goodrich, *Priestesses* (New York: Harper Perennial, 1989), 172–90, for a discussion of Medusa as African and Atlantic priestess.

28. Morrison, *Beloved*, 188.

29. Marjorie Suchocki, *God, Christ, Church: A Practical Guide to Process Theology* (New York: Crossroad, 1992), 28–36, 39, 49–61, 109–10, 203–6.

The Scandal of GOD with a Body

XODUS Perspectives on Jesus

A s HOWARD THURMAN noted many years ago, African American Christology has focused on Jesus of Nazareth, the oppressed first-century Jew.[1] Unlike orthodox Christianity's Jesus, understood in terms of the Passion week themes of death and resurrection, the Jesus of Black folks — from Harriet Tubman, Sojourner Truth, Anna Julia Cooper, Martin Luther King, Jr., to Jesse Jackson and Bernice King (Martin's youngest and "anointed" daughter) — is and was the one who performed miracles of healing and exorcisms, who preached love and forgiveness. This Jesus of Nazareth was that same controversial oppressed Jew who dared to extend forgiveness even to one's enemies! Such a thought remains controversial even now. He earned fame and renown, but his radical politics and self-understanding apparently threatened the powers-that-were in first-century Palestine, and he was murdered as a political criminal by the occupying "police force" of his time — the Romans. The power of Jesus as the Disinherited One whose message spoke to the disinherited of his time remains vital to the followers of Jesus even now. Even now those who follow Jesus believe that GOD had the "last word" on the whole messy business of Jesus' death, raising him from death to Life. The movement from the fully human "him" to glorious Lord "Him" rests on the faith-assumption that "even death couldn't hold Him in the grave."

Ethically, because Jesus arose from a certain and verified cessation of life into Eternal Life, there is the theological assurance that no obstacle, no problem, no negation of life has to have the final "say." Because He arose, all of us who have suffered the slings and arrows of oppressive misfortune, systemic violence, negation, and erasure can be confident in the GOD who is Able to "make a way out of no way" as the famous Black Christian faith-proclamation announces. Because Jesus arose on the first

94

"Easter Sunday," the followers of Jesus are empowered to do "all things" in His name, with love, with fervor, and with conviction. Resurrection is GOD's *Yes!* to the totalizing power of tyrannical No's! It is a Divine limiting of intimidating power, of imperious threats and the illusions that they comprise. With such assurance human life is freed from the manipulations of coercive power and freed to act on the deeper impulses of loving service.

What do such musings mean to XODUS theology and ethics? Universal faith-statements such as those in the preceding paragraphs are given specificity as we examine the Scandal of GOD having a BODY. The underlying theological and philosophical "scandal" of Christianity lies precisely at this critical juncture, that the GOD-of-Many-Names who is both Spirit and immanent in Creation could materialize the Divine Self into one human form. More sharply, the scandal of Christology, the Incarnation or in-fleshment of the Divine, is intensified in XODUS because XODUS theology insists that if GOD is really GOD and not "God," then we must respecify and reclaim GOD's difference-within-identity.

The Scandal of GOD's enfleshment presses sociopolitical overtones into the very fabric of christological reflection. GOD is most assuredly Black for Black people, Italian for Italians, Jamaican for Jamaicans, German for the Germans, Arabic for the Arabs, and Irish for the Irish, all at the same time. GOD's *personal* Being is "all things to all people," simultaneously, without contradiction or preference. Such an embodied GOD, a GOD with the Rainbow of "flesh" tones cannot "belong" to or be "owned" by any single people. In this way GOD is ever on "our side" as well as undermining the pretensions of ethnic-nationalist chauvinism — at the same time! GOD, in the Scandalous BODY of "Christ," truly fulfills the meaning of "Christ," *anointing* all humanity with GOD's presence, while affirming and relativizing our particularities. Through the Rainbow of GOD's embodiment a political standard of difference-in-solidarity is symbolized.

In XODUS the BLACKness or AFRIKANness of GOD does not erase or negate the REDness of Native-Americanness or the ASIANness of various Asian understandings of GOD. The scandal of GOD having a BODY is that GOD sanctifies human bodies by in-dwelling within flesh and blood in all its many-colored hues and textures. GOD privileges human bodiliness by being "incarnate," to use the traditional theological expression. Therefore, in the event of GOD becoming flesh through Jesus Christ we can make the bold theological assumption that all human shades and varieties of Flesh are sanctified. This is ethically scandalous because such a theological assertion subverts sociopolitical patterns of preference for certain groups over others. It is ethically scandalous as well because it disrupts the idolatrous racialized aesthetics of dominant groups which influence standards of beauty and ugliness within societies.

The Flesh of GOD, GOD's BODY, ought never be confined to or privileged by any particular association with the Varieties of the human form. Such human Variety is properly reflected in the many kinds and types of ethnicities which adhere to representations of Jesus as Chinese, Nigerian, English, or any other particular ethnic grouping. It is because we assert the theological "truth" that GOD's FLESH can be represented in every kind and type of human being that we learn the SCANDAL of Christ, that GOD has revealed GOD-self to *all*, even to those too illiterate to read about it, to those too removed from power centers to profit from the news, and to those whose genetic ancestry has socially foreordained their status to that of inferiority in human society. The moral import is clear — because GOD has taken on a BODY, no set of laws or customs can deny GOD from reaching every person because GOD's compassionate outreach includes all flesh. The ethical upshot which follows radicalizes this theological truth by insisting that social, political, and economic patterns and institutions must be challenged to conform to this Christ-like pattern of inclusion. *Christ-like inclusion is a processive expression* into the ways in which we live our lives, create laws to govern ourselves and institutions to embody our ideals.

XODUS Christology employs both the traditional African American adherence to the flesh-and-blood Jesus of Nazareth become Glorious Savior and the incarnational GOD who moves out into various nations, colors, and textures of humanity. This "both/and" valuing is important because, on the one hand, it encourages a universal appreciation for who and what Jesus did as a Jew, thus qualifying false appropriations of Jesus as only a German (as the Nazis' perverted Christology proclaimed),[2] or as a Euro-American male with blond hair and blue eyes (as the Hollywood portrayals of Jesus directly imply). It even tempers certain ideological celebrations of a Black Jesus which reify the "color" of Jesus without any kind of symbolic excursus as to the nature of "Black" as an ontological symbol of oppression. Misappropriations of James Cone's "Black Jesus" or Albert Cleage's "Black Messiah" can become such reified symbolizations. On the other hand, XODUS Christology can give an unqualified affirmation of any and all kinds of visions of Jesus (from Ghanaian to Chilean to North American) which *celebrate the symbolic multiversity of embodiment* that obtains from the incarnated GOD represented by the name "Jesus." *It is morally appropriate in this historic period of racialized retrenchment, fear-mongering, and scapegoating of Brown peoples in purportedly*

"White" America for African Americans to embrace a Black Jesus. To affirm Jesus' Blackness is to re-cognize, that is, re-appreciate and re-envision the divine groundedness of our BLACK skins. We do have BLACK skins, and if racism has devalued the beauty of that skin color, idolizing any and every other hue that is lighter than jet black, then it is completely necessary for us to place BLACK skin at the forefront of a subversive christological irruption. Why? An XODUS answer would be that it is in affirming "the least of these my sisters and brothers..." (Matt. 25). *It is necessary that the least valued of all skin-tones in the world be lifted up to make visible the very likeness of Jesus Christ.* Thus the SCANDAL of saying Jesus is BLACK is both *theologically meaningful and sociopolitically valid!*

At the same time, we ought to examine this Black Jesus in light of the historic Jew Jesus of Nazareth in order that we not simply project all of our needs, ideals, and social desires onto a normative model of spiritual heroism and then name it "Jesus Christ." Some would say that I am making a distinction between the historical "Jesus" and the universal "Christ" of faith, but such a distinction would not be true to the energetic church rituals, living images, and naming of Jesus in African American communities. When one says "Jesus" in most African American Christian contexts, the historical Jew Jesus of Nazareth and the Jesus usually called "Christ" in theological circles are being cited. Focusing on the Jewishness of Jesus helps us to understand the profoundly rich religious traditions which shaped Judaism of the first century. There, caught between the iron claws of the Roman Empire, Jewish life was severely compromised. Political leadership was coerced to follow courses of expediency rather than what we would call "self-determination," because whenever political uprising occurred, massive destruction and crucifixions soon followed. Jesus based all of his teaching and preaching on the Torah and could well be viewed as a preacher-in-parables, as were the great rabbis Gamaliel and Hillel. His rhetorical patterns were those of a Jew. His self-understanding of his mission was of healing, delivering, and exorcising the demonic from his own people, even though he did not refuse his gifts to others.

Many Africentric scholars have contested the Europeanizing of Jesus and Jews, reclaiming Jews as African peoples.[3] A careful reading of the Exodus narrative (Exod. 12:37–38) reveals the often overlooked, mostly downplayed line that states that the six hundred thousand who departed from Egypt were a "mixed crowd." The Hebrews, the Semites, were not merely a "race," but a concatenation of various kinds of peoples, including Africans. Moses, after all, married a black-skinned ("Cushite") Ethiopian woman, Zipporah! Jews, like many peoples who arose on the land bridge between Africa and Asia, were *Afro-Asiatic people.*[4] An unprejudiced view of a map or globe will tell anyone this *fact.* Like contemporary African Americans, ancient Hebrews probably ranged in skin tone from very dark brown to yellow, with hair ranging from kinky to semi-straight, and with a variety of other features and body configurations. It is difficult for Euro-dominated persons, of all colors, to even *consider* that Jesus might have been "Black" in our sense of the term. In order to exorcise our minds from Euro-heteronomy and from the hegemony of imagination imposed by centuries of erasing the Afro-Asiatic heritage of Jesus' Jewishness, an XODUS Christology simultaneously lifts up both Jesus' Blackness and his Jewishness.

Yet most African American churches struggle to affirm Jesus' Blackness and Jewishness. Why is it that we have a hard time seeing the SCANDALOUS GOD WITH A BODY as possessing a "Black" body? Why is it so difficult to note that Jesus was not a "Christian" but a Jew? An even more troubling question combines the two ideas: what is the connection between our inability to love our Blackness and the rising anti-Jewishness within Black churches? Michael Lerner, a leading liberal Jewish intellectual speaks about growing up as a Jew from the 1950s through the 1970s as being difficult because, while assimilation into mainstream American life was the ostensible strategy for Jewish flourishing, there were also intentional attempts to maintain Jewish distinctiveness.[5] His autobiographical narrative strikes this African American as resonating with the kind of "double-consciousness" — being "American" and something else — that W. E. B. Du Bois spoke of in *The Souls of Black Folk:* "two warring souls, one African, the other American."

Is it possible that the struggle for Jewish identity and our struggle resonate so closely on the social-moral plane that our communities inevitably irritate and clash with one another in our attempts to define what it is that we are experiencing? Or to be more precise, is it possible that the social experiences of Jews and Blacks in America are just similar enough to resonate, while at the same time there remains enough of a significant difference (the economic and skin-color differences being the most apparent) for conflicts to be exacerbated? I continue to find myself jolted by sermons in Black churches where otherwise unprejudiced preachers drop unflattering portrayals of Jews as "cheats" and "in charge of the money" while fighting racism in the next breath. Michael Lerner and Cornel West provide an exemplary model of honest, respectful, and sometimes conflictual dialogue that moves toward the goal of creating a healing between the two communities. Such a goal has implications for the kind of

Jesus we envision. I believe that a second-generation Black theology must encourage Black churches to explore both the Blackness and Jewishness of Jesus as a way of exploring the theological dimensions of a broader Christology. As we broaden our definitions of Christ we may find ways to affirm the presence of those Jews who have been in solidarity with Black self-love and Black self-determination all along. Thus, while the Journey of XODUS is one of an enriched consciousness of Afrikanity, it inevitably draws us into specific discourse, dialogue, and solidarity with other peoples. In order to develop an XODUS Christology that does not deepen anti-Semitism in Black churches, the Jewishness of Jesus must be formulated as part of our reconstructive task.

Creation-Centered Christology in XODUS

Karen refers to Jesus the Christ in ecological terms directly tied to Creation itself. Such a naming extends GOD's em-BODYment toward its ramifications in the natural world. In XODUS language Karen's thought pushes the Scandal of GOD having a BODY outward into even more scandalizing directions because such theologizing nudges rather uncomfortably against a comfortably "human" face of Jesus! The entire notion of GOD reaching out to all "flesh" expands the comfortably human-centered assumption that "flesh" refers only to human beings. "Flesh" includes the entire Creation which GOD has made. A Creation-centered Christology expands a traditionally human "Jesus" into a model of Christ which encloses Jesus' human flesh with the cosmological "FLESH" of the entire world. Such a model of Christ might be called "Jesus-in-Nature." Jesus-in-Nature has "feet" that look a lot like the roots of trees and seaweed. Jesus-in-Nature has "arms" which reach out to the world like branches of a tree. Jesus-in-Nature "breathes" in the tiniest rustling of the wind, sometimes rising to "voice" in the powerful declamations of hurricane and tornado. To encounter Jesus-in-Nature is to reanimate Nature's "voices" from the silence of empirical observation and thereby to move toward a mystic harmony with the Earth. While speaking of mystical harmony with GOD, it is very traditional to speak about being "in Christ," but we radicalize the idea when we re-conceive being "in Christ" as learning to "listen" to Jesus-in-Nature as manifested in ripples of a pond, the majesty of autumn's colors, and the sponginess of black dirt.[6]

If XODUS theologizing is truly a JOURNEY, then I see the cleansing "Blood" of a Jesus-in-Nature as in the salty depths of the ocean waters. The pierced side of Jesus hanging on a Cross, from the vantage point of this Creation-centered Christ Jesus, may indeed be the place from which flow the ruptured blood-red landslides caused by unregulated strip-mining of originally pristine landscapes. Did the pouring forth of "water and blood" from Jesus' pierced side have any moral bearing on the destruction of nature? When I survey the "wondrous cross" of Jesus, I must take account of this unconventional naming of "the Blood" because it compels the spiritual imagination to consider the interconnections between the suffering of Jesus caused by humanity and the suffering of nature caused by humanity.

That phrase "the Blood" is one of the most revered and most often used within African American Christian churches. Its high place within our spirituality may have something to do with the drawing of blood from being whipped by cruel overseers and masters as slaves. For instance one of the verses of the communion spiritual "I Know It Was the Blood" reads:

> Well they whipped Him through the night,
> They whipped Him all night long,
> They whipped Him through the night for me
> One day when I was lost He died on the Cross
> I know it was the Blood for me

One of the most startling revelations of recent research on the period of enslavement has been the excessive brutality by which the enslavers controlled Africans. In a nineteenth-century cartoon a naked African woman is shown tied to a tree limb, completely exposed, with the caption that she was whipped two hundred times! If we are to believe this account, then this slave woman endured a scourging worse than that which Jesus suffered (with the Roman custom of thirty-nine lashes) the night before He was crucified on the Cross. If she survived, which the cartoon does not tell us, then she surely may have been viewed as Jesus was by His disciples, as one resurrected from "the grave." Such a woman gives credence to Jacquelyn Grant's claim that the Black Woman *is Christ* for our times. An XODUS Christology affirms the notion that all those who have suffered "unto death" — from the savagery of human-created famine to the brutality of intertribal genocide (as in Rwanda between the Tutsi and Hutu tribes in 1994) — and *survived* are living examples of the *Power of GOD revealed in Christ Jesus.* Jesus became "Christ" when He was experienced as a living embodied Presence after His certified "death" on a Roman instrument of torture and death, the Cross.

But what does all this have to do with "the Blood"? The Blood of Jesus is a theological symbol for the most precious life-giving substance which flowed through his Body, which He shed "for us." Conventional African American Christians buy into the sacrificial Atonement theory of Jesus' substitutionary death. Delores Williams decries such a theory as inimical to the psychospiritual health of Black folks, particularly Black women, who have been historically conditioned and socialized to bear the bloody crosses of surrogacy, violence, and abuse "for" their community. Williams's critique of Atonement is creatively addressed by Karen. I would want to add an XODUS reconfiguration to "the Blood."

I struggle with notions of redemptive "sacrifice" in a way similar to that of Delores Williams. My father spilled the blood of a chicken on the foundation of our home as it was being built, explaining to me that "the old folks said...a sacrifice of blood" was required at the start of every new building lest "someone be taken" by death during the process of the building. He said this matter-of-factly, solemnly, and with a sense of the IS-ness of things that in my child's mind I simply accepted. In my studies many years later I learned that such a religious sacrifice of a chicken (or other animal) had similarities to rites of sacrifice in traditional African religions, Voudon, Santeria, and other New World African spiritualities. My father did not teach me anything about such religiosity; he simply *performed* the rituals intrinsic to these neo-African religions! He was a deacon in the church, an exemplary Christian, but...he still "remembered" what the "old folks" had to say, and kept their traditions alive for me.

Later, before he died in 1984, he related to me in terse phrases that he had to "go on before" me in order to "make it possible" for me to have a good life. With lymphoma cancer completely metastasized throughout his body, each word, each breath was difficult to catch, but I distinctly heard him tell me that *his death* was going to have a salvific and empowering meaning for my life. Such notions resonate with traditional African notions of ancestorhood, which I did not really understand at the time. An ancestor is one who "goes before" into the realm of Ancestors to "make a way" for those still remaining here in this realm. Ancestors communicate with us through dreams, signs, and occasionally more spectacularly. Without divulging any of the "appearances" of my father, suffice it to say that my spouse and I have both experienced both my father and my mother as "ancestors" making a better way possible on "the other side" for us remaining here "on this side." Notice that death and sacrifice are reconfigured here not as focused on the suffering, blood, and the gory details of how my parents died, but on the salvific effect of their deaths. *When I consider "the Blood" then, it is recast in such a way that it is a symbol of the ongoing family ties that I have with my ancestors, so the*

*BLOOD of Jesus symbolizes our ongoing ties with the Ancestor of our Faith
who has gone on before to "make a way out of no way."*

> *It reaches to the highest mountain,*
> *It flows to the lowest valley,*
> *Oh the blood that gives me strength from day to day,*
>   *it will never lose its power.*

> (refrain from "The Blood Will Never Lose Its Power,"
>   one of the favorite hymns in Black churches,
>   particularly during Communion Service)

The ethical upshot of the sentiments voiced in the above hymn imply
that the BLOOD of Jesus symbolizes a power of GOD that can extend
itself to the uttermost reaches of human humiliation, depravity, and need.
The "highest mountain" of life might be understood in several ways:
(1) the greatest moments of exaltation and human joy, (2) those greatest moments of human striving which need to be overcome, (3) the most
arrogant, god-less persons, civilizations, or cultures, or even (4) specifically for African Americans those seemingly insurmountable obstacles
placed before us in a society that negates persons of color. The BLOOD
reaches *even* to these "highest" of obstacles. The imagery of "valley" in
hymnody often represents the lowest points emotionally, spiritually, and
even physically, such as times of great trial, sickness, and disease. The
BLOOD reaches to these points as well. The climactic message of the
refrain is that this sacred BLOOD strengthens *on a daily basis*, and that
its power is inexhaustible. Such a re-presentation of the BLOOD implies an *ongoing atonement theory*, not a simplistic buying into traditional
Anselmian "satisfaction" notions of Jesus' atoning work as "once and for
all," satisfying the sullied "honor" of a monarchical God. This BLOOD
is being shed continually, experienced daily, and is needed by followers/
believers of Jesus on an ongoing basis.

So what are we to say to persons like Delores Williams, who rightfully criticize the theo-ethical manipulation of sacrificial christological
theories, particularly in regard to historically enforced surrogacy roles of
African American women? The critique that Williams presents in *Sisters in the Wilderness* ought not to be decried or denied out of turn, for
it is one of the most specific, thoroughgoing ethical criticisms of how a
theological notion can be used oppressively to legitimate unjust behavior.
Williams rightfully connects Christologies whose understanding of Jesus'
work emphasizes sacrifice with the coercive practices of males demanding that women incarnate Christ's sacrificial role in society. Sacrificial
Christologies have been used demonically to imprison abused women

in violent relationships. Sacrificial Christologies have indeed borne several deformed and malnourished ethical norms within traditional church teachings about what is considered "normal" Christian behavior. The question really comes down to whether entirely excising theologies and norms of sacrifice will sufficiently purge unjust practices within Christianity. I hope that by showing how the BLOOD is understood both within a Christian home and in Black church worship dialogue might be encouraged about the positive and complex valences of "blood" rhetoric within African American Christian spirituality. The BLOOD is a very concrete and "real" experience for many African American Christians, much more than rhetoric about "sacrifice" for the sake of sacrifice:

- For a people who have had to go to every length, even being willing to give one's life in order to be free, notions of "sacrifice" for others is not a theological abstraction. In the concrete flesh-and-blood struggle to make life a little bit better for our "children," African Americans have experienced ideas about sacrifice for the good of the future as an unwelcome but inevitable possibility.

Karen Baker-Fletcher turned my head around about the issue of sacrifice as tied to male understandings of ultimate value when she stated that one ought to *find something worth living for* during the early days of our marriage. It seems to be a particularly "male" construction within our community that one must be willing to "die" for something in order for it to be valuable. Even Martin Luther King, who David Garrow interpreted as embodying the martyr norm of "bearing the cross," used to say that a person who had not found something worth dying for has not found anything worth living for. Such martyr norms, when proclaimed in the powerful eloquence of a preacher, need to be examined closely in our time of gang warfare, casual handgun use, and the prevalence of the street rhetoric of threat. Gangs also believe in a norm of sacrifice, but it is a norm emptied of the kind of generational significance and hope for eventual social transformation that King and others spoke of during the Freedom Struggle of the mid-twentieth century. Gang sacrificial norms appear to lift up death as an inevitability that one must face with hardness and a determination to "take as many wit' cha" as possible! Such a casting of sacrifice implies that one faces certain death with a warrior's dignity. Yet such a norm has encouraged Black young men to destroy each other in record numbers! Without a doubt being a "street soldier" means embracing an ethos of death-dealing that threatens to empty the meaning of "future" for all but a remnant of African Americans if we cannot find a way to overturn the momentum that has set in.

Williams emphasizes the norms of life-giving and healing that Jesus incarnated in His life. She lifts up the *living* Jesus of Nazareth, as well as the *living Christ of faith.* XODUS Christology must agree. In XODUS we JOURNEY toward the future *following a living Jesus,* not tied to a Cross of death.

XODUS Cross

What then becomes of "the Cross" for XODUS Christology? In the most hard-headed fashion I must insist that "Crosses" in life seek us out, and invariably seem to find us. We do not have to seek sacrifices, the demands of life will place "Crosses" on our backs. What the BLOOD symbolizes is that inner strengthening which the *Living Jesus* provides to His follow- ers to withstand the strain, stress, and bearing-down forces — otherwise symbolized as "Crosses" — which threaten to destroy us. The Cross of Jesus of Nazareth is empty. The nails no longer pierce any body parts of Jesus of Nazareth. But in the contemporary social world we are nailed to Crosses of injustice, racism, sexism, and other forms of oppressive vio- lence daily. The physically challenged experience their "difference" from norms of physical "able-ness" as a Cross. We experience life oftentimes in the same way that Jesus did as depicted on Roman Catholic crucifixes, as piercing our bodies, draining away our life energies, and pointing toward the inescapability of death. Yet the Cross, in XODUS, is empty because no matter how inevitable the "Crosses" of life may be, they are not more powerful than the BLOOD of the *Living Jesus.*

The crossing of two lines in either a " + " or an "X" has important ramifications for XODUS christological reflection. There has been a his- torical, cross-cultural, and interreligious JOURNEY of the crossing of lines. As I have written in *XODUS: An African American Male Journey* (Fortress, 1995), the "X" harkens back to an ancient cryptic greeting of "illegal" Christians. By drawing a "line in the sand" during an ostensi- ble salutation, an invitation was subtly proposed to the person greeted to draw a crossing line over the first line, thus identifying oneself as Christian during a time when the Roman Empire had outlawed Chris- tianity. The crossing of lines has had a universal religious import from ancient times, often symbolizing the four compass directions. After the remarkable public career of Malcolm X, the "X" represents for African Americans something of Malcolm's "lost-found" JOURNEY toward re- claiming and reinventing one's self in an audaciously symbolic fashion. The "X" of Malcolm X represented his "lost" African tribal or ances- tral name; these names had been stripped away from all Africans who were kidnapped and taken into North America as slaves. The movement from his "slave name" of Malcolm *Little* to Malcolm *X* enabled Malcolm to find a new name and a new sense of self within the Nation of Islam under the radical teachings of the Honorable Elijah Muhammad. His JOURNEY eventually led him away even from the Nation of Islam to an embracing of orthodox Sunni Islam, which he symbolized by taking on yet another name, El Hajj Malik El-Shabazz. Each of these name changes represented yet another step along his JOURNEY, a JOURNEY which I believe we might call his X-ODUS away from Euro-hegemonic definitions and impositions to a more African self-definition and centered-ness.

The "X" for contemporary African Americans is a "CROSS of LIFE." Embracing the X of XODUS represents a psychospiritual "death" to Euro-heteronomy and a rebirth into the NEW REALM of Afrikan-centeredness. Afrikan-centeredness is not a racialized chauvinism, reverse discrimination, or "skinocracy" (a term used by Kortright Davis in his *Emancipation Still Comin'*). As we have "died" to the love of all things, all values, all visions of European derivation, so we "rise" to the NEW LIFE of dis-covering/un-covering the suppressed layers of Africanity which we were previously too ASLEEP to notice. Such a psychospiritual resurrection is a lot like waking up from a four-hundred-year NIGHTMARE. It is an AWAKENING. Such an event is, in fact, akin to a "second birth" because it bursts forth within the consciousness as a SURGE of cleansing ANGER. This ANGER is righteously energized by the wave upon wave of new information pouring forth from both printing presses and archeological digs about what exactly happened to our people, and why we were even coerced to support the so-called "Enlightened" capitalists who stole our bodies from African shores. Yet ANGER soon subsides into a more productive form of ongoing CREATIVITY as we learn to channel ANGER's energies through disciplined reflection. CREATIVITY no longer needs to repudiate Europeans or Euro-Americans, but begins to build itself on a critical reappropriation of the forgotten/neglected/stolen remains of great African cultures. Such CREATIVITY is *critically appreciative*, a dynamic hermeneutic that continually sifts through the cultural evidences, sorts out the distances between uplifting ideals and dehumanizing practices, and presses toward finding ways to appropriately bring the ancient remains of ancient African traditions back to life. As such, CREATIVITY embodies Afrikan-centered XODUS **resurrection** of the boldest and most innovative sort.

Christological CREATIVITY is underway in this text, reclaiming the ANKH, for example, as one of the possible originating inspirations for

Christians to invert the meaning of the death-dealing cross of crucifixion into a CROSS of Life. The ANKH was an ancient Kemetic (Egyptian) symbol of Ma'at, the sevenfold ordering virtue and moral law of the Cosmos. As the Cross of Life it symbolized both male and female creativity joining together at the crossbars to represent the ongoingness of living generations which were the fruit of the union of both principles. XODUS CREATIVITY scours through ancient texts, bringing the philosophical riches of ancient Medu Netcher into the postmodern period with a vengeance.

Jesus the Rider on a White Horse

> Ride on, King Jesus,
> No man [sic] can a'hinder me
> Ride on, King Jesus, Ride,
> No man [sic] can a'hinder me.
> For He is King of Kings.
> He is Lord of Lords,
> Jesus Christ, the First and Last.
> No man [sic] works like Him.
>
> — African American spiritual

There is a militancy in these lyrics that always used to energize me in church on Sunday mornings. Here we find no Jesus meek and mild, head bowed, whipped and chastised... like a slave! Rather we see a celebration of the Conquering King of the book of Revelation returning to pass judgment on "sinners." Somehow it always was clear to me that these "sinners" were not ordinary sinners, who had ordinary faults and weaknesses, but were the crafters and maintainers of injustice, misery, greed, and oppression in the world. The sermons and the music I remember from my childhood and participate in even now seem to celebrate Jesus' return not as one who will punish those who are the "ordinary sinners" of life, but will "set things right" in the world. Of course the language is vivid, militarist, and violent. So is oppression.

Why do such words sound so strangely out of place in a Christology? Is it because we do not want to place *anything violent* near the nonviolent Jesus of orthodoxy? Surely, one might say, it is not only theologically unsound but immoral for a Christian ethicist to advocate a Conquering Jesus in an era when radical right-wing militias believe that "Jesus was not a Pacifist" — thereby manipulating Jesus into a gun-toting Warrior supportive of their own causes. I am sensitive to such charges. Yet it is the Conquering Jesus who still intrigues my imagination because He is not merely a symbol of social justice violence. Rather, it was the *personal energizing* of King Jesus that allowed oppressed Black folk to recognize that no powerful race, political machine, or social custom could "hinder" them. Such a casting of Jesus did not erase the nonviolent teachings of Jesus, but placed them into position within the formation of one's own spirituality where they could be understood as *necessary penultimate ethical strategies* for surviving in a violent world.

Whereas contemporary televangelists use Jesus the Conquering King in such an individualistic fashion that one can "claim" Jesus against personal poverty and for wealth and prosperity, the "Ride On King Jesus" of Black folks enabled us to survive tremendous psychic assault and often physical threat. There is a huge social distance between the two understandings. The televangelist can often use Jesus as Conqueror as a foil for questionable exegesis on North America's role as a "Christian country." It is surprising how often the symbol of King Jesus is used by a variety of these telepreachers as a way of making a way for an individual to achieve the "American dream" of prosperity. But prosperity, bolstering flagging patriotism, and a "gospel of wealth" remain far from the minds of oppressed Black folk who clap their hands and tap their toes to the spiritual "Ride On King Jesus" on Sunday mornings.

The Jesus of the spiritual "Ride On King Jesus" is the same one who "rides in the middle of the air" (compare this lyric with the reference to Rev. 14:14) coming to judge the earth. But this eschatological figure of judgment is *not* merely the One we await. This Jesus is accomplishing something in the here-and-now realm of existence that deserves some XODUS reflection:

- The Horse-riding, Cloud-Riding Jesus is an image that might originally have reminded the African composers of this spiritual of the storm gods such as Shango (Yoruba god of lightning and thunder) and Oya (orisha/goddess of winds and rain) or other divinities in the various pantheons of Yoruba and other West African religions.[7] If such a phenomenon of religious transference did occur, then the Jesus of Horse-Riding and Cloud-Riding would have appeared to be much more akin to traditional divinities with which Africans were acquainted.

- Theophus Smith's *Conjuring Culture* insists that Africans used Christian categories to surreptitiously (and oftentimes *unconsciously*) maintain direct spiritual ties with their stripped-away African spiritual roots.

- The Jesus who can Ride a Spiritual Horse and comes in might Riding a Heavenly Cloud *opens up a creative SPACE* within which, however momentarily or fragmentarily, a sense of Divine Freedom could be experienced during worship.

- Such a Space for sensing the spiritual reality of Divine Freedom was not and is not something to be overlooked or downplayed. If in the presence of worshiping a Conquering Jesus oppressed African Americans could achieve a state of momentary UNION with that to which the Divine was calling them to BECOME, then the Horse-Riding/Cloud-Riding Jesus is worth considering positively. I would call the creation of such a Space the process of XODUS Space, that is, the JOURNEY toward which Space-making takes on great significance. May it be noted that I am not referring here to ecstatic "shouts" or trances of worship merely, but rather to the entire spiritual experience of oppressed Black folk lifting up "King Jesus" whom no "man" — including the White "man" — could hinder.

- The celebration of Jesus' unhinderability implied that being a Child of God, a follower of this Jesus, meant that one did not have to be "hindered" by all those apparently insurmountable obstacles which racism, sexism, and classism put in one's way.

If we continue to explore the image of the Conquering King Jesus from the vantage point set forth above we see a very different understanding of "conquering" and "kingship" than is held by those who do not question the injustice of the status quo.

Notes

1. Howard Thurman, *Jesus and the Disinherited* (Nashville: Abingdon-Cokesbury Press, 1948).

2. This the demonic perversion of Christology in the works of Emmanuel Hirsch, criticized very effectively in the ongoing work of Prof. Clark Williamson of the Christian Theological Seminary, Indianapolis, Ind.; cf. *A Guest in the House of Israel* (Louisville: Westminster/John Knox Press, 1993).

3. This is particularly true in the extensive works of Dr. Ben Joachanon. See particularly *We the Black Jews* (Baltimore: Black Classic Press, 1983) and *The African Origin of Major Western Religions* (Baltimore: Black Classic Press, 1970).

4. A major scholarly support of such a redefinition of traditionally "European-ized" Hebrews comes in the ongoing work of Cain Hope Felder of the Howard University Divinity School, as well as several other African American biblical scholars including Randall C. Bailer, Charles Copher (the "Father" of the movement by most accounts!), Renita Weems, and John Waters. See Cain Hope Felder, ed., *Stony the*

Road We Trod: African American Biblical Interpretation (Minneapolis: Fortress, 1991), and Cain Hope Felder, *Troubling Biblical Waters: Race, Class, and Family* (Maryknoll, N.Y.: Orbis Books, 1989).

5. Michael Lerner and Cornel West, *Jews and Blacks: Let the Healing Begin* (New York: Grosset/Putnam Books, 1995), 27–28.

6. Such theo-poesis builds on the formidable scholarship of Sallie McFague in *The Body of God: An Ecological Theology* (Minneapolis: Fortress, 1993) as well as the formative feminist theo-ecological writings of Rosemary Radford Ruether: *Sexism and God-Talk* (Boston: Beacon, 1983); and *Gaia and God: An Ecofeminist Theology of the Earth* (San Francisco: HarperCollins, 1992).

7. Robert Hood writes about this very clearly in *Must God Remain Greek: Afro Cultures and God-Talk* (Minneapolis: Fortress, 1990), 60–61.

Dialogue on CHRIST

Karen

As you point out, the saying that one must find "something worth dying for" is dangerous. I agree that whether it is desirable or not, those who struggle for justice often end up sacrificing their lives because of the risk involved. But the "something" that young people choose to die for is often infected by consumerist lust and is devoid of spiritual depth. Does XODUS thought leave itself vulnerable to glorifying death and the blood of violence rather than the power of God to overcome death?

KASIMU

Your question is both profound and disturbing. The depth of concrete sociopolitical struggles for justice often involves wrestling with questions of self-sacrifice for the sake of a future realization of social "justice." Black male and female freedom fighters throughout our historical sojourn here in the "New World" have faced this question in numerous desperate situations. XODUS *faces* the ghastly possibility of self-sacrifice, as one faces the dangers and pitfalls of every positive moral act bent toward freedom from tyranny, oppression, and injustice. The "powers-that-be" never give up their privileges without violent repression, and those that lead the movement are always targeted first by the slayers of dreams. History proves this. Christ's death on a Cross is but one manifestation of this horrible human, or rather, institutional reality. Yet I believe that the real *power* of the Christ narrative is in the belief that GOD does not glorify death, but overcomes death with life. Death is not the final word even for those who have lost their lives in a justice struggle.

Karen

I agree with you that, like it or not, those who struggle for justice bear a kind of cross. You still have not answered my question about whether

XODUS thought *glorifies death*. What role does the resurrection play in your thinking?

KASIMU

All right, I will answer the charge of glorification of death directly. I affirm the Christian belief in the resurrection of Jesus' dead body to life as an affirmation that the power of GOD is greater than the power of death and self-sacrifice. I think that an XODUS Christology must make this a central point. If I have spoken of blood and sacrifice in relationship to traditional African religiosity too much, then perhaps I *have* glorified death in that sense.

Karen

I cannot think about Jesus' blood without thinking about Mary's blood. To discuss the blood of Mary's womb is taboo. But where did Jesus' blood come from if not from Mary? One can see the blood and water of the womb, like the blood and water shed on the cross, as symbols of life. Isn't this the deepest scandal of Christianity's enfleshed God? Is there room for this in XODUS?

KASIMU

Yes there is plenty of room for enlarging the "scandal of an enfleshed GOD" to include the humanity of Mary's blood as an aspect of Jesus' sacred Blood. As a matter of fact, I think that reflecting on the "Blood of Jesus" as Mary's blood intrinsically lifts up blood-imagery from the mire of traditional atonement theory's glorification of the self-sacrificial "meaning" of the shedding of blood. Women "shed blood" every month as a *possibility for life and not death*. The womb gives birth through a dramatic "shedding of blood" from which a new life is celebrated. Imagine how the introduction of *these kinds of images of shedding blood*, taken from the concrete life experiences of women, could enrich our Christologies.

Karen

Is womanist Christology more ready to affirm the image of Jesus as female than XODUS Christology? While you refer to the possibility, you do not flesh it out. Even in conservative churches I have heard pastors lead parishioners to sing songs that proclaim "I see Jesus on each face." To see Jesus on each face is to say, in effect, that not only is Jesus Black, African, Asian, Latin American (*male*), or historically Jewish, but Jesus is also male *and* female. Why is it difficult for male clergy to fully affirm this?

KASIMU

With a firm commitment to greater theological equality between female and male images and symbols, I still must confess a certain loss of nerve when it comes to exploring female symbolizations of Christ. Having been raised in the thoroughly patriarchal theological mores of Black Baptist traditions, I find myself assenting to the need for female understandings of Christ intellectually, without knowing how such images can be appropriated into the everyday depths of Christian worship practices. Your challenge requires of me a willingness to really "see Jesus" in the eyes, faces, arms, and hands of women. To "see Jesus" in this way necessarily requires a different understanding of how Jesus communes in the hearts, souls, and bodies of *all* believers.

One of the ways in which I find myself wrestling with Jesus-as-Black-Woman symbol is to reexamine certain biblical symbolizations of Jesus as the "wisdom of God" in 1 Corinthians 1:24 in this light. Here the Apostle Paul insists on affirming that *the foolish, weak, and stumbling crucified and resurrected Christ is both the power of God and the wisdom of God.* Such a bold conflation of terms brings all of the known intellectual and spiritual cosmos together into one human being, Jesus Christ. Yet the Hebrew proverbial imagery of Wisdom as the female cohort with God in Creation found in Proverbs 8 and 9 is directly suggested. There are overt connections between Jesus as the Logos of God who was with God from the beginning (John 1:1) and the Female Sophia/Chokmah (Wisdom) who proclaims in Proverbs 8:22, "The Lord created me at the beginning of his work, the first of his acts of long ago" (NRSV). Throughout Proverbs Wisdom is personified in the female imagery and rhetoric of "she" and "her," a distinct departure from the prevailing male images of God. If Jesus is the Wisdom of God, then theologically and scripturally we ought to be able to affirm that Jesus (at least as the experiential "Christ") can be *both* male and female. What has become increasingly significant for me is the need for all Followers of Jesus to embrace the radical possibilities for broadening our spirituality. It is not necessary for me to completely affirm the Christa in order for me to embrace the female symbolism of both Jesus (as Wisdom of GOD) and his work (as a Labor of love akin to the labor pains of women) that are already in Scripture.

How does this Scripture tie into Black women's experience of a Black female Christ? Throughout the literature of African American writers we find rich tomes celebrating our mothers and grandmothers as the embodiment of our community's wisdom. If Jesus *is* the Wisdom of GOD, and Black experience recognizes Black women as the wisdom of our people, then there are possibilities for re-cognizing GOD's Wisdom through Christ as the same Wisdom that African American artists have come to represent in our Mothers and Grandmothers. Such symbolism would have to take care not to put motherhood on a pedestal, thereby devaluing those many Black women who are not mothers. Nevertheless, this symbolism provides christological weight to the concrete existential reality of Black women's Wisdom as rooted in GOD. In this sense, also, we may say that each of us has experienced Christ every time we have been blessed with the Wisdom of our Mothers/Grandmothers. Such a re-casting of Jesus requires open-mindedness. I am open-minded, however, because such openness is a sign that I am still willing to risk the XODUS JOURNEY.

Although there are several "cutting edges" to your christological chapter, your insights into Jesus as DUST is a promising area of new theological imagination. To connect the elements of air, water, and fire with the lowly "dust" of the earth signals a new way of viewing Jesus' humanity in relationship to Divinity. Yet you press us to consider how Jesus brings together SPIRIT with DUST. This moves us to reconsider one of the most revered traditional symbolizations of Christ—Jesus as the Revelation of GOD. A terse reconstruction of Jesus as DUST may evoke in contemporary sensibility an analogous sense of shock as the phrase "God became flesh" might have for first-century Hellenists. Since most of us think of dust as "dirty," how do we rethink of DUST as the holy element which GOD as SPIRIT uses?

Karen

Do we really think of dust as dirty if we stop to think about biblical references, particularly in Genesis 1? The metaphor has shock value because it does require us to stop and think of where we came from, what we are made of — the same elements that comprise earth, water, air, and fire (heat). There was a time when African Americans as a whole lived closer to the land. Since Black migration to urban centers over well more than three-quarters of the twentieth century, we have distanced ourselves from the land. According to the synoptic Gospels Jesus spoke freely about earth *and Spirit*. We tend to forget that we, like all people, are dependent on the land for our physical sustenance. Not only that, but we are dependent on the land for our spiritual sustenance as well. When we and others love the land, more often than not it returns sustaining power to us. When we and others treat it poorly, we suffer the consequences. The industries that our people often work for all too frequently pollute our air and neighborhoods. It is important that more of us join in with those in our communities who are demanding both jobs *and* environmentally conscious industrial practices. In doing so, we recover what our ancestors knew and what our elders still know — the livelihood of our spirits *and* bodies is interwoven with the livelihood of the cosmos.

KASIMU

If Jesus "feels" with humanity, then is He also the *Epiphany of SPIRIT as Feeling?* An "epiphany" is another way of speaking about a "revealing" or "uncovering of something hidden." How does this Jesus, who has come to reveal the hidden things of the SPIRIT, relate to the traditional understandings of Christ as the Revelation of GOD?

Karen

Yes, I would say that Jesus Christ is indeed the epiphany of *Spirit as Feeling.* Such revelation continues today through the Spirit of Christ which is ever-present. Jesus Christ reveals God as Spirit who *feels with* humankind, the earth, the rest of creation. It is the revelation of that which *knows* all because it *feels all.* Feeling with, empathy, is the deepest form of knowing, so strong that humankind cannot contain it except for brief, rare revelatory moments.

KASIMU

Your work inspires one to pursue the problem of theodicy by the christological "answer" of Jesus as "feeling" so much *with* and *for the cosmos* that the final victory over pain, suffering, death, torture, and all of the various hosts of evil is assured. Because I know that SPIRIT "feels" with me, I am mysteriously opened to the possibilities for acting as Jesus did as a healer, liberator, and freedom fighter. That is what you mean by "compassion." Yet how does this "feeling" Jesus relate to the suffering of oppression and nature? Does the Jesus who "feels" with the cosmos activate something within us that refuses to be silent in the face of horrid injustice? How are we moved by this Jesus to act as healers to the sick and providers of food to the hungry?

Karen

I would like to say that this Jesus who feels with the cosmos activates something within humankind that refuses to be silent in the face of injustice. Unfortunately that is not always true. If it were, we would not see so much violence and disregard for others around us. It is more accurate to say that Jesus *can* activate us to resist injustice *if* we are open and willing. It is *possible* to be activated to participate in personal and social transformation. There are, however, conditions involved. The primary condition is one of willingness. Even then Paul's dictum that the good he would do he did not and the evil he would not do he did is true for all of us. We are not clones of Jesus Christ. We make mistakes even when we strive to do good. The second condition is that we must be willing to learn from our mistakes. Among other conditions, we must be willing to repent and ask forgiveness for those mistakes we are aware of as well as for those that only God and/or others recognize.

KASIMU

Your answer focuses on *our* response but does not address the *theodicy problem of a "feeling" Jesus in relationship to a suffering Cosmos*. Is this Jesus powerless before the movements of destruction and hatred?

Karen

You asked a similar question in response to my God chapter. No, Jesus Christ, the revelation of God as Spirit who feels with us, is not powerless. Jesus Christ as revelation of God, however, *shares* power with us. Therefore, we are not powerless either. This is where the problem comes in. Because we have the power (specifically the power of freedom) to choose to participate in good or evil, we are beset with problems of sin versus righteousness. It is possible that only if God determined to cease such sharing of power would we have a world devoid of injustice. But to ask God to do so is asking God to do everything for us, with humankind exempt from responsibility for love and justice. I wonder if we would be as loveable or interesting to God and one another if we did not share power to choose to align ourselves with good over evil? What amazing love God sheds upon humankind to allow us such freedom. What amazing love God shares to create us in God's likeness insofar as we have this freedom to choose whom we love. It makes us subjects with God, who shares power with us, rather than objects to be manipulated. Jesus, the revelation of God's power of freedom and love, is not powerless. Jesus reveals the source of power, which we share in limited ways.

KASIMU

So then, does Christ become a primary moral Exemplar of our human responsibility to choose GOD's power by participating in acts of loving justice?

Karen

Yes. But Christ is also something more than that. I certainly see the historical Jesus as an exemplar. But historically, when we look at the understanding of Christ in the lives of African American women and others who emphasize religious *experience*, Christ is more than an exemplar. Christ can be experienced in the hearts of believers in every generation. Here I would make a distinction between the historical Jesus of Nazareth and the living Jesus as Christ who fully transcends history, incarnate in the hearts of believers and revealing the power of life in all of creation in every era and beyond time.

Part III

HUMANITY

Seven

Only "Human" Nature

XODUS Anthropology

Q UESTIONS ABOUT the meaning of human life to a people who perceive themselves to be edging toward possible extinction take on a
distinctive urgency. With over 70 percent of the nation's male prison
population and 46 percent of the female inmates being African American, while representing only 15 percent of the general population of
the United States of America, incarceration and imprisonment are major factors in considering African American humanity. Are we a people
whose humanity is being heteronomized — determined by forces outside of our communities, forces determined to depict us negatively? More
pointedly, have African Americans really been accorded the status of
being "human," or are we being coerced to accept the status of "useful tools" which we had during slavery? XODUS anthropology cannot
begin with abstract intellectualism. It is abstract intellectualism for an
Afrikan scholar to begin with the kind of careful logic forwarded by
Gordon Kaufman as he discusses the groundedness of a normative humanity in the "biohistorical" emergence of evolutionary development of
human culture, combining evolutionary biology with a sophisticated theory of culture.[1] In a time of crisis, such a turn to the scientific discipline
of evolutionary biology would be a betrayal of compassion, an intentional
attempt to be "respectable" at the cost of being irrelevant. Even discussions of the biblical fundamental of being made in the "image of GOD"
(Gen. 1:26–27) can become abstract intellectualism if not grounded in
the turbulent *sociohistorical context and continuing legacy of African subordination.* James Evans says this well when he notes in *We Have Been
Believers:*

> The true nature of black humanity has been veiled by a litany of
> stereotypes endemic to western European culture. People of Af-
> rican descent have been described as inferior, savage, profane, and

119

invisible; they have been called outsiders, intruders, interlopers, and subhuman beasts.[2]

With justifiable rage, XODUS theology insists that our humanity *is* being heteronomously defined by those outside of our community who care little for its future flourishing. In order to properly explore a theological anthropology from an XODUS perspective it is important to *examine the fundamental problematic of social dignity in light of the negative heteronomous imposition of thingification as experienced by the continuing legacy of slavery on the one hand, and the positive reclamation of humanity and dignity which African Americans created for ourselves on the other hand.* The narrative of our painful encounter with dehumanizing practices is not wholly negative, for it is flavored with the creative efforts of a people who moved beyond the psychic boundaries of their sociopolitical and economic oppression. Out of a masterful synthesis of the discarded tatters of recognition thrown our direction and the memories of African mythoforms as transmogrified by enslavement, Africans living in North America forged a unique vision of humanity. Yet through the continuing retrenchment legacy of racialized narcissism there remains the threat of thingification by criminalization even a generation after the Freedom Struggle of the twentieth century. XODUS anthropology insists that African peoples living in the USA must experience both a historical excavation of what we have done, and a contemporary psychospiritual migration "back to Africa" by which we might found a firm sense of humanity not dependent on amending a three-fifths of a person Constitutional appraisal of our human beingness. This psychospiritual migration "back to Africa" is complex because it involves the forging of a new understanding of the role of work, self-criticism, and responsibility for the well-being of all Community — human and otherwise. As such I do not call for a romanticized return to the glories of ancient Kemet, nor do I resurrect Garvey's call for a massive emigration back to the Motherland. Rather, the JOURNEY of XODUS begins in the small steps of creating a liberating, nonsexist, enlivening SPACE for the flourishing of our selves, our family relationships, our children, our people, and then expanding that circle of concern to include all peoples and the Earth.

XODUS theology and ethics problematizes the role of gender discrimination as well as racial subordination as necessary components for reclaiming our human beingness. Care must be taken to criticize those aspects of "manhood" inimical to the flourishing of humanity, yet finding ways to embrace and revive the good and beautiful even in "gangstas" who visit violence on the streetz on a daily basis. Ultimately the aim of

XODUS anthropology is *reclamation and revival of the good and beautiful, which is the freedom we have as GOD's "children."*

An essential part of reconfiguring a nonpatriarchal masculinity is naming one's economic status and making it distinct from one's appraisal of human worthiness. Men in capitalist cultures particularly tend to conflate their sense of worth with their economic state. So doing, those who are laid off permanently by company "downsizing" are left with a shattered sense of self, destroyed by the mingling of job evaluation with human valuation. The task of XODUS reclamation and revival must be to aid men to see their lives as a JOURNEY filled with various challenges, joys, and pains, and not as a quest for economic stability. The *terra firma* of our humanity is beyond the control of profit assessments because it is DIVINEly implanted.

Construction: "Twenty Million Black People in Prison"

The first step in creating an XODUS anthropology is to look at the socially grounded symbols of *imprisonment* and *criminalization* in contrast to the religiously grounded counter-symbols of *awakening* and *freedom*.

Malcolm X's address on January 23, 1963, to a group of students at a Michigan State University rally reveals the power of the imagery of imprisonment in considering African American humanity. It is an interpretation of Black humanity in the United States as existentially grounded in the slave experience. The slave experience, for Malcolm X, was paradigmatically divided between the relatively privileged place of the "house Negroes" or those whose work kept them physically close to the Master performing the duties pertaining to maintaining the domicile such as butler, cook, valet, and driver; and the "field Negroes" who labored out in the cotton fields, the backbone of the slavemaster's unpaid workforce. Malcolm saw a paradigmatic difference between the psychic loyalties of the two types of "Negro": the "house" Negro completely identified all that is meaningful and significant with the "Master," and the "field" Negro identified with the masses of hard-working, disenfranchised, nononsense Black folk. In the humorous style which made him such an unforgettable orator, Malcolm X described how the "house" Negroes were in the minority, were well fed, well-dressed, and lived close to "Master" in Master's house; while the "field" Negroes had to fend for themselves, wore the tattered bits of cloth thrown their direction, and continually prayed that Master and his house would burn! From these two types of Black humanity Malcolm discerned that the house Negro became the favored, intellectual, well-educated, and chosen-by-Whites "representative" of *all* Negroes, even though this person's values, loyalties, and goals had nothing to do with the masses of Black folk. Deeply criticizing those descendants of house Negroes, Malcolm denounced such persons as ignorant of their historical heritage of leadership, culture, and civilizations like ancient Egypt, Mali, and Carthage in Africa because their minds had been imprisoned by the educational process of racist propaganda.[3] Such persons — Uncle Toms — are like well-trained "watchdogs" preventing fellow Blacks from entering the "house" of opportunity:

> He [the Uncle Tom] is like a watchdog or a hound dog. . . . Now that dog, when he's out in the street, only his own life is threatened, and he's never been trained to protect himself. He's only been trained by his master to think in terms of what's good for his master. So when you catch him in the street and you threaten him, he'll go around you. But when you come up on — through the gate when he's sitting on the master's porch, then he'll bare his fangs and get ready to bite you. Not because you're threatening him, but because you threaten his master who has trained him not to protect himself but to protect the property of the master.[4]

Such persons believed themselves to be defenders of "the White man" and the "American government" set up by "the White man" according to Malcolm. Further, such persons were delusional in their inability to accurately discern the difference between genuine friends to whom one ought to be loyal and enemies:

> The Uncle Tom can't see his enemy. He thinks his friend is his enemy and his enemy is his friend. And he usually ends up loving his enemy, turning his other cheek to his enemy.[5]

Such deluded African Americans had been used by the "Christian religion" and its emphasis on nonretaliatory love as pawns of White power in Malcolm's view. He called on the "new type" of Black, one who rejected Christianity and embraced respect for one's body and soul, as the effective counterpart to the imprisoned and deluded Uncle Tom. The New Type of African American, in XODUS as in Malcolm's view, recognizes that African Americans are a people who "were brought here and put in a political, economic, and mental prison."[6] The New Type of African American stood up and debunked the premise of integrationist tokenism as the privileging of the former "house Negroes" rather than genuine reclamation of full human freedom. Malcolm believed that the "integration-intoxicated Negro" was merely being given more room to roam inside the confines of the "prison," and not any actual power of self-representation:

> Now you have 20 million Black people in this country who were brought here put in a political, economic, and mental prison. This was done by Uncle Sam. And today you don't realize what a crime your forefathers have committed. And you think that when you open the door a few cracks, and give this little integration-intoxicated Negro a chance to run around in the prison yard — that's all he's doing — that you're doing him a favor. But as long as he has to look up to someone who doesn't represent him and doesn't speak for him, that person represents the warden, he doesn't represent some kind of president or mayor or governor or congressman or anything else.[7]

This stunning criticism places *all* African Americans in the "prison." The United States, in such a view, *is a PRISON*. Such rhetoric has tremendous import for creating a contemporary XODUS anthropology because it employs the confining concrete facticity of imprisonment as an operative metaphor for the cultural, sociopolitical, economic, and spiritual life of African Americans. It reminds us that the chains by which we were enslaved and reminded of our inferior social status historically as slaves remain more than an image of a dim and unfortunate past for Blacks today. Every evening news program shows young Black men bent over with their arms locked behind their backs in handcuffs, and sometimes their legs bound together in chains. Imprisonment is more than symbolic; it is a visceral everyday experience for all African Americans. An XODUS view of humanity, therefore, highlights the spiritual significance of Imprisonment as a way of describing the reality of African American life experience. We are Imprisoned by the systemic perpetration of Euro-heteronomy, intellectually compelled to accept the vaunted "superiority" of all things European and "White," and thereby devaluing (whether we are conscious of doing so or not) all other values, accomplishments, and cultural heritages. We are Imprisoned by a lack of economic care, confining African Americans and various Brown peoples to the bottom levels of job opportunities. To name Imprisonment this way is not to demonize the technological, philosophical, scientific, or theological achievements of the various nations which comprise Europe. Demonization and Victimization are not the intent of the symbol Imprisonment. Rather, it is to make crystal clear the actual historical complex of practices and discourses whose overall historic inertia continues to reproduce a dominant cultural "belief" that there really is nothing valuable or worth studying *outside of*

Europe and America. Imprisonment is a state of be-ing which enchains the minds of Europeans as much as it does the minds of Native Americans, African peoples, Asian peoples, the so-called "minority" peoples inhabiting the American "center" of power.

To concretize Imprisonment in this way is one side of an XODUS anthropology. The other side of Imprisonment resonates with certain aspects of traditional views of "sin," although it upholds such views *from within a cultural and societal view which insists that one must name both the social structures which bind and blind our best moral intentions, and our various individual responses and moral choices within the set social structures.* To cast Imprisonment in this way is to express it as a symbol of a state of sinfulness.

Sin has been defined by various theologians throughout Christian history in a multitude of ways. In Augustine's *Confessions* he uses the image of a spiritual "chain" binding his will, keeping him from turning his entire volition toward a full and complete rest in the revelation of Jesus Christ. Now that is a powerful image of Imprisonment! For Augustine the power of Christ's grace was enough to break open this "chain" and set humanity's continual desire for spiritual "rest" at ease. In later writings Augustine spoke in a metaphysical way about all things being created good but not perfectly good; thereby sinful acts are the manifestation of the corruption or privation of the good, rather than an expression of some ontological evil force in the cosmos.[8] Aquinas also located the seat of sin in the will and in actions which spring from the will, noting that "every sin is voluntary,"[9] yet his description of sin did not emphasize imagery of Imprisonment as much as describe it as an *inordinate desire of a temporal good rather than God who is the Supreme Good.*[10] Luther extended the theological imagery of Imprisonment even further by noting that there can be no free will since human sinfulness, as described in Pauline terms, is so utterly complete and thorough that *the human will is forever in a bondage which only faith in Christ can break.*[11]

For XODUS such views of human sin have usefulness in constructing a view of the power of Imprisonment as a metaphor for the human condition. But the Imprisonment we have experienced as a people was not merely the inordinate desire for a temporal good rather than the Good which is GOD, although surely Black bodies were desired, used, and abused because of the inordinate desires of capitalists for more wealth. Inordinate desire is part of the picture, but not the whole. Women's lives and bodies are not used and abused by systems of patriarchy because of inordinate desire alone, even though one might attribute a great deal of a *theological* explanation of sexism to this kind of answer. Rather, *both*

sexism and racism are perpetuated by (1) an inherent bent within human-
ity toward repression and violence, and (2) the socially organized, societally
transmitted value systems embodied in systemic and institutionalized forms.

XODUS anthropology resonates, on the one hand, with the sensitive
analysis of the propensity within the human psyche toward aggression,
which expresses itself in repressive violence as articulated by Marjorie Suchocki,[12] and, on the other, social gospel giant Walter Rauschenbusch's
definition of the social solidarity of "sin." Sin, for Rauschenbusch, must
always be understood as a *social phenomenon*, not isolated or contained
in the private foibles and vices of individuals.[13] Further, Rauschenbusch
believed that the unjust institutionalized practices and customs of one
generation are passed on to the next, and in this the Kingdom of
Evil strives to defeat the justice work of the Kingdom of God. Thus
Rauschenbusch focused attention on the transmission of sinful behaviors
as one of the consequences of socialization, noting that those discourses
and practices which perpetuate injustice are the "super-personal forces" of
group evil rather than any kind of spiritualized idealization of "demons"
as such.[14] The oppression whereby entire sectors of a people are set aside
for the cathartic practices of scapegoating is a form of Imprisonment in
XODUS thinking.

The metaphorical symbolism of Imprisonment has a self-critical valence which undercuts any tendencies toward pleas of victimization.
While African Americans see ourselves as Imprisoned by centuries-old
patterns of prejudicial behavior by racist, sexist, and class oppression here
in the United States, we are not wholly innocent. Spinning an elaborate tale of Euro-domination is too facile a critique of the experience of
human sinfulness in African American and Afrikan communities. Various
tribes in Africa suffer from systemic forms of traditional Imprisonment
in the form of generations-long intertribal hatred which feeds genocidal energies. Afrikan women, despite the gains of the global women's
movement of the last two decades in which Black women have participated, continue to lag far behind Afrikan males in overall wage-earning
capacity. African American males found ourselves publicly confessing the
sin of irresponsibility, abusiveness, and sexist behavior during the Million
Man March in October of 1995. At a very fundamental level, we were
repenting of our self-Imprisonment to the sinful sociocultural patterns
of traditional patriarchy, with its concomitant patterns which support
the subjugation of women and occasional outbursts of physical abuse as
means for shoring up one's "rightful place" of unassailed dominance in
the household! XODUS anthropology, if it really is committed to being
prophetic, decries patriarchy as that manifestation of Imprisonment which

destroys the possibility for wholeness, liberation, and salvation. The violence of young Black males against each other is a manifestation of the deadly reality of Black sinfulness, a reflection of the lethal ways in which one can participate in self-Imprisonment. The power of Imprisonment resides in its capacity to convince the self that one has no good, righteous, beautiful, and uplifting choices. When people are self-Imprisoned, their ethical process is thwarted and their moral processes issue forth in both self-destructive and antisocial behaviors.

The problem of self-Imprisonment is not confined to Afrikans or people of color. Those who suffer various forms of physical/mental challenge, for example, continually struggle with the enervating power of Imprisonment by images and subtle "messages" which connote our "difference" as a sign of inferiority. The problem with such a grim symbol is that it could collapse in upon itself, emptying itself even of descriptive authority, unless we can name a way out which rings true both to the Gospel message and the experience of the Folk. Before we do so, however, we need to address a growing concrete social manifestation of Imprisonment in the Black community — criminalization.

Criminalization

There are more young African American males in prison cells than in college classrooms (677,000 in jails versus 436,000 in higher education). While much of the population of the United States mouths easy platitudes about "law and order," African American communities experience the bloody consequences of genuine lawlessness and moral nihilism. Those precious "ties that bind" which have kept the spirits and hopes of the Folk alive have become unraveled with the increasing disillusionment and despair rampant in post-Civil-Rights-era USA. Instead of seeing "the Promised Land," as described so eloquently by Dr. King in 1968, we have witnessed the unfolding of an ever-growing American nightmare, with the bodies and souls of Black Folk being lifted up as fit Sacrificial Offerings on Altars of Postmodernity. Are Black men inherently "criminal," or is this a status imposed by those forces of Imprisonment which reign in the "land of the free, home of the brave"?

Amos N. Wilson provides a controversial, thought-provoking explanation for the underlying psychosocial dynamics of White supremacy which drive the push for criminalizing African Americans, especially Black males. In his *Black-on-Black Violence: The Psychodynamics of Black Self-Annihilation in Service of White Domination* (1990) Wilson pens a stunning thesis which states, in effect, that *the European American dom-*

inant population encourages disaffected and disenfranchised young African American males to engage in self-destructive behaviors as a way of reinforcing unconscious perceptions of their cultural-racial superiority and, likewise, of inherent Black inferiority. Through a carefully constructed argument Wilson presents the idea that as the image of Blacks as "criminal" and "rebel" are projected into society they are *introjected* (individual internalization on the part of the young African American male of "the prohibitions, values, attitudes, and commands of others as his own even when their acceptance and incorporation may work against his objective interests").[15]

Racialized narcissism in Euro-populations globally has engendered a situation where the genuine historical damages and cultural genocides propagated by various European nations are overlooked, neglected, ignored, and ultimately "forgotten" by the *projection culture.* The act of projecting negative expectations, stereotypes, and rewards reinforces self-annihilating behaviors in the introjected groups. For Wilson, then, the Black-on-Black violent person has allowed himself to become the ultimate tool of White supremacy, having so dissociated himself from pertinent loyalties to kin and kind that no healthy sense of identity, somebodiness, self-respect, or self-other regard remains. In effect Wilson calls the Black-on-Black violent individual the ultimate "Tom," the race traitor who has sold out his humanity and fundamental loyalties in order to imitate the very image of racialized narcissism which has destroyed his proper dignity![16] Such a person is the embodiment of the archetypal *CRIMINAL* that the projective racialized narcissist has intended. In the dominant society's effort to control these CRIMINALS, the building of more jails and more prison staffing make criminality a multibillion dollar growth industry profitable for those who have perpetrated the image of CRIMINAL in the first place.[17]

What is helpful in Wilson's argument for XODUS theo-symbolizing of human beings is the way in which he reveals the connections between the psychodynamics of an oppressor with their self-destructive internalization by the oppressed. The CRIMINAL is a psychocultural construct created not merely by those who do not view Afrikans as fully human Subjects but as the Objects of their proper economic self-interest, *and* by those within the oppressed community who fail to responsibly struggle against the powers of introjection. What Wilson fails to argue persuasively, in my XODUS view, is the proper role of Black Subjectivity and individual agency. Most persons who are poor, disenfranchised, and illiterate struggle to maintain and nurture the loyalties, values, and norms of their communities. They do not introject themselves into CRIMINALS.

Do all African males suffer from the demonization of Criminalization?

Yes and no. Yes, as described by conservative African American social critics Shelby Steele and Stephen Carter when they observe the terrified reaction of a lone White woman meeting them in a secluded hallway or elevator. Whether Ph.D. or "No D," criminalization is *the projected perception of illegal intent glued to every and all African persons simply because we are "Black."* On the other hand, no, we do not suffer to the same degree and intensity. Even as educated and relatively "privileged" persons such as Steele, Carter, and myself may be compelled to suffer through such moments of mis-recognition, our educational status, our financial position (or ties to those with socioeconomic power), and our abilities to rally progressive European American and African American legal representatives to bolster our outrage make our *experience* of criminalization completely different from that of those off the streetz who may have been imprisoned behind jail bars at one time or another. Affluent African Americans can hire competent attorneys to defend themselves against unjust charges; our poorest brothers and sisters must settle for overworked public defenders and take their chances.

In light of both the psychosocial reality of criminalization and the theo-symbolism of Imprisonment, African Americans face a distinctive challenge in affirming ourselves as human beings. Two alternatives present themselves as initial directions in XODUS construction: Awakening and Liberation. Countering the suggestion that XODUS may be preoccupied with victimization symbolism, Awakening and Liberation provide insight into the ongoing struggles of African Americans to counter indignities with dignity and resist cruelty with self-loving practices.

Awakening

Malcolm X was a particularly rigorous member of the African Americanized Moslem faith, a member of the Nation of Islam. His answer to the imprisonment reality for African Americans was to "awaken" them to their "true" African self. The nature of this Awakening for Malcolm was to turn to the true GOD, ALLAH, and find one's recognition in AL-LAH rather than in the self-denying, suffering-glorifying ethos of "the White man's" Christian religion. Yet Malcolm believed that while the needed Awakening was grounded in spiritual conversion, even comparing the Islamic conversion ethos to that of Christianity,[18] he believed that it involved some very specific political aspects as well. Awakened to their African roots and broadened by a globalized, pan-African international consciousness of being "Black," the New Type of African American Malcolm described is confined no longer by the restraints of the "prison" which is the United States of America. Such a one's thinking reverses the standard custom of Blacks in America to call ourselves a "minority." Rather "by seeing that the majority of the people on this earth are dark" we no longer regard ourselves as an American minority but "as part of that vast, dark majority."[19] Malcolm ended his speech by noting that once we have understood the freedom movement of the dark peoples throughout the world, we will also believe that GOD is on the side of the dark oppressed majority and will right the "crimes" of the oppressive minority.

In the XODUS anthropology I am writing there is no need to reject Christianity in order to be Awakened. We can critique versions of Christian conversion that are radically privatized and intentionally stripped of sociopolitical significance. In XODUS I remind followers of Jesus that turning to Jesus actually means that Christians ought to be at the forefront of dynamic international struggles against oppression and for peace. XODUS Christian humanity embraces: *PEACE* "because Jesus is *our peace*" (Eph. 2:14); *FAMILY* because the *One who Shed Blood* makes us one people and no longer strangers (Eph. 2: 13–19); *LOVE* expressed in concrete deeds for brothers and sisters (1 John 5:7, 19–21); *COMPASSION* (Matt 25: 31–46); and *ANOINTING* because Jesus is *Anointed Proclaimer* of GOOD NEWS to the poor (Luke 4:18)! Malcolm X might never have had to denounce and reject Christians if we lived such lives. On the other hand, XODUS Christianity affirms with Malcolm X that American Blacks are ASLEEP to our fundamental dignity as GOD-granted, as well as to our African ties, the roots and the possibilities for making all Afrikans more powerful globally through the joining of our resources in a pan-African consciousness.

Black Americans are still ASLEEP. Often the worst representatives of this spiritual-cultural-psychological SLEEP are those in leadership positions in local Black churches, since they make no visible attempts to teach the people about our African cultural past, nor visibly stand against domestic abuse, nor help establish economic programs to empower those locked out of opportunities.

We ought to aspire toward the exercising of AWAKENED IMAGINATIONS to be able to reappreciate the variety of ways in which African Americans can reconnect ourselves to African cultural traditions, to envision a healthy sense of maleness not dependent on the subjugation of women, and to create a new economics capable of transforming the majority of impoverished people. Ron Maulana Karenga used such AWAKENED IMAGINATION to develop the *Kwanzaa holiday* (held during the seven days between Christmas and New Year). Based on an extensive cross-tribal and cross-cultural study of various "first-fruits" festivals held in West Africa, *Kwanzaa* lifts up traditional principles of *community-building-in-balance-with-individual-responsibility.* Of particular relevance to this part of the discussion are the themes of the second, third, and fourth days — *Kujichagulia,* or "self-determination," can come to be only with the aid of *Ujimaa,* "collective work and responsibility," and *Ujamaa,* "cooperative economics." Karenga models an appreciation for African categories of thinking, while simultaneously laying the foundation for a different kind of economics theory different from that of individualist, competitive market capitalism.

The 1984 publication of James Cone's *For My People* challenged African Americans to expand our vision of humanity not only by becoming more economically sophisticated, but by demanding fundamental change in the system of capitalism. Citing Cone's challenge as the reflective result of his encounter with the powerful Marxist social critique of Latin American liberation theologians, George Cummings developed a sophisticated economic theory.[20] Drawing on the formative theoretical works of Amilcar Cabral, Antonio Gramsci, and Cornel West, Cummings insists that Black theology ought to transform traditional Marxist "economic determinism" by noting how the factors of race and class function in a *dialectical fashion* within multiracial, multiethnic societies such as that found in the Americas.[21] Cummings further insists that the "counter-hegemonic culture" of resistance and struggle emergent from Black American experience may contribute yet another positive dynamic to a new economic analysis. Such theo-economical creativity rings with an AWAKENED view of the relationship between economics and a liberating view of human beings.

AWAKENING, as a positive counter-symbol to Imprisonment and Criminalization, can be traced to practices of resistance and empowerment throughout our history in the United States. Second-generation Black theologians such as Dwight Hopkins, George Cummings, Will Coleman, and Arthur C. Jones make a point of teasing out elements of resistance from those spirituals, narratives, and practices from the time of slavery that refused to submit to the lethal self-hatred promulgated by that oppressive system. Dwight Hopkins quotes a former slave, Charlie Moses, as expressing a resistant theological anthropology: "God Almighty never meant for human beings to be like animals. Us niggers has a soul an' a heart an a min'. We ain't like a dog or a horse."[22]

Roundly condemning the practices of slaveholders as "white heretical faith," Hopkins goes on to insist that the slaves understood their *souls and minds as sacred spaces created for GOD to inhabit in a transformative fashion.* This is an important insight because Hopkins bases it on his reading of the slaves' active belief in their "God-given humanity" and "God-createdness."[23]

George Cummings analyzes the presence of the Spirit in slave worship and conversion narratives as indicative of *Blacks attaining a sense of resistant personal identity and wholeness through the agency of the Holy Spirit.* Cummings attributes several positive psychological and spiritual virtues to the presence of the Spirit in the lives of slaves:

- affirmed "independence and selfhood,"

- "sustained hope for freedom as embodied in their [the slaves'] prayer life"

- functioned as the "basis of love within the slave community"

- "assisted slaves in their desire to escape to freedom."[24]

Arthur Jones examines the spiritual "Oh, Freedom" as indicative of the powerful psychological resistance to enslavement which slaves presented:

> *Oh, Freedom! Oh, Freedom! Oh, freedom over me!*
> *And before I'd be a slave I'll be buried in my grave*
> *And go home to my Lord and be free!*

Jones sees the singer of this song as an active agent engaged in the struggle for freedom. Jones interprets this passage to mean that such a person would rather fight unsuccessfully to attain freedom than to live in acquiescent servitude.[25]

AWAKENING is not merely a psychocultural reappropriation of an African "past." Rather, AWAKENING requires attentiveness to our sinfulness, willful irresponsibility, and woeful lack of boundless self-determination. We are Awakened when we can be self-critical without feeling that the "White media world" is looking over our shoulders, searching for new information with which to humiliate and publicly degrade us.

Liberation

Liberation connotes an awareness of a struggle to free oneself of the imposed constraints of existence of which one has become aware. African Americans cannot literally return to our home "people" because "Africa" is a *continent,* a geographical location inhabited by many various, often conflicting types of cultures and peoples. We are no longer Ewe, Ibo, Igbo, Ashanti, or Yoruba. We are a new people, a "New World" tribe whose variety of colors, shades, and body types bespeaks the powerful trans-mogrification of various kinds of West and Central African peoples into "African Americans." Yet the psychospiritual PATH of liberation beck-ons us to Re-Turn to HOME, and HOME is not located within the SPACE defined and confined by European American cultural parameters. HOME is a SPACE of freedom and ought to be supported economically as well as financially. HOME is the place to be embraced and supported, materially and physically.

XODUS liberation is *pan-African*, embracing the multicultural real-ity of *Afrikanity*. From the curry-flavored reggae rhythms of Jamaica to the afternoon "tea" of Great Britain, from the barbecue-smoked down-home textures of the southern United States to the dawning "Rainbow" elegance of a South African breakfast, Afrikanity is global. We are not monolithic. Just as one would not expect all Italians to be identical, so the pan-African reality holds that our differences are as precious as our similarities.

Why is it "liberating" to affirm our Afrikanity as a symbol of XODUS humanity? To affirm our Afrikanity is to say, in no uncertain terms, that GOD [the true GOD] created *us* in GOD's *Imago* or *image*. That all humanity is created in the *Image* of GOD is described in Genesis 1:26–28:

> Then GOD said, Let us make humankind in our image, according to our likeness; and let them have dominion over the fish of the sea, and over the birds of the air, and over the cattle, and over all the wild animals of the earth, and over every creeping thing that creeps upon the earth. *So GOD created humankind in his image, in the image of GOD he created them; male and female he created them.*
>
> GOD *blessed them,* and GOD said to them, "*Be fruitful and mul-tiply,* and *fill the earth and subdue it; and have dominion* over the fish of the sea and over the birds of the air and over every living thing that moves upon the earth." [italics added]

XODUS theo-anthropology affirms three distinctive dimensions of human beingness from this passage. First, humanity is GOD-created. The origins of humanity are not merely the accidental evolutionary prod-uct of conflictive emergence from mindless bacterial sludge into complex bio-specific matter. Rather, there is a "something" about human beings which is distinctively connected to THAT which has created all LIFE. That "something" has been variously described as our capacity to reason, our mind, our *Geist* in the philosophical tradition of Germanic ideal-ism, and as the transcendent aspect of humanity by Reinhold Niebuhr.

Recent developments in feminist theology have helped all of us to recognize that there is *not* such a fine distinction between the invisible "spirit" within the body and the body itself. Beverly Harrison has called this the "bodyself."[26] If we take another look at the Genesis passage from the perspective of human beings as GOD-created bodyselves, there are some profoundly controversial affirmations possible. For instance, if GOD created *us* in the DIVINE image, then GOD must be *male and female* [*and "more"*] since the term "human beings" includes both male and female.

Our GOD-created origins imply something about the concrete source of our *moral* life as well. In line with the Augustinian-Thomistic notion of "law," which notes that all genuinely just laws are in conformity with the Eternal or Divine LAW inscribed by GOD in human "nature," XODUS lifts up LAW as those laws in the moral cosmos whose origins are GOD. Such LAW is that which bends all the strife and confusion of human processive law-making toward a DIVINE end. Martin Luther King described this LAW, "The arch of the universe is long, but it bends toward justice." Therefore "right" and "wrong" are contested claims in the human sphere only insofar as they are discerned as being in conformity with the LAW inscribed in the moral universe. Such a vision of Moral Law recognizes that traditional interpretations have been used as a way of justifying unjust treatment of women and various nations/colors of people as "inherently" inferior to some other class and race. Such is not the claim of XODUS Moral LAW. Rather, in line with the Niebuhrian ideal of Love as that which beckons all forms of human love and justice toward its ideal telos or goal, XODUS envisions Moral LAW as GOD's ultimate standards of just treatment: human beings toward each other, and humanity toward nature. This leads us to an important element of XODUS reflection.

An XODUS reading of LAW turns to ancient Egypt as another rich source for understanding our role as GOD's children. Why turn to Egypt? one might ask. Isn't Egypt portrayed as the archetype of enslavement, corrupt civilization, and sinfulness in the Bible? A deeper reading and acquaintance with the vast history of this mighty African civilization reveals that its high ethical standards, the code of Ma'at, often stood at odds with its practice of enslavement. As is true for every powerful and creative nation, its practices often overtly contradicted its espoused beliefs in much the same way that the violent imperialism of so-called "Christian States" betrayed the ideals of universal love and forgiveness espoused by Jesus the Christ, or the egalitarian movement that led to the formation of a United States of America also (contentiously) tolerated transgenerational slavery. Aware of the fact that ancient Kemet was not a morally perfect nation, XODUS reflection turns to Kemetic thought in much the same way that traditional Christian scholars have turned to Greek philosophy or Roman law. This is particularly significant in light of recent historical research indicating that Egypt was, at the very least, *influential* in the historical development of Western ideals of virtue.[27]

The code of virtues in ancient Egypt (Kemet) was derived from the cosmic moral LAW called Ma'at. Ma'at was believed to be "the principle that bound all together, from the universe to humans, to the fish in the sea and the chick in the egg, as Akhnaton's Great Hymn to Aten (RA) so poetically expresses."[28] Ma'at was a cosmological imprinting of duty and obligation binding all that is together. In XODUS we bring the Ma'atic understanding of cosmic LAW into a Christian form of theo-ethical reflection. Moral LAW is revealed to us in the unfolding of history in Ma'at. The sociocultural customs which justified slavery in Egypt as well as the United States have been destroyed by the revelation of LAW. LAW moves societies and cultures in an XODUS JOURNEY away from the enslaving practices. *XODUS reflection stands, paradoxically, both with the Hebrew slaves escaping bondage in Egypt, and with the Ma'atic LAW (of Egypt) whose unfolding condemned the un-Ma'atic practices of Egypt!*

The second dimension of human beingness that the Genesis passage articulates is the concept of our being GOD-blessed creatures. We are "blessed" by GOD. Human beings are blessed with experiences of GOD touching our hearts, moving our intellects, and inspiring our consciences. GOD is alive and capable of communicating with us. This DIVINE communication or "presence" among us we call the "Holy Spirit." The experience of the Holy Spirit is what enables human moral excellence despite the negativity of an impoverished social environment, or a hate-filled family, or physical/mental challenge. A GODly or Christ-like character is developed over time, in the slow march and growth of a human bodyself in contact with the Holy Spirit aiding and guiding our moral agency. Such a GODly and Christlike character bears the "fruit of the SPIRIT," those nine qualities listed in Galatians 5:22–23: "By contrast the fruit of the Spirit is love, joy, peace, patience, kindness, generosity, faithfulness, gentleness, and self-control."

The last virtue in the list, *self-control*, may be elaborated in XODUS conceptuality as consonant with the ancient Kemetic ethical goal of one's life — becoming *geru* or "self-mastered." One who was *geru* had attained the ideal moral character, which according to the ancient Kamites was being calm, silent, controlled, modest, wise, gentle, and socially ac-tive.[29] A *geru* was the opposite of an *unrestrained person*, one ruled by hot-tempered and aggressive instincts and influenced by *isfet* (the op-posite of *ma'at*).[30] Critically, the aim of *self-mastery* negated the reason for lusting after the power which comes from *other-mastery of isfet —* *the tendencies toward imperialism, domination, and practices of enslavement.* Unfortunately, as was the case even in the democratic ideals that forged the founding ideology of the United States, sociopolitical and economic practices in Kemet fell far short of its noble moral ideals.

The import of elaborating a Kemetic understanding of *geru* for our contemporary XODUS is apparent in a contemporary discernment that *isfet* has manifested itself everywhere. In ancient Kemetic terms, we are living in an age which does not seek the wisdom of *ma'at*, but is driven by the basest and cruelest of *isfet*-inspired moral impulses. The violence of brother against brother, the abusiveness of many men in their homes towards women and children, the cruelty of contemporary business prac-tices which value economic efficiency more than human life, and the calculating coldness of current politics which shamelessly privatize and blame the poor for their poverty — all are signs of *isfet* reigning, rather than *ma'at*.

In Christian terms we might say that the current outpouring of vi-olence, abusiveness, cruelty, and coldness are signs of a demonic spirit rather than the Reign of GOD's wisdom. For XODUS Christians, a spirit of Isfet is a demonic and anti-GODly spirit. Our humanity is ef-faced and diminished by Isfetic politics and policies. We Turn away from our GOD-blessedness every time we consent to following the ways of Isfet rather than the Re-Turning to the ways of Ma'at — order, balance, righteousness, truth, justice, harmony, and propriety. XODUS humanity proclaims that the streetz need to be Re-Turned to ways which empha-size self-mastery rather than hot-headedness, calm rather than panic, and social-activeness rather than quietistic resignation.

Finally, the third human dimension revealed in the Genesis pas-sage has something to do with our God-ordained Status of being in-relationship-with-Nature. Human beings are commanded by GOD to be fruitful, multiply, fill the earth, subdue it, and have dominion over all living creatures. Such a command could be viewed as biblical justifi-cation, even *explanation* for exploiting the earth and conquering nature or as a justification for "Christian" Europe to label both the earth it-self and various peoples of the earth (brown, black, and olive-skinned) as resources in the rightful "fulfillment" of a biblical command. XODUS takes these criticisms seriously. The conflation of imperializing schemes with this biblical aspect of our human beingness has been a source of a great deal of confusion and loss of faith in the Bible as speaking for "truth" and not just for the interests of the conquerors. "Dominion" over nature has walked in the march of history with subjugation over peoples and cannot be appropriated uncritically in an XODUS reading of our human relationality.

An XODUS view of humanity believes that human "dominion" over the earth must be critically rearticulated as *stewardship for the earth*. Human beings are GOD's stewards. We are a part of the earth, our bodies being composed of the same chemical compounds that make up the soil, water, and air. Human beings are "earth creatures," in Hebrew *ha adam*, related to the earth, *ha adamah*. XODUS consciousness is vigilant in reminding Afrikan (and all) peoples that whether we live in urban, suburban, or rural environments, we are *earth creatures*. Despite the fact that earth-killing, earth-raping, and earth-denying practices have devastated not only various African lands, but also various nations in Asia, South America, and North America, we must re-member our earth-connected Ways.

Earth-denial and earth-disconnectedness have been ingrained in Euro-hegemonic practices, yet such earth-hating practices are not the sole product of Euro-hegemony in the modern period. Human practices of "civilization" have tended to use up Nature's resources faster than could be naturally replenished. There is excellent speculation that the magnificent structure which is called the Great Zimbabwe in southern Africa was eventually abandoned because of the excessive deforestation and erosion of soil produced by human practices, including massive cattle-farming.[31] We need to remember that Nature, with all of its wild animals capable of harming or killing human beings, was never viewed as the Space of peace, retreat, and serenity that it has become in our crowded, technicized, and industrialized contemporary existence. Nature was an "enemy" to be tamed and "subdued" in order for human beings to live safely, without the threat of bodily harm, for most of history well into the so-called "Enlightenment" period. So we ought not to romanticize Nature, or make "Her" a benevolent goddess of absolute mercy. XODUS earth-connected values denounce essentialist claims that suggest an "inherent" African cultural trait of earth-connectedness, demonizing all things European/American. Instead, with a view toward the seemingly unavoidable historic tendency of humanity to mis-use and abuse Nature, XODUS attempts to re-member and Re-Turn Afrikans (and all in solidarity with Life) to a profound sense of rootedness with Earth from which more humane understanding of Nature might flourish.

A liberating XODUS view of humanity borrows from many traditional West African cultures that teach that Life itself is animated with the SPIRIT; therefore every creature and living thing is "spirit." LIFE, as such, is SPIRIT. SPIRIT consists of the multitude of the spirits of trees, rocks, birds, mountains, rivers, oceans, the wind, air, water, and humanity. Traditional African religions (throughout Africa) teach that humans can gain a cosmic awareness of SPIRIT. Western anthropologists mistakenly called this cosmic awareness "animism," and Western missionaries condemned African peoples as primitive worshipers of trees — "idol worshipers!" A more accurate term for this cosmic awareness, philosophically, would be "vitalism." The vitalist conception of the earth insists that all that is may be understood as surrounded by the SPIRIT which is LIFE. While vitalism has been decried in traditional Christianity as Nature worship, an XODUS vitalist conception flows into a kind of reverential awe for LIFE in its massive Fullness and ever-changing majesty. Such reverential awe is *a consciousness of LIFE*, the LIFE which GOD created.

In XODUS a properly vitalist human life is *cosmocentric* rather than *anthropocentric*. Peter Rukungah's definition of "cosmocentric" suggests that those who are cosmocentric have oriented their lives in accordance with the wholeness of the cosmos, of nature, rather than toward what is good only for human beings.[32] A cosmocentric decision looks toward the entire relationship of the community of LIFE rather than toward the private good of an individual human being. To privatize moral choice and decision making would be to violate the fundamental ontology of community that obtains in a wide host of African cultures. In Bantu cultures of the south and southeastern portion of Africa this sense of communal personhood is symbolized in the phrase *umuntu ngamuntu ngabantu*, "I am because we are, and because we are I am," or "I am a person through the community of persons." This communal notion of personhood has come to be known as a *Muntu* conception of humanity — an eco-humanity according to Rukungah. The Sotho in South Africa have a similar saying: *Mothoke mmotho ka botho babang*, "A person is only a person through people." The Venda people reveal this community-personhood slightly differently in their saying *Myuthu u bebekwa nunwe*, which translates "A person is born for the other."[33] In XODUS we take the communal-personhood ethos embedded in so many African cultures and explicitly recognize that part of this communal ethos is our inherent relationship with Nature. The Community is ALL — people, earth, water, animals, macroscopic and microscopic.

Resistance as Liberation

From the time of slavery African Americans have learned that RESISTANCE to dehumanizing stereotypes and crippling expectations sustains our dignity and self-regard, albeit in a surreptitious fashion. I end this chapter looking at the particular forms of RESISTANCE developed by our forefathers. Instead of buying wholeheartedly into a view of themselves as clowns and fools, our forefathers created double-edged images of ourselves in order to survive with dignity intact.

Sambo the Clown is perhaps the longest lasting and most representative double-edged self-representation of Black manhood. Reveling in self-mockery more akin to the court Jester than an idiot, Sambo pranced his way into the hearts of racist Americans, who had no idea that they were being laughed at while they were laughing. The Sambo caricatured and exaggerated certain features of African American life on the one hand, holding them up as something to be laughed *at*, while on the other, creating a space wherein humor could be a useful tool for traversing the tremendously dangerous and wide social gap between European Americans and African Americans. The genius of the Sambo character is that those persons who have placed themselves into the "clown" paradigm, from the earliest accounts in the late eighteenth century right down to our present moment, provided a way to deliberately mock Euro-American ignorance and fears about Blacks (males in particular), while providing "entertainment." Sambo degraded himself in the eye of the public, but not in his own self-understanding. Though well-paid to entertain and acting in ways that no human being ought to be expected or required to act, *his very existence challenged the humanity of "Enlightened" slavemasters who clung to egalitarian principles of democracy in one hand and a whip in the other!* Some of the Sambo characters used this staged mockery as a way to "get back" at their bosses and masters, mocking their arrogance, and doing so in a way that would not result in punishment. This is not to affirm the Sambo as humanizing, but rather in XODUS I want to reveal how even the most accommodated of social representations might have actually been the paradoxical locus of intensive public resistance.

Even African Americans renowned for their RESISTANCE occasionally used a strategy of accommodation, assimilation, and what the old folks call "go along to get along" to creatively resist degrading stereotypes in their particular class strata. For example, the first African American Ph.D. from Harvard, W. E. B. Du Bois, was renowned not only for his intellectual brilliance and stunning writings, but also for his impeccably Teutonic dress and manner! Accounts of his immaculate attire —

gold-tipped cane and aristocratic bearing — reveal strenuous attention to such matters and a spirit resistant to degrading stereotypes of the Sambo entertainers' depictions of a "Black professor." While Sambo depictions often used outlandish costumes, loudly exaggerated dialect for speech, and long-winded ridiculous "discourses" filled with intentionally mispronounced "long words" (e.g., "unlitened" for the word "enlightened") Du Bois, Monroe Trotter, and others like them worked at presenting themselves as refined, urbane, and sophisticated gentlemen.[34] Du Bois might be slighted by contemporary standards of Afrikan pride for being too "Eurocentric," yet such a charge would not recognize the nature of his resistance to prevailing stereotypes during his time. By being *more "European" than American Whites* in taste, dress, and manner, Du Bois presented a resistant front behind which he could compile massive sociological evidence of Black aptitude, skill, and genius with his prolific pen.

The utterly rebellious posture of persons such as David Walker, Nat Turner, and Sojourner Truth in the nineteenth century and Martin Luther King, Malcolm X, and Fannie Lou Hamer in the twentieth century indicate that African Americans have also chosen not to cooperate whatsoever with our heteronomously imposed status of inferiority. Nat Turner's violent slave rebellion and fiery apocalyptic eschatological rhetoric presage a kind of character-symbol akin to the Sambo, namely, the Rebel. Examples of the Rebel abound in Black literature, one of the best recent examples being the social-justice activist preacher Reverend Rice in Bebe Moore Campbell's *Brothers and Sisters.*[35] Modeled after a real Christian Rebel preacher, Cecil "Chip" Murray of First A.M.E. Los Angeles, Reverend Rice is a no-nonsense community activist whose church, the "Solid Rock Baptist Church," interweaves evangelical Gospel outreach programs with economic development initiatives and an Africentric philosophy. Actual historical Rebels like Nat Turner, David Walker, Malcolm X, and Martin Luther King, Jr., have been killed for their ability to inspire masses of people to organize and resist.

A more easily identified character-type symbol of Black maleness is an extension of the mythological figure John Henry. As in the John Henry myth, a contemporary John Henry can out-run, out-jump, and out-"man" all others who would dare to challenge! As John Henry could out-work even a steam drill, dying in the process, so the contemporary John Henry challenges conventional ideas of what *one person* ought to be able to accomplish. We have seen the proliferation of multiple-sport superstars, like Bo Jackson, who "knows" everything! Yet Bo fell victim to a vicious tackle in a football game, and after hip-replacement surgery and an abortive attempt to restart his legend in baseball, seems to have had his superstardom cut short in much the same way that John Henry's superstar work abilities were ended abruptly with his cutting-through-a-mountain competition. John Henry is a troubling model of Black manhood because it suggests that *the only truly honorable African American male is one whose body exudes supernatural strength, resilience, and the capacity to work unto death for one's "boss."* The model appears to equate the sacrificial loss of one's life energies for the tasks determined by European American authorities with a kind of sacrificial Christology. John Henry is a suffering Christ-figure, but he is not allowed the dignity of dying for anything more than a contest between human brute strength and the efficiency of a machine. The implications of such a symbolism for contemporary Black males are disquieting, to say the least.

The famous West African folk tale Trickster Ananse was transmuted into a supernatural spirit named "High John De Conquer" in the New World experience. Humorous stories of High John's exploits can be found in a number of sources, but fundamentally High John was said to be:

- a "Spirit who crossed de water [the Atlantic] just when we [African folks] needed him";

- one who could outfox and trick "Massa"; and do so with such *panache* that "Massa" had to laugh in spite of himself;

- one who enabled the slaves to be hopeful and encouraged despite the grinding psychic wear of enslavement; and finally,

- a kind of "liberator" whose "powers" were believed to be accessible to those who knew the secret "conjure words" to open a particular root buried in the ground.[36]

The High John character-symbol has Christ-like qualities unlike the sacrificial traits of John Henry. High John "rises" from the ashes of despair, riding the winds of agony from Africa to those suffering Children of Africa enslaved across the Atlantic. High John knows how to "deal" with those shrewd kidnappers and "man-stealers" (the nineteenth-century abolitionist term for slavers), stealing from them, teaching the slaves how to sing songs of hope and freedom, and so forth. High John is a symbolization of something irrepressible and unstoppable in human character, that "singing something which rises up" that Anna Julia Cooper spoke about in *A Voice from the South.*[37]

XODUS theo-anthropology values High John because the subversive strength of humor is part of High John's liberating arsenal, as is the inner drive for freedom "by any means necessary" that typifies the Rebel. High

John did not arise except at times of great distress and woe. Such is our time. The African American community needs to reclaim its powerful spiritual-historical resources and find a way to summon High John from his buried "root." The global pan-African Community languishes in the grip of petty tyrants, neo-colonialization, and an enduring legacy of underdevelopment. The Cosmic Community is choking from the filth of wasteful human exploitation of Nature. It is time for an XODUS human being to come forth.

Notes

1. Gordon Kaufman, *In Face of Mystery: A Constructive Theology* (Cambridge, Mass.: Harvard, 1993), 97–140.

2. James H. Evans, Jr., *We Have Been Believers: An African American Systematic Theology* (Minneapolis: Fortress, 1992), 100.

3. Bruce Perry, ed., *Malcolm X: The Last Speeches* (New York: Pathfinder, 1989), 37.

4. Ibid., 36.

5. Ibid., 39.

6. Ibid., 41.

7. Ibid., 41–42.

8. Augustine, *Enchiridion* in *The Nicene and Post Nicene Fathers*, vol. 3: *St. Augustine* (Grand Rapids: Eerdmans, 1980), 240.

9. Peter Kreeft, ed., *Summa of the Summa* (San Francisco: Ignatius Press, 1990), 490.

10. Ibid., 497.

11. Timothy Lull, ed., *Martin Luther's Theological Writings* (Minneapolis: Fortress, 1989), 173–226.

12. Marjorie Suchocki, *The Fall to Violence: Original Sin in Relational Theology* (New York: Crossroad, 1994). Suchocki builds on Rauschenbusch's understanding of the social solidarity of humanity and the transgenerational passing on of oppressive structures.

13. Walter Rauschenbusch, *A Theology for the Social Gospel* (Nashville: Abingdon, 1981), 50.

14. Ibid., 61ff.

15. Amos N. Wilson, *Black-on-Black Violence: The Psychodynamics of Black Self-Annihilation in Service of White Domination* (New York: Afrikan World Infosystems, 1990), 65.

16. Ibid., 78. The above sentences summarize Wilson's argument (64–80).

17. Ibid., 41.

18. Perry, *Malcolm X*, 43.

19. Ibid., 45.

20. George C. L. Cummings, *A Common Journey: Black Theology (USA) and Latin American Liberation Theology* (Maryknoll, N.Y.: Orbis Books, 1993), 102–10.

21. Ibid., 160.

22. Dwight Hopkins, *Shoes That Fit Our Feet: Sources for a Constructive Black Theology* (Maryknoll, N.Y.: Orbis Books, 1993), 36.

23. Ibid., 36.

24. George Cummings, "The Spirit and Eschatology," in Dwight Hopkins and George Cummings, eds., *Cut Loose Your Stammering Tongue: Black Theology in the Slave Narratives* (Maryknoll, N.Y.: Orbis Books, 1991), 49.

25. Arthur C. Jones, *Wade in the Water: The Wisdom of the Spirituals* (Maryknoll, N.Y.: Orbis Books, 1993), 57.

26. Beverly Wildung Harrison, *Making the Connection: Essays in Feminist Social Ethics*, ed. Carol Robb (Boston: Beacon, 1982).

27. See the bold scholarship of Cheikh Anta Diop, particularly *Civilization or Barbarism*, as well as the stunning critique of Greek philosophical developments as "stolen" in some respect from Egyptian Mysteries by George C. M. James, *Stolen Legacy: Greek Philosophy Is Stolen Egyptian Philosophy* (Trenton, N.J.: Africa World Press, 1992). While many of my most esteemed colleagues such as Cornel West and bell hooks simply dismiss these authors, I believe that XODUS conceptuality must critically dialogue with all of the credible aspects of their arguments. Despite a certain "romanticism" in Diop and James, their fundamental assertions about the cultural and intellectual contributions of ancient Kemet remain persuasive to me.

28. Maulana Karenga, *The Book of Coming Forth by Day: The Ethics of the Declarations of Innocence* (Los Angeles: University of Sankore Press, 1990), 100.

29. Maulana Karenga, *Selections from The Husia: Sacred Wisdom of Ancient Egypt* (Los Angeles: University of Sankore Press, 1984), 91. To become *geru ma'at* was to be the master or teacher of the self-mastered, a goal even beyond becoming self-mastered.

30. Ibid., 91.

31. Interview on CNN with African scholar Ali Mazrui, October 1988.

32. See Peter Rukungah, *Towards Becoming Muntu* (Nairobi, Kenya: Act Print Limited, 1993).

33. These quotations and translations are taken from Peter Kasenene, "Ethics in African Theology" in *Doing Ethics in Context: South African Perspectives*, ed. C. Villa-Vicencio and John DeGruchy (Maryknoll, N.Y.: Orbis Books, 1994), 138–46.

34. See my chapter "The Council of Ancestors" in *XODUS: An African American Male Journey* (Minneapolis: Fortress, 1995), 47–72.

35. Bebe Moore Campbell, *Brothers and Sisters* (New York: Putnam, 1994).

36. Zora Neale Hurston's "High John De Conquer" in *Book of Negro Folklore*, ed. Langston Hughes and Arna Bontemps (New York: Dodd, Mead & Company, 1959), 93–102 as cited also in *XODUS: An African American Male Journey*.

37. Karen Baker-Fletcher, *A Singing Something: Womanist Reflections on Anna Julia Cooper* (New York: Crossroad, 1994).

Eight

Womanhood

It's a Way of Being Human

S INCE BLACK WOMEN were stolen and forced from the shores of Africa into ships to make the crowded, chained, and stench-filled passage to the shores of America as slaves, they have been required to reconstruct womanhood — to redefine themselves in the face of racial and gender stereotypes of what it means to be Black and female. In the midst of doing so, they have not escaped stereotypes. The struggle continues. The popular icons are well-known: mammy, matriarch, whore. There is also the myth of the *superwoman*, which many Black women unwittingly perpetuate ourselves. The false myths of *mammy, whore,* and *castrating bitch* are obviously degrading and unhesitatingly fought against. Michelle Wallace, bell hooks, Patricia Morton, and Patricia Hill Collins are just a few cultural theorists who have criticized such images in popular culture. For the moment, I want to focus on the myth of the superwoman, which is particularly deceptive and insidious. Many women are easily tempted to identify themselves with it, making it a popular icon that seemingly has spiritual and moral value. While the other stereotypes are undeniably disparaging and degrading, the myth of the superwoman has a pseudo-exalted character.

I have noticed that I and other working-mother/scholars are sometimes asked by older and even young White women with no parenting responsibilities, *"HOW* do you *do it?!"* While Black women are well aware of the struggles involved in working and parenting, they rarely ask this question in a tone of amazement, because they either are or have been in the midst of working and mothering themselves. Or they remember their own mothers, aunts, and sisters who performed a multitude of roles. Nor do working White mothers ask me this question, because they already know that such an existence for women is quickly becoming normative in the United States. Working mothers ask the question with a different tone of voice and for different reasons. They are genuinely interested in strategies for mothering, working, putting bread on the table, maintaining a job and raising children, possibly with a fulfilling career. Their intonation does not suggest that working and mothering is a supernatural, extrahuman enterprise. They ask rather matter-of-factly, "How do you do it?" and go on to share their own plans, dreams, and strategies.

The question *"HOW* do you *do it?!"* carries a host of presuppositions. In America today, few families can survive on one income. Historically, for working-class White women, such a way of living has always been normative just as it has been for Black women. Recent statistics show that 64 percent of mothers work and 70 percent of those work full time. Not all of them are scholars or have careers, but work is work and the time it takes is time taken from the self. Implicit in *exaggerated* queries of *"HOW* do you *do it?!"* is the suggestion that working mothers are extraordinary or exceptional. While I hope that every woman has some extraordinary or special gift she can offer, since I believe in spiritual gifts and the calling of the Spirit to a specific life-work, it would be incorrect to suggest that such mothers are *superwomen.* To do so implies that they are not quite human (presumably more than human), which falls into the old trap of denying that women who do not fit into traditional categories are fully women. It is as *sexist* to suggest so-called nontraditional women are *more* than human as it is to suggest they are *less* than human. The truth is that today *"being conventional" for most women means working and mothering.*

To suggest that working mothers are or ought to be superwomen renders them goddesses, isolating them from the rest of humanity, denying their humanness and their womanhood, imprisoning them in the cell of a stereotype that is smothering and repressive. While the bearers of such queries claim to be speaking in admiration, and perhaps that is the intention of some, to suggest that Black working mothers are superwomen who can do the impossible is tainted by *sexist, classist, and racist presuppositions.* From the perspective of Black or working-class White women, what is the questioner really asking? It often sounds as if she means, "I, a White middle-class woman, can't imagine myself doing that. I don't think I could do it. So *HOW* can *you [a Black woman or working-class White woman] do it?"* The implication is that only a few White women (with "old money" and live-in nannies perhaps), being superior and exceptional, can work and mother. This is not far from the traditional expectation that only men (mostly White and upper middle-class) can be professionals.

Christian social ethicists like Marcia Riggs refer to a common, shared phenomenon among Black women and the Black community generally. In *Arise, Awake, Act: A Womanist Call for Black Liberation,* Riggs writes of the powerful social myths internalized by Black people. One is the myth of "personal exceptionalism." Those of us who resist the myth, having long seen its cubic-zirconium-like (false) award of honor for what it is, balk when well-meaning White Americans seem to foist it upon us. The myth of "personal exceptionalism" as Riggs describes it is derived "from the notion of individualism, which is at the heart of liberalism and the concept of private property. For African Americans, it has meant striving to be, or to be labeled as, an exceptional Black person standing apart from the larger mass of poorer Black people."[1] During the Harlem Renaissance, Zora Neale Hurston wrote with sharp criticism and bold humor about upper-class White liberal Americans' love for the "pet Negro."[2] Others have written of White Americans' preference for the "exceptional Negro, African American, Black Person, etc.," Feminists have criticized tendencies to treat women who break with convention in their gifts and abilities as exceptional. The "superwoman myth" buys into the myth of the exceptional woman. It is problematic across racial lines, but exacerbated by racialized stereotypes of the normative behavior of Black women as slothful, immoral, inept, ignorant.

Note that people rarely ask the exaggerated question *"HOW* do you *do it?"* of men in the workplace, although more fathers are sharing child-rearing and homemaking responsibilities. There are families in which if the male partner's job allows more flexibility for picking up kids from school and childcare, he is the one with primary responsibility for those duties. Single mothers and fathers explore other alternatives — extended family networks, friends who become kin. Same-sex parents share responsibilities in whatever way is practical. The truth is that most women don't have a choice about work and family. Those who have the opportunity find work that promises the fulfillment of a career or vocation as well as income, while numerous others struggle in low-paying, pink-collar jobs. The cultural mindset of some Americans, even those who believe themselves to be progressive or feminist, lags behind the reality.

It is important to debunk the stereotype of the superwoman because it is the most deceptive and insidious stereotype of all. The problem is that it can be tempting for White women and women of color alike to accept the idolatrous image of the superwoman as a positive model of womanhood. As far as stereotypes go, it is seductive in its benign, seemingly positive appearance. This is a problem for women whose work is at home centered on the family as well as for those with outside jobs, vocations, and careers. The diverse authors in Evelyn White's *The Black Women's Health Book* astutely observe the various ways in which African American women fail to adequately take care of ourselves in the midst of taking care of others. Emilie Townes in *In a Blaze of Glory* likewise admonishes Black women for not loving ourselves enough in the midst of loving others. Renita Weems, biblical scholar, contemplates the problem women have in loving others to the virtual exclusion of ourselves in *I Asked for Intimacy*. Alice Walker emphasizes that a womanist loves herself regardless in her careful definition of womanism. Cheryl Townsend Gilkes and others build on this theme of loving oneself regardless in anthologies such as *A Troubling in My Soul* and *Living the Intersection*. The problem of loving oneself and taking time out from playing superwoman emerges again and again in womanist and Black feminist writings. Womanists and feminists in general are concerned with self-actualization and self-love in the midst of a relational understanding of the world.

Perhaps the superwoman syndrome is the flipside of our will to survive when taken to an unhealthy extreme. We are so accustomed to toughing it out, being self-reliant, being dependable for others, concerned with the salvation and wholeness of family, friends, community, and strangers that we become ill from lack of self-nurture and sometimes die early deaths as a result. The same will for survival that enables us to persevere through pain and oppression can also numb us to the realities of pain and illness if we are not grounded in God as Spirit who loves us, body and soul, as well as our loved ones. There is a thin line between survival and denial. As Weems, White, and so many health educators have pointed out, the higher incidence of deaths from breast cancer among Black women in relation to White women because of late detection is a paramount example of Black women's tendencies toward a stoicism that is all too often grounded in denial of illness — denial of the reality that there is something wrong. Such misguided stoicism keeps women in all kinds of unhealthy situations from untreated disease to abusive relationships to oppressive social situations. As the authors in *The Black Women's Health Book* point out, we are vulnerable to diabetes, heart disease, strokes, obesity, cancers, domestic abuse. Many of us go untreated because we have few or no resources. Sometimes those who have resources available to them simply are not aware of them or unsure of how to access them. Too often those of us who do possess and know of resources fail to use them, ignoring symptoms of illness or remaining in abusive relationships until it is too late.

The irony is that the ability to ignore disease in the effort to "keep on keepin' on" is a distortion of our gift to survive and overcome oppression. The same gift that is a source of healing and wholeness is a source of illness and death when misused and distorted. On the one hand the kind of spiritual strength that many of us seem to be raised to embody from birth is the stuff which makes entire freedom movements possible and eventually successful. There is the famous example of the woman who responded to how she felt about participating in the Montgomery Bus Boycott by saying, "My feets is tired, but my soul feels good." This woman spoke the feelings of thousands. The movement depended on thousands of such women, men, and children with tired feet but liberated, healed hearts. In the context of social action strategies like the Montgomery Bus Boycott and the many marches of the Civil Rights movement, such asceticism is appropriate and necessary. The Civil Rights movement was a forum in which Black women and men applied their social understanding of Christian asceticism to the best of their advantage in a powerful, transformative way. There is a time and a place for such asceticism — walking even when our feet are tired. It is good not to be self-indulgent when one is fighting for the children to be fed, for economic opportunity, for social equality. In the midst of struggling for social justice, however, it is also important to love our bodies by taking care of them so that we will be both physically and spiritually strong enough to live into the future with the children whose rights we struggle for.

While admiring the spirit and courage of an attitude that says, "My feet are tired but my soul feels good," I also hope that the speaker of these words soaked her feet in hot water at night, soothing them with Epsom salts and massaging them with lotion, if she could afford it, before she went to sleep. I wonder if she had someone who could do that for her and for whom she could return the favor. We too often neglect these small acts of self-love and love for others. I remember the account of Jesus washing the feet of his disciples and the account of the woman who washed his feet with her hair. In our everyday lives we need not be nearly as dramatic, but it is important to remember that Scripture indicates that the body, precisely because it does become tired and dusty in the work of justice, needs loving care. Some of the most loving, nurturing women do not take care of their own bodies very well. Black women extend our training in the Christian ascetic practice of sacrifice for others to the extreme that we suffer unnecessary illness by neglecting ourselves.

Slowly giving in to death by denying our own physical well-being cannot contribute to survival and liberation of family and community in the long run. There is a difference between stoicism and genuine strength. While it is good to teach our daughters to be strong by word and example, we can ensure a better quality of life for them by teaching them that true strength is not the same as stoicism, which requires an acceptance of evil and suffering. True strength transforms evil and suffering. Evil and suffering are not accepted. They are recognized for what they are, confronted, and challenged. It is good for Black women to be strong. But we need not be superwomen, a revision of the amazon myth which dehumanizes us by ignoring our need for equal opportunities of health and nurture.

The stereotype of Black women as amazons during slavery meant that slaveowners had no need to feel remorse for sending women into the fields to work before healing from giving birth to their new infants. Infants sometimes died from exposure to the harsh sun in the fields where they were laid while their mothers labored. It meant that mothers were discouraged from complaining about their pain or even admitting to it. Even today in relative socioeconomic freedom, Black women are slow to admit to pain, illness, and suffering. Moreover, Christianity as taught in many churches teaches us that it is good to be long-suffering. The problem is that we interpret the meaning of "long-suffering" in unhealthy ways. It is one thing to sacrifice the comfort of one's feet for a bus boycott. It is another to sacrifice one's health out of a sense of low self-esteem and lack of self-love. The first practice is a form of asceticism and prophetic action. The second practice implies that our bodies, minds, and spirits have less value than that of husbands, boyfriends, brothers, girlfriends, sisters, children, and friends; it presupposes, at an unconscious level, that others are worthy of the love, nurture, and compassion of God — oneself is not. The first practice, then, is a form of faithfulness. The second practice is a form of faithlessness. Whether in churches, other religious organizations, or in secular society, the task of revisioning Black womanhood continues. Below I consider the ways in which womanist moral virtues or powers apply not only to the salvation of the larger community, but to the personal bodily and spiritual salvation of Black women.

Womanist Powers (Virtues)

Metaphors in historical resources and contemporary works of womanist scholars that describe Black women's understanding of their participation in God's creative activity say as much about a womanist concept of God as they do about womanhood. The two are dynamically interrelated. A reconstruction of womanhood requires a reconstruction of God. Concepts of God directly impact our understandings of human beings and of creation.

A classical concept of God as all-powerful perpetuates a subjugative concept of womanhood, humankind, and creation. A concept of God as *most powerful* and as *sharing power*, which emerges from Whiteheadian metaphysics, is in keeping with Christian scriptural concepts of a God who shares gifts of power among the body of believers (1 Cor. 12–14; Eph. 4). 1 Corinthians 12:4–7 in particular suggests a concept of a God who shares gifts of power with believers:

> There are varieties of gifts, but the same Spirit; and there are varieties of services, but the same Lord; and there are different kinds of working, but it is the same God who activates all of them in everyone. To each is given the manifestation of the Spirit for the common good. (NRSV)

1 Corinthians refers to a specific set of gifts: knowledge, wisdom, healing, working of miracles, prophecy, discernment, tongues, and interpretation of tongues. While historical Black Christian women like Jarena Lee, Zilpha Elaw, and Julia Foote have referred to some of these gifts in their writings (particularly gifts of healing, wisdom, knowledge, and prophecy), there are also other types of gifts that Black women have discussed in the past and in the present as part of the everyday faith activity of African American women. Drawing on process theology, *Muntu* cosmology, and biblical sources, I presuppose an integrative understanding of the relationship between sacred and existential reality. If humankind shares in God's creativity as certain Christian Scriptures, process theology, and African Bantu *Muntu* philosophy suggest, what are some of the metaphors that might describe Black women's participation in such creative activity?[3]

While there are a multitude of symbolizations of Black women's participation in God's creative activity, there are seven that I find particularly important to consider: faith, which has to do with the power of belief in a God of infinite possibilities for fulfillment in creation; voice, which has to do with the power of prophetic speech and naming; survival, which includes gifts of healing, resistance against evil, "making do," and "making a way out of no way"; vision, which has to do with prophetic sight; community building, a form of social salvation and healing; regeneration, which requires memory and the passing on of wisdom, knowledge for survival, healing, and liberation; and liberation, acts of struggle for freedom and social reform.

One might refer to the above gifts as "gifts of power."[4] The phrase is from Jean Humez's title for her publication of the autobiographical writings of Rebecca Cox Jackson, who painfully taught herself to read and write so that she could record her thoughts in her own words without depending on others who might change her meaning.[5] Jackson referred to her ability to teach herself to read and write as a gift from God. The

Latin word *virtus* means "power," so one might describe this as an aretaic ethic — an ethics of virtue or, better, an ethics of *power.* However, like many African American scholars, I am uninterested in examining ethics apart from theology. My interest in *gifts of power* begins with theological questions. What does it mean for Black women to reflect God's likeness and to share in God's creative, sustaining, and freeing activity? How might one examine creative power in the midst of injustice among Black women in relation to the creative power of God?

Gifts of Power for Survival and Wholeness in Black Women's Narratives

Much has been said about Black women's situation of oppression and the denial of their humanity that emerged out of White supremacist and sexist ethics. But what of Black women's gifts of power for survival and wholeness in the midst of such oppression and dehumanization? And what can we learn about such powers from Black women's narratives? There are a multiplicity of gifts of power for survival and wholeness in Black women's social-historical experience. Black women have survived in the midst of an oppressive social system historically, beating the odds and regenerating spiritual power in the midst of political-economic powerlessness. This is an important point to remember, because all too often discussions of power cast all power as negative, political, destructive, dominant. What of positive manifestations of power?

A concept of power that is wholly negative or that makes a distinction between political-economic power as oppressive and all spiritual power as salvific is inadequate. Not all political-economic power need be oppressive and much evil has been enacted in the name of spiritual power. It is important to be more nuanced in our discourse on power. All too often Black women are cast as the victims of power. Black feminist and womanist theory nuances such half-truths to clarify that Black women have been the victims of an *abuse of power* in disproportionate numbers. Such *abuses of power* require a counter-hegemonic exercise of powers of survival and wholeness on the part of Black women. Historically, Black women have exercised such counter-hegemonic powers and struggle to continue such activity.

It is important to consider Black women's embodiment of the sacred in their everyday lives. Because both Blackness and womanhood historically have been disparaged as evil, such reflection is important to an understanding of what it means to be human. In considering metaphors for a positive reconstruction of womanhood,[6] one might begin with the metaphors of "A Singing Something" and "Voice" from the writings of Anna Julia Cooper.

1. Voice. Anna Julia Cooper introduced an interesting metaphor of God in relation to voice in her doctoral defense, where she described God as a "Singing Something" that rises up within humanity in every nation to cry out against injustice. On the one hand she had a traditional understanding of humankind being created in the image of God. Human being was a "divine spark" whose source was God — the Creator of all.

Cooper's metaphor of a "Singing Something" suggests an epistemic shift. Human being is not simply created in the image of God. Human being is created in the voice of God. This suggests the presence of a prophetic element within humanity that must be exercised with wisdom and discernment.[7] Voice is an important metaphor for the power of prophetic speech in Cooper's work as well as in the writings of other Black women: Jarena Lee, Zilpha Elaw, Maria Stewart, Ida Wells-Barnett. For Cooper there is a *Singing Something* in humankind that can be traced back to the Creator. It rises up in the face of injustice and cannot be squelched. Because prophetic speech is traceable to the Creator, one might say that prophetic Black women reflect the voice and message of God. How do we know this? For Cooper it is evident where there is a transformation of injustice into justice, of social inequality to equality. Moreover, moving beyond Cooper to womanist thought one might say that it is evident when such speech effects healing and wholeness in a community with positive global effects. A collectivity of voices, across class, color, and international lines, offers a fuller representation of the meaning of spiritual and social freedom.

Emilie Townes has recently published an article in which she observes that one might turn to the symbolism of the "ringshout" to represent the importance of a community of voices among women, Black and White.[8] This resonates with Anna Cooper's understanding that the world needs to hear all of women's voices across color lines, while moving beyond it to appeal to symbolism from African American folk culture.

Whereas Cooper emphasizes an anthropocentric concept of God's embodiment in creation, today it is necessary to seriously address the ecological realities that affect African American women and men who live in environments affected by environmental pollutants in disproportionate numbers. Today, we must continue to consider the sacredness, worth, dignity, and value Cooper's metaphor attributes to human being. But we must also consider such sacredness, worth, and value in relation to all of creation — the air, water, and land with which human beings are interdependent. Such concerns cannot be separated from economic concerns, since environmental abuse — like race and gender oppression — is based in large part on economic factors involving industry and the production of capital.

2. Vision. Delores Williams emphasizes the gift of the power of vision in the life of Hagar. For Williams, God has functioned primarily as a God of survival in the life of the biblical slavewoman Hagar and in the history of Black women in America. Black women, Williams demonstrates, have participated in God's creative activity of survival by engaging in survival practices. However, survival requires vision. Moreover, by survival Williams has in mind a specific form of survival that stands in stark contrast to the dog-eat-dog survival ethics of oppressive socioeconomic structures. This must be clarified, for it is easy for those who are unfamiliar with Williams's employment of the term "survival" to interpret it as brutal, bare-bones, amoral existence. To the contrary, she pairs survival with quality of life to indicate a form of survival that includes healing, wholeness, community building, and faith.[9]

Williams's attention to the biblical story of Hagar suggests that the capacity to envision resources for survival in the midst of scarcity involves more than the human will alone. It involves revelation from a God that provides insight and vision into one's social-historical and geographical situation. There is always a potential for despair, but the gift of vision allows for renewed hope in the midst of wilderness experiences.[10]

3. Naming. I referred earlier to Rebecca Cox Jackson's understanding of her power to teach herself to read and write as a gift from God. While she also wrote of gifts of the power to heal others, it is important to note that the gift of writing increased her *power of naming*. She could *name* reality as she experienced it in her own words, without the disruption of others interpreting her experience, thought, and practice for her. Naming is a recurring theme in womanist theology and ethics. Most explicit is Delores Williams's work in *Sisters of the Wilderness*, in which she emphasizes that Hagar, often referred to as an ancestral *sister* by womanists, is the first and only woman in Hebrew and Christian Scriptures *to name God*. Moreover, Hagar *names God* differently from her oppressors, Sarah and Abraham. She names God *El Roi*, God who gives vision, sight.[11] What does God give Hagar vision to see? God provides the power of vision to see resources for survival where it seemed none could exist.

The power of naming is also evident in contemporary womanist *self-naming*. Caught between the gaps of feminist and Black male theology, many Black women religious scholars and clergy in the 1980s began referring to themselves as womanists to connote both continuity with and distinctiveness from feminist and Black male history, experience, and theological reflection. Cheryl Sanders astutely observes similarities between the significance of naming in Afrocentrism (*nommo*) and self-naming in womanist discourse, commenting that the "self-affirmation and self-assertiveness of womanism and Afrocentrism should be regarded not in individualistic terms but as indicative of the self finding expression in harmony with others."[12]

Emilie Townes discusses the significance of *confrontation* — to face together as equals. Confrontation involves naming areas of injustice without apology and engaging in dialogue with acceptance of diversity.[13] The tradition of exercising the creative gift of naming is evident in a number of biblical, historical, and contemporary resources drawn on by womanist theologians and ethicists.

4. The "tar/glue" qualities of community building. Community building is emphasized in the work of Theressa Hoover, Delores Williams, and Jacquelyn Grant, and in historical writings by figures like Maria Stewart, Anna Julia Cooper, and Ida B. Wells-Barnett. In Boston in the early 1830s, Maria Stewart emphasized community self-development.[14] Some sixty years later Anna Julia Cooper, working primarily in Washington, D.C., emphasized that the development of Black women was as essential to the development of the Black community as the development of Black men. Ida B. Wells-Barnett pioneered an anti-lynching campaign and championed women's rights in an effort to realize a wholistic vision of healing and wholeness for Black and White communities, male and female alike. Contemporary figures like Congresswoman Maxine Waters, Marian Wright Edelman of the Children's Defense Fund, Surgeon General Joycelyn Elders, and the Rev. Suzanne Johnson of Mariner's Temple Baptist Church continue such community building activities.

Two metaphors that capture well the community building activity of historical and contemporary Black women have been employed by contemporary Black women writers. Theressa Hoover describes Black women as the "glue" of the church. The metaphor "glue" in Hoover's work represents Black women's creative energies for holding the church together.[15] Toni Morrison has employed the metaphor of "tar" to refer to Black women's creative power of holding together things like church and community. She calls such creative powers "ancient properties." Her novel *Tar Baby* provides extensive narrative that examines the "tar baby myth" from several angles. In the U.S. South, it became a denigrative term for young Black girls. However, in interviews Morrison points out that she was inspired by an African tale of a tar lady. For her, the myth came to represent Black women who were in touch with their ancient properties of community building. She remembered that tar or pitch was used to hold together Moses' little boat, build pyramids — and therefore is sacred in its quality of holding together that which is sacred.[16] Black women who have engaged in coalition and community building then, one might say, participate in the sacred power of coalescence. They embody what Christians might call the power of *koinonia*. Today this must be extended to consider the ecological environment — land, water, air, plants, animals — as part of the community in the tradition of African cultures such as the Bantu. Peter Rukungah, for example, in his work on African Bantu cosmology explains that according to *Muntu* worldview, all of creation has being and is to be treated with dignity.[17] As mentioned earlier, abuse of the ecological environment affects the poor disproportionately.

5. Regeneration. Regeneration is the power to pass on wisdom, knowledge, and Black women's cultural heritage from generation to generation. Walker's definition of "womanist" is descriptive of the ways in which women in African American culture have often passed on wisdom from mother to daughter, from generation to generation.[18] One sees evidence of this when the mothers, missionaries, deaconesses, evangelists, exhorters, and other women elders in Black churches have schooled girls and younger women in Christian personal, social, and political thought and practice. Today, this tradition is being continued not only by women in traditional gender roles in Black churches but by women pastors and deacons. Such passing on of wisdom requires the prophetic element of "voice," which I referred to earlier. The passing on of wisdom through prophetic voice is evident in the work of churchwomen like Anna Cooper, Ida B. Wells-Barnett, Mary McLeod Bethune, and Fannie Lou Hamer, who are best known for their work in educational, civic, and political affairs. It is also evident in the work of women like Nannie Helen Burroughs, who transformed understandings of women's roles in the church as well as women's roles in movements for social reform.

Such women saw their work of reform as consistent with God's aim for religious and social progress. Anna Cooper contended that reformers, "after all, but think God's thoughts after him" [sic].[19] She believed that each generation had its own work to do in God's activity of reform. In this sense, God's creative power is not only a power that makes something out of nothing; it is regenerative. It grows, continues, and changes from generation to generation in history. No one generation gets the full picture of God's plans for the life and development of a people, humankind, or the planet humankind is dependent on.

An important task for womanists is to consider how one might best interpret the symbols of faith that have provided wisdom, healing, and wholeness in the past for present and future generations. How do we apply that wisdom to the needs of our present context, mindful of the near future? Are we willing to change as our situation changes, preserving something of the old belief in a God of reform who is concerned with both personal and social salvation, but understanding God's intention for reform in new ways for the needs of each new day? For example, today it is necessary to move beyond Cooper's emphasis on race and gender oppression to consider more fully its connection with economic and ecological oppression.

6. Rememory. The wisdom and knowledge required to make decisions that promote survival, healing, and liberation are dependent on the power of *memory*. The creative power to make meaning out of the past is necessary to give a sense of direction for present and future generations. Womanist theologians and ethicists participate in such activity by grounding their thought in historical and contemporary studies of Black women's religious thought and practice. I refer to this activity as *the power of memory*. Memory — or what one character in Toni Morrison's novel *Beloved* refers to as "rememory" — involves the power of reconnecting those memories that have been forcefully dismembered from community consciousness. It involves an uncovering and insurrection of subjugated knowledges about the history and ancestry of Africans in Diaspora. For example, Morrison's character Beloved in her novel *Beloved* symbolizes the problem of *disremembered* myth and history in African American culture as well as the psychic disruption experienced during the trans-Atlantic slave trade and beyond. Beloved, believed by Sethe to be the ghost of her baby girl whose neck she severed in an effort to rescue her from slavery, is described as being "disremembered" and "unaccounted for." Morrison's novel is based on the actual historical figure Margaret Garner, who, in a nihilistic act, tried to spare her children the brutalities of slavery by killing them. As the novel progresses, it is evident that Beloved is something more than the ghost of Sethe's murdered daughter. The disrememberment of Beloved, a figure who has memories of being on the slave ships during the trans-Atlantic slave trade, involves a dismemberment — a fragmentation — of history and myth.[20] Whether or not the exorcism of Beloved from the community is good or effective remains a question. An individual like Sethe could not contain the painful memories of an abusive past without falling into madness. Yet Beloved, representative of the history and culture of a people, cannot be completely exorcised. The struggle to forget is futile. A more subliminal form of haunting persists in the collective consciousness of those who make up the culture Beloved belongs to. Beloved is not truly exorcised, but erupts into her separate parts, symbolizing a fragmentation of memory. The Black community in *Beloved* has become a new people, separated from Africa, freed from slavery, and moving forward to create new meaning in a context of relative freedom and subjugated, fragmented memories. The abuse of slavery as well as preslavery memories of venerating the ancestors recede as paramount aspects in the collective memory of a new community, although never completely forgotten. But how do we know who we are if we do not remember more fully who we have been?

The novel raises questions about the suppression of the past, denial of history, and the will to forget. Has active disrememberment brought on such angry haunting by the ancestors in the first place? Are there methods for *re-membering* and *re-collecting* the past, with all its terror, that can lead to healing and wholeness? The community in *Beloved* does not consider that Sethe's problem is that her remembering activities take place in profound isolation. How could an individual remember the terror of the bodily and psychic abuse of millions without suffering the kind of insanity Sethe endured? Perhaps the solution is not exorcism, but recollection of the past in community, holding one another together with tar-like power of community building. Could one then emerge with new understanding of the insane terror of the past and the blessedness of survival? Morrison reworks ancient myth and fragments of history to challenge understandings of complicity with good and evil. The power of memory is important for celebrating creative, liberative gifts as well as recognizing complicity with oppression. Applying Morrison's work to womanist theology and ethics, one might say that remembering mythic and historical ancestors is both dangerous and vital. The narrative in Beloved notes the importance of remembering to forgive and receive forgiveness for acting in complicity with oppression.[21] Without forgiveness and connectedness in community, memories of abuse are destructive. The purpose of memory is to build strengths and correct weaknesses in community relations in order to more effectively challenge sociopolitical and economic injustice.

7. Interlocking Powers of Survival, Resistance, and Liberation.

a. *Survival.* Survival is a creative quality that is discussed in the works of womanist theologians and ethicists like Delores Williams, Katie Cannon, Jacquelyn Grant, and Kelly Brown Douglas. It has been metaphorically referred to as the power of "making something out of nothing" in the work of Katie Cannon and "making a way out of no way" in the work of Delores Williams. In *A Singing Something*, I refer to this particular quality of God and Black women in my grandmother's words as "making do."[22] All three metaphors refer to what Williams calls an ethic of survival and quality of life among Black women. The activity of the God who enables them with vision for such survival traditionally has been described as God's *sustaining activity*. For Williams God is a God of survival and quality of life. One might interpret this God as a God of sustenance who provides vision for survival in the midst of oppression. In this way God sustains communities for whom liberation is long in coming.

Williams emphasizes that God provides Hagar with *vision* to see resources where it seems none exist. God does not exercise sustaining power apart from human responsibility. Humankind is responsible for exercising gifts of vision and sustenance with God. In this way, one shares in God's sustaining power. Historically, Black women who have made a home for themselves and their families out of scarce food and material supplies share in the creative power of God to seemingly make something out of nothing.

b. *Resistance.* While womanists like Katie Cannon and Delores Williams give emphasis to survival, they also refer to resistance. Cannon, for example, refers to the unctuousness involved in Zora Neale Hurston's sense of dignity as she "pushed against the structural limits which did not adhere to her own standard of self-fulfillment."[23] Delores Williams writes that:

> African-American women have not been passive in the face of the threat of destruction and death. The Hagar-in-the-wilderness symbolism directs attention to African-American women's history of resistance, which has been especially rich from the time of slavery until this present day. Like the slave woman Hagar, many African-American slave women had belligerent attitudes expressed in the numerous slave insurrections they instigated.[24]

The power of resistance involves active unwillingness to perpetuate injustice. In my understanding, it involves subtle and explicit rebellious and insurrectionary acts against systems of oppression. The idea and practice of resistance recurs in womanist theology and ethics. Various historical figures — Ida B. Wells-Barnett, Anna Julia Cooper, Sojourner Truth, and Fannie Lou Hamer — are examples of women who employed legal, journalistic, physical (Wells-Barnett kicked and fought when a conductor tried to remove her from the segregated car of a train), and political strategies to *resist oppression*.[25] Resistance may also involve more subtle acts such as Rebecca Cox Jackson's refusal to have others interpret Scripture or write her thoughts for her, or it may involve physically resistant and liberating acts such as Sojourner Truth's and Harriet Tubman's abolitionist activities. Williams cites little-known women as examples of resistance activity: Jenny Slew, who successfully sued her Massachusetts owner for unlawfully holding her in slavery; Lucy and Charlotte, women who participated in Nat Turner's revolt in Southampton County, Virginia, in 1831. The women who Williams describes were not passive, but engaged in explicit defensive measures such as legal suits, kicking, biting, fighting, and other acts to defend self and community.[26] *Resistance* against oppression is a difficult task, because gender and racial discrimination are easily internalized. Internalized oppression is the most dangerous and insidious form of oppression because it seduces the oppressed to comply with their own oppression. Moreover, it is necessary to resist not only racism and sexism, but classism and environmental abuse. All of these forms of injustice must be resisted internally in the Black community as well as externally in relation to dominant social structures.

c. *Liberation.* Liberation is the act of reclaiming the power of freedom. What kind of freedom? What kind of liberation? What do we mean when we use these terms? We are familiar with historical African American emphasis on social, economic, and political freedom and equality. But along with these come Du Bois's and Cooper's emphasis on the freedom of the mind to think, to enjoy intellectual exploration — freedom from the colonization of the *minds* and *souls* of Black folk and humankind around the globe. For Anna Cooper and other Black leaders — Henry Highland Garnett, Alexander Crummell, Frederick Douglass, Harriet Tubman, Ida B. Wells-Barnett, Martin Luther King, Jr., Fannie Lou Hamer — God is a God of freedom. For Anna Cooper freedom and equality were inherent, universal principles in humankind whose source was the Creator of all. In her thinking "progress in the democratic sense" was an "inborn human endowment" and "a shadow mark of the Creator's image," a "Singing Something" traceable to the Creator.[27] Humankind is created in ontological freedom and equality, one might say. God's aim for society was fuller realization of freedom and equality in the thinking of Cooper and her contemporaries in the Black women's clubs and racial uplift movements.

Today we must further define what we mean by freedom and equality. It is important, for example, to engage in fuller economic analysis as well as cultural, historical, and social analyses of freedom and oppression. Moreover, ecological issues must be given further attention, as Alice Walker's work suggests. This is particularly important since environmental abuse has a particularly direct impact on the poor. Finally, "liberation" must be balanced with powers of survival, resistance, and the other six gifts of power I have referred to. Such a balance is often overlooked, so that liberation becomes isolated from the other gifts, which is problematic. A diversity of gifts sustains hope in God's liberating power and is salvific by thwarting the threat of nihilism when full freedom seems too long in coming.

Reflections

I have sketched seven gifts of power that represent womanist participation in and embodiment of the creative power of God, which we all have the freedom to participate in. When I examine womanist theology and ethics — e.g., the works of Katie Cannon, Delores Williams, Jacquelyn Grant, Kelly Brown Douglas, Emilie Townes, my own work, and writings by historical Black women — I see attention given to three powers or virtues in particular. These are the powers of survival, resistance, and liberation. Katie Cannon and Delores Williams give more attention to the power of survival, while continuing to appreciate the power of liberation. However, each avoids exalting liberation into a position of primacy. It is a power alongside the power of survival. In fact, Williams's writings in particular suggest that survival is a sustaining and nurturing quality that maintains the lives of individuals and communities until liberation actually comes. Why, Williams challenges her readers, does God not liberate all the oppressed all the time?

In contrast, womanist theologian Jacquelyn Grant focuses on a God of liberation who is reflected in the faces of ordinary Black women. This God is a God of the least of these who provides liberation from oppressive structures of institutional oppression. Finally, elements of the power of resistance can be seen in the lives of historical Black women like Sojourner Truth, Nannie Helen Burroughs, Anna Julia Cooper, Ida B. Wells-Barnett, Jenny Slew, and Lucy and Charlotte.

Rather than choose between an emphasis on liberation, survival, or resistance powers, I prefer to embrace all three in my own theological work. It is often noted that womanist theology and ethics is in a stage of development. As that development takes place, it is important to be attentive to a community of ideas and articulations of Black women's cultural, religious, and sociohistorical realities. Ideally, womanist theology is written in community. A wholistic womanist concept of gifts of power for survival and wholeness embraces a community of womanist *gifts*, a diversity of symbolizations of power that lead to the healing and wholeness of entire people, male and female.[28] Further reflection on womanist gifts of power requires moving beyond the three most frequently cited activities of liberation, survival, and resistance.

The seven gifts of power I have cited here are interrelated. The six metaphors of voice, naming, vision, tar/glue, rememory, and regeneration refer to related gifts that are empowering and sustaining for the work of liberation, survival, and resistance. Without them liberation, survival, and resistance could not take place. Finally, the undergirding power for the seven gifts I have discussed here and the multiplicity of gifts beyond them is the *power of belief* in God as Strength of Life. God is empowering Spirit. While God as empowering Spirit is eternally present, we humans are called to believe in and have faith in empowering Spirit in order to fully realize God as the strength of our lives on a daily basis.

Anna Cooper discusses the power of belief extensively in the last chapter of *A Voice from the South*. "That is power," she argued. "That is the stamping attribute in every impressive personality, that is the fire to the engine and the moter [sic] force in every battery." She described the words "I believe" as the power of Paul, Muhammad, Luther, and St. Ignatius of Loyola. The words "I believe," in her thinking, form the first act of faith. They are "the live coal from the altar which at once unseals the lips of the dumb." They "must be our strength," she argued, "if our lives are to be worth the living."[29] What must one believe in? One must believe in a "God of history" who "often chooses the weak things of earth to confound the mighty"; believe as Jesus did in "the eternal development of *the best* in [hu]man[ity]." The concept of God that emerges throughout Cooper's *A Voice from the South* is a God of freedom, equality, compassion, and power. In contrast the power of finite "dilettante speculation" was far from adequate for realizing the fullness of human potential.[30]

Cooper saw religious belief around the world and across the centuries as foundational to the strength, power, and value of human life and existence. Without such belief one would lose sight of the worth and value of human life, falling into destructive patterns of relationship with self and other. She did not develop a theodicy, which gives her work a tone of optimism. Today one must more fully consider human potential for evil as well as for good. There is a challenge to creatively communicate the power of belief in something in the universe that is greater than classism, greater than racism, greater than sexism, greater than environmental racism, greater than xenophobia in all its manifestations. Such a challenge has to do with the work of regeneration — not only the regeneration of belief but the generative work of creating new socioeconomic and political realities that promote healing and wholeness. Such healing and wholeness is not only for the others that Black women have traditionally struggled for. It is also for ourselves as Black women who are called to love ourselves *regardless* of the stereotypes and unrealistic expectations others may have of us. Such healing and wholeness is not only for minds and hearts; it is for bodies. Just as Hagar found water in the desert for physical sustenance along with renewed faith, so are Black women called to new vision for healing of their bodies *and* souls, as well as the bodies and souls of their loved ones, on a daily basis. We are called to speak out against injustice not only as it affects the many others in our lives (traditionally brothers, fathers, uncles, sons), but we are called to speak out against sexism, domestic violence, environmental racism, classism, and heterosexism as they affect Black women and girls. We are called to speak on behalf of our own right to be treated as fully human, not as superwomen, but as participants in a wholistic praxis of vision for survival, liberation, and wholeness through resistance against injustice that threatens the abundance of life promised to humankind and all creation.

Body and spirit are interdependent. We cannot enact concrete social change without engaging the strength God as Spirit provides for our entire selves as individuals and community. Moreover, realizing a wholistic vision of survival, liberation, and resistance against injustice requires the participation of entire communities, male *and* female. Black men are called to share in these gifts of power, adding their own gifts, working in partnership with Black women. Finally, the entire church, whether it realizes it or not, is called to participate in God's activity of making a way out of no way, in liberation and resistance against injustice wherever it may be and whomever it may afflict.

Notes

1. Marcia Riggs, *Arise, Awake, Act: A Womanist Call for Black Liberation* (Cleveland: Pilgrim Press, 1994), x–xi.

2. Zora Neale Hurston, "The 'Pet' Negro System," in Alice Walker, ed., *I Love Myself When I'm Laughing and Then Again When I'm Looking Mean and Impressive: A Zora Neale Hurston Reader* (Old Westbury, N.Y.: Feminist Press, 1979), 156–62.

3. I am influenced in part by process theology as articulated by Marjorie Suchocki and Henry James Young, in which God and humankind are described as being made of the same stuff, so to speak, although each functions differently. They are within one another, although humankind is limited in its capacities of knowledge and power. Yet God shares power with all of creation. Created in freedom, humankind may choose to participate in or live in disharmony with God's initial aim for creation. See Marjorie Suchocki, *God, Church, Christ* (New York: Crossroad, 1992), and Henry James Young, *Hope in Process* (Minneapolis: Fortress Press, 1990). See also the *Muntu* concept of cosmology as described in the dissertation of Peter Mwiti Rukungah, "The Cosmocentric Model of Pastoral Psychotherapy: A Contextualized Holistic Model from a Bantu African Worldview, a Perspective for Post-Modern Pastoral-Psychotherapy," School of Theology at Claremont, 1994. Rukungah's work is distinctive in its introduction of a pre-Whiteheadian African worldview that has much in common with process theology.

4. Karen Baker-Fletcher, *A Singing Something: Womanist Reflections on Anna Julia Cooper* (New York: Crossroad, 1994), 185–206.

5. Jean McMahon Humez, *Gifts of Power: The Writings of Rebecca Jackson, Black Visionary, Shaker Eldress* (Amherst: University of Massachusetts Press, 1981).

6. The expression "reconstruction of womanhood" is derived from Hazel Carby's book, *Reconstructing Womanhood* (New York: Oxford University Press, 1987). Carby explains that in nineteenth-century ideologies of womanhood, "black womanhood was polarized against white womanhood." Thus, Black women writers "had to define a discourse of Black womanhood that addressed their exclusion and rescued their very bodies from a persistent association with illicit sexuality" (32–36). Black women, then, historically have *reconstructed* "womanhood" to mean something different from dominant stereotypes of Black women in American culture.

7. Baker-Fletcher, *A Singing Something*, 16, 66–67, 189–95.

8. Emilie Townes, "Keeping a Clean House Will Not Keep a Man at Home: An Unctuous Womanist Rhetoric of Justice," in David Batstone, ed., *New Visions for the Americas* (Minneapolis: Fortress Press, 1993), 122. On womanist-feminist conversation, Townes writes: "The relevance of our worldviews is more of a challenge than we are willing to accept.... A monologue is not enough, a dialogue is better, a chorus is wonderful, but a ringshout is what a womanist ethic of justice seeks. The are no observers, only pilgrims in the ring." The same criterion could be applied to womanist conversations in general.

9. Delores Williams, *Sisters in the Wilderness: The Challenge of Womanist God-Talk* (Maryknoll, N.Y.: Orbis Books, 1993), ix–xii, 5–6, 20–22.

10. See ibid., chaps. 1, 2, and 5. See esp. 20–23.

11. Ibid., 28–32. Williams discusses the account of Hagar's naming of God as "El Roi" ("God of seeing") in Genesis 16:13 and of her second encounter with a God who provides vision in the wilderness as she struggles for survival with her son Ishmael in Genesis 21:18–19.

12. See Cheryl Sanders, "Afrocentrism and Womanism in the Seminary," *Christianity and Crisis*, April 13, 1992, 124.

13. Townes, "Keeping a Clean House," 140.

14. See Marilyn Richardson, *Maria W. Stewart, America's First Black Woman Political Writer* (Bloomington: Indiana University Press, 1987).

15. Theressa Hoover, "Black Women and the Churches," in James Cone and Gayraud Wilmore, eds., *Black Theology: A Documentary History, 1966–1979* (Maryknoll, N.Y.: Orbis Books, 1979), 380–81. See also Jacquelyn Grant, "Black Theology and the Black Woman," in Cone and Wilmore, eds., *Black Theology: A Documentary History, 1966–1979*, 423.

16. See Thomas LeClair, "The Language Must Not Sweat," in *New Republic* 184 (March 21, 1981): 26–28. See also Judith Wilson, "Conversation with Toni Morrison," *Essence*, July 1981, 85ff.

17. See Peter Rukungah, "The Cosmocentric Model of Pastoral Psychotherapy: A Contextualized Holistic Model from a Bantu African Worldview," dissertation, School of Theology at Claremont, 1994.

18. See Alice Walker, *In Search of Our Mothers' Gardens* (San Francisco: Harcourt Brace Jovanovich, 1983), xi–xii.

19. Anna Julia Cooper, "Woman versus the Indian," in *A Voice from the South*, ed. Mary Helen Washington, Schomburg Library of Nineteenth-Century Black Women Writers (1892; reprint, New York: Oxford University Press, 1988), 118–19.

20. Toni Morrison, *Beloved* (New York: Alfred Knopf, 1987), 132, 267. Beloved is aware that "it is difficult keeping her head on her neck, her legs attached to her hips when she is by herself." By the end of the novel, after she has been exorcised from the community by a group of praying women, she "erupts into her separate parts" and is "disremembered," but there is a period during which "the rustle of a skirt hushes when they wake, and the knuckles brushing a cheek in sleep seem to belong to the sleeper." From an African ontological perspective (e.g., Yoruba), one such symbolism could suggest that Beloved has passed from the realm of the ancestors to the realm of the spirits whose names are no longer remembered. One might say Beloved exists in the collective unconsciousness of a people.

21. See ibid. In reference to dismemberment and disrememberment, see pp. 206, 211, 215, 181). See also p. 132 in reference to Beloved: "Among the things she could not remember was when she first knew that she could wake up in any day and find herself in pieces."

22. See Katie Cannon, *Black Womanist Ethics* (Atlanta: Scholars Press, 1987); Delores Williams, *Sisters in the Wilderness;* Jacquelyn Grant, *White Women's Christ and Black Women's Jesus* (Atlanta: Scholars Press, 1988); Kelly Brown Douglas, *The Black Christ* (Maryknoll, N.Y.: Orbis Books, 1993); and Karen Baker-Fletcher, *A Singing Something.*

23. See Cannon, *Black Womanist Ethics,* 108–9; Williams, *Sisters in the Wilderness,* 130–39.

24. Williams, *Sisters in the Wilderness,* 136–37.

25. See ibid., 130–39; Emilie Townes, *Womanist Justice, Womanist Hope* (Atlanta: Scholars Press, 1993); Grant, *White Women's Christ and Black Women's Jesus* (Atlanta: Scholars Press, 1988); Cannon, *Black Womanist Ethics;* and Baker-Fletcher, *A Singing Something.*

26. Williams, *Sisters in the Wilderness,* 136–39.

27. Anna Julia Cooper, "Equality of Races and the Democratic Movement," privately printed pamphlet (Washington, D.C., 1945), 4–5.

28. See Walker's definition of "womanist" in *In Search of Our Mothers' Gardens,* xi–xii.

29. Cooper, "The Gain from a Belief," in *A Voice from the South,* 301–3. See also Karen Baker-Fletcher, *A Singing Something,* 97–99.

30. Cooper, "The Gain from a Belief," 298.

Nine

Dialogue on HUMANITY

KASIMU

In keeping with your first book, *A Singing Something*, it is entirely appropriate that you focus our attention on the particular issue of womanhood.[1] You "break the silence" concerning women's human-beingness, particularly Black women's articulation of their own humanity, subverting traditional theological anthropology's abstract presentations of "man" or "humanity" exclusively from a male point of view. I see the "Womanhood" section of this book as a systematic extension of the family stories and accounts found in *A Singing Something*. In particular you take on degrading myths of Black womanhood, focusing on deconstructing and demystifying the popular mythic image of the superwoman. You draw a distinction between a psychologically healthy "will for survival" and the unhealthy aspects of "denial" and "misguided stoicism" which are the hallmarks of a true superwoman. Do you see an equal need in the African American male community to deconstruct and reconstruct the "superman?"

Karen

Yes, I do see an equal need in the African American male community (and male communities generally) to be freed from the "superman" stereotype. First, it is important to acknowledge that a Black superman image exists, since the image does not appear in popular media. In contrast, the myth of Black superwoman is very present in the media. Both images, whether perpetuated by the media or not, are passed on in Black families. The Black superman holds down two or three jobs, for very real economic reasons. It is not holding down the jobs to support his family, however, that makes him a superman. It is the expectation that he must deny the toll such work takes on body and spirit to be a "man" that requires him, in effect, to be a superman. It is the superwoman who is expected to feel his feelings for him, the family, the community at large, even though she

164

also may hold down two jobs or work at night while he works during the day. Moving toward a wholistic understanding of human being requires that we all allow ourselves to be more open and vulnerable to ourselves, to God, and to trusted loved ones.

KASIMU

The terms "open" and "vulnerable" are almost annihilated from male self-understanding. XODUS theology and ethics seeks ways for Black males (and all men who are in solidarity with the Folk and the "Hood") to reconnect our selves with our GOD, our feelings, and our bodies. To put it more sharply, since men are socialized to deny pain, push the body even when it cries out for rest, and negate the effects of sickness or disease, the health of Black male bodies depends on our ability to honestly assess our needs, and then find just and loving ways to go about meeting those needs. I am interested in developing an ethic of Black male health which would require honest self-body appraisal and would fulfill the same physical, emotional, and spiritual parameters found in *The Black Woman's Health Book* by Evelyn White.

In order for Afrikan bodies to be healthy we must

- understand the devaluation of Black bodies in its larger socio-historical context;

- take care of our own bodies;

- become attuned to the rhythms of our bodies, spirits, and minds;

- become responsive to the signals of our bodies;

- demand adequate health care officials and courteous staff; and

- insist that more be done to insure the institutional longevity of health and medical facilities in African American communities.

What else would you see as necessary for an XODUS and womanist ethic of health?

Karen

First, I am most intrigued by your comment that "openness" and "vulnerability" are virtually annihilated from male dialogue. I think that men need to speak to other men about this. Before womanists and Black male theologians can begin to develop ethics of health that are truly mutual, it is necessary for men and women to think in new paradigms so that we are able to communicate with each other more effectively. We must be able to address issues regarding health of body and spirit in relation to the diversity of perspectives across gender, class, cultures, and experience that is present in Black communities. I would place conversation at the top of my list. Some would say that before men and women dialogue with one another, it is necessary for women to be in conversation with women and for men to be in conversation with men. Alice Walker asserts that a womanist is *not* a separatist, except on occasion for reasons of health. For me, this suggests that there will be times when women will need to meet separately to discuss particular issues relating to women. The same is true for men. But it is also important for women and men to come together and engage in conversation with each other about their particular understandings of spiritual development in order (1) to understand differences and (2) to discover and share some common themes. A relationship of trust needs to be built in which all are heard with respect for integrity of others in the midst of both agreement and disagreement. This relationship of trust must be built before we can even begin making an adequate agenda for addressing spiritual and physical health in Black communities.

I think that building trust occurs over a period of time. This means that Black women and men need to be in conversation in a covenanted relationship and on a regular basis. I realize your question asks me what strategies I would add for attaining healthier lives in Black communities. I respond with comments on trust and conversation, because I am concerned about the *process* required for setting up such an agenda. I find your agenda helpful. I would add that educational programs regarding health providers in Black communities be provided by churches in affiliation with health providers. Education about *psychological* health services is necessary and often neglected, because until recently psychotherapy has maintained a Eurocentric bias. It would be helpful for communities to be informed of Black or multicultural mental health services that are available. Again, before such education can be productive, I believe that a process of communication needs to be developed that includes scriptural, African, and African American texts (oral and written) as foundational resources for interpreting the relationship between one's spiritual life and one's mental and physical well-being. Workshops could be presented — some for men, some for women, some for both groups together.

While I am intrigued by your discussion of Ma'atic principles as a solution to the disparagement of dignity and self, I would like to see further discussion on how similar principles are already present in Black American culture. You hint at this in your discussion of liberationist

Christianity in relation to Ma'atic principles, but I would like to see the connection fleshed out.

KASIMU

Actually some of the most conservative and traditional elements of Black American culture might resonate most with Ma'atic principles! For example, those lessons we all learned from our grandparents on self-reliance, working harmoniously with persons in positions of authority over one's self, and — the one on "righteousness" — "what goes around comes around" are all similar to the cosmologically grounded ethical imperatives of the Ma'atic code. The principles of Ma'at have the potential to bring together liberationist Christians with more traditionalist elements within the increasingly conservative mood of African American communities.

Karen

Your discussion also leaves me wondering about the ways in which Malcolm's understandings of Islam (early and late) are similar to or different from Ma'atic principles. At times you seem to conflate Ma'atic principles with Malcolm's "X." But you are really reconstructing Malcolm's "X" to interplay with Ma'at and Martin Luther King's theory of dignity. How would you argue that such a synthesis is tenable?

KASIMU

This is an excellent question because it goes right to the heart of XODUS theo-ethical idealism. XODUS theology and ethics builds on the original premise of first-generation James Cone's idea that a "Black" Christian reflection appropriate to the sociopolitical upheaval of the late Freedom Struggle (1960s and early 1970s) had to combine the important progressivist Christian elements of King's thought with the Black nationalist/ Black Power ideologies represented in the dynamic life-journey of Malcolm X. XODUS attempts to update Cone's original imperative by bringing the combination of Martin King, Malcolm X, and Howard Thurman into a dialogue with womanism, the "New Male" movement, and the expressive "art" of the "streetz" found in Rap. Ma'at does not demonize any ethnic-cultural grouping, as the Nation of Islam's teaching about White people still does. It is not anti-Semitic, as is the Nation of Islam to this day. Malcolm X grew out of the demonizing ideology of the Nation, but never lost his forthright prophetic denunciation of racism and injustice. He always couched his denunciation of sociopolitical and economic injustice in religious terms. Ma'at couches its criticism of social injustice in cosmological terms. Both use proverbs and stories to promote their ethical stance.

Karen

These distinctions are helpful. And yet not only did Malcolm X grow out of the ideology of the Nation of Islam, but he also became El Malik Hajj El-Shabazz as a convert to Sunni Islam. Your understanding of XODUS, however, relates more clearly to Christianity and ancient African principles than to Islam and African principles. How is XODUS related to other religions of contemporary Black people, including Islam and Judaism, since, after all, XODUS derives in part from the Exodus of the Hebrew Bible as well as the exodus of African American slaves?

KASIMU

The lack of explicit references to the religious principles of Sunni Islam and Judaism are the result of my attention to building up connections between contemporary liberationist Christianity and (1) ancient Kemetic moral philosophy and (2) traditional African religions. I believe that XODUS ought to be able to JOURNEY outwards rather than retreating to an enervating provincialism, so I hope that Moslems and Jews as well as representatives of other religions might find a framework in XODUS work tenable for doing some of their own reflecting.

Karen

As we lift up the problem of the dehumanization of Black men and women, I find it important to lift up both the anonymous and well-known resisters against such dehumanization. How are these principles already present in ordinary people?

KASIMU

The strength and beauty of living in a community, caring for one another, and learning to negotiate our differences with calm resolution are principles of both Ma'at and everyday Folk. Ma'at is not elitist, even though many "ordinary people" in Black communities have never heard it mentioned!

Karen

Are Ma'atic principles, in your view, liberating both for women and for nature?

KASIMU

Nature is always lifted up as the realm created "by the love and tears of RA (GOD)." Teachings on women are more ambiguous. On the one hand, the principles of Ma'at are most often directed to the specifics of male understandings of how to live a wise and moral life, as were most ancient moral texts like the biblical Proverbs. Women appear as "wife," "mother," and "strange woman" — in reference to both prostitutes and women of known sexual promiscuity. The texts were obviously written from a traditional male point of view. On the other hand, there are many more proverbial teachings on fair and just treatment of wives and mothers than are found in the Bible, with its predominant tone of domination and submission. They stressed *self-mastery rather than mastery over the female in one's life*, even suggesting that men learn to *silently watch and appreciate* the women in their lives before speaking to them! I hope to spend time with you and other womanists in doing a more extensive analysis of how women view the Kemetic proverbs.

Karen

I am struck by your use of the metaphor "dust." You write, "Our bodies, souls, and cultures were ground into dust as part of a plan of subjugation done in the name of this kind of interpretation of 'dominion.'" I find this use of the metaphor "dust" striking because it is a reminder that "dust" is not always a positive metaphor. "Dust," which I use primarily as a symbol of the life-giving power of earth and its elements, can also be a symbol of death. There are expressions such as "another one bites the dust" in popular culture or "ashes to ashes, dust to dust" in the biblically based funeral rituals of Christian culture. It strikes me that it is necessary to explore further the double-edged nature of the metaphor. It is at once a symbol of life and of death. While it is important not to overwork the metaphor of "dust," I find it important to consider how to breathe new life into dry bones. How might we answer Ezekiel's question: "Can these dry bones live?"

KASIMU

I examine "dust" because of my appreciation for your use of the term as a christological symbol of Jesus' humanity. Yet "dust" is most commonly alluded to in a negative way by Black Americans in relationship to dry skin — "being ashy!" No doubt the word carries an ambivalent meaning for most, especially in light of its funereal context. Traditional Yoruba myth about the dust of the earth being impregnated by the falling dust-like personalities of the *orishas* (similar to Christian angels) who fell to earth as the Creator Obatala climbed down his golden ladder remakes "dust" into a *positive* sacred symbol of life rather than death. Yet one will not immediately think of *this sacred story* unless one has heard it. It will take a concerted effort by womanist and XODUS thinkers to promote the positive connotations of "dust" from the particular point of view of one informed by Afrikan spirituality.

Karen

Isn't that also true of Ma'at? Aren't African American scholars generally challenged to communicate in plain speech our more seemingly esoteric ideas. I say "seemingly esoteric" because they are often parallel to or even derived from practices and beliefs already present in our communities.

KASIMU

Yes, it takes time to bring a new word, idea, and phrase into the everyday language of the Folk, but then isn't our job to be "culture workers"? I am intrigued by the beauty and potential of Ma'atic principles for reforming Afrikan life, but I do not advocate a full-scale romanticized and uncritical appropriation of ancient Kemet and its myths. One cannot resurrect a long-dead civilization, but perhaps its greatest ideas may yet have life.

Karen

Well, then, it is possible to breathe new life into dry bones, especially if they yet have some life in them!

Notes

1. Karen Baker-Fletcher, *A Singing Something: Womanist Reflections on Anna Julia Cooper* (New York: Crossroad, 1994), 102–31.

Part IV

GENERATIONS

Unto All Generations

Mothers, Other Mothers, and Honoring the Ancestors

To BE WOMANIST is to be generational. Generation has to do with more than the biological activity of child-conception and childbearing. It includes childrearing and moves beyond that to consider care for elders and remembering ancestors. Generation has to do with time, space, and creative activity. To be engaged in generational activity requires concern with the past (history), the present, and the future. It requires attention to space or place because it is concerned with the land in which the events of everyday and extraordinary life take place. It has to do with creative activity because it involves the creation of new life and the renewal of already existing life. It involves the nurture of children and all of creation, young and old, plant and animal, sky and earth in a way that sustains communities and the planet we are all dependent on.

Biological Motherhood

While mothering involves more than biological tasks of childbearing and breastfeeding, it is important to acknowledge and respect the work of women's bodies. Since I write this chapter within weeks of the birth of my third child, Desiree Aisha Dawn (trans.: "dawning of greatly desired abundant life"), who is named after several ancestors and elders, I would find it artificial to write a chapter on generational activity without considering the theological significance of childbearing and breastfeeding. While not every woman desires to or is able to engage in such activities, for those who do it is important to consider the sacredness of such life-giving, life-affirming activity. To engage in such activity is to engage in embodied spiritual labor.

The act of bearing a child is a sacred act, the act of bringing new life into the world. Moreover, nursing or even feeding a child with formula is a sacred act because it participates in God's activity of spiritual and physical sustenance. That women are able to feed young infants from their own bodies, as well as with the work of their hands, says something about the embodiment of God's sustaining activity in human beings. Today women are gaining new respect for the life-sustaining capacity of their bodies. It is one of many ways in which women can embody Spirit. Moreover, the time, patience, and physical labor involved in such work teaches that participating in God's sustaining activity is no easy task.

It is easy for young first-time mothers, for example, to assume that it all comes naturally, that raising and nurturing the life of a child is an innate skill all women possess. The larger society, after all, assumes that this is what women are primarily created for. One's head may be filled with the romantic pictures that overflow in magazines of dreamy, smiling mothers tenderly cuddling round, expertly nursing babies to the breast in rocking chairs, surrounded by sunlight and lace. Such images of mature babies with their mothers populate the media, including hospital literature.

In past generations, Jesus and God have been imaged as nurturing, breastfeeding mothers, even when flesh-and-blood mothers were deemed impure, unclean, profane in their bodily functions, creatures who were whole and holy only in relation to husbands.[1] Whereas in the past God has been envisioned as perfect mother, while real mothers were disparaged, today it is important to consider that flesh-and-blood motherhood is sacred. Flesh-and-blood mothers reflect God's sustaining, life-giving, life-affirming activity. Women participate in such activity with God whether they are biological and/or breastfeeding mothers or not.

Even as I speak of such activity as sacred, it is important to further deromanticize the activity of mothering. One of the problems Americans face today is the number of teenage girls who purposefully become pregnant because they desire confirmation of their womanhood and a warm person in their lives to love, little knowing the real rigors involved in parenting and adult responsibilities.

The church is reticent to speak about human sexuality, let alone offer courses on the true demands of parenting. While there are plenty of sermons that condemn sex outside of marriage, "the problems of the youth today," and the irresponsibility of "some parents today," and that celebrate "the way we used to do things," little concrete constructive teaching is taking place. There are some Black churches, however, that have manhood and womanhood initiation programs. It would be helpful if there were more of these programs, emphasizing the fullness of manhood and womanhood as including but involving far more than childbearing and childrearing. Preaching alone is not enough. Preaching that makes young males and females feel unacceptable to or unwanted in the church can even perpetuate the problem. Unwed teenage mothers, for example, have been excluded from church Mother's Day activities in an effort to shame them into repenting before the church. This ritual of isolation all too often has the desired effect of making such mothers feel bad about themselves, worse than they have already been made to feel by murmurs and gossip. But it does not demonstrate what it means to be a good mother. While the intent of acts of shaming may be to discourage youth from irresponsible sexual behavior, it can be destructive to the self-esteem of the one who is shamed. Unfortunately, the isolation of the teenage mothers is reactive rather than proactive. Moreover, it is extremely sexist when the mother is singled out for rebuke while the father is to all appearances rendered blameless. It provides no real solutions or answers to the problems and questions young people wrestle with in their transition to mature bodies, minds, and feelings.

Fortunately, rites of passage programs for males and females are emerging in Black churches. Such programs on the transition from childhood to adulthood provide healthy rituals for young people to honor and celebrate what it means to become a responsible adult. They need to become even more widespread, in small churches as well as in large ones. It would also be helpful if teenage mothers and fathers took part in rituals that emphasize the sacredness of parenthood, the responsibilities of parenting, and the understanding of generativity as a creative power that is not only biological but cultural and spiritual. Moreover, programs especially geared toward mothers and fathers of various age groups can help create a community that truly implements the African proverb, "It takes a whole village to raise a child." We need less shaming of youth and more loving programs that deal honestly with their concerns, questions, and realities.

Teenage mothers are among the most vulnerable, most often condemned mothers in society. In reality, however, and in sharp contrast to sensationalized media portraits, they make up a very small percentage of single mothers. Most single mothers are adults, age eighteen or older, and they are predominantly White. The unwed fathers are often several years older than the mothers, so male abuse of sexual responsibility needs to be addressed. The church across the racial spectrum must come to terms with issues of sexuality and parenting.

Other Mothers (and Fathers)

Generational activity requires the commitment of entire peoples, male and female. We live in a changing era in which women are learning that we do not have to do it all, and men are more actively engaged in parenting responsibilities. Black women, who have always had to work in greater numbers than White women, continue to combine work and parenting responsibilities. Single Black men who are raising their children are rarely acknowledged by the media, but in fact many are doing a fine job. The workplace is required to have far more generous family leave policies for women and men than before. More workplaces have paid paternity leaves as well as paid maternity leaves, although this practice is not at all common enough. This is important, because sexism is a systemic problem affecting both women and men. While new models of womanhood and manhood are changing at an individual level, new visions cannot be fully realized unless socioeconomic practices in the workplace change at a more far-reaching systemic level. Too many women continue to struggle with employers who see childbearing and maternity concerns as an inconvenience. Men find themselves required to cooperate with employers who either do not offer paid paternity or family leave or who offer it but still expect them to work during that time to the point that the "leave" is eroded. There is still an overall expectation in the larger society that "the burden falls on the woman."

Womanist generational thought challenges sexist assumptions in relation to women *and* men. Womanist thought is distinctive in relation to feminist thought, with its attention to questions regarding care for the community across the generations, including parenting as mothers and fathers. While womanism is critical of stereotyped prescriptions of women's roles as nurturers and mothers, it is also constructive in its understanding of nonsexist, nonstereotypical revisioning of what it means to mother, nurture, parent. It is not that feminism is indifferent to such concerns. Popular feminists like Gloria Steinem and Susan Faludi have made it clear that feminism today is concerned with the liberation of men as well as women, particularly in relation to the workplace. They have addressed larger socioeconomic concerns as they affect the freedom of both women and men in relation to the family. But until recently twentieth-century feminist literature (particularly in academia) has tended to shy away from the topic of mothering in its effort to move beyond stereotypical understandings of women's roles as exclusively those of wife, mother, nurturer. Black feminists, womanists, and Black women writers like Patricia Hill Collins, bell hooks, Delores Williams, Emilie Townes, Toni

Morrison, J. California Cooper, and Alice Walker all give attention to the reality of the activity of nurturing and mothering among Black women even as they criticize sexist thought and practice that would relegate women exclusively to the roles of nurturer, mother, and mammy.

Most Black women and men are mothers and fathers to somebody. Many are what Patricia Hill Collins has called "other mothers." Hill deftly debunks the myth of the "superstrong Black mother," agreeing with Renita Weems that it is as false as the myth of the happy slave.[2] An "other mother" may be an aunt, sister, grandmother, friend, or one of the many Black Americans who have traditionally adopted children, formally or informally. For example, like many Black Americans, I grew up in an extended family network. My grandmother was my "other mother." We lived in the same neighborhood. When I was not at home I was at my grandparents' house. My parents rented the home we lived in from my grandfather. His barbershop was attached to the house. We looked after his shop when it was closed. He looked after us and our home when he was at the shop. Occasionally when boys wanted to make trouble for me as I walked to or from my grandmother's house, they left me alone when they learned I was Baker's granddaughter. Grandpa Baker was feared and respected. Whether I like the sexism involved or not, his reputation as one not to be messed with, along with the tough attitude a city girl must develop, went a long way. My grandmother played a very important role in my upbringing. She was so intricately interwoven into the fabric of my family's life that she raised me every bit as much as my own mother. She was an "other mother" not only to me, but to my mother whose own mother lived a few hundred miles away. Likewise, my grandfather functioned as an "other father." A generation later, my aunt was "other mother" to my children when I lived in my home town. Now that I live in southern California, far away from blood kin, a neighbor who my children call "Aunt" has become an "other mother" to them. I received a card from a friend's children, thanking me for being, as they put it, "our other mother."

Such extended family patterns until very recently were normative in African American culture. There are stories of schoolteachers known for truly loving children, sometimes collecting children's clothes and giving them to children from families in financial difficulty. Such teachers take time to get to know the children and their families, becoming part of their lives, not charity workers. There are teachers who have combed a student's hair in the morning because her mother was not able to. Such women are "other mothers." Today, even when flesh-and-blood family is not present, many Black Americans form networks with "fictive kin."[3]

While the extended family tradition has received some wear and tear, it has not died out. Black communities, however, must work at perpetuating its survival. The Million Man March on October 16, 1995, was a mass symbolization of the extended family tradition in Black America. Women and men speakers for the day addressed the million or so men as "sons," "grandsons," and "nephews." The men addressed one another as "brothers," "fathers," "grandfathers," and the women as "mothers," "grandmothers," and "sisters." The extended family tradition is so deep within Black American consciousness that I believe that if there is firm commitment, the kind of commitment the Million Man Marchers professed, it can be revived to function in full health.

One does not have to be a biological parent to nurture the young. The Ashanti proverb "It takes a whole village to raise a child" expresses well the concept behind "other mothers" and "other fathers." It debunks the notion that parenting is an individualistic, biological act or a role performed best by nuclear families. Most important, it presupposes that there is more to being a parent than biological acts of conception and birthing. The most difficult part of birthing is the *lifelong* birthing process of raising a human being from childhood to adulthood for twenty and more years, allowing children to enjoy childhood but moving them toward age-appropriate responsibilities in attitude and action as they mature. True parenting, as elders in diverse communities often teach young parents, is a lifetime responsibility. True parenting requires the gifts of wisdom that an entire community of individuals has to offer. While *responsible* biological parents or a nuclear adoptive family may play a very important, primary role in a child's life, there are others in the community who have wisdom and knowledge that is enriching for all.

Generational Activity and the Womb of Life

Black folk across the generations have passed on wisdom from mother to daughter, father to son wherever we have been. On a plantation, on a slave ship, on a farm, in the city, in the suburbs, in the church, in a mosque, in the wilderness — we have found and must continue to find ways to carve out sacred time and space to pass on tools of wisdom and survival to our children, our children's children, and one another. Such activity must not be romanticized.

It is necessary to consider such passing on of wisdom as a challenge in a complex world, where it is not easy to carve out space or time to do so. Such activity, however, is necessary for revitalizing self, friends, family, and community. Carving out space and time for honoring the many generations that make up our communities and remembering the spiritual ground that sustains individuals and communities has often been performed against all odds by African American ancestors. J. California Cooper captures in graphic and poetic form the survival practices involved in passing on wisdom and worshiping the Spirit on a slave plantation in her novel *Family*.[4] She describes the kind of activity that has been described in numerous slave and ex-slave narratives. She presents the practice of praying into a large pot in the hush harbors or wildernesses on the edges of plantations so that the pot would catch the sound of one's voice. Praying was a subversive act to be hidden from slaveholders. Gathering to worship and to share wisdom tools of survival, liberation, strength, and faith was exercised in an *invisible institution*, as Albert Raboteau reminds us. In a new and hostile environment, slaves searched out a kind of XODUS space in which the generational activity of spiritual renewal, creativity, and re-creation could take place. To live in XODUS space requires generational activity. To be generational involves more than the biological acts of conceiving and bearing children. To be generational is to be mindful of the effects of one's everyday and extraordinary acts for future generations. It involves concern for those children one has physically borne into the world and for the children of entire communities.

There are mothers and there are other mothers. Mothering has to do with the care and nurture of children by aunts, sisters, neighbors, elders, cousins, friends. XODUS space is space in which children can survive and hopefully flourish with the rest of creation. Not only are the generations important, as far as time — past, present, and future — is concerned, but space is also sacred. The womb and the village, the embryo and the environment communities live in are interrelated, whether urban, rural, or suburban. The physical, socioeconomic, and political environments in which we raise our children are as important as generating new life. New life cannot flourish in oppressive conditions. Space and place are as important as time.

If we are children of dust and spirit, then we are concerned not only with our own future but with the physical environment our children live in. This means that environmental issues are not simply "White concerns" but "Black concerns." In passing on wisdom it is necessary to pass on not only the value of struggle for socioeconomic and political equality, but the value of struggling for clean air, clean water, environmentally safe neighborhoods. Recent criticism of the tendency to place toxic waste sites, powerful electromagnetic fields, and other disease-generating forces in poorer neighborhoods — urban, suburban, and rural — is directly related to the survival and wholeness of present and future generations. As community activists involved in protesting such injustices recognize, much of the disease — cancer, for example — in poor and Black communities has as much to do with environmental waste as with balanced meals. The air we breathe and the water we drink is as important as the food we eat. Generationalism has to do with more than bringing babies into the world. It has to do with generating new abundance in the quality of life — more justice, more freedom, more equality, more socioeconomic opportunities, cleaner water, cleaner air, less cancer, less heart disease, cures for sickle cell anemia, diabetes, and AIDS.

The environment we live in must be given the kind of love, nurture, and care that an expectant mother desires for her own body as she looks to her physical well-being and the well-being of her developing child. The physical environment we live in is like the womb of an expectant mother. Everything placed in it — toxic or healing — affects us for ill or for good. To say it plainly, just as expectant mothers risk birthing children with physical defects if they smoke, drink, abuse drugs, eat improperly, or have no access to balanced meals, so we heap risk upon risk of physical and spiritual illness upon ourselves and our children unto our children's children if we do not work for positive transformation of our physical environments. Such transformation goes hand in hand with the traditional socioeconomic and political transformation which Black communities have struggled for in the United States.

Remembering Who We Are and Whose We Are

In *Daughters of the Dust* by Julie Dash, Nana Peazant proclaims that "ancestors and the womb are one." These moving yet curious words suggest that we are connected by time, by spirit, and by body. The living and the dead are one. There is a continuity between present, past, and future generations. This requires a responsibility to remember the legacy of blood and sweat, labor and love, body and soul that has preceded us. It means that the living and the dead alike are held within the one great womb of the Spirit, where there is no difference between the dust of graves and the flesh of new mothers.

The womb of the Spirit is vital and greater than the womb of the ancestors and of the environment. It precedes all that is and is everlasting. It is Creativity-Itself, which cannot be contained by space or time. It is at once immanent and transcendent, with us and beyond us, infinite and within the limits of creation all at once. It is that which holds us and sustains us in the times when the earth groans and shakes, uprooting families from their homes. It provides survival for many and new meaning in the midst of loss. It is that which suffers with us when we are in physical, spiritual, or emotional pain. It is that which rises up in joyful praises inside of us in spite of all obstacles and in times of celebration. The Spirit is necessary because even when we have succeeded with care to create a healthy physical environment nature sometimes seemingly fails us with its tornadoes, hurricanes, floods, fires, freezing cold, blizzards, and earthquakes. The Spirit is also necessary because not everything the ancestors have done has promoted our health and well-being. Living elders and we ourselves are not perfect in our care for one another. We are less-than-perfect, complex people who struggle to do that which is truly healing and nurturing for our children and for one another.

Both Alice Walker and Toni Morrison are interested in mothers and daughters. For Walker, a womanist passes on the wisdom of what it means to be womanish to the daughters. To be womanish or womanist is to be audacious and courageous, concerned with healing and wholeness of entire people male and female. It is to be feminist, but not separatist (except occasionally "for reasons of health," as Walker explains). It involves loving self, creation, and the Spirit. For Morrison, it is necessary to be a good daughter in order to become a good mother. This is a central theme in her book *Tar Baby*. Like Collins and Walker, Morrison does not limit motherhood to its most liberal connotations: "You don't need your own natural mother to be a daughter. All you need is to feel a certain way, a certain careful way about people older than you are."

The male character, Son, in *Tar Baby* wants to make protagonist Jadine remember her funkiness and her ancient properties of tar which connect her to Black women elders and ancestors. Son wants Jadine to live in the all-Black town of Eloe, where women hang sheets on the line. Jadine wants Son to seek educational and economic success. Son remembers community responsibility but resists applying the ancient properties of Black culture to his contemporary situation. Neither Son nor Jadine realize it is possible to be both economically successful and responsible sons or daughters who remember their ancient properties. Aunt Ondine regrets sending Jadine to private schools without teaching her enough about being a daughter. Therese insists that Jadine has "forgotten her ancient properties."[5]

By "ancient properties" the narrative in *Tar Baby* particularly has in mind the qualities of "tar" to hold things together. Morrison reexamines the tar baby story of the South in the United States to reconstruct what it means to be a "tar baby" from several different perspectives: the Westernized plantation version of the story, an original African version of the story, and a contemporary understanding. Morrison explains that the Western version of the story has a tar baby used by a White man to catch a rabbit. She further explains that White people call Black children "tar baby," especially Black girls. It is a name similar to "nigger." In her research, however, she found that "there is a tar lady in African mythology."[6]

Inspired by the tar lady in African mythology, Morrison has reenvisioned the African foundations of the southern folk tale of Br'er Rabbit and the Tar Baby. In so doing, she explores the wealth of Black women's spiritual and creative heritage. According to Morrison, the "tar lady" who predates the "tar baby" of southern folklore was originally a powerful symbol of Black womanhood. She is a Black woman who holds things together — a builder and cohesive force. Tar in this interpretation has a sacred quality. Moreover, by considering the "tar" qualities in Black women, Morrison suggests that Black women's activity of holding things together is a sacred quality and a spiritual power. In her eloquent novel, *Son* associates such spiritual power with the women who bake and sell pies in the church basement — ordinary women involved in the everyday work of being what Theressa Hoover has called "the glue" that holds the church together.[7] As the narrative unfolds, such ancient properties are associated with woman as mother and as daughter. But first one must learn to be a good daughter, which as Aunt Ondine explains, involves feeling a certain careful way about one's elders.

In traditional African and African American cultures, respect for one's elders is an important moral value. It involves respecting not just anything about someone who is older, but respecting the wisdom gained through life experience and survival by those who have struggled for and celebrated life before you. It involves respect for the heritage the elders have to offer, the life-learning they have to pass on, and care for their physical and spiritual well-being. One does not need one's own natural mother to feel this way, Aunt Ondine explains. The powers to nurture and hold family and community together are the sacred properties of Black *women*, not just of biological mothers.

But Jadine resists Ondine's expectation that she return the gift of nurture and holding things together by standing by her elders in their old age. She has no understanding of her night visions of Black women, ancestral and contemporary, who bare their breasts as symbols of the ancient properties to nurture and bear culture.[8] When confronted by her ancestors, she resists their sacred properties. She is caught up in a mass consumer, acquisitive, mainstream culture that is thirsty for wealth and material success. Such values compete with effective nurturing among rich, middle class, and poor alike. They conflict with strong values of care for elders and children alike among women and men. Such conflict is visible across class and gender lines. XODUS space, womanist space, and generational wisdom compete with the American dream of material products. The very poor whose desire is only a balanced meal are too easily forgotten altogether in a false exodus into this American dream. Morrison reminds us that to be concerned with the well-being of the generations involves not only the care of children but also the care of elders. It is often said that "the children are the hope of the future." But the elders are also the hope of the future. Without respect for those who have paved a way before us, we cannot adequately understand the present. Without adequate understanding of our history and present, we have no direction for the future. We disconnect ourselves from the full cycle of life.

On the subject of mothers, biblical scholar and writer Renita Weems moves beyond romanticized notions of motherhood. Not all of us, she reminds her readers, have had mothers who were fully present for us. Some of us had mothers who left us or who could not provide for us. Some of us had mothers we would rather forget. It pains Weems to admit that her own mother was an alcoholic and died an alcoholic. And yet her mother also loved her children. She explains:

> Over the years I have tried to forget my mother. There are many Black women who have not been able or eager to talk about our less-than-perfect, our outrageous, mothers. It would be like playing the dozens on ourselves.... We have simply sat and nodded while others talked about the magnificent women who bore and raised them and who, along with God, made a way out of no way.... We paid to hear them lecture about the invincible strength and genius of the Black mother, knowing full well that the image could be as bogus as the one of the happy slave. The easiest thing in the world would be to romanticize my mother's drinking, see it as the muted need of a repressed artist who sought to drink in the fullness of life.... But the truth is never that simple ... I cannot forget my mother. Though not as sturdy as others, she was my bridge. When I needed to get across, she steadied herself long enough for me to run across safely. For that I am grateful.[9]

In remembering the importance of caring for elders and children, respecting the sacredness of the lives of each, it is also important to confront the realities of complex human relations in which all is not ideal. Weems's reference to "less-than-perfect mothers" applies not only to the alcoholic or drug abuser but to all mothers and fathers. To be human is to be less than perfect. When we idealize the elders we learn far less of what life has taught them or can teach us than if we learn from their strengths and their weaknesses. Weems is one of many who was raised not only by a biological mother, but by other mothers, including her stepmother. She describes her stepmother, neighbor women, colored school teachers, and friends — other women — as helping her put her relationship with her mother in perspective. The stepmother, for example, explained to Weems that she could understand why her biological mother found it difficult sometimes to cope with the challenges of being a woman and a mother in an oppressive society. She helped Weems understand that some women are not able to find adequate coping skills to handle the heavy responsibilities involved in daily mothering. At the same time, by being a stable presence in her stepdaughter's life, she demonstrated to Weems that women do have the capacity to find such healthy coping skills and spiritual/emotional strength.

The kind of complexity Weems refers to in her writings is the kind of complexity we see in Morrison's literature, in which neither mothers nor daughters are perfect. Where there are heroes there are no unflawed heroes. Baby Suggs Holy, in the novel *Beloved*, comes closest to sainthood in her sermons on loving oneself, loving one's body, and loving one's heart. But in the end, even she is not immune from faith crisis, despite her powerful role as elder and one who gathers the community, holding it together in spiritual revival meetings. Help often comes from unexpected people in unexpected places in the larger community. In Morrison's work it takes an entire community to bring about healing and wholeness. At the same time, the community is not perfect either. It too is vulnerable to complicity with evil out of feelings of jealousy and envy. Just as individuals can be selfish and hurtful toward others, so also can communities be cruel, ostracizing, painful forces. Yes, it takes an entire village to raise a child. But what kind of village do we have in mind? Not just any kind of village will do. It must be a village — a community — that respects the difference of its members and encourages survival, healing, wholeness, and liberation for all. This requires what W. E. B. Du Bois referred to as a spiritual striving. Yes, faith is also important — the belief in some power greater than ourselves as individuals and communities. But spiritual striving — a desire for and commitment to greater wisdom, greater spiritual perfection within the body of the community — is also required.

Weems reminds her readers that her mother had choices to make. She had a choice not to drink, not to give in to the bottle, to struggle with the difficulties of being a very young mother of five children in creative, healing ways. As a mature woman and a mother herself, Weems has chosen creative outlets — writing essays, poetry, sermons which bring healing to body and soul for herself and others. While her mother loved her and her siblings, her love functioned very differently because of the choice to run away from pain and problems. Weems does not hold herself higher than her mother. Rather she has learned from her tragic flaws as well as from her strengths of hard work, of being a good provider, of her laughter, and of her friendships with other women. There are other women and men who have had even more complex relationships with their mothers or fathers, women and men who were thoroughly neglected or continuously abused, for example. But as Aunt Ondine points out in *Tar Baby*, being a good daughter — or a good son for that matter — does not require a strong relationship with a natural or biological parent. It has to do with returning care and nurture to whatever elders have provided care and nurture for you. I think it is important to add, however, that such a maxim is a two-way street. It means that adults in the community are called into good parenting activity, called to elderhood, and must take committed action to be present for young folk who doubt there's anyone to turn to, anyone who really cares.

Humankind is a complex creation. Within all of our lives we wrestle with tragic flaws in ourselves and relationships even as we celebrate rich, diverse gifts in one another. The problem of alcoholism that Weems points to in her own mother's life is an obvious tragic flaw. But what of some of the less obvious flaws like the ones Morrison's literature reveals: jealousy, envy, apathy, spitefulness, selfishness — the kinds of flaws Christians and other religious people have referred to as vices, moral sinfulness? These are the everyday obstacles that must be overcome and more often than not underlie visible habits like alcoholism or drug addiction. As Weems does so carefully, it is important to consider the underlying feelings of despair and frustration that make addictive behavior an appealing escape for some parents. At the same time the less obvious escapes that other mothers and fathers choose are not any more healthy or any less problematic. Even the tough kind of speech that families sometimes engage in to rib and tease one another can be harmful, painful, as bell hooks warns in *Sisters of the Yam*. Humor can be a healthy release, but when it amounts to picking on another's weaknesses and insecurities, perceived or real, it no longer promotes healing but woundedness within families.[10]

In past generations spanking and whipping was an accepted form of discipline in Black and White families alike. Black families look with skepticism at White, privileged, liberal middle-class families who frown on spanking. More are willing to concede that old-fashioned whippings with belts and switches are extreme and likely to result in welts, burns, and scars and can easily degenerate into abuse. Indeed, many Americans across racial lines struggle with such issues. While most would agree that whipping is excessive, total agreement has not yet been reached on the matter of spanking. However, given our history of slavery, Black Americans must ask questions regarding the legacy of slavery in relation to corporal punishment for children. In certain African cultures, spanking is not practiced. Other methods of counsel and discipline are employed that involve the passing on of moral wisdom and reason. The Spirit, the energy of re-creation (new creation), promotes those ways that lead to healing and abundant life.

Ancestry

While there has been much talk about claiming and naming the ancestors by Black cultural critics and writers in recent years, more attention needs to be given to the question "Which ancestors do we claim?" Alice Walker answers this question most honestly and openly in her book *Living by the Word*. She observes the sharp criticism she received after publishing a poem in which she named all of her ancestry — Black, Indian, and White. She laments the stereotype that Black Americans who acknowledge their Indian and White ancestry as well as their African ancestry do not really want to be Black and are secretly ashamed of their Black heritage. The challenge of Walker's approach to her spiritual, ancestral, and cultural heritage deserves more serious consideration than it has received. It is of particular importance for womanist and Black male theologians because it raises the question of what it means to be a Black feminist or Black person generally in terms of one's ancestral heritage? What does it mean to be a feminist of color or person of color generally as far as one's ancestral heritage is concerned? Walker touches a nerve, because she reminds us that race is but a construct. She does not allow us to forget that the honest retrieval of one's history is both rich and painful, because history is not simply an accounting of individual heroes and fiends or even of socioeconomic, political institutions, but a complex web of sexual and familial relationships between women, men, and children, some borne of love and choice, others born of exploitation and violence.

For Walker to name the truth that she had a White ancestor who raped one of her Black ancestors, as is the case for a vast number of Black Americans, does not mean she would rather be White, as some critics have irrationally charged. It means she is taking care to confront her entire history. She does this using an approach that is both critical and constructive. At the very least, Walker's work demands that we admit that our honoring of ancestors is selective and that not all of them deserve honor. Although some may not deserve honor, their destructive acts must be remembered so that we ourselves do not perpetuate such destruction in new ways. Walker observes that the White ancestor, for example, who raped her earliest known Black ancestor is someone she pities. Such an attitude allows her to forgive him, not for the purpose of forgetting his destructiveness, but for the purpose of strengthening herself to acknowledge the ways in which destructive behavior can be passed on from generation to generation. She suggests that by facing the full truth of the past one can better discern both the seeds of creativity and the seeds of destructiveness in the self.

Walker does not *honor* her grandmother's rapist or the memory of his act, but she does openly and consciously remember him in order to *learn* about humankind's potential for violence, evil, sin. From the historical materials and oral histories available, it is evident that most of the White ancestry Black Americans possess was the result of the rape of Black slave women by their slavemasters. There were occasional, but rare, interracial relationships in which Black and White people, men and women, chose each other and loved each other. Anti-miscegenation laws were instituted to prohibit legal marriages between Blacks and Whites. These laws were necessary because love transcends races and cultures. Once such laws were instituted, affected Blacks and Whites who desired to marry did so illegally and secretly. Such relationships have rarely been written about or discussed because of a sense of shame emerging from the lack of freedom or privilege to be legally married. Dorothy West, a Harlem Renaissance writer who has continued to publish into the 1990s, has written a controversial novel called *The Wedding*, which addresses this aspect of racial identity in American culture. Writers like William Wells-Brown, Dorothy West, and Alice Walker tell the stories of ancestors who have contributed to both good and evil in order to tell a *whole* story. It is necessary to tell the stories of as many ancestors as possible in order to better discern the good and evil acts we might learn from. While it is important to *remember* as many ancestors as possible, I would suggest that it is not helpful to *honor* all of them. We choose who we honor according to their contributions of healing and wholeness to our historical and contemporary communities.

I find that Walker's writings *honor* those ancestors who have contributed to the *healing and wholeness* of communities. For example, she writes often of the contributions that both Native American and African heritages have made to her developing spirituality. Her first novel,

Meridian, referred to both sets of heritages in the life of the protagonist, Meridian. Black Americans have been discouraged from claiming their entire ancestral and cultural heritage, as Walker writes in *Living by the Word.* And yet many, perhaps most, African Americans know that Indian ancestry is an integral, vital part of our heritage. New research on "Black Indians" promises to clarify missing portions of written Black history. Willie Adams, a Creek Indian, emphasizes that Black people with Indian ancestry must not "be embarrassed about it." They must be "whole," people. "I am a human being he says," while also proudly claiming his Creek heritage. "You are an American — a whole person."[11]

With all the attention to the ancestors that has been a part of much of our practice historically and has been given new emphasis through rituals such as Kwanzaa, we need to ask which ancestors we are to remember. Of those we remember, how do we discern which ones to honor? While African American relationship with European relatives has historically been one of conflict and struggle, relationship with Native Americans was predominantly one of friendship, help in escaping slavery and the segregated South, marriage, family, and sharing of moral values and wisdom.

There is much that African and Native American heritages have in common in respect for nature, family, and communities and in understandings of the sacred. Shouldn't we honor all of those ancestors who have contributed to our survival, wisdom, and positive moral heritage? If so, it seems disrespectful to "disremember" and fail to honor our Indian ancestors. For me, this means I need to name my great-great-grandmother Jane Finch as the Native American ancestor that she was. It is important to learn about the tribes and nations such ancestors came from in order to better understand the moral wisdom they exchanged with wise African ancestors.

Native Americans often married African Americans, in part, to escape the threat of exile to reservations. While some Black Americans were being offered educational opportunities and/or jobs (however menial) on or near the land where their slave parents had birthed them, Indians were being forced off the land and onto reservations. Marrying a Black American often meant being able to live in the land where one had been born. Those who chose this route of escape from exile tended to say little about their race, culture, and tradition. They raised their children as "colored" or "Negro," sometimes calling themselves "colored" or "Negro." There were those who felt it was safer in certain respects to be Black than to be "Indian." Others who identified themselves as Indian felt it was better to hold on to land and tribe.

Black Americans have woven the moral and cultural values of all our ancestors into a rich tapestry. Reconnecting, sustaining connections, and learning more about the African and Native American peoples of today who are our relatives and friends can give clearer meaning to the new tapestry we are and continue to become. Such remembrance and knowledge can help discern the threads that will lead to healing and wholeness from those that will not. Much of the weaving that we have done has been unconscious. We have remembered without being able to clearly name. But we have also woven in some destructive threads like materialism and self-hatred, which need to be pulled and restored with richer, healthy threads. The fact that we often share common ancestral heritage and similar cultural traditions is evident in a variety of areas — color, features, drums, syncopated music, syncopated dance, testimony, valuing creation as sacred.

Honorable Choices and Rainbows

To honor one's ancestors is to honor a set of cultural values that contribute to moral understandings that promote the survival of one's people. I mourn the death of millions of Africans who died during the trans-Atlantic slave passage, as much as I mourn the millions of Africans who survived but were enslaved, as much as I mourn continued genocidal and suicidal practices that bring slow, steady death to young Black and Indian people. Moreover, I feel a deep sense of longing and loss for those Indian ancestors who once inhabited this land called America in great multitudes. I mourn the killing of millions of Native Americans as I celebrate the survival of a remnant. For me, it is not enough to search for God in a church building. God is not confined to buildings. I see evidence of the presence of God as Spirit in the lives of African American, African, and Native American ancestors as well as in all of creation. The caressing of the earth with feet and hands through dance accompanied by the rhythmic syncopation of drums is a practice among both Afrikan and Native American peoples. Traditional Black churches participate in the rhythmic beat of gospel music to celebrate God who is Spirit and who lives in the hands, heart, feet, and minds of the people. Likewise, I have found in pow-wows that there is a kindred respect for the movement of Spirit in the hands, arms, feet, and minds of the people and in the earth. One Saturday I went to a pow-wow where there was remembrance of Native traditions and practices respecting people and earth. One woman was claimed by a tribe, who saw not only her dark-brown skin but the features of their people in her face. Black Americans met people who looked like their aunts, uncles, grandparents. One woman informed me that you can-

not tell who is Native American by the way they look. It is a culture. The
flower-garden range of colors that Walker describes in her definition of
"womanist" holds true not only for Black people but for Indians. Many
Aztecs in southern California are African American in appearance, Native American in culture. There is also blending of cultures. On Sunday
morning I went to my traditional Black church where we clapped, patted
the ground with the rhythmic steps of our feet, and lifted our hands in
praise as we remembered traditions that are healing for our community.
The pow-wow and church each offered spiritual renewal and revitalizing
fellowship.

While participation in pow-wows is a small, superficial step toward
reconnecting with a buried heritage and while I am aware that not all Native Americans or Black Americans feel any sense of kinship or identity
with one another, participation in such events offers valuable lessons. I
have learned that Native American parents of Black children often denied
their heritage as they sought to assimilate into "American" culture in order
to have access to educational and economic opportunities. While such access was limited for Black Americans, it was even more limited for Native
Americans, who were placed on reservations, often on the least desirable
land and far from adequate economic opportunities. I find this compara-
ble to isolating African Americans in projects. On the other hand, there
are also Native Americans who have denied their African heritage.

The most important thing I have learned from participating in such
events is that while the music and food are different, in the ceremonies
of both Black and Native American culture there are warnings against
materialism, division, and passing on empty values to children. There
is a charge to pass on traditions of community, work, and respect for
life to the children. In each ceremony, praise and teaching are accompanied by the syncopated rhythm of the heart and the pulse of life. In
each ceremony, strength is found in the memories of the elders, who
pass on wisdom to the generations. The forms are different while the
rhythms and messages are similar. Participating in both ceremonies, I experienced them as antiphonal, a kind of call and response from culture
to culture, ancestors to ancestors, body of wisdom to body of wisdom. In
each ceremony, people felt touched by the Spirit.

For me, it confirmed that Black Americans need to continue doing
what we have traditionally done, which is to teach not only that Euro-
Americans stole our African ancestors from their native land, but that
they stole people and land from the Native Americans of this country as
well. Moreover, some of these people are among our ancestors and are
persons with whom Black people often found mutual refuge and solidar-

ity to fight oppression. It would be helpful to learn not only about the specific African nations from which we are descended but to also learn about the specific Native American nations of some of our ancestors. In this way, we honor all those who gave life, nurture, and love to our African-Americanness, learning more about those who are most truly, natively, American even as we also explore our African heritage. The challenging task is to implement the proclaimed values of community and caring these cultures have contributed to our African-*Americanness* in our everyday lives. Today, we must consciously remember and honor a diversity of those ancestors who have identified with our families and communities, who have shed blood and tears to ensure our well-being.

Notes

1. See for example, Caroline Walker Bynum, *Jesus as Mother: Studies in the Spirituality of the High Middle Ages* (Berkeley: University of California Press, 1982); and *Julian of Norwich: Showings*, trans. Edmund Colledge, O.S.A., and James Walsh, S.J. (New York: Paulist Press, 1978).

2. See Patricia Hill Collins, *Black Feminist Thought: Knowledge, Consciousness, and the Politics of Empowerment* (New York: Routledge, 1990), 115–37.

3. Carol D. Stack, *All Our Kin: Strategies for Survival in a Black Community* (New York: Harper and Row, 1974).

4. J. California Cooper, *Family* (New York: Doubleday, 1991).

5. See Karen Baker-Fletcher, "Tar Baby and Womanist Theology," in *Theology Today* (April 1993): 29–37. See also Toni Morrison, *Tar Baby* (New York: Plume, 1981), 91–281, 305, and Missy Dehn Kubitschek, *Claiming the Heritage: African-American Women Novelists and History* (Jackson: University Press of Mississippi, 1991), 141.

6. Cited by Thomas LeClair, "The Language Must Not Sweat," *New Republic* 9 (March 21, 1981): 26–27.

7. Theressa Hoover, "Black Women and Black Churches: Triple Jeopardy," in James Cone and Gayraud Wilmore, eds., *Black Theology: A Documentary History, 1966–1979* (Maryknoll, N.Y.: Orbis Books, 1980).

8. Morrison, *Tar Baby*, 258–59.

9. Renita Weems, *I Asked for Intimacy* (San Diego: LuraMedia, 1993), 34–37.

10. bell hooks, *Sisters of the Yam* (Boston: South End Press, 1994).

11. Conversation with Willie Adams, Claremont School of Theology, Fall 1994.

Unto the Fathers' Fathers

XODUS Generations

B EING A FATHER and a parent is the hardest work in the world. There are no time restrictions, no hours at which one may turn off one's "Daddy-hood" and ease into forgetfulness. You may well look wistfully at the child in your arms sleeping peacefully and wonder to yourself, "How did I ever get myself into such a mess!" Yet the joy of being a parent far outweighs the risks, sleepless nights, fretful anxieties, and pressures to "do right" by your children and spouse. In our society there are not the special rewards, incentives, or honors bestowed on fathers, especially African American fathers, that might provide an added incentive, additional encouragement, or even a needed "pat on the back" to help us maintain our composure under pressure. Dr. Alvin Poussaint notes that media images of Black fathering are highly ambiguous. On the one hand movies and television shows often intensify negative stereotypes of Black males, portraying us as "irresponsible, out-of-wedlock, and/or absent, hustling fathers," while on the other hand, Bill Cosby of *The Cosby Show* fame and author of the bestseller *Fatherhood* remains ensconced in the popular imagination of most Americans as "America's favorite father."[1] No wonder so many Black men wind up drinking themselves into oblivion, having high blood pressure, and suffering disproportionately from ulcers. In the psychospiritual JOURNEY that is XODUS, meditating on parenthood in general and fatherhood in particular is one of the most important ways to carve out a SPACE for building a viable future for Afrikan peoples.

So am I merely whining the "VICTIM" song that can no longer be received by the dominant population? Not really. Most of the men I knew in various socioeconomic strata throughout African American communities in Cleveland, Ohio, from the 1950s through the 1980s were stay-at-home "dads." Whether factory workers like my own father, lawyers like one of my best friends, teachers, sanitation workers, truck drivers, or preachers, they were married men who loved their wives fiercely, overworked, sometimes drank too much, blew off plenty of loud "steam" at parties, and mostly were faithful to their marital vows. The men of my home church, Antioch Baptist, were proud of their children and told everyone except their children about the wondrous deeds, progress, and sayings of their offspring. These were men who had rough voices, smoked smelly cigars, yelled at us children when we did "wrong," and complimented us with smiles when we did "right." They practiced the old Ashanti proverb "It takes a whole village to raise one child" assiduously, even though most would not be able to tell you that they were being "African" in any particular way. Yet I looked up to each one of these men as a "father" to me — not a "flesh-and-blood" relative, but a spiritual father who had the "right" and "duty" to correct me when I was inconsiderate, mean, fighting, or in the wrong place at the wrong time. In solemn tones they would remind me that they *knew* my grandmother and grandfather, my mother and father, and all of their "ways." With such rejoinders I was re-minded of *who I was* and *whose I was! I could not just act any sort of way because I was "Superia's son, Kenneth's boy" and not just anybody "off the streets"* as they would say. These were the men who had no compunctions about reprimanding ill behavior on the one hand and complimenting successes on the other. Theirs was a tough, textured "love," not sugar-coated or passive, but active, interventionist, and rugged enough to handle all of our childhood silliness and promise. I loved them, even when I did not quite understand them, because even as they reprimanded my "wrongs," they did so with such a look of concern that one could not miss their intent.

Lest it seem that an XODUS view of fatherhood and manhood is uncritically celebratory, I bring the critical wisdom of a womanist voice as indicative of the dialectical "yes and no" movement of the XODUS JOURNEY. In the writings of Alice Walker men are presented as taking a long time to mature into places of nurture, justice, and egalitarian concern for women and themselves. In *The Color Purple* "Mister" abuses Celie for years. It is only after suffering the malevolent effects of her "curse" of him — as she is leaving him — and his "making things right by her" that Mister finally matures into a kind and considerate person. Walker has taken much flak from concerned African American male leaders who believed that her portrayal of Black men, particularly Mister, helped to reinforce negative stereotypes about Black males.

This concern, while wrongly avoiding the prophetic critique of Black male abusiveness which Walker provides, may have a slight justification. As a graduate student in the mid-1980s, when Steven Spielberg's movie adaptation of *The Color Purple* was released, I found myself constantly being glared at angrily by Japanese, Korean, and European students who eventually confronted me as an "abusive man" because their viewing of *The Color Purple* in their native movie theaters before they came to the United States gave them a strongly negative *pre*-judgment of *all* Black males! They actually believed that *all* Black males were like Mister! When other Black male students received this treatment they angrily denounced Walker, feminists, and the obvious racialized ignorance of whatever their accusers were facing them. For my part, I found myself working overtime to disabuse these accusers of their false stereotypes — often with only mixed results.

It is apparent that Black men have an "image problem" across the globe, and movies like *The Color Purple* add fuel to that fire even as they accurately portray the real problem of Black male violence. However, one would be remiss not to note that Spielberg's *Purple* significantly departs from Walker's novel, especially in his treatment of Black males. Harpo, in the movie, becomes a Sambo clown rather than the struggling young man trying to find his own way that Walker presents. Harpo falls through roofs, shucks and jives in broken English, and glares his eyes in Spielberg's imagery. Walker presents a much more complex picture. In the novel Harpo imitates his father's (Mister's) abusive treatment initially, and then is reformed when Sophie strikes him back. Further, in Walker's writings she treats Mister much more sympathetically. She pulls no punches about his abusiveness, but in the end Mister and Celie are portrayed sitting together, sewing, and enjoying conversation with each other! Spielberg's movie does not resuscitate Mister as completely, leaving him gazing at an idyllic reunion of Celie with her Africanized children from across a very wide field. So the movie presents a much more brutal and less redeemed portrayal of Black maleness than does Alice Walker, and Black males who are not abusive must deal with the after-effects of a famous Euro-American male's reading of a Black female novelist's writings being enlarged to cinematic proportions.

What are Afrikan peoples to do when Euro-domination so often intervenes in our relational process with distortions of our artistic and prophetic creativity, as Spielberg did with Walker's novel? We must honestly begin a kind of dialogue and public discussion very different from what the larger-than-life abuser portrayals of movies can afford. Such a dialogue can take place in XODUS SPACE because it is a "safe" SPACE, that is, a SPACE where ideas, difference, and occasional agreement can be encouraged and allowed. The active imagining and psychospiritual disengagement from the competitive, violent, and monological dynamics of

Euro-Domination which entail XODUS SPACE-MAKING are operating even now as the reader reads this text, and we, the writers, engage one another.

In order to construct a comprehensive XODUS view of transgenerational fathering, one needs to begin with a critical note. XODUS Space is pan-African, but as it affirms the loyalties, values, and norms regnant in Afrikan communities globally, it debunks, deconstructs, and reconstructs those practices which do not forward the ongoing inclusive, liberating, and salvific health of all the Folk. Some of the ways in which fathering has been practiced, in Africa and in the Americas, have deepened oppressive patterns of father-privilege in ways which XODUS JOURNEY cannot condone. XODUS SPACE creates anti-patriarchal SPACE for men, women, and children to grow into lovingly just Community. Its energies of grace, communion, inclusion, and wholeness run counter to exclusionary, dominating, and hierarchical social patternings.

BABA-Hood

I first became interested in addressing the issue of maleness as a topic of concern as I was reading feminist texts in graduate school. I was astounded by the ferocious creativity, righteous anger, and what Katie Cannon would call the "unctuous"-ness of the writings. By unctuous-ness Cannon referred to a bold, audacious ("Bodacious" in Black English), and determined way-of-being in the world. Not only were women taking apart the oppressive dynamics of patriarchy (the privileging of maleness and men), but they were going about the business of renaming, revisioning, and reconstructing womanhood and female-ness outside of the parameters of male definitions. They did not ask permission from men to do this; they simply did it! African American women were just beginning to name as "womanism" their own critique of White women's racism and Black men's sexism and movement into affirmation of Black womanliness "regardless...." They took the term from Alice Walker's now-famous definition in *In Search of Our Mothers' Gardens.* My father developed a fatal lymphoma in 1983 and by April 1984 he was dead. It was a perfect time to re-cognize myself, and perhaps other males....

I realized that men were not writing about how we felt about this insurgent insurrectionary tide of woman-feeling swirling about us. There was a lot of pent-up rage voiced by males, to each other, and occasionally the anger boiled over into some very ugly scenes in the classroom, but men were not writing a thing. At least that is what I thought originally. I discovered in my search for a creative, nondefensive, and life-affirming word, book, or creative expression about maleness that there was a "new male movement" afoot. It disappointed me much more deeply than the occasional outbursts of "angry White males"! It turned out to be a group of middle-to-upper-middle-class predominantly Euro-American males who spent exorbitant amounts of money on weekend nature retreats where they would strip off their clothes, paint their bodies and hoot and holler. In searching for their "deep masculine" the favorite culprit (not surprisingly) turned out to be "the feminists," who were alternatively blamed for "feminizing" men and castigated for "castrating" and weakening male "vitality."

What I saw in this movement was a powerful male "backlash" to what I took to be women's rightful claims to a full and complete humanity. Further, at least initially in the 1980s, there was wholesale ripping-off of Native and Afrikan cultures taking place, with no Black or Brown male bodies present! The beating of drums, vision-quests, and "sweat-lodges" all became part and parcel of one's "new male" weekend experience, without even the courtesy or consciousness to inquire whether such activities might be appropriate for the children of conquerors of Native and Afrikan cultures. I saw such activities as neither liberating nor creative, but as a new form of the conquering, stealing, and destructive mentality which my ancestors — female and male — had fought so hard to eliminate in the Freedom Struggle.

In Black churches increasing alarm over the criminalization and incarceration of young Black males in the 1980s has led to an African American "male movement." This concern, deeply rooted in the dire statistical reality of Black American experience, has deepened the already powerful male control of Black churches, silenced what had been growing egalitarian inroads concerning Black women's issues, and increased the stridency of male-domination rhetoric in many Black churches. I became disenchanted by the "Black women step back..." attitude of the main proponents of Black male liberation in Black churches, the pastors. It seemed to me that womanists were right when they insisted that if our community is to be liberated, then the *whole* community must be liberated, men and women together. For many pastors the sole concern was for "lifting the Black man" so that he could "take his rightful place as head of the family." This Headship rhetoric, while appearing to empower Black males, actually cripples us. It disables our intellects from actually perceiving where our concrete strengths and weaknesses reside, fuzzing reality and genuine love with so-called "biblical" family models which were actually Pauline applications of oppressive patrimonial models of family taken from the Roman household codes of his time. Headship is a culturally confined metaphor with as much currency as Levitical codes of "uncleanness" in regard to the issue of women's blood. It was useful in Colossians 3 and Ephesians 5 for describing family relations for early church participants in order for the church to gain a strong cultural foothold.

We are facing an entirely different set of historical circumstances. The Christian movement is now global, well entrenched historically, and instead of defending its claims against charges of "atheism" by not worshiping "god" Caesar, now must defend its moral and religious claims against centuries-old accumulations of horrors, murders, wars, and conquests all done "in the name of Christ." For our time "Headship" language participates in the same kind of domination rhetoric used to justify enslaving millions of Africans in Christ's name in order to Christianize them, murdering millions of Jews in order to "purge and cleanse" Christian Europe, and destroying the Five Hundred Nations of native peoples in the Americas because they were considered the "spawn of the devil." Headship means that when the one deemed "in charge" decides that it is time to take action, no matter how immoral, how unrighteous, or unChristlike, those "under" him must obey or be threatened. Headship is not what Christians ought to be emphasizing. We need a new and different reading of biblical models of fatherhood than the single model of Headship.

As my father was dying my mother deepened her understanding of Swahili. The Swahili word for father, *Baba*, became a fresh way of re-understanding who and what a "father" could and should be. It became for me a way of naming the beginning of a psychospiritual JOURNEY, a re-envisioning of masculinity which took on a special urgency as I watched him die. After reading the creative and cutting rhetoric of Mary Daly, with her use of words as double-edged axes ("labrys") in *Gyn/Ecology* and later in *Pure Lust,* I realized that my own surging male-creativity reached out to the Swahili word *BABA* as a way of renaming, reinscribing, and resignifying maleness.

To be a BABA is to reassert the traditional community responsibility for raising children ascribed to in various West African and Native cultures. It is to widen the notion of "fathering." The biological insemination which results in a child is the most minimal and least valued of traits pertaining to genuine fathering. To be a BABA is to embrace the notion of *communal parenting* — embodying the Ashanti proverb "It takes a whole village to raise a child." Why try to recapture something which may have been permanently devastated by the horrors of enslavement? Even the horrors of coercive deculturation and violent enslavement did not strip most Africans here in the USA of our sense of communal parenting. As shocking as it might be to say it, it was the very cultural "success" of the assimilationist strategy originally called "integration," combined with rapid deindustrialization and the influx of drugs as a seductive economic underworld, which has gutted African American bonds of communal responsibility. The way in which the Freedom Struggle for equal access and opportunity worked itself out in concrete history has resulted in the dissolution of parenting memory for so many. The scope of this tragedy can no longer be merely mourned or spoken of in wistful sentimentality.

In the prophetic conceptuality of XODUS SPACE I dare to cry out that it is time for our people to stir ourselves up and remember WHO we are, and WHOSE we are! It is time for the "real" men to stop blathering on about "Headship" nonsense and start to make real the very powerful cultural-spiritual calling of BABAhood which our forefathers and foremothers practiced. Thus being a BABA is not the imaginative fancy of my individual imagination, but is the re-membering of communal practices which our purported "success" and "acceptance" into Euro-American middle-class culture has denuded. Our ancestors in this violent and unfriendly land knew how to raise their children, without the aid of degrees, affirmative action, or the massive legislature of legal recourse now available to us. To our shame we have dishonored their memory by not "holding to God's unchanging hand" (as the phrase goes in a beloved hymn of the church).

To speak in this public way to my own community is not a casual affair. I recognize up front that there will be many who may point to their own individual attempts at communal parenting and say that this text is not accurately portraying their personalized "reality." I applaud you. The XODUS applauds your untiring efforts. But ours is not a time for comforting pats on individual backs. If there were more individual men remembering BABAhood, we would not be in such a forsaken place. Rather let my words be a catalyst for stirring us, rousing us out of handwringing, nay-saying, and hollow back-biting. If we are truly committed to the liberation and future health of our various Afrikan communities, then it is time for the BABAs to rise up and take a stand.

I take great reassurance in recognizing that my words represent a vast silent majority of unorganized, overworked, and often overly responsible males who are already doing their very best just to survive. What the XODUS offers Brother Everyman is the opportunity to stand with somebody else, usually that brother who sits silently across the way from you on the subway going to work, or who drives his car filled with his children by your house every morning on his way to school, and then to work. Brother Everyman needs to know that his struggle ought not be so solitary a hell or so lonely an agony. Brother Everyman needs to hear somebody say something strong enough, angry enough, and clear enough for all of us to unite and become stronger because we are finally organized.

BABA-HOOD and Black Churches

The resurgent interest in reclaiming Black males into active participation in Black churches is fundamentally positive if it can be divorced from mistaken patriarchal ideals. BABAhood offers African American males the opportunity to explore the many ways of being a "man" and "father" without reinscribing patriarchal values into their meaning. Whether we have biologically sired a child or not, BABAhood opens the door to concrete affirmation of the many things that fathers actually do both in the home and at work. For example, there are many men who enjoy cooking for their families at least as much as and often more than the women who are their spouses. Such men are a mixed lot. Some of us are middle-class and highly educated, but just as many are hard-working blue-collar men. We do not see anything "sissy" or "feminine" about actually preparing the food which sustains both our spouses and our children. In fact we relish learning the many ways in which to prepare the most mundane of foods as something savory and delicious. The pleasure of hearing one's children smack their lips and say "UMMMM, delicious!" is not confined to the female gender. By the same token, the back-breaking monotony and drudgery of preparing meals *every day* demoralizes and discourages males as much as it does women. Thus becoming a BABA is not a romanticized ideal, but fleshes itself out in the humdrum ordinariness of contemporary family life.

BABAhood is not an invitation to become a "SuperMAN." A Super-MAN "can bring home the bacon, fry it up in the pan...," clean the house, never be late for a business appointment, and be "in charge" in his career — all at the same time! Like his female counterpart, the Super-WOMAN, a SuperMAN tries to be all things at all times everywhere, and excel in all areas at the same time! While it may be admirable for brothers to sincerely engage ourselves in things not traditionally held as proper to the "male" role, such stress-producing self-motivation is ultimately self-destructive. One cannot be all things to all people all the time. Many theologians have even debunked that idea when applied to GOD! Rather, BABAhood is the fervent daily JOURNEY of a committed, depatriarchalized masculinity to be connected to his family, his

spouse, his friends, and his career/job/vocation. Since all of these different spheres of relationship and connection at times demand one's full and
complete attention, a BABA struggles to find ways of prioritizing his life
energies so that he can really be "present" to the activity at hand. Many
times I have failed to reserve enough energy for my children at the end
of the day and found myself despairing as I watched their little eyes fill
with disappointment that their daddy just couldn't seem to rouse himself
out of his easy chair. Many times I have found my mind wandering away
from what feels like a monotonous droning on of meaningless words at a
business meeting because my mind was working out a problem with the
family. One does not claim one's BABAhood; one Be-COMES a BABA.
It is a process of growth and discernment, learning how to sort through
the various miasmas of shifting loyalties and commitments.

Black churches ought to join the JOURNEY toward BABAhood
rather than staking out in a territory of patriarchy claims that are not
only anachronistic, but place African American males in the ironic position of defending oppression in the name of biblical obedience. If we
have been willing to struggle against the oppressive social effects of various particular scriptural passages which overtly sanctioned slavery in the
name of Jesus Christ when Euro-Americans used them against us, why
in the world can we not fight now in regard to certain biblical texts
used to justify women's oppression? We shall never be liberated with a
group of patriarchal males Heading the crowd, subjugating the women
and children in their families under the banner of Christian obedience.
We cannot be free in Christ until all of us are free, the men, women,
and children. It is incredible to think that calls for Black men to assume
their "rightful place" echo the same kind of "stay-in-your-place" language
that segregationists used a generation ago in the Freedom Struggle of the
mid-twentieth century. Have we not learned that all rhetorics of "place"
translate into somebody calling all of the shots, while an entire other
group of human beings is coerced into silence? African American males
will never be free with their children and spouses handcuffed, gagged,
and shoved into the background. Liberation just does not work that way.

Black churches must be courageous enough to reexamine biblical
teachings in light of our current historical period, trusting that as it took
the Spirit of GOD almost nineteen centuries after the resurrection of
Jesus to enlighten human culture enough to abolish slavery, so twenty
centuries after He told Mary Magdalene to tell the Disciples the Good
News of victory over death, women must no longer be treated as spiritual second-class citizens. Anna Julia Cooper called this progression of
liberating revelation the germination of the "germ-cell" of the message

of Jesus Christ.[2] Why spend so much time speaking about the liberation of women while discussing BABAhood? We are connected, female and male. Our community's humanity consists of both male and female aspirations, hopes, dreams, and desires. To be a BABA is to affirm a common humanity, a common and shared destiny in GOD, and to lift up those connections shared by *all* human beings.

I suggest that the first place Black churches can reexamine how women and men are to live together as a just family unit is in the Spirit-filled vision of the post-Pentecost community found in Acts 2. In Peter's famous address to the amazed crowds who heard the Galilean disciples speaking to them in their own "tongues" he quoted the prophecy of Joel 2:28–32 as a fitting explanation for the Pentecost outpouring of the Holy Spirit:

> Indeed these are not drunk, as you suppose, for it is only nine o'clock in the morning. No, this is what was spoken through the prophet Joel: "In the last days it will be, GOD declares, that I will pour out my Spirit upon all flesh, and your sons and your daughters shall prophesy, and your young men shall see visions, and your old men shall dream dreams. Even upon my slaves, both men and women, in those days will I pour out my Spirit; and they shall prophesy." (Acts 2:15–18)

The vision of community which this biblical passage presents is one that embraces male and female, free and enslaved. It is a vision in which the outpouring of GOD's Spirit enables all in the community to become prophets. Black churches who participate in XODUS are the ones who affirm the community of saints as prophets. We are all empowered by the Holy Spirit to prophesy the Good News. What Good News? It is that same Good News which Jesus proclaimed when he read from Isaiah 61 in his home synagogue after being tested, tried, and refined by his wilderness-temptation experiences in Luke 4:14–19. Jesus proclaimed to his own local community that because he was "filled with the power of the Spirit" (Luke 4:14a), He had been *"anointed to bring Good News to the poor . . . to proclaim release to the captives and recovery of sight to the blind, and let the oppressed go free"* (Luke 4:18). In the Prophetic community which the church is called to be, BABAs and MAMAs (the Swahili term for "mother"), married or single, childless or child-many, are to set as their first mission-priority the proclamation of the Good News.

An XODUS vision of family arises out of the primary duty of proclaiming the Gospel which sets aside hierarchical "terms of endearment," replacing them with the language of mutuality. For example, the famous "Subjection" text often read by ministers to "put the women in their place" and exalt men to "their rightful place" — Ephesians 5:22–33 — does not begin on vs. 22, but on the mutual admonition of Ephesians 5:21, "Be subject to one another." The entire section of this admonition, therefore, is misheard and misunderstood if one does not begin with vs. 21! It is a call to *mutual subjection.* What is this mutual subjection? Tradition has often used the most oppressive and domineering interpretation of the word "subject" as meaning "to be placed under or below . . . being under the power or dominion of . . . submissive, obedient." To affirm only these kinds of definitions takes power away from one's agency and compels decision making to be placed into the hands of another. In XODUS conceptuality one can take this same Scripture passage and find in it the seeds for a liberating vision of BABAhood and family. Why? The word "subject" can also mean "owing allegiance." To owe allegiance to another, in the context of mutual allegiance, affirms the moral quality of mutuality rather than submission.

Webster's notes the following about the term "subject" when referred to in its philosophical valence:

> 7. In philosophy, that in which any characteristics inhere; a thing considered as apart from its attributes or qualities; hence the ego; the *thinking agent; the self, or personality of the thinker, as distinguished from everything outside of the mind.* [italics added]

What fascinates me about the philosophical definition is that it *reverses* the other meanings of the term! To be a subject, in philosophy, is to be considered one who can act, think, and choose based on one's own thinking, feeling reflections, A "subject" so envisioned is the opposite of an "object," or one who is acted upon, coerced, and is never allowed any place from which to make one's own decisions. If anything, traditional interpretations of this passage would appear to say, "Wives, be *the objects* of your husbands!" Yet Scripture does not say this; it says be subject to one another. In XODUS conceptuality I take this to mean that *husbands and wives are to owe allegiance, love, and inherent respect for each other's choices, decisions, and actions.* We *owe* these things to each other because we do not act *on* each other, nor is the male required to be the sole decision maker and moral actor in the relationship. Rather, to move the philosophical definition of "subject" to front stage, we *reverse subjection/ subjugation language and become SUBJECTS,* one with the other. Such a definition resists the Headship-domination connotations explicit in v. 23, reenvisioning the notion of being "subject" to the Lord as *becoming a spiritually empowered actor, thinker, and self before a GOD who loves, honors, and respects us.* This interpretation transforms (X-forms!) the hierarchical arrangement of Christ-husband-wife-children, which mimics Roman household codes of the time, from an oppressive pyramid to a *circle of accountability, connection, love, and respect.*

If such a reading of Ephesians 5:21–33 seems unorthodox, it is, and our dire situation requires that we reexamine the "household texts" in the Bible with New Eyes. A BABA looks at his spouse and children as Subjects, not as Objects of his power, physical strength, and intimidating manner. Rather, as Ephesians 5:28–29 notes, a BABA is one who ought to love his spouse and children with the same kind of detailed concern and attention with which he loves his own body and self, analogous to Christ's love of the church (which is Christ's "Body" according to 1 Cor. 12). If it is true that "there is still fresh Light" to break forth from the Holy Scriptures, it would seem that perhaps this XODUS LIGHT may be GOD's prophetic answer for us in our time. Black churches on XODUS ought to dare to reverse traditional oppressive readings of this kind of Scripture, particularly in relationship to how we understand ourselves as Christian BABAs. As Prophets and Subjects we co-participate in the ongoing process of be-coming and unfolding that is part of the genuine work of the Holy Spirit acting in history.

BABA Values in XODUS

Our values, according to ethicist Charles Kammer III, are those things through which we derive purpose, direction, and meaning in our lives.[3] Norms, accordingly, are those rules, guidelines, and ways of being which enable us to accomplish our values. What are the values and norms entailed in XODUS JOURNEYing toward BABAhood, or is the purpose of this concept only to serve as a kind of ideal telos, unattainable but necessary as a spur for personal growth and development? Part of the self-conscious intent of XODUS conceptuality is to be creative according to our own integrity, which in my particular case means writing as a highly educated, middle-class African American follower of Jesus. The XODUS JOURNEY toward BABA-ness is a psychospiritual development, which, in my view, ought to find a way to build bridges across the widening chasm of class division and educational privilege which is tearing asunder even the ideal of community for Blacks and other ethnic groups. So a primary value for a BABA would be to hold precious the need for different types and classes of men and women finding ways to work together toward the greater good rather than for their individual good. The individual good, that which encourages and forwards the interests, material accumulation, and well-being of an individual, is vaunted in Euro-American culture as *the* Highest Good. When African Americans gain a certain level of affluence and education, we can be seduced by this negative aspect of the so-called "American Dream" if we are not aware of the value of holding to the greater good of Community. Community is a stated norm of capitalism which can never be actualized comfortably because of the inherent individualistic thrust of capitalist structural process. Therefore, while it might be an ostensibly positive value for all African Americans to be partakers of the American Dream of material "success," such success is premised on the abrogation of communal good in favor of individualist and privatized goods.

The good of Community cannot be confined to the human community but urges and presses outward toward all of creation in an XODUS Baba norm. In South Africa I witnessed an elder African theologian, Gabriel Setiloane, reminding us that the land belonged to the ancestors and that we are responsible for its use in order to become ancestors. The land is part of Community. Without the earth there can be no possibility for future Community. Thus decisions about how to use the earth are generational. No decision ought to be made that disrupts the possibility for future generations to flourish.

Setting the good of Community as a fixed norm as well as the ongoing value accompanying our every decision must be at the center of XODUS revaluation because of those factors of individualization and privatized pleasure which threaten the fabric of Community. Community, Us-ness rather than Me-ness, is never a settled state. It cannot be confined to one racial grouping or class status. Community is an ongoing accomplishment which is ever so fragile but far more satisfying to the deeper urges for fellowship in human beings than the hedonistic pursuit of individual goods sanctioned as proper to capitalist value structures and practices.

The BABA ought to be that brother who is unafraid to recognize the import of lifting up communal good as necessary for the exercise of justice in both the public and private spheres. Lifting up what is good for maintaining, nurturing, and fostering a stronger sense of the communal good, it must be stated, is not a simplistic call for group-think. Neither does holding to the communal good negate private or individual goods. It is, rather, to recognize the delicate balance between the inherent Is-ness of the individual person and the conflictual Is-ness of groups of persons. Among many of the Bantu peoples of Southeastern Africa the cosmological community principle *muntu* states that "I am because we are, and because we are I am." Many authors have cited this as a pan-African view of community personhood, setting it in radical distinction to the solipsistic individualism of René Descartes's famous dictum, "Cogito ergo sum" (I think therefore I am). What is significant about the *muntu* proclamation from an XODUS moral vantage point is that it states in shorthand the kind of harmonious balancing of the "I" and the "We" which I take to represent what entails the *communal good.*

Virtue and Character

> And now abide faith, hope, and love, these three; but the greatest of these is love. (1 Cor. 13:13)

In moral philosophy a discussion of virtues is typical, but in our conservative "family values"–charged era an analysis of virtue and character is a necessity. There can be little depth in a discussion of fatherhood, parenthood, and family without looking into the place of virtues and character. In the last chapter of *A Singing Something* Karen brings up this ethical concern in the midst of an extended discussion on womanist character. Taking her cue from the Latin root of virtue, *virtu,* meaning "power, excellence," Karen elaborates on womanist "powers" of character. In Karen's interpretation of womanist character, the *telos* of life is "survival and liberation" as attained by five "powers": (1) voice, (2) making do, (3) memory, (4) holding things together, and (5) generation.[4] This is not a traditional casting of virtue or of character.

Traditionally the Western discussion of virtue derives from Aristotelian understandings of *arete* (αρετη) which is variously translated as "goodness," "excellence," and "virtue." Martin Oswald notes that the history of the word is deeply embedded throughout the development of Greek moral ideas, but that it evolved into the denotation of "the functional excellence of any person, animal, or thing."[5] He goes on to note that *arete* is "that quality which enables its possessor to perform his own particular function well," and thereby "virtues" ought to be understood as that complex of qualities which make persons "function well" in relation to other persons, thereby playing "their part in human society."[6] Aristotle's discussion of "virtue" arises from his anthropology, in which he discusses the division of the "soul" into two elements: rational and irrational, of which virtues arise from the rational faculty. From this fundamental division arise the divisions of virtue: *intellectual* virtues, which are "theoretical wisdom, understanding, and practical wisdom," and *moral* virtues, which entail "generosity and self-control."[7] For Aristotle the intellectual virtues develop primarily from the experience of training, teaching, and the time it takes for this kind of excellence to form. Moral virtues, on the other hand, are "formed by habit, *ethos*, and its name, *ethike*, is therefore derived, by a slight derivation, from *ethos*." Aristotle is concerned to note that none of the moral virtues are "implanted in us" naturally, but are acquired by means of socialization.[8]

Aristotle further clarifies the meaning of virtue by calling it the middle ground, or "mean" between the two "emotional" vices of *deficiency* and *excess*. For Aristotle this middle ground, or what in XODUS I would call Middle Space, is a space of excellence and goodness because it involves the rational principle of choice, of discernment in the relation of parties and situations to each other.[9] Thus, for example, the virtue of fortitude (courage) is the mean between the excessiveness of behaving recklessly and the deficiency of being a coward.[10] This doctrine of the "golden mean" is thus the traditionally held "classical" view of virtue.

In Christian ethics one traditionally turns to Thomas Aquinas's Christianization of Aristotle's views on virtue. Thomistic reformulation notes that all human beings are created with the four cardinal virtues of prudence, temperance, justice, and fortitude. These cardinal virtues enable human beings to live *morally*, but they cannot enable us to attain to a measure of "natural happiness."[11] Yet Aquinas discerns in Christianity another happiness, "superior" to this natural happiness, one based on 2 Peter 1:4 whereby human beings are made to be *partakers of the Divine nature*. The cardinal virtues cannot take us into this sphere, but *God can infuse us with God's excellence*. Aquinas calls this "supernatural happiness," which is not possible without God's assisting human beings by the "additional principles" of the *infused* or *theological virtues*.[12] These Divinely imparted virtues Aquinas draws from the last verse of Paul's famous "Love Chapter," 1 Corinthians 13: faith, hope, and love. Aquinas believes that Love (or "charity") precedes the other two virtues in the "order of perfection; . . . thus charity is the mother and root of all the virtues, inasmuch as it is the form of them all."[13] The "form" of something is how it exists ideally, which *is* the "real" world in Aristotelian metaphysics. So Love is the most Real virtue in Thomistic moral theology, from which flow faith and hope.

Karen's discussion of womanist "powers" is concretely embedded in African American women's experience. It is nontraditional. XODUS conceptuality also seeks a nontraditional way of discussing virtue although I do so by reexamining pre-Graecian roots of Platonic and Aristotelian ethics — the ancient Kemetic moral ideal of Ma'at. I do this in order to displace, undermine, and subvert those "foundations" within my mind which have fostered a Hellenocentrism in Western thinking, as was elaborated in part 3 above on anthropology.

As *arete* served in Graecian society as that which enables one to function well, so Ma'at was considered the "spirit and method of organizing and conducting the relations of human society."[14] While virtue became a privatized matter of individual excellence, thus distorted from its original social meaning in *arete, Ma'at is preeminently relational. Ma'at is generational* as well, passing on the wisdom of the ancients to each new generation through the use of story and proverbial instruction. *The Book of Khun-Anup* passed on moral wisdom through the narrative of an "eloquent peasant" who confronts the High Steward of Pharaoh named Rensi, appealing "for relief, justice, and righteousness" from Rensi. In the narrative Khun-Anup initially praises Rensi as a righteous man who has acted as "father of the orphan, husband of the widow, the brother of a divorced woman, and a protective garment for the motherless."[15] After the praise section Khun-Anup challenges Rensi by criticizing him for not acting as one who represents Ma'at, but in the end Rensi renders a judgment favorable to Khun-Anup.

Karenga's translation of *The Book of Khun-Anup* emphasizes that Ma'at is the plumb-line of balance and order from which all justice flows. Notice how Khun-Anup addresses Rensi, Pharaoh's High Steward, as one who ought to embody the balancing that is Ma'at:

> The balancing of the land lies in Ma'at — truth, justice, and righteousness. Do not speak falsely for you are great, do not act lightly for you have weight; be not untrue for you are the balance and do not swerve for you are the standard. You are on the level with the balance. If it tilts, then, you will lean too.[16]

Such words need to be understood from within the *incarnational principle* of all Egyptian religion. As Pharaoh was understood to be the "Son of RA (GOD) living on earth," so the High Steward was believed to embody the ordering principle of all life: Ma'at. While there is a danger that such a belief could lead one to abuse one's power, the existence of this narrative seems to point to another interpretation, namely, that as the embodiment of Ma'at, the High Steward could be criticized to his face for not living up to his role! While many may have been punished, imprisoned, or even executed for such "impertinence" by less honorable High Stewards, this narrative seems to demonstrate that at least Rensi tried to live up to his ma'atic responsibilities.

As one embodying Ma'at, Khun-Anup counsels Rensi in both personal morality and in issues of societal justice. The following is a list of *personal* maxims:

- There is none quick of speech who is free of hasty words.

- None light of heart and mind whose thoughts have weight.

- Be patient that you may learn righteousness.

- Restrain your anger for the good of one who enters humbly.

- No one hasty achieves excellence.

- One who is impatient is not leaned on.

- Let your eyes see and your heart take notice.

- Do not act harshly with your power lest a misfortune fall on you.

The list of *societal* ma'atic maxims reads, to contemporary eyes, like something from Proverbs, the Prophets, and liberation theology, yet it predates even the Hebrew wisdom tradition found in Proverbs:

- Rob not the poor of their goods, the humble you know. For the poor's belongings are breath to them and to take them away is to stop up their nose.

- One who lessens falsehood encourages truth.

- One who supports good diminishes evil — even as satisfaction comes and ends hunger as clothing removes nakedness.

- He who cheats diminishes justice. *But* justice rightly given neither falls short nor brims over. [Notice the notion of a balancing mean between extremes embedded in this saying.]

- Do not delay; deal with the matter at hand. If you separate who will join?

- People fall low through greed.

- Those who prey on others achieve no real success. Their success is, in *truth*, loss.

- Do not listen to everyone, but call those who have a just cause.

On the other hand a few statements could make excellent "law and order" platform statements for contemporary conservative politicians!:

- Punish the robber and save those who suffer.

- Punish those who should be punished and none shall equal your righteousness.[17]

I believe that the XODUS JOURNEY cannot be fully realized in the present until and unless we vigorously excavate the vital ethics, cosmologies, and theological precepts of the Kamites as a creative way of reenvisioning a contemporary connection with valid moral ideals from Africa's history. If it is true, as Plato says in the *Timaeus*,[18] that Greek philosophers were educated and trained in ancient Egypt for a certain period of time (sixteen years say some sources), then XODUS work uncovering ancient Kemetic ideals of Ma'at is part of a counter-process of Irruptive Truth whereby buried narratives, stolen thoughts, and long-neglected idea-forms are dusted off, brought out into the light of day, and given their first taste of intellectual "air" for over a thousand years. If generational knowledge claims any "truth" value, then our retrieval is a bold step in a process of moral resurrection. As Ma'at is resurrected in XODUS, so its power may enliven the "dry bones" of our troubled times. One cannot witness the ethos of self-destruction and violence engulfing urban neighborhoods and the cultural suicide of the Black affluent in corporate workplaces without looking for a fresh injection of African views of virtue.

The underside of the post-Civil-Rights era for African Americans has been a loss of passing on those virtues of hard work, sticking to one's job even if the "boss" was a rabid racist, and always remembering to be loyal to GOD and the dignity of one's people. Perhaps we have tried to assimilate so much of America's "mainstream" values that we have drunk at the fountain of unbridled greed, avarice, self-centeredness, and "success-by-any-means-necessary" — the negative values associated with the so-called "American Dream." Those fathers celebrated in *Faith of Our Fathers*, like Cornel West's loving, self-giving, and dependable father, have not been followed in this generation. Many of us have failed to follow their example, a matter for public repentance. The Million Man March of October 1995 was a public recognition of this failure on a massive scale, but though it was impressive as a beginning, a genuine *movement of male responsibility* remains at a nascent stage. In its best moments — such as the men's fellowships in local churches like the one in Primm A.M.E. in Pomona, California — small groups of men gather once or twice a month to genuinely support, encourage, and advise each other. The men of the Primm A.M.E. Men's Fellowship are incredibly open to each other's emotions, careful to hold each other's vulnerabilities with a sense of grace and trust. The older men advise the younger, but not in a heavy-handed fashion, while the younger men share their lives with each other without fear of ridicule. Such a model of male fellowship is indicative of the possibility for developing what XODUS reflection calls a BABA, a revolutionary Ma'atic male, rooted both in Christian ideals of love and gentleness and the ancient principles of balance, harmony, and righteousness.

For a BABA, character is formed over a long period of time. It is passed on in mother's milk, father's advice, grandfather's and grandmother's front-porch talks, and the guidance of all the "mothers" and "fathers," sisters and brothers one picks up along the rough and tumbled ways of life. Character is not merely the environment we are surrounded by; it is our personal response and sense of duty and responsibility to both the self and community. We choose to follow certain pathways of living and reject others. Sometimes we choose amiss. We may choose to emulate the worst moral nihilism of "gangsta Rappers," having no compunction that prevents us from degrading ourselves by calling ourselves "Niggah!" and the women we love "Ho's" and by preferring to shoot our guns rather than to preserve the dignity of life. Coming from the same neighborhoods, others of us may choose a different path. We may decide that only certain kinds of Rap music are acceptable to us because we believe that lyrics can either uplift and edify or pollute our mental-moral ecology. We may organize feeding programs instead of joining gangs, get involved in a church or a mosque rather than hunting for somebody to "jack up" (Rap-English for "rob") and so be known in "the Hood" (neighborhood). Still others of us may choose to erase all the signs of "street" or "black" from ourselves that we can short of bleaching our skin. Such self-conscious deculturation is often followed by a zealous attempt at Euro-American middle-class reculturation, with a vengeance. Such persons may choose to marry someone not of their race as an intentional act of racial uplift, or they may have convinced themselves that marriage to "anybody" is the "right" of every American. Such views are not necessarily "caving in" or "selling out," although often the persons who state such things are judged by the majority of African Americans in this way. Rather, they are the radical possibilities of choice which Africans living in America face throughout our lifetimes.

A BABA in XODUS attempts to find common ground with all the various ways of being human, "Black," and alive in the United States. To live and create a SPACE of sharing-our-humanity-despite-radical-differences is part of the FLUIDITY that comprises BABA character. FLUIDITY is another BABA virtue. Through exposure to the many different and conflicting types of "Black" cultural-personality types, I have grown into the FLUIDITY realization that the genuine BABA is a Bridge-Builder in the community because he is able to "be with the Folk" in all the various ways that the Folk are the Folk! One cannot hope to educate, enlighten, and teach anything about BLACKness in this Euro-hegemonic, sexist, and class-conscious world if one is not able to love and accept the Folk for their struggles, joys, and victories. Even when it would be easier just to withdraw from certain persons and resort to name-slinging, an XODUS BABA cannot afford the luxury of withdrawal because to withdraw from the Folk is to accept psychospiritual and cultural defeat. If there are no XODUS BABAs out there loving the Folk, teaching, revealing these truths, where and when will the Folk hear the word?

For the Fathers and the Generations

XODUS parenting embraces what Karen calls a "revolutionary" way of being because the passing-on of the gifts of "makin' do, holding things together, and calling for social reform"[19] connects our children with all of the heartaches, tears, and joys-in-the-midst-of-the-struggle which our parents and grandparents taught. To be generational, or to be *generationing*, is to honor the most precious African retention within American Black[20] communities, *the honoring of our elders*. The wisdom of life experience which elders possess has been highly valued in a great variety of African nations and peoples. Before the Civil Rights/Integration era most of us lived near our elders and had direct access to their wisdom. Now, post-Integration, we find ourselves catching bits and pieces of sage advice in our short visits, phone calls, and occasional letters. Many of us no longer live so close to our grandmothers and grandfathers, so it is harder to teach our children about elder-honoring, or even the learned skill of *how to listen* to elders! The unique story-forms and endless repetition of the same sayings of most elders can grate on the nerves of TV- and MTV-trained persons who have never had to slow down their minds long enough to savor the wisdom and richness of elder experiences.

Our family struggles to preserve a sense of the passing-on of wisdom from one generation to another in spite of the vagaries of contemporary work possibilities. We live thousands of miles away from my spouse's parents and grandparents, our children's grandparents and great grandparents. We find ourselves continually mourning the immediate source of our direct kinship elder experiences. Yet in true African tradition, at least insofar as it has been translated down through the generations here in the United States, I have found myself "adopting" various women and men into an ever-growing circle of "family." Female friends become "Aunt" and close male friends become "Uncle" to my children. Their children call me "Uncle." So while my own parents have departed to the next life and my spouse's family lives across the country, we build kinship networks which serve as family. The things which we share together — from Thanksgiving meals to Christmas presents, Fourth of July parties to occasional weekend romps to amusement parks — knit our lives together into a very powerful fabric of fellow-feeling, mutual concern, and interdependence. In XODUS I still find the JOURNEY lonely, yet such kinship networks provide a Space of GRACE in which the wisdom is passed on from fathers to sons, fathers to daughters, mothers to daughters, and mothers to sons.

It is a special joy and responsibility to accompany one's pregnant spouse through the various trials, tribulations, and occasional moments of bliss which precede the birth of a child. Fears of one's own weaknesses can haunt one's thoughts in daylight and harass one's sleeping hours at night. Anxieties press in on all sides. Worries about whether one's financial resources will be taxed beyond their capacity loom large, particularly in our society where traditional understandings of "being a Man" are enmeshed in a jumble of ideals about the "Man" taking "care" of the house financially. No matter how "liberated" one may believe oneself to be, when that pregnancy evolves from the first blush of excitement into the discomfort and misery of seeing one's beloved swelling with the growing life inside of her, one realizes that "my part" in this whole affair seems to revolve around "taking care of business." In XODUS there remains the obligation to try to disentangle this confused web of positive feelings of responsibility from negative patriarchal notions of being a "take-charge" male. Even more importantly, we must move beyond a mere "paralysis of analysis" toward finding ways to act our SELVES into a new REALM of Be-ing/Do-ing. The Be-ing/Do-ing of accompanying our beloved during that sacred time of pregnancy is a special stage of BABAhood which has nothing to do with "taking charge," but has everything to do with discovering and reinvigorating certain vulnerable inner SPACES which, more often than not, have been covered and eviscerated by years of macho socialization.

The Be-ing/Do-ing Space of BABAhood has much to do with some traditional understandings of the continuing relationship of the ancestors with us who remain on "this side" of life. While in South Africa during the summer of 1995 I rejoiced in the stories of women and men who accounted the events in their lives to be signs of their ancestors' continuing presence in their life. The stories brought together both recountings of dreams and the unexplained "events" which were attributed to the powers of ancestors to influence and shape our lives for good or ill. For example, one story was told of how a large boulder seemed to continually roll back to a place which blocked the construction of a roadway. After consultation with the "traditional healer" (*sangoma* in Zulu), it was determined that the site over which this particular rock was located must be the location of a particularly strong ancestor. The next day the living relative of this ancestor showed up saying that his great-grandfather had been coming to him in dreams telling him to remove his remains because machines were going to desecrate the site! Since the road was being built through the traditional homeland area of this man (which he himself had never been to because of the apartheid Relocation Acts), he could not determine where this site was. But after a removal ritual was performed by the *sangomas* of the area, workers removed the rock and found the remains of a body which bore the garb and markings of this man's ancestor. The remains were removed and transferred to another site away from the road and the developers. Then the construction of the road continued apace.

Such a story, one of several I heard during my sojourn, reveals a sensibility that ancestors still have something to do with how we are to make our decisions. To our Westernized understandings of empirical events, such a story is entertaining, but not to be taken seriously. To Africans such as those who taught me, such stories are not "tales" but "signs" which require the careful spiritual discernment of those gifted in HEARing the "things of the Spirit." To HEAR in this way requires *reviving the intuitive mind.* This intuitive mind can make "connections" between events which go beyond the sensory data of empirical observation. To be connected to the ancestors requires an ability to HEAR with our intuitive "ear," or what Westerners would call "being psychic." Yet this Sixth Sense, as it were, is ingrained in the language and culture of many African peoples. For example, the Xhosa people of South Africa have *sixteen* different greetings in their language. There is one for greeting a man who has just had an argument with his wife, another for one who has just had intimate sexual relations, another for one who has just ridden his favorite horse, and so on. Such states of mind are expected to be accurately discerned by the person offering the greeting. To present the "wrong" greeting is viewed as a sign of either illness or malice, since every member of that tribe "knows" what is "proper etiquette"! Persons not raised in the group are not expected to "know" in this way, and are excused. Perhaps the greatest contribution Afrikans have to the rest of the world may be the rekindling of this Sixth Sense as normative to the discernment of how we ought to think and act in Be-ing/Do-ing Space.[21]

By uncovering this Be-ing/Do-ing Space and reigniting the suppressed psychic fires of our Sixth Sense, we open up opportunities to genuinely pass on the deepest things of ourselves to our children. Even more importantly, by Being/Do-ing, we create a REALM of CO-INTIMACY with our beloved ones in this present world and the next. XODUS JOURNEY cannot be healthy without developing this REALM of CO-INTIMACY. The ma'atic character foundation, in combination with those Christian virtues as elaborated in Galatians 5:24, creates a far more supportive SPACE than trying to become a "take charge" father. With our Sixth Sense extended to HEAR the VOICE of GOD, and those voices of our ancestors living in the realm of GOD, we may yet develop a keener sense of responsibility, a deeper commitment to our families, a stronger faith to envision the future, and a gentler touch as we interact with our children — the next generation.

Notes

1. Alvin Poussaint, foreword to *Faith of Our Fathers: African-American Men Reflect on Fatherhood*, ed. Andre Willis (New York: Dutton Books, 1996), xiv. The outpouring of support for Cosby on the death of his son Ennis in the winter of 1997 only proves the point that America loves Cosby. Even after nasty speculations about his paternity of a daughter emerged during the week of the murder, Cosby's "star" as a popular father figure remains.

2. Anna Julia Cooper, *A Voice from the South*, ed. Mary Helen Washington, Schomburg Library of Nineteenth-Century Black Women Writers (1892; reprint, New York: Oxford University Press, 1988).

3. Charles Kammer III, *Ethics and Liberation* (Maryknoll, N.Y.: Orbis Books, 1984).

4. Karen Baker-Fletcher, *A Singing Something: Womanist Reflections on Anna Julia Cooper* (New York: Crossroad, 1994), 188. Karen elaborates each of these "powers" on pp. 188–204.

5. Aristotle, *Nichomachean Ethics*, trans. and ed. Martin Oswald (Indianapolis: Bobbs-Merrill Library of Liberal Arts, 1962), 303.

6. Ibid., 304.

7. Ibid., 32.

8. Ibid., 33.

9. Ibid., 43.

10. This is elaborated in relationship to soldiers and their response to the heat of battle in Aristotle (ibid., 70–71).

11. From *Summa Theologica* Ques. 62.I. as exegeted in the marvelous text edited by Peter Kreeft, *Summa of the Summa* (San Francisco: Ignatius Press, 1990), 465.

12. Ibid., 465–66.

13. Ibid., 467.

14. Maulana Karenga, *Selections from the Husia* (Los Angeles: University of Sankore Press, 1989), 30.

15. Ibid., 31.

16. Ibid., 32.

17. Ibid., 33.

18. *Stolen Legacy*, 42. James notes the following: "Concerning the fact that Egypt

was the greatest education centre of the ancient world which was also visited by the Greeks, reference must again be made to Plato in the Timaeus who tells us that Greek aspirants to wisdom visited Egypt for initiation, and that the priests of Sais [an order of Kemetic priesthood] used to refer to them as children in the Mysteries."

19. Baker-Fletcher, *A Singing Something,* 204.

20. The phrase "American Black" is one I have heard from many Africans. It humbles me to be thought of as "American" first, since the Euro-Americans who vastly determine the distribution of cultured acceptability have historically locked Africans out of the picture. Yet I use the phrase as a way of remembering that there are many ways in which I am perceived, for good or for ill.

21. This complicated way of exercising one's Sixth Sense was explained to me by our guide in South Africa, "Martin," who had traveled around various countries in Africa and the world as a monk for over twenty-five years. The story was told by a friend of Bishop Tutu's wife named "Mama Lindy." Her long experience in the struggles for Black South African and women's liberation was lifted up as an inspiration to all of us younger people.

Twelve

Dialogue on
GENERATIONS

Karen

I take oppression and domination by European and Euro-American cultures very seriously. However, I think that there has been some positive sharing as well. I find it important to name the reality that we African Americans *are a mixed people*. Western heritage is part of our cultural and ancestral heritage along with Native American and African cultures and ancestries. While I advocate casting off the blinders that Euro-American values have imposed on African American vision of our native traditions as well as rejecting the horrors of slavery, racism, sexism, classism, imperialism, and conquest that form the *demonic* aspects of Euro-American historical practice, I also embrace the underside of that history which includes the John Browns, the F. W. de Klerks, the William Lloyd Garrisons, the anonymous abolitionists, the frowned upon and outcast interracial spouses and partners who are also part of African American history, ancestry, and culture. I would challenge XODUS and myself to embrace interracial relationships that celebrate diversity, difference, and the gifts of the many. I celebrate the opportunity for cultures to learn from each other, even as I reject cultural imperialism. Is there room for the ironies of cultural exchange in XODUS thought, the possibility for God to bring good out of relationships that have often begun in evil circumstances?

KASIMU

Your question brings to mind a subtle interrogation made by Pastor Thomas R. Noon of *XODUS: An African American Male Journey*. He wondered if XODUS could become a call for a "new kind of Black provincialism."[1] A careful reading of my writing reveals, I think, a fundamental irony at the core of XODUS similar to the call for intercultural appreciation that you have issued. This irony, simply stated, expresses the

216

intrinsic dissonance brought about when one combines the forthright, no-nonsense, unapologetic criticism of Malcolm X with the irenic, Christian, progressive, and intercultural/global envisioning voice of Martin Luther King, Jr. How does one combine biting criticism with calls for former enemies to come together in a future "Dream" world? How does one stand up for those who have been stood upon for centuries, while at the same time seeking to find ways to reach beyond the true and real complexities of oppression? All those in the "oppressor" group are not oppressive, this is certain. XODUS calls on solidarity with all those who would cast their lot with the oppressed. At the same time, the "psycho-spiritual liberation" I so often write about is pointed at ferreting out those aspects of self-oppression, self-hatred, and introjected self-doubts that continue to cripple Black Folk today even after the *legal restraints* of racism have been lifted. The "battle" today is not legal but cultural, economic, and spiritual.

Karen

I see that you emphasize inner cultural, spiritual journeys as well as economic change. This is very important. And yet there are points where one could interpret XODUS as demonizing Euro-American culture as a whole, which would be hypocritical since African Americans play jazz on European instruments *and* African drums, while Euro-Americans play country and western music on the African guitar and banjo. Beauty emerges even in the midst of ugly circumstances; by the grace of God the music of angels surges forth even out of the depths of hell. While I understand the importance of emphasizing love of African heritage, what about the American part of African-Americanness? Also, is interracial marriage always a matter of deculturalization, as you imply? If so, among which cultures?

KASIMU

I do not believe that pointing out the historical genesis of the particular social practices surrounding issues of "race" and the predominantly negative experience of one group meeting another is "demonizing" Europeans. Europe has been a major "player" on the world's historical stage for at least half a millennium, and many of the world's problems *right now* are tied to European adventures. I try to speak frankly, recognizing that "race" is a large concern for me, but by no means the only one. I am equally disturbed by gender discrimination and the undermining social influence of class oppression. I see these latter concerns as historically predating the largely modern five-hundred-year historical trajectory of racism. African patriarchy has been a long-term source of oppression; the example of female genital mutilation looms as a particularly heinous example of African oppressive behavior. Poor people, no matter what ethnicity, suffer because of the exploitative practices of the rich. As a Christian I recognize that we are all children of GOD, created in GOD's image, and part of *one human race*. As an Afrikan man I take responsibility for my own discriminatory ways, prayerfully working toward becoming a more loving partner. XODUS thought also recognizes the "demonic" element in all civilizations. Even the beauty of ancient Kemet was marred with vicious slavery during certain periods, and the glory of a newly independent Uganda was marred by the genocidal madness of Idi Amin. Finally, intercultural marriages tend either towards the deculturizing of one partner for the sake of the other or the more difficult merging and transformation of two cultures into a new one.

Karen

Feminists have argued that it is important not to conflate womanhood with motherhood. Would you say that it is also important not to conflate manhood with fatherhood? I can imagine that some men who are not in fathering relationships may want to see more on XODUS understandings of maleness *in contrast* to fatherhood. Not all men are skilled at fathering, just as not all women are skilled at mothering. Can you name some specific ways in which we can all contribute to parenting beyond the conventional functions that most often come to mind?

KASIMU

Yes, it is important not to conflate maleness with fatherhood, yet the issue of fathering is a primary one for Black men in particular. With Mike Wallace showing a teenage "homey" celebrating the birth of his *twentieth* out-of-wedlock child, the popular depiction of Black fatherhood is woeful. Instead of ignoring our public disgrace, many Black male authors like Earl Ofari Richardson and Haki Madhubuti, have written books critically celebrating real Black fathers. At the same time, not all men are *skilled* at fathering, not because they do not try, but because it is not their *forte*. I see men mentoring little boys in their churches as "fathers." The single and elderly man who looks after everyone's home on the block is a "father." Fathering can be communal and public, in a nondominating way.

Karen

You seek to rend the veil that patriarchal rhetoric of hierarchy has cast over a co-equal, mutual principle of connection between women and men. I continue to find the language of being "subject" problematic, because of historical misuse. Why do you find it possible to reform understandings of "being subject" while you seem to dismiss the possibility of reforming concepts of headship?

KASIMU

Actually I dislike the rhetoric of "headship" and wish it had never been used in the Bible! Because such rhetoric is used by the churches, particularly Black churches, to refer to male responsibility in the family, I am compelled to "work" with it. I *reverse* the language of *subjection,* i.e., to be *in subjection* to someone, to that of *working toward subjecthood with each other.* Becoming Subjects to one another is a possible model of co-equality only because it empties the language of subjection of its oppressive quality and rediscovers what I believe to be the *real spiritual and theological meaning* that is buried in traditional hierarchical renderings.

Now I have a question for you. In what ways are the majority of African Americans enriched by our reconnecting with the lost Native American traditions which are a neglected aspect of our ancestry? Is *reconnection* or *recognition* important, or is *creating solidarity* even more important? What positive political and economic ramifications do you envision for greater African/Native American solidarity, especially in relationship to the generational activity of passing on traditions in our families?

Karen

I question whether it is possible to create solidarity without also engaging in reconnection or recognition. At the same time, there is more that needs to take place than reconnection. One must allow for the fact that African Americans and Native Americans have traditions and cultural values that are distinctive for each group. In this sense, I would say that solidarity, which requires appreciation of both similarities and differences, is what we must aim for. Some reconnection with shared histories and contemporary plights, however, is necessary for understanding why solidarity is especially important between the two earliest groups of color who were exploited on the North American continent. Both groups have been dispossessed of homelands; one group was stolen from the land and one group had its land stolen from them. Each group within its own set of cultural values and traditions believes that land and people belong to God, or Spirit-Itself, not to humankind. Solidarity between the groups has not been and is not easy. While we have much in common, there are also strong ambivalences on the part of each group. Given the ambivalences, solidarity is more realistic than reconnection. Reconnection can emerge more powerfully from solidarity which involves strong socioeconomic and political support of one another.

KASIMU

I noticed that you extend your discussion of both the natural physical environment and the spiritual realm as a kind of "womb of an expectant mother." This imagery is rich. Symbolic language about wombs and space, it seems to me, give mothers a concrete *embodied experience* of space as sacred. It is a "natural" imagery emergent from our bodies. Do you believe there are any dangers to employing such symbolism? Do males have an analogous holy space in our bodies to reference symbolically?

Karen

There are dangers involved in employing any symbolism. No symbol, including the symbolization of the natural and spiritual realms, is exempt from misunderstanding, abuse, or exploitation. *All* symbols must be used with care and discernment. Humankind has a tendency to take symbols literally and to accept them at face value. As Paul Tillich has cautioned, when we do this symbols of the sacred lose their religious depth. Likewise, I would say, symbols of nature or of humankind lose spiritual depth when taken literally. The womb as a symbolization of God or nature is no more sacred than the eagle as a symbolization of God, of father as a symbolization of sky, or of mother as a symbolization of earth. In response to your second question, yes males do have an analogous holy space in their bodies to reference symbolically. Around the world and across the centuries among diverse religions and cultures the phallus has been an important symbol for the generative power of the divine. In the biblical tradition, the "seed" or sperm of men is held sacred. In the Hebrew Bible, great emphasis is placed on male circumcision, which is a sign of covenant and is associated with increased spiritual power. My concern is that *as men explore the sacredness of their own bodies they do so in a way that deconstructs abusive, subjugating understandings of male power and reconstruct male bodily symbolizations of the sacred that are consistently affirming of all life.* Symbolizations of God as womb, ovum, phallus, or seed share the danger of being misunderstood. As feminists have noted, God incarnate as man has too often been reduced to suggest that man is God. Likewise, God as woman can be reduced to mean that woman is God. The problem, however, is not in the symbols themselves. The problem lies in human tendencies to treat symbols as if they actually *are* the reality to which they *point.*

KASIMU

While you speak of "being generational," I wonder if perhaps you mean "transgenerational." In what ways is being "generational" related to being "transgenerational?" Which term would you prefer, or could you use both? If so, then could we also speak of *generationing activity* in a theological-ethical manner?

Karen

There are instances where "transgenerational" would appropriately describe my meaning. For example, when I refer to the importance of remembering the ancestors, respecting elders, and passing on wisdom from one generation to the next, that is indeed transgenerational activity. There are other instances, however, where this would not be an appropriate synonym. For example, when I talk about male and female powers of generation, I have in mind the power to create, which may take on biological, artistic, or intellectual forms; I also have in mind the power to produce physical and spiritual goods that are necessary for everyday survival. Therefore, the terms "transgenerational" and "generational" are not always interchangeable. I find the distinction between the two terms helpful and may indeed employ both terms to clarify my meaning in future writings. As for "generationing activity," I prefer to say "generational activity." You and I have very different styles. You are in the midst of developing a new lexicon (LX-ICON?!) for XODUS space. In the midst of playing with words you create new ones. For a future book, you could publish a lexicon similar to radical feminist Mary Daly's *Wickedary*, which she published so that readers could better understand the new language she has developed in the midst of creating a philosophy for women's space. This is a radical undertaking.

In my case, I think my ideas and use of images are more radical than my use of words. At this point, I have not begun to develop a new lexicon. I am more interested in using old words and images in new ways. In my hesitation to create new words I see myself as more reformist than radical. There is value in creating new words like "generationing," which is not in the dictionary, but it sounds awkward to my ears. "Generational activity" means the same thing. "Generational activity" involves (1) the transgenerational activity of passing on wisdom from one generation to another, respecting ancestors, elders, self, and children; (2) the power to create new life, whether in the form of ideas, art, children, or products for everyday sustenance (agricultural products, tools, shelter, etc.). If I lived with the word "generationing" for awhile, I might come to appreciate its succinctness and become less distracted by its novel sound. For now, I find it challenging enough to encourage people to understand familiar images and words in new ways, without adding the challenge of introducing people to newly created words.

I do appreciate your questions. I wonder if some of the difference in our styles is gender-related. In contemporary Black culture, Rappers, who are more often male than female, have great liberty to create new words. While there are women Rappers, few are given respect for their creativity, and it is difficult for women to break into this field. As in ministry, there is the exceptional woman, like Queen Latifah, but Rap is a patriarchal and unapologetically sexist industry. We need to consider whether or not there are different and unequal levels of freedom to create new language across gender lines. Alice Walker was bold to create a new word, "womanist," which I find I must defend *ad nauseam* for each new audience. It is gaining very gradual familiarity and acceptance in Black communities. I believe that this very slow movement of the term into general use is due in part to its challenging, woman-centered content and in part to the fact that it was created by a woman who is often charged with male-bashing by Black men. Reflecting on all of this challenges me to consider that Black women need to take greater freedom in creating new lexicons as a form of resistance to patriarchal domination of *naming* and as an act of liberation. Even so, I don't see "generationing" as a term I would use.

Notes

1. Pastor Thomas R. Noon, Review of Garth KASIMU Baker-Fletcher, *XODUS: An African American Male Journey,* in *Augsburg Fortress Book Newsletter,* no. 568 (Spring 1996): 8.

Part V

CHURCH

Thirteen

SPIRIT-Church

Justice-Making Virtuous Energy in XODUS Community

THERE COMES A TIME in every person's life when the inconsistencies, lies, and hypocrisy get to be too much. We are living in such a time. Americans are sick and tired of being sick and tired. We are tired of all the violence, sickened by reported abuses of power, angry at leaders who switch positions with every opinion poll, and fed up with a political process which seems hopelessly deadlocked. As a nation we have thrown both parties out of power within two years and are restlessly waiting to see whether any political solution can be found. Faith is being drained out of Americans of all races like water out of a wrung sponge. Whenever things are "wrong" with the European American community, they have already reached a disastrous level in the African American community. The old adage still rings true: "When White folks catch a cold, Black folks have pneumonia!" The sickness I want to address is our loss of a freedom vision.

The Bible says that without a vision the people perish. When Black folks got settled into our new "civil rights freedoms," we seemed to get distracted from our deeper, spiritual roots. We sought to gain more cars, bigger houses, finer clothes, more elaborate hair styles, wealthier spouses, and every other material thing. We appear to have forgotten the long and terrible struggle for freedom of our grandparents. We have forgotten their faith and perseverance. We have neglected to teach our children, and our children's children, the things that our grandparents taught us that kept us climbing life's harsh crystal staircase. And so now we face cultural suicide/genocide. While we have consumed our energies making the competitive grab for material gain, those quiet porch-talks where the wisdom of the mothers and fathers was passed on to future generations have been forgotten.

If cultural suicide were not enough, we face a kind of creeping spir-

225

itual and physical genocide as well. Seventy-seven percent of the newly reported cases of AIDS afflict African American women and Latinas. We have allowed millions of our sons to be incarcerated, sending barely half as many through college. A people cannot flourish if their women are dying and their men are imprisoned. We have exchanged our birthright heritage forged by the likes of Frederick Douglass, Harriet Tubman, Sojourner Truth, Malcolm X, and Martin Luther King, Jr., for a mess of materialist pottage. Our hopes and future dreams are being compromised and we sit by quietly and let it happen. Where is our inner strength? Why have we fallen into such a historic crisis and seem so unwilling to fight? *We are here because we have lost our freedom vision.*

Why have we lost this freedom vision? Our central institution is the Black church, and the Black church is too busy preaching a "feel-good" "get-saved" half-Gospel. The Black church spends millions of dollars every year to recarpet, build larger sanctuaries, and robe our glorious choirs in brighter finery instead of creating economic opportunities for ourselves. We complain when someone is abused by police or a racist comment is made, but seem unable to mount any serious campaign to transform dingy streets into golden roads of opportunity. We have mastered the art of *reaction,* but shy away from the challenge of *organized pro-action. We celebrate Dr. King's birthday, but fail to put our lives on the line, on the streets, as he would have.* We have seen the "enemy," and it is "us" more than "them." When will we wake up and remember that the Gospel call for "redemption" comes from an ancient Hebrew word whose root meaning is rescue? Our Gospel message must be delivered with an intention to *rescue the lost* — which means the crack addict, the gang member, the sick and shut-in, as well as those regular church members who tithe and attend our sanctuaries every week. We need freedom fighters who bring the freedom Gospel of Rescue to the streets, not robed messengers of "pie-in-the-sky-by-and-by"! If Jesus came to bring "eternal life," then let's see what committed and organized Christian people can do to demonstrate that the abundant, powerful love of Jesus is more than a Sunday thing.

Sermonic rhetoric announces that it is time to Wake Up! It is time for a "new thing" to break forth from the settled comfortable walls of "the Old Ship of Zion"! There is too much pain, too much grief, and not enough time for us to be subtle or to wait for everybody to come with us. Perhaps our church-based mindset needs to change from the "Old Ship of Zion" to the "Ark of Hope." But XODUS ecclesiology takes seriously the challenge of saving our communities from the despair that stalks our streets and the violence that destroys our children's lives, so seriously, in fact, that the whole enterprise of writing a "church theology" must be bent toward recovering the lost freedom vision. The object of the sermon is to learn to build a New Ark of Hope out of the shattered remnants of the "Old Ship." In this New Ark those who are keen enough to detect the coming flood of neglect, racial backlash, and outright politicized anti-Africanism can find not only safety, but salvation for the future. Our work is but a small part of the massive ethical and theological re-visioning required.

Ecclesiology in XODUS starts from outside the walls of church sanctuaries. It has an ear for the cadences of "streetz" criticism, in the hope that the people of GOD and the FOLK of the Streetz can come together to find sufficient common ground to save the lives of our children. By situating church theology in the multiple overlapping crises arising from the Streetz we then move toward explicating the *specifically theological engine* of all vibrant and relevant churches: the activity of GOD's Spirit operating in the lives of believers, the liberating activity of Spirit. We end where most traditional ecclesiologies begin: with the (in)famous apostolic "marks" of church authenticity. Leaving behind Euro-dominated discourse on XODUS JOURNEY, in this chapter, means inverting church tradition in order for it to "fit"! I do this by examining the sustained critique of "church" by Rappers.

Prayer, Praise, and Powerlessness

All Rappers, even those who perform "Christian Rap," fault the church for being irrelevant, unconcerned, and an impotent SPACE for genuine transformation. This is a stunning fact which ought not to be ignored by pastors, preachers, and members of Black churches. How can the most important and influential Black institution in the history of African Americans be looked upon with such disdain by its children? What has happened to the urgent social-action "fire" of the former Freedom Struggle generation so that now it is viewed as a joke, an insult, or something not worth attending? How could the formidable center of progressive massive social change in the 1960s be so massively abandoned by the most prolific and expressive artists of the 1990s? For those who would look to the one or two large, popular, and progressive churches in their city and see it as having a vibrant youth ministry, I say that the one or two will not do! It is time for a massive theo-ritual transformation of the church in which the criticisms of the streetz can transform narrow presentations of the Gospel. Such transformation has begun in the electrifying Christian Rap of groups such as Disciples of Christ and LA J, whose presentation of the Gospel brings the cadence of the streetz within the four walls of the church.

Christian Rapper LA J represents what one might call an "internal critique" of the church, which Christian Rappers feel they have the spiritual privilege to undertake. LA J *is* a Christian, a strong evangelizer, who takes the notion of *taking the gospel to all the ends of the world* with great earnestness. In "Get Involved" he calls for church members to "get up out of that pew" and "get involved." His is a message of exhortation to the faithful, calling them to "take it [the Gospel message] to the streets." He criticizes the insularity and exclusivism of church members as *proof of their hypocrisy,* a bold lyrical move to be sure! How, he asks, can one believe the message of the Gospel and stand in judgment of those who have not been reached? Further, he sees the church as being inherently *unfaithful* to the message of the Gospel if it sits in a community being choked with drugs and violence and does nothing. Repeatedly he cries out, "Move . . . get involved, let's move, take it to the streetz y'all!"

The Gospel for LA J is "bread" which he sees as needed by everyone. He "breaks bread with the Bloods and the Crips," the two most notorious gangs of Los Angeles streetz. LA J believes that as Jesus broke bread with prostitutes, so church members are required to "hang out with" prostitutes today. His vision of the church is one without the "four walls," reaching out to meet people on the streetz and byways of life.

Rappers like Arrested Development reveal that while they were raised in the church and retain a strong belief in the DIVINE, the institution and ways of the church are inimical to the "real needs" of Black peoples. In the Rap-song "Fishin 4 Religion" we find the lyricist, Speech, saying that Baptist churches do not present a revolutionary or liberating vision of the Gospel. He condemns Baptist preachers as encouraging prayers and shouts to a passive, irrelevant God who seems unconcerned about the great material needs of the faithful. Such a God enables one to "cope" rather than "Change." *Change* for Speech is the primary ethical-spiritual "ought" of church and GOD. If a particular church or group of churches is not preaching a message of spirituality which emphasizes concrete "change" in the social-economic structures which keep people miserable, then one ought to keep "fishin 4 a new religion" rather than stay in such an institution.[1]

Paris, a Moslem Rapper, finds that churches represent a form of European racist ideology — with White Jesus and so forth — that ought to be utterly condemned as lies and anathema by any self-respecting person of African descent. Believing that Allah is a Black God, Paris roundly condemns all forms of Christianity as inimical to Black liberation.[2]

XODUS theology and ethics can affirm the disillusionment with and critique of the Europeanization of Black churches which Rappers express without joining in a wholesale condemnation of church. We ought to hear these words with a deep concern, however, because the elements of spiritualized pacification, ritualized escapism, and routinized Afrikan-erasure which remain in Black churches must be exorcised. XODUS ecclesiology proclaims that the salvific center of Black churches must be, and be-come LIBERATION, especially the kind of self-exorcising liberation that comes when we cast off the internalized "White Jesus" which contaminates our churches. As Black theologian James Evans, Jr., states so powerfully, liberation has been a central tenet of Black churches from their inception, but it is not merely missiological (related to the *mission* of the church). Rather, Evans states that liberation is the *essence* of the church, it *is* the church, and not merely what it *does*.[3] Our spirits cannot be "free in Jesus" if the Jesus we pray to and praise is nothing but a Hollywood interpretation of the New Testament account complete with blue eyes and blond hair! Our very *salvation* depends on the exorcism of Europeanization. Not only is this an Afrikan (pan-African) concern, but it ought to be the concern of all Christians! Jesus of Nazareth was an Afro-Asiatic Jew who probably shared more physical similarities with Middle-Eastern, African, and Asian persons than with Europeans. Yet it is not merely the *color* of Jesus which is so important for Black churches' self-understanding, but our ability to envisage WHO and WHOSE Jesus is, for ourselves, without the permission or blessing of Europeanized theological imagination. Our prayers will not be truly purifying, our hearts will not be genuinely "washed in the Blood" until we have exorcised Europeanization from our souls. Lest our prayers turn back upon us and fall unheard at our feet, let us ask the SPIRIT to give us the courage to pray for EXORCISM!

SPIRIT

Insofar as womanist and XODUS theology and ethics are based on a profoundly ancient Afrikan (pan-African) notion of SPIRIT as the fundamental basis for all of REALITY, so too Black church spirituality is grounded in this ancient Afrikan belief. Helping African Americans to recognize the extent of this particular Africanism in our various forms of worship becomes part of the educating concern of a text such as ours. Womanist theology takes as one of its strong theological basepoints that portion of the definition of womanism provided by Alice Walker which says that a *womanist loves the Spirit*. Such a "Spirit" is not confined to the

Christian use of a "Holy Spirit," but leaves open the possibility of communing with the "Spirit" as SHE expresses and IS in all of Nature. Have African American church-going folk forgotten the extent of our ancient communion and connection to Nature? Perhaps some of us have. Therefore, while Alice Walker does not write as a Christian (by any stretch of the imagination!), her words have a prophetic "word" for us to hear. As an XODUS follower of Jesus who is male, I must respond to the womanist "love of Spirit" in a way that can move our Community forward toward greater Love of SPIRIT. The following are a few ideas that are called forth from my "inner spirit" about womanist "Spirit" and its relationship to ancient traditional African understandings of SPIRIT.

Africans — whether we are the descendants of those stolen from the forests of Central and Western Africa or are the descendants of those who were conquered by colonialists but who recently arose to throw off the manacles of foreign imperialists and who now often wrestle with native-born tyrants — have been affected by an anti-nature consciousness for the last five hundred years. We have not been alone, for even Europeans themselves were more earth-centered in consciousness before the so-called "Enlightenment." Even as recently as fifty years ago most African Americans retained strong ties to Land and SPIRIT. Now most of us are thoroughly urbanized, often having little patience for hearing about "nature" except as a temporary place for a vacation for those few of us who can afford it! As Black churches have wrestled to meet the demands of urban life, they must find ways to reconnect ourselves and our People to the Land which has always sustained our souls.

The SPIRIT and the Land are intertwined. They do not exist separately from one another. The SPIRIT can be experienced as we find Land, no matter how small an area, no matter how devalued it might be by urbanized thinking. And yet I do not write these things as a way of chastising the Black church per se, but as a way of reconnecting forgotten and ancient Land-based memories into our daily practices.

Black churches cannot begin to reenvision what our role ought to be in African American communities unless we are willing to "get back to our roots," as one often overhears from the great pulpiteers. What is "getting back to our roots" if not reconnecting to our ancient ties to the Earth, SPIRIT, and Nature? WHY? African Americans suffer disproportionately from environmental abuse. I am not calling for Nature-romanticism, but I am warning against building our homes, apartment complexes, and communities in places that are not suitable for healthy life. As Emilie Townes has documented in a recent text on womanist spirituality, *In a Blaze of Glory* (1995), a high percentage of toxic waste dumps and landfills either are near or underneath Black people. It is time for Black churches to cry out against violating the lives of both Nature and Afrikans. Townes cites the 1984 General Accounting Office study of four hazardous waste sites in the Southeast, noting that three of the four locations were in places whose majority population was Black, and that the largest one was in the "predominantly Black and poor Sumter County in Alabama."[4] Townes also notes that African Americans and the poor who are confined to living in cities often bear as much as five times the pollution levels of surrounding suburbanites.[5] Townes's research has led her to the conclusion that the Southeastern African American and poor populations bear a disproportionate amount of the nation's hazardous waste effects, some 59 percent.[6] Since the southeastern corner of the United States of America remains the "roots" of most Black Americans, it is important to understand the import of Townes's research. If we "get back to our roots," we ought to recognize that our "roots" are dying from exposure to toxicity and neglect. If Black churches do not "Arise, Awake, Act!"[7] for a wholistic vision of justice, then we will not have any "roots" or future.

The Liberating SPIRIT's Ole Ship of ZION

The call for authenticity in the SPIRIT lies at the heart of James Cone's formative Black theological reflections on church. Writing in a prophetic mode, Cone throws out the challenge, "When do the black church's actions deny its faith?"[8]

It is not enough for the officials of Black churches to sing the praises of the Ole Ship of Zion, says Cone, without pausing to address several questions:

- What direction is the SHIP going, toward freedom/liberation, or is it merely trying to shore up its own petty individual institutions?

- Who is the "Captain"? Jesus, or the bishop? GOD, or the pastor?

- What are the political interests and economic program of the "Captain," or is "He" merely interested in souls?

- What activities and deeds of the church need to be rejected as "un-Christian" and exposed as "demonic?"[9]

For Cone the *faith* underlying Black churches must lay claim upon all of its members, transcending mores which might prevent exposing the sins of church members and leaders. *The plumbline which we are required to use, in Cone's mind, is the ethical factor of liberation.* The SPIRIT empowers us to be "agents of liberation," and Black churches are to be those sacred SPACES of liberation wherein the eschatological joining together of spiritual power and the struggle for earthly freedom are momentarily realized. Yet Cone sharply reminds Black churches that we will come under DIVINE judgment, as did the children of Israel when they forgot the Exodus liberating power of GOD, if we do not continue to focus the mission of the church on uplifting the poor and oppressed.[10]

Cone suggests that the SPIRIT will find another "instrument" or institution to use in the ongoing liberation struggles of the poor throughout the world if Black churches, and others in Africa and Asia, do not remember WHO and WHOSE they are. So doing, one might say that for Cone the SPIRIT *is* the underlying "church" that incarnates itself in particular churches. He notes that the tension between the imperfect moral obedience of church-goers and the SPIRIT dynamism of the Church-as-SPIRIT-of-Liberation gives all of the churches who serve the poor and the oppressed a global "credibility problem" because of their concern for "institutional survival" rather than creating a "new society."[11] Citing pan-Africanism as an important indication of the global dimensions of the Freedom Struggle, Cone insists that liberation is a universal which embraces the yearning of all peoples. Thus lifting up liberation as normative comprises an important distinguishing norm of one model of Black church — the model of *Liberator-Prophetic Church.*

Cone's theological rhetoric falls into the category of prophetic denunciation and is always unpopular with those to whom it is directed! XODUS theology affirms Cone's critique insofar as he emphasizes the role of the SPIRIT as central to the ethical value of liberation; an XODUS ideal of church ought to incorporate the norm of liberation in the same way as does the Liberator-Prophetic Church model. An XODUS ecclesiology, however, believes that the church must be about the business of both sustaining liberators *and* creating a SPACE for liberation to inhabit. There *is* an important function directly related to the power of the SPIRIT which enables XODUS to affirm individual and institutional survival as being eminently important to the generational struggle for liberation. Persons cannot achieve any sustainable form of "liberation" if they are not concerned about the preservation and nurture of their institutional SPACE. An XODUS affirmation of institutional survival involves affirming those spiritual capacities, organizational gifts, and economic skills required to create and maintain both a liberating SPACE and a wholistic concern for the flourishing of all members of that SPACE. Liberation is a *telos* to be fervently lifted up, but it cannot be the *only* value by which the SPIRIT is discerned.

Pastor Howard McClendon of Massachusetts Avenue Baptist Church in Cambridge, Massachusetts, once commented that he discerned in the Black church an underlying "message of liberation which from time to time breaks forth into outright organized resistance, but most of the time rests quietly in the praises of the people every Sunday morning." I think that this is an XODUS insight because it discerns in the everyday praise proclamations the underlying SPIRIT-based creation expressed so beautifully in the Scripture "You shall know the truth, and the truth will set you free!" (John 10:10). Cone's prophetic voice necessarily awakened those whose moral outrage was focused primarily on "those racists" outside of the Black community rather than on the real problems which resided *within* the Ole Ship of ZION. In XODUS we are not ashamed to appreciate his contribution and still move beyond his thought to see the ways in which Black churches must be awakened. Since we stand on the shoulders of those who have come before us, we ought to turn to another first-generation Black theologian for help as we continue a critique of the Black church.

GOD's Colony and FAMILY on Earth

J. Deotis Roberts is a senior colleague in the struggle to awaken Black churches to their mission. Roberts's writings demonstrate *the mutually critical and necessary interrelationship* between Black theology and ethics, on the one hand, and Black churches, on the other. He notes that the church is both a divinely appointed institution and GOD's "colony on earth" in his recent political theology of ministry, *The Prophethood of Black Believers.* One of the more engaging observations Roberts makes about Black churches regards a similarity he detects between the peoplehood and community building mission of the Jewish synagogue and that of Black churches.[12] As the synagogue arose during the Babylonian Captivity as an institutional center for "rallying and worship," reading Scripture, instruction in Torah, and a refuge shelter for the homeless and destitute, so too have Black churches arisen during a time of enslavement, have remained the center of our life as a people, have provided for the concrete needs of the homeless and destitute in our communities, and have functioned as our centers of worship, praise, and instruction.[13] Roberts is fascinated by the rabbinic emphasis on family, noting that the Black preacher historically has proclaimed the values which strengthen and nourish family life. Both institutions have the highest regard for the teachings, stories, and authority of the Hebrew Bible, and their mission emphasizes what Roberts calls an "ethical theology." Roberts seems to believe that these similarities between synagogue and Black church are worth mentioning because they demonstrate that when the political power of the Prophets' teachings is lifted up, even disparate communities such as African Americans and Jews can find common ground in their outreach to the dispossessed.

Throughout *The Prophethood of Black Believers* Roberts elaborates ways in which Black churches have been involved in economic-political life, from the particularities of male-female family relationships to church-state praxis. His intention is both descriptive and prophetic. Descriptively he briefly summarizes the role of the church across the range of issues, from education, faith development, pastoral care, music, and women in the ministry, to the even broader social issues of economics and politics. In his prophetic voice Roberts challenges Black churches to find ways to constructively engage the issues of Afrocentrism, ecological crises, sexism within and outside the church, multiculturalism — moving beyond various ideologies of social analysis to praxis strategies for education, solidarity, and ministry to the oppressed.[14]

Roberts was one of the first Black theologians to emphasize the importance of family as a key metaphor for Black church. Defining ministry to Black families as a singularly essential expression of the church's *priestly function*,[15] Roberts has developed a rich ecclesiology of family throughout the entire corpus of his thought. By "priestly function" I take Roberts to mean those aspects of ministry which nurture healthy psychological and spiritual values and lifestyles. In *Liberation and Reconciliation* Roberts notes that "family life is universal; it answers to universal human requirements."[16] He understands family to be more than an economic or social unit, but also a "moral and religious school for children when it functions properly." The Black church, analogously, has functioned in the lives of its members as an "extended family" for those who had their strong sense of direct genetic-family ties shattered in the experience of slavery. Black church, therefore, allows for the rediscovery of the rich extended family concept of kinship which pervades all of Africa, according to Roberts.[17] Through the empowering presence and power of the Holy Spirit, Roberts says the church:

- is a hospital for sick souls;

- can mend broken lives;

- brings succor and comfort to the anxious and the oppressed.[18]

Through an extended analysis of New Testament terms associated with the church such as "brother," "neighbor," and "philadelphia" (which he translates as "brotherly love"), Roberts notes that Black theology's norm of liberation must always be modified to include the New Testament Agapic norm of *reconciliation*. In XODUS terms, Roberts draws a powerful image of both the family and the extended family known as "church" as the consummate operating SPACE for the liberating and reconciling love of Jesus Christ.

Resonating with XODUS theology, first-generation Black theologian J. Deotis Roberts calls on Black theology to be true to its deepest spirituality as a "church theology" and a "practicing theology" whose source, methods, and witness arise from the "living faith and lifestyle of black believers."[19] Further, he challenges Black theology in our time to plumb the deepest spiritual resources of Black church spirituality, its music in particular. Dwight Hopkins, second-generation Black theologian, has noted the same thing, deepening the arguments forwarded in James Cone's *The Spirituals and the Blues* in his two recent works, *Cut Loose Your Stammering Tongue* and *Shoes That Fit Our Feet*.[20] Together these various voices seem to be saying that it is time for Black theology to remove the veil of ideology which academicizes it and puts off the Folk and to get its hands dirty with the grit and sweat of the Folk's churchly spiritual powers.

If Roberts's theo-ethical insights ring true, then it is time for Black churches to Wake Up Black theology and ethics! We cannot sit idly by while the poor, illiterate, and dispossessed of our communities are chewed up by a heartless shift in the economy which values "the bottom line" of profitability more than human compassion. Inasmuch as Black churches may require the awakening rhetoric of XODUS prophecy, so XODUS theology and ethics will dry up and wither unless energized by what Roberts calls the "spiritual taproot" of pan-African spirituality. As GOD's Colony on Earth all churches have a role to be in solidarity with the dispossessed in line with their ability to deliver redemptive resources to those in need. Black churches are really front-line "Souljahs," fighting "the good fight of faith" on the battlegrounds of gang warfare, teenage pregnancy, AIDS, and the epidemic outbreak of violence which threatens the entire fabric of contemporary American life. Black churches, as GOD's FAMILY, shore up the shattered pieces of humanity which the violence in our world has made and remakes us into Somebodies capable of love, forgiveness, reconciliation, and freedom. As GOD's Colony on the front-line of social misery, Black churches need to hear words of criticism that build and do not tear down, critique that heals and does not wound, and a message of Love which incorporates and does not disintegrate all the years of struggle, pain, and accomplishment. So in XODUS, I speak to Black churches as one of their own sons, as one whose critical views are meant to help in much the same way that one would expect

a grown son to speak to his family. Black churches need to speak as
FAMILY, one to another. We are, therefore, both Liberator-Prophets
and FAMILY.

Usually systematic ecclesiologies begin with an elaboration of the Nicene creedal affirmation of the church as "one, holy, universal ['catholic'],
and apostolic." I have begun by articulating the dire cultural crises which
threaten the life of a particular segment of GOD's people — Africans living in America. By an Iconoclastic reversal we now turn to the "classical"
ecclesiological matters.

The "MARKS"

An XODUS ecclesiology must define and name itself, questioning what
is called "proper" ecclesiology. Historically the church's identity has been
characterized by the four "marks" summarized in the Nicene and Apostolic Creeds — "one, holy, catholic, and apostolic." The second "ancient
claim" of ecclesiology refers to the mission of the church in the Greek
words: *kerygma* (*preaching/proclamation*), *koinonia* (*fellowship*), *diakonia*
(*service*), and *didache* (*teaching*). Evans notes that the identity and mission
of the church has been forever interrelated, and XODUS agrees.

The One-ness of the church surely is not in its variety of dogmatic
proclamations but in its organic SPIRIT. We are, as the famous contemporary praise song goes, "one in the Spirit, we are one in the Lord."
Our "one-ness" is not a pseudo-harmonizing of our various differences.
It is not a spiritual "melting pot" wherein we embody the American creed
"E Pluribus Unum" (Out of many one). Rather, we are "One" in mind
and spirit because of *the SPIRIT,* who enjoys and weaves our many-
ness into a marvelously complex "ONE" unlike any earthly imitation. It
is a "One" which only GOD can discern. It is a "ONE" which has a
kerygmatic center in proclaiming Jesus. Its moral norm is that of service
(*diakonia*), its ethical *telos* is that of fellowship (*koinonia*), and its means
of attaining that end is the function of teaching (*didache*).

The Holy-ness of the church comes from its status as a community of
those "called out," *ek klesia,* to serve, teach, preach, and be in fellowship
with GOD and each other. I envision an XODUS church as a "called
out" Space. XODUS church is GOD's FAMILY of LIBERATOR-
PROPHETS, *made holy* by the SPIRIT which in-breathes every inch
of their be-ing. In this way an XODUS church is, to quote the famous Gospel song Aretha Franklin sang and Marvin Gaye wrote, *made
WHOLLY HOLY.* To be WHOLLY HOLY is to be filled with that
SPIRIT. It is not enough to make token academic abstractions about

the "activity and work of the SPIRIT" if one is not willing to risk the life-changing, life-jarring, and life-affirming FULLness that SPIRIT demands. It is a theological demand because without it all our talk about "being transformed" or being "born again" is hollow rhetoric. It is an ethical DEMAND because once one confesses the need for the pleroma of SPIRIT and experiences the SPIRIT in Her FULLNESS, then one cannot re-turn the SPIRIT-less decisions and deeds of one's past. To be "filled with the SPIRIT" is both the goal of the fully Christian life and the means whereby we might achieve that goal.

Being filled with SPIRIT is not a privatized experience. Any careful reading of 1 Corinthians 12–14 will remind us that the gift-bearing, gift-inspired LIFE of the church is really the in-breathing of the SPIRIT into the living bodies of church folk. Part of the WHOLLY HOLY experience of church is to recognize it as a "Body" which *is* Christ on the earth. This "Body" language has become troublesome for many of those who see its reified and oppressive potential more than its liberating theo-ethical meaning. The "Body of Christ" can become another way of speaking about a hierarchically ordered, patriarchal family whose "Head" is Jesus, and we the human members are "His" blushing "Bride." In such an understanding, which is a reified and frozen inaccuracy from an XODUS perspective, "He" gives the orders and we obediently follow. Holy-ness, is not being WHOLLY HOLY in such a view, but is rather the conforming of one's "rebellious" will to obedience. An XODUS view of the *Body of Christ* turns such an understanding upside down because SPIRIT-filled lives are driven by the risky challenge of *following Jesus as He goes out into the world.* To *follow* Jesus is difficult not because we are "rebellious" as much as because we are afraid. We are afraid to follow anyone who can courageously go into crime-ridden communities, meet the violent, the outcast, the diseased, and the un-wanted. We are afraid because we do not have such a capacity for unlimited patience, untiring zeal, unflagging hope, and unflappable equanimity. It requires a deeper anointing, a more thorough in-spiritedness which only being WHOLLY HOLY can provide for us. As we are filled with the SPIRIT we become WHOLLY HOLY and enabled to proclaim the liberating freedom of the Gospel (*kerygma*), cast away our self-centeredness and really attend to the needs of others (*diakonia*), open up our hearts to embrace complete strangers as sister and brother (*koinonia*), and fervently work to inform and train others to do the same (*didache*).

XODUS is a universal movement. It is "catholic" in this sense. An XODUS church, therefore, embodies this universality. There is no boundary to the revelation of God, no borders past which the salvific powers of Jesus cannot go, and no chains that the liberating energy of the SPIRIT cannot break. The church is forever incarnating, or embodying, itself in a multiplicity of forms. Church in-culturates, it transmutes the form of the Gospel variously, from one culture to the next. No single culture has the "right" view of the Gospel because each way that Christ embodies Gospel revelation/salvation/liberation has the in-cultured power to reach those in that particular culture. And yet there is a ONE-ness to the Gospel which transcends the particularities of cultures. This, of course, sounds like nonsense to those who have never experienced the powerful communion which Christians can experience with each other when we worship together. Even though I do not speak Korean, Tonga, Japanese, or Spanish (very well!), when all of us place our hearts and minds before the altar in sincere open catholicity, we hear the universe of multiple languages as a cosmic paean to our GOD. Such "universality" does not efface our many languages or cultural perceptions, but there is "something" in the air which enables us to experience this multiplicity in a manner that widens our spirits. This too is a gift of SPIRIT. This marvelous event is church in its most "catholic" and inclusive joy.

The last "mark," that of apostolicity, is a hotly contested arena these days. Christians everywhere are arguing about more than the succession of leadership, but are, as James Evans puts it, struggling to understand that the mark of "apostolicity" has to do with the character of the succession of the faith itself.[21] Do we extend apostolic privilege to women? What would Jesus say about the laying on of hands to confer apostolic status to those of homosexual orientation? These are questions which are revealing the fragile nature of the catholic and holy ONE-ness of the church as it has previously understood itself. Such questions are beyond the scope of this small section to discuss with thorough reflection. Rather, in XODUS I would say that the apostolic character of the church is always coming under challenge and pressure to modify both its understanding of how the faith is passed on, and how the succession of leadership is to be determined.

In the fourth century there was a great deal of controversy about whether one could be ordained if one did not believe that Jesus was both "fully God and fully human." While this formulaic phrase became a formal statement of faith in the creed of Nicaea, where one stood on the issue determined the succession of leaders chosen by various church bodies. In other times the primary controversy revolved around whether the true representative of Jesus Christ was the Roman pope or a local bishop. In the early years of the African Methodist Episcopal Church Richard Allen struggled with how to recognize the obvious calling of GOD on the life of a woman, Jarena Lee. The question of women's ordination has been settled favorably for African Methodist Episcopal churches, but still hangs in doubt for most Black Baptist churches.

If the controversy surrounding women's ordination is unsettling, the demand by homosexuals for complete affirmation of their humanity (as well as sexual orientation) before GOD by allowing them access to apostolicity within mainstream denominations seems an even greater challenge. *A pertinent initial question for all churches is whether the homosexual challenge is of the same nature as that of women's ordination.* We are required to pray and listen to all sides, seeking both specific scriptural references and theological exegesis of biblical principles concerning these matters.

The second pertinent question is this: What does an ordained person symbolize for your particular incultured understanding of ministry in the church? Evans has rightly pointed out that in most Black churches both what I would call the "ontological transmutation" model and the "common priesthood" model of ordained ministry are lifted up. The ontological transmutation model of ordained ministry understands ordination as a fundamental, or ontological, change in the character, nature, and "being" of the person upon whom the church "lays hands" in the act of ordaining. The common priesthood model of ordination emphasizes the shared ministry of all believers, pointing to ordination as a singling out of a person "on the basis of innate gifts and abilities to serve the community as pastor."[22] Both models can be used to deny women ordination, because the ontological argument sometimes leads to a reductionist biological argument that "Jesus was a man; therefore women can never be ordained because they are not male." The common priesthood model can also become a stumbling block for women's ordination if one holds males and females to traditional and hierarchical functional social understandings wherein the role and "place" of males is in the public sphere of leadership, thus relegating women to the private sphere of motherhood and the home.

At this present moment I do not see a happy conclusion for the move toward homosexual ordination in the current configuration of denominational Protestantism. Gay and lesbian persons will continue to be an "invisible" church within the "visible" church, consciously keeping their bedroom business out of public view. Black church practice is like President Bill Clinton's approach toward homosexuality in the military, we "don't ask" and we really don't want anyone to "tell" on themselves! Such a posture places homosexual ministers in pulpit, choir loft, and pew in continual denial and jeopardy, because someone can "out them" (homosexual subculture's way of saying that their sexual orientation has been made public *without* their consent!). Being "outed" can have disastrous effects on the life of a church, because while most persons in the church will continue to turn their "blind eye" of denial, the strict biblical literalists will demand action in conformity with what they take to be a seamless condemnation of homosexuality in the Bible. I have seen vibrant and SPIRIT-filled churches lose their pastors, inspiring music ministers, or committed lay members when such purging actions take place, all in the name of obedience and conformity to the Bible! Is the best way of representing Jesus Christ found in throwing out all the gays and lesbians, or is there a different way which we have not yet discovered, beyond denial?

The passing of time and the interaction between the continual unfolding of Gospel revelation with scientific "discovery" will answer these questions. Future generations may look back on this time and pity us that we did not have their "scientific" data, which will persuade most church-folk in the future that homosexuality is a minority biological configuration. Current research already points to distinctive differences in the size of hypothalamus and pituitary glands in homosexually oriented persons. Just as some New Testament accounts of demon possession clearly reveal what we now call an epileptic seizure rather than heteronomous spirit-agents possessing a body, so attitudes toward homosexuality may also change. Such a view is not entirely optimistic, however, because it is clear that many Black churches have already made the question of homosexual ordination a *status confessionis* ("that upon which the confession rests").

It is entirely possible that in the next five to ten years various denominations will split over this issue in much the same way that the Methodists split over slavery in the nineteenth century, Presbyterians split into "New Light" and "Old Light" over the issue of how the SPIRIT ought to be experienced in the Great Awakening revival movements of the eighteenth century, and the Roman Catholic Church split in the sixteenth century over Luther's declaration that "faith alone" saves persons. Unfortunately, when Christians disagree over what they consider to be *essential* to the *faith*, division in the church occurs, and new churches are formed. Peace over this issue may not occur within even our children's lifetimes, but someday the "Affirming Methodists" and those who did not "affirm" (and all their other denominational counterparts) will look at this issue with New Eyes and weep.

An XODUS church needs all of its members to bring their gifts of ministry to the altar for consecration. We need preachers who are inbreathed with the WORD of GOD, singers whose voices can mend brokenness, organizers who can plan and bring about events impossible for anyone who did not have such a gift, and committed lay members who are willing to go where the SPIRIT leads. In a time of crisis we do not need to build walls but breach them. In a time when our children's future hangs in a precarious balance XODUS church proclaims that the ANOINTing of GOD's SPIRIT must lift ALL the Folk, not some of the Folk, and that representatives of that ANOINTing shall go forth by twos, announcing that the Reign of GOD is Coming.

Will the denominational churches, as Delores Williams calls them, be willing to join in the empowering mission that IS the invisible "Black church"[23] or will we destroy ourselves fighting over issues which do not directly pertain to the future flourishing of the Folk, the Community, and LIFE?

XODUS ecclesiology suggests that there are many more than four "marks" of African American and pan-African churches' authenticity. One cannot have gone through the horrors of slavery in this hemisphere, or the degradations of colonialism and its evil twin, neo-colonialism, in other parts of the globe without recognizing that a "church" needs *more than* the traditional "marks." The following is an initial musing meant to spark conversation. It is neither complete nor exhaustive, but aims at being suggestive. Further, it builds on the very same high regard for biblical verse and principles which regulated the formation of the historic "marks":

- a church must be faithful;

- a church must persevere in times of death, danger, and crisis;

- a church must model GOD's *Agape.*

These three XODUS "marks" arise from the purifying forge of African American historical experience — from slavery to the present. There would be no "Black church" (in Delores Williams's sense of the term) without the followers of Jesus coming together to remain *faithful* in spite of everything in this life that stood against believing in anything more powerful than raw might, *persevere* in the struggle of life regardless of obstacles, and finally *grow in GOD's Love* because it was *the* expression of GOD's SPIRIT on the move. Faithfulness, perseverance, and GOD's Love stood by African Americans as they moved from slavery through Jim Crow, from lynching to marching, and from cotton fields to corporate offices. Despite the crises of violence threatening the present, there are spiritual "roots" represented in these "marks" which traditional ecclesiology should respect.

In the end Faith and AGAPE issue forth into HOPE. HOPE is the eschatological in-breaking of GOD's power into the reality of life. HOPE is a "mark" of an XODUS church because it is a movement of LIFE, SPIRIT, and *Agape* operating in the faith-filled lives of those who have been called out by GOD.

Notes

1. Arrested Development, *3 Years, 5 Months, and 2 Days in the Life of....* (New York: Chrysalis Records, 1992; FA-21929).

2. Paris, *Guerilla Funk* (Los Angeles: Priority Records, 1994; P453882).

3. James Evans, Jr., *We Have Been Believers: An African American Systematic Theology* (Minneapolis: Fortress, 1993), 135.

4. Emilie Townes, *In a Blaze of Glory: Womanist Spirituality as Social Witness* (Nashville: Abingdon, 1995), 56.

5. Ibid., 55.

6. Ibid., 56.

7. The title of Marcia Riggs's book on Black Women's Club movement.

8. James Cone "Black Theology and the Black Church" in *Black Theology: A Documentary History 1966–1979* (Maryknoll, N.Y.: Orbis Books, 1979), 1:354.

9. Ibid., 354.

10. Ibid., 354–55.

11. Ibid., 355.

12. J. Deotis Roberts, *The Prophethood of Black Believers: An African American Political Theology for Ministry* (Louisville: Westminster/John Knox Press, 1994), 23.

13. Ibid., 29–30.

14. Ibid., 131–46. While this sentence summarizes the main challenges of the entire text, most of the points contained are briefly summarized in the last chapter, "Faith and Praxis: What about the Future?"

15. J. Deotis Roberts, *Black Theology Today* (New York: Edwin Mellen Press, 1983), 188.

16. J. Deotis Roberts, *Liberation and Reconciliation* (Maryknoll, N.Y.: Orbis Books, orig. pub. 1974, 2d ed. 1994), 29.

17. Ibid., 30.

18. Ibid., 64.

19. Roberts, *Prophethood of Black Believers*, 138.

20. Dwight Hopkins and George Cummings, eds., *Cut Loose Your Stammering Tongue* (Maryknoll, N.Y.: Orbis Books, 1991); Dwight Hopkins, *Shoes That Fit Our Feet: Sources for a Constructive Black Theology* (Maryknoll, N.Y.: Orbis Books, 1993).

21. Evans, *We Have Been Believers*, 137.

22. Ibid., 138.

23. Delores Williams, *Sisters in the Wilderness: The Challenge of Womanist God-Talk* (Maryknoll, N.Y.: Orbis Books, 1993), 204–6. Williams eloquently describes as "invisible" the "Black Church" in contrast to "African American denominational churches."

"Having Church"

A Womanist Perspective

S HUG AVERY'S observation in Alice Walker's *The Color Purple* that God is not something you find in church but something people bring in with them is a cautionary statement. It requires that people be responsible for their relationship to God as *active* rather than *passive* believers. In other words one's relationship with God involves more than passively waiting for God to show up while sitting in a church pew or kneeling at the altar. While church pews and altars are sacred places where Christians encounter God, God is not limited to such spaces. One actively searches for God by being open to the Spirit, which is not limited to a particular location or body of people. The human spirit seeking Spirit finds Spirit and is found by Spirit in church pews, altars, prayer closets, hospital beds, on a morning walk, and millions of other places because it actively engages the will in seeking relationship with God. Moving beyond Shug's observations, I would add that because people bring God with them to church it is possible to find God in church. God is found wherever people sincerely seek connection with God, the strength or power of all life. Moreover, God is found wherever people sincerely seek to evidence their love for all life in harmony with God, the strength of all life.

Because God is everywhere, one can find God in church or on a mountaintop, in a synagogue or in a garden. Jesus could be found in both places, according to Scripture. The synagogue was an important place for interpreting Scripture and sharing the Spirit of God, but so were mountains, if we recall the account of the sermon Jesus gave on the mount, which we know today as the beatitudes. Mountains and gardens are also represented in Scripture as places of solitude, retreat, prayer, meditation, and communion with God. Jesus' sojourn in the desert is famous for the temptation he experienced there, but it is in this same wilderness that he also became one with God, fully committed to his calling. There are places that we humans hold particularly sacred because of momentous movements of the Spirit in those locations in human history. Such places seem to hold power, to pulse or vibrate with empowering Spirit and the prayers of believers. For this reason pilgrimage is an important tradition not only among Christians, but in a diversity of religions — Islam, Buddhism, Hinduism, Judaism. Although space is important, it does not, cannot limit God as dynamic, empowering, creating Spirit. What is most important is the history and tradition of spirit connecting with Spirit in such places. In the end, however, this is something we are called to do wherever we may be. Church is not merely a place; it is a happening — an event. It is a particular kind of event involving movement of the Spirit. It can happen in a storefront, in a temple, in a basilica, in a cathedral, in a small country or urban church edifice, in the wilderness, or in a park. Ultimately, faith must emerge from something deeper and more ancient than denominational churches — fallible human institutions comprised of people of limited knowledge and understanding in relation to God. One must be grounded in the source which the churches claim to represent, the divine ground of all creation, of all that is and all that will be — God Godself.

I have witnessed the strength and stability churches can provide for women, children, and families. I have also witnessed the struggles that take place within churches between people of diverse personalities and backgrounds who all wrestle with profound questions and the difficulties of understanding difference. Church is a place where human inadequacies inevitably become starkly apparent because idealism runs so high. However, this does not mean that the church is unnecessary or unimportant. There is a story about a woman who said she did not need to go to church because there were too many hypocrites there. The minister responded, "There is room for one more."[1] More than one new Christian has determined to leave the church because its members did not live up to all their expectations based on the ideals they proclaimed. In such an idealistic context, the warts and imperfections of those who claim to believe in the highest scriptural principles seem starkly apparent. It is not so much that the church is full of hypocrites. Most people are not hypocrites, people who boldly proclaim one set of beliefs and do something altogether different. Churches are simply full of people, not gods. They are full of people who seek to imitate Jesus but are not Jesus, people who are on the road to godly perfection but who are not perfect because only God is perfect.

People are imperfect and often fall short of their beliefs and the spiritual goals they aspire to. For this reason, it is important to think of the church as an ongoing transformative event. Change is not sudden; it is continuous and never-ending. Living up to our fullest potential in relation to God as empowering Spirit is a life-time process. For this reason, it is necessary to understand that forgiveness and patience are necessary virtues not only in relation to "the world" but in relation to believers. Church as event is a process of working out faults, problems, foibles. It is not a place of escape that one runs away to in order to avoid those problems in others and in oneself.

The church is vital for realizing the interrelatedness and interconnectedness of believers and the sacredness of life. It moves believers beyond an individualistic form of faith experience and activity to communal faith experience and activity. The church is wherever the people and Spirit are in all times and beyond time. It is an empowering event that involves spiritual transformation, growth, and change. While the church cannot be limited to or contained by time and space, it includes time and space. The sacred spaces where we praise and worship God, the empowering Spirit, source, and power of all that is, are very important. Also important are those times we set aside for special remembering and reverence of God as Spirit. Church happens whenever and wherever such worship, communion, and fellowship takes place. For this reason, there is a saying among Black Christians: "We're having church today" or "We had church today." Going to church and having church are not the same thing. Just because the people attend church on a Sunday morning does not mean that church will take place. Church *happens* when people come "prayed up" to worship God in spirit and in truth and the Spirit moves through the service.

Another often quoted saying in Black churches is "the Spirit was high."[2] Delores Williams explains that the criteria for determining that the spirit is high include active and obvious presence of the spirit.[3] Church is a spiritual event and care is taken to welcome the Spirit. Many traditional churches have a devotion and/or testimony time prior to the official church service to ensure that everyone is "prayed up" and in the Spirit before the scheduled liturgy begins. Again, this reinforces the understanding of church as more than space, place, or a time-slot in a schedule. Church is an experience that believers live into through prayer and devotion to God and through spiritual sharing with one another. When this happens, church is liberating in many areas of believers' lives.

From a womanist perspective, to speak of church as "event" or "happening" moves beyond a romanticized, religion-addicted, feel-good motivation to one that looks to the movement of Spirit in relation to *spiritual praxis*. Local churches participate in Church Universal when their members actively participate in God's aim for healing and wholeness of self, family, community, and world. Such healing and wholeness involve spiritual, socioeconomic, and political well-being. Church Universal, as the body of Christ, is a continuous series of ongoing events that involves the words believers say not only on Sunday but throughout the week. It involves not only the liturgical acts of praise and worship during the weekly church services, but small acts of kindness toward others daily. It has to do not only with the movement of the Spirit in the hearts of believers, but with the way believers apply their gifts of the Spirit. Such gifts include not only the traditional gifts of preaching, teaching, healing wisdom, knowledge, prophesy, and interpretation, but gifts of listening, feeding, clothing, caring for children in the community, lifting someone's spirits, mopping a sick friend's floor, sharing survival resources.

Emilie Townes gives a very careful analysis of economic and environmental crisis among Black Americans and the responsibility of Black churches to ongoing socioeconomic and environmental inequities. Refuting several economic myths regarding welfare, the welfare state, and poverty, she debunks the notion of the "emerging" Black underclass to observe that a certain segment of Black America has been poor ever since the end of slavery. Today's class is an expansion of a problem that was not adequately redressed more than a century ago. Although 28 percent of the Black population is poor, poor Whites outnumber poor Blacks by two to one.[4] While acknowledging that the Black middle class has responsibility for continuing the transclass traditions of previous generations, which did not abandon working and lower classes, she refutes the notion that the Black middle class alone can hold together the Black underclass, because the middle-income groups of any race or culture historically have never had the economic clout to bring about radical socioeconomic transformation. "The middle may not hold," Townes asserts.[5] The problems of poverty are systemic problems within a larger, complex socioeconomic structure in which an elite few (1–3 percent) hold a majority of wealth. The Black middle class is not the fundamental problem. Systemic economic class exploitation is the problem. From the time of indentured servitude American economics has been dependent on the exploitation of lower classes. Such is the nature of a "free-market economy" such as ours in the United States. Opportunity *is not* for all, as things are and historically have been.[6]

Given the gross inequities Black communities face (and that Black women face disproportionately), Townes warns that "the Black Church cannot lapse into or continue to advocate a spirituality and a social witness that preaches and teaches self-abnegation and moral intolerance."[7] This does not mean, she explains, that Black churches should advocate an "anything-goes" spirituality. Rather, "the church must gain a clearer understanding of the nature of tolerance and intolerance and begin to question the structural moral universe in which it exists and for which it is responsible."[8] As it is, the smaller storefront churches and lower-class mainline churches are left as sociomoral guardians of the community struggle with the Black underclass in an often valiant effort to attain and maintain viable living standards. Moral dictates of these churches provide straitjackets of moral dicta that function to draw "another circle around the church that leaves out substance abusers, single parents, homeless, gay men and lesbians, the mentally ill," and the physically challenged. On the other hand, middle-class Black churches all too often reflect the moral judgment of the larger socioeconomic order against the poor and dispossessed, Townes observes. The crux of Townes's argument is that more Black churches of all traditions and socioeconomic walks must cease separating *church and community.* Building on Townes, I would add that the church as embodiment of Spirit is communal. This communality is not something the church can keep to itself. The church can move toward full embodiment of Spirit, the source of empowerment for all creation, only if it embodies itself within society as a whole. This means, as Townes observes, that the church must engage in *radical societal criticism as well as radical self-criticism.*[9] Moreover, such societal criticism must be proactive, involving strategies for realizing *a new creation, the reign of empowering Spirit,* in the lives and entire environments of the dispossessed.

According to 1 Corinthians the greatest of all gifts is love. Love is a complex word, not easily defined. But it involves all of the acts of compassion and care on an unconditional basis I describe above. It seeks to do what only God does perfectly and what we humans are called to do more perfectly. As the church hymn goes, God looks beyond our faults and sees our needs. As participants in God's redemptive, compassionate work believers are called to look beyond the faults of others (real or imagined) and see their needs. In doing so, we allow the Spirit that moves through us during worship to move through our hearts, hands, and words to empower others.

Denominational Churches: Liberating or Oppressive?

Denominational Christian churches and the God-talk that emerges from them are sources of both liberation and oppression for women. I am very aware of both phenomena in my life and the lives of others. Since women tend to be outsiders in terms of leadership in the very churches and other organized religious institutions that they hold together as subordinate insiders, I am aware of myself as both insider and outsider, supporter and critic. Because of this dual experience of oppression and liberation, the church is not my only or even primary source of spiritual strength except in some ideal, utopian sense. Black churches, like any human institutions, are places of celebration and struggle, healing and pain.

As Delores Williams points out in her groundbreaking work *Sisters in the Wilderness,* it is necessary to make a distinction between the Black church and Black churches.[10] By Black churches she has in mind the everyday practices, beliefs, ritual, music, and art of local denominational churches. By the Black church she has in mind a larger sense of what Black churches sometimes claim to be about, struggle to become, and in certain moments actually embody. Her focus and mine is on God-talk that promotes survival and wholeness for entire communities, male and female. Because the churches are complex systems of liberation *and* oppression for Black women, ultimately it is God, not churches, who is the strength of one's life. God transcends the evils of patriarchy and oppression wherever they exist. To move toward such God-talk it is necessary to consider God-language that emerges from the lives of Black women, making it an integral part of what is heard in sermons on Sunday morning as well as in prayer meeting on Wednesday evening.

The oppression of women in Black churches, and churches in the general population, is not the sole domain of male pastors, preachers, deacons, and other church officers. Internalized oppression is a recurrent problem among those who live in cultures where the subjugation of their group is normative. *Sometimes women themselves are the most avid supporters of women's subordination to men, citing 1 Peter, Galatians, and Ephesians to drive home supporting biblical arguments.* What women hear on Sunday mornings and in prayer meetings on Wednesday evenings affects their understanding of Scripture and its authoritative message on women's roles. I have found, however, that introduction to overlooked Scriptures on women's leadership in religion, family, and community is often well received and appreciated by women who have previously been exposed only to those household Scriptures that emphasize the submission of women, particularly when respect is given for their own leadership in traditional women's roles. Other womanists, like Prathia Hall-Wynn, have likewise found that when the *whole* of Scripture is analyzed in relation to the *whole* spectrum of women's callings and ministries, even women who have been most traditional in their understanding of women's roles and adamantly opposed to women pastors, deacons, preachers, etc., become more supportive of women's equality in churches, family, and community.[11] Sometimes, these are the first women to respond to a call to ministry that has been "like fire shut up in their bones" for decades. For the first time, some of these women realize that their own call to a ministry comprises more than traditional women's roles. Others remain confident that their own callings are more traditional but become more open to peers and younger women who claim a call to pastoral ministry.

It is important to affirm a diversity of women's ministerial callings, traditionally female and nontraditional. Some of the arguments against women in ministry among church women have as much to do with a fear of displacement and competitiveness between women as with scriptural correctness. Attention to Scripture passages that support women's ministry as clergy and in more traditional roles is important for acknowledging a diversity of gifts among women in the church. One of the challenges for women called to traditionally male roles in ministry is to communicate as clearly as possible an inclusive vision of women's ministry that honors the work of women elders, many of whom may have responded to a nontraditional call to pastoral ministry themselves had they lived in a context where that was an option. At the same time, as church women (lay and clergy) we are challenged and called to support one another in our diversity of gifts of ministry.

Another way in which we oppress one another as women is, as several Black women writers have observed, our tendency to subscribe to the very superwoman syndrome that many of us claim to be critical of. Alice Walker writes about the rich culture, wisdom, and courage that Black mothers pass on to their daughters. But there is also something that she calls "women's folly" which must be acknowledged as well.[12] Women's folly includes those statements of apparent wisdom that are not really self- or other-loving at all, but lead to a kind of stoicism that ends in poor health physically, mentally, and spiritually. Granny, in Zora Neale Hurston's *Their Eyes Were Watching God*, informed her granddaughter Janie that the colored woman was the mule of the world as far as she could see. Those who internalize this expectation, believing it to be true at some level, are more likely to give into oppressive social forces that insidiously lure them into believing they should be treated like mules, even whipping themselves into action when on their last leg. Whereas those who have seen women of color as means to their own gain may have treated them as beasts of burden, God sees women of color not as chattel but as women. The challenge for womanist theologians, Christian and across a diversity of religions, is to consider the type of God-talk that leads to true liberation and wholeness for entire communities, male and female.

There is a kind of stoicism Black women are taught and expect from one another that is passed on from mother to daughter. We need to encourage one another to love ourselves *regardless*, as Walker puts it, far more often than we do. Many of us know churchwomen who are close to death before they see a doctor (often for economic reasons) or the mother in the church whose commitment is so reliable that she returns to church less than a week after a heart attack, diabetic crisis, or some other major medical emergency. The preacher calls attention to this dedicated church-woman, thanking God that she is alive and praising her commitment. In the meantime, the church nurse is on hand to take her blood pressure and administer first-aid in case of an emergency.

While such dedication is breathtaking and awe-inspiring, it is also dangerous. Such acts move beyond long-suffering to self-negligence and nihilism. They teach girls and young women to love their bodies little more than slave masters loved the bodies of Black foremothers when they commanded them back into the fields when seriously ill or within days of delivering babies. How joyous to come into a place of worship to praise God for one's life which is an entirely different act from working in the fields. But God does not require that women abuse their bodies in the process. Job learned that while one may indeed experience evil in the world, God is not a taskmaster or evildoer. God as empowering Spirit who dances as a fierce whirlwind in our midst requires only that we receive the grace s/he has to offer. There is enough of God's grace, love, and compassion to wait for yet another Sunday and truly "lean on the everlasting arms" for a change rather than lean on our own when God seems to be saying it is time to rest! For all the talk in churches about "tarrying on the Spirit" and "waiting on the Lord," church women could learn to "tarry on the Spirit" and "wait on the Lord" a little bit more for the sake of their own well-being and that of the church. Churches need whole, healed people, male and female. Healing takes time and we need to receive the grace of God we claim to believe in. Such grace is not just for "other people," the sister or brother in the pew next to us. God does not demand that we be burnt-out workers. God provides grace and rest not only for others but for the self. It is important to love oneself, accepting God's love in one's own life, in order to remain alive long enough to share God's love with those who are within reach of the full life-span God intends for us.

For the church's part, the altar prayer is an important moment for looking to the Creator and Healer of all to heal those with illness in their bodies. Such prayer is a life-affirming, life-loving, life-promoting moment. But churches should not stop there. The ministry of denominational churches must include counsel about health care. Such counsel does not involve medical diagnosis, but information about medical resources. Money, food, and clothing are often available for those who are in need of resources to clothe and feed themselves and their families. It would be further life-affirming and helpful to offer information, and funding if necessary, for those who are ill and lack resources for medical attention. It is important for the churches to be at the forefront of movement for universal health care in the United States, because health is a core part of Christian ministry. Jesus was known as a healer. Spiritual healing of body and soul is at the heart of Christian ministry. Such spiritual healing occurs through a variety of means. While prayer and the laying on of hands of the elders are important, the hands of doctors and nurses are also resources that God has made available.

The Generations and the Church

A diversity of generations is necessary for the life of churches. Older members provide stability, history, tradition. Younger members provide enthusiasm for the continued life of churches and new programming. Unfortunately, the reality is that often these two groups come into conflict. Older members are threatened by the changes young members inevitably recommend. Younger members feel held back by tradition and feel that their visions are suppressed. The pastor is in the position of holding the visions of the two groups together. Such a task takes great skill. Even among the most skilled pastors personality conflicts sometimes turn into tumultuous discords. Diverse generations must recognize the importance of each generation — the value of both tradition and new vision. According to Scripture, "without a vision the people perish." At the same time, without knowledge of the church's history with God the people are also at risk; they risk losing sight of who they are as a historical body; they risk losing sight of the wisdom of the elders, which is born out of years of experience in relation to God and one another. While it is true that God is always creating "a new thing," God creates the new out of the old. We are called to carry the wisdom of the past with us into the future. Without young women and men, churches slowly die as membership falls off through death, remaining members become embedded in the past and ingrown relationships, and spiritual torpor sets in.

For young women, families, and children to feel welcome in the congregation it is important to have or at least express interest in planning adequate facilities for them — a nursery, a private place to nurse, children's church, a youth program, or simply a pastor and congregation that welcome the cries of babies as "a joyful noise unto the Lord" rather than as a nuisance and disturbance. Without such facilities or at the least an expectation that children belong in church as *children* and not as miniature adults, mothers (and fathers) of very young children are discouraged from participating in church services. To attract young adults there must be adequate programming for them. For youth to feel welcome and included, they cannot be met with suspicion, distrust, and discouragement, but rather must be met with love and affirmation for the vitality they bring.

The old wine skins of tradition and "we've always done it this way" threaten to break under the vigor of the new wine of fresh ideas for programs, music, events. Impatience emerges on both sides, which becomes problematic when neither side is willing to learn to work cooperatively in a give-and-take relationship with the other, allowing the God they claim to believe in to work as mediator rather than judge. In the Spirit of Christ there are no old wine skins, because in Christ there is no age. We are created anew daily and moment by moment. Ageism must give way on either side. Neither the elders nor the young can hope for a stable, vital church if they treat each other as enemies. Joel 2:28 reads that "in the last days your daughters shall prophesy; your old men shall dream dreams; your young men shall have visions." All ages and genders are called to bring gifts to the living body of Christ, which is the church.

Church as the Living Body of Christ

The body of Christ is living. The body of Christ resurrected is comprised of all believers. It is comprised of the energy, vision, and hope of youth as well as of the wisdom, experience, and dreams of elders. It is not a White body, a Black body, a Red body, a Brown body, or a Gold body. The body of Christ today, like the body of Jesus of Nazareth, is of Dust and Spirit. It is a body made up of the diverse bodies, gifts, and spirits of believers of many colors. In its physical manifestation today, the body of Christ is a rainbow body, God's symbol of covenant in the midst of the pain, and in many respects this body of Christ is visible in the faces of those who believe. In other respects it is invisible because we cannot see all believers who live and walk in every part of the globe. We simply do not know all believers or even who they are, as Augustine observed in *The City of God*. Moreover, as Romans 8 observes, some believers walk according to laws written upon their hearts and are not part of a local church or familiar with Christian Scriptures. The body of Christ is known and unknown, visible and invisible, palpable and beyond our reach. This living body of Christ is the Church Universal, which we come to know in part through our particular experiences of it.

As the body of Christ, the spirits and bodies of those who make up the church embody God as Spirit, who is the Strength of Life. This God as Strength of Life is empowering Spirit, which enables the multitudes who make up the body of Christ as Church Universal to participate in God's work of salvation, wholeness, sustenance, and liberation within creation. Believers participate in God's work in a number of ways. The prayers of believers affect the way humans choose to feel and think about our actions. One ought not underestimate the power of prayer. Scientific studies show that prayer effects detectable chemical changes within the body. Such biochemical changes affect the brain, the neurological system, the cardiovascular system, the immune system, the organs, all parts of the body. These biochemical changes affect the way we feel about our bodies, if we have been physically ill, and the way we feel about life circumstances. Prayer and meditation lead to faster healing, prolonged life (cancer patients who have a strong prayer life, for example, have been known to live longer than predicted), and to positive, proactive responses to the vicissitudes of life. As those who comprise the church seek to effect social change, prayer and meditation are very important for maintaining a strengthened psychospiritual state and for preventing the infamous crisis of "burn-out." The prayers of the church are also important for maintaining a sense of centeredness in God who is the Strength of Life. Such centeredness is necessary not only for a sense of well-being, but also for discerning and focusing on God's aim for creation.

Ideally the church seeks to be in accord with God's aim for creation. History, however, reveals that the church has not always worked in harmony with God's aim for creation. European expansion into Africa in the fifteenth century was commissioned by papal bull. English and Spanish expansion into the Americas, North and South, appealed not only to the names of nation and state for their authority but to Christendom. The Christian holy wars against Muslims in the Middle Ages waged violence against those of another faith in the name of Christ and church. The church as a human institution has participated in the moral corruptions of human heart and hand. As Reinhold Niebuhr has observed, as human beings form larger and larger social groups they have a tendency to be self-serving, self-interested, and selfish. They have a tendency to rationalize that which is evil as good, to legitimate oppressive acts, one might say, as liberating, redemptive acts.[13] In the late nineteenth century, Anna Cooper observed the complicated role the church has played in human history. Ultimately, she suggests, the proper locus of faith for Christians is not so much in the church but in Christ:

Individuals, organizations, whole sections of the church militant may outrage the Christ whom they profess, may ruthlessly trample under foot both the spirit and the letter of his precepts, yet not till we hear the voices audibly saying "Come let us depart hence," shall we cease to believe and cling to the promise, *I am with you to the end of the world.*[14]

Observing that there were "some corruptions and incongruities against which the Bride of Christ has had to struggle in her past history,"[15] Cooper maintained that she had no doubt that the source of the vitalizing principle of woman's development was the church "so far as the church is *coincident with Christianity.*"[16] In other words, the church, which claims to be a Christian body, does not always act according to Christian principles. Cooper lambasted the church's relegation of marriage to an inferior position in relation to celibacy, arguing that it resulted in hypocrisy on the part of clergy and in the discrediting of women. At its best, however, she saw the church as embodying acts that were in accord with the gospel of Jesus Christ. She made a distinction between the gospel teachings of Jesus and the diversity of the church's practices and teachings. For Cooper the gospel message was a message of freedom. She interpreted the synoptic Gospels as presenting a message that showed "reverence for woman as woman regardless of rank, wealth or culture" and that came "from that rich and bounteous fountain from which flow all our liberal and universal ideas — the Gospel of Jesus Christ."[17] In her interpretation, as well as in the interpretation of other women who were active in the Black Women's Club movement, Jesus taught principles of equality and freedom in relation to women and men, people of diverse colors. The gospel as she read it was a social gospel. Only as the church acted in accord with this social gospel that taught the equality of persons across racial, gender, and national lines did it walk in accord with Christianity.

Whereas Cooper envisions the church as the Bride of Christ, feminizing it, I see the church as the embodiment of God, who is Spirit. Moreover, building on 1 Corinthians 12, I would say that the church embodies Christ. As I noted earlier in the discussion on God, Spirit belongs to both Christ and God. As Augustine suggests, it is the gift of each. The church embodies God and Christ, who are Spirit. The church is called to do this as a follower of Jesus, who was a perfect incarnation of God. As the body of the resurrected Jesus, who is Christ, the church aims toward such perfection, although unlike Jesus it is imperfect.

While the church is comprised of women and men, it transcends all cultural notions about gender. The church is at once male and female and neither male nor female. In the ordinary affairs of daily living it is comprised of men and women who may or may not ascribe to cultural gender norms and roles. In its ultimate sense, the church as Spirit, while it is incarnated in women and men, is neither male nor female. Galatians 3:28 supports such spiritual transcendence of cultural norms of maleness and femaleness: "There is neither Jew nor Greek, slave nor free, male nor female, for you are all one in Christ Jesus." Traditionally, Black churches have taken this passage to prove that slavery is not of God or Christ. The problem is, churches from a diversity of cultures, including Black culture, have not extended this teaching to its logical conclusion that God does not give preference to gender either. In Christ there is neither male nor female. Not only is God not a racist; God is not a sexist. Moreover, God gives preference to neither Greek nor Jew, which is a reminder that God is not anti-Semitic. The people of the church are people of Spirit. They are also people of dust. They are bodily creatures. God affirms us as *whole* people, body and spirit. God as Spirit is not concerned with the sociocultural restrictions we humans have placed on our bodiliness in terms of race, ethnicity, religion, denomination. God as Spirit embraces all such differences. At the same time, God transcends them. Because the people of God are born of Spirit as well as of body (John 3:3–8) they are whole people, wholly loved, wholly affirmed.

The conditions that are normative for material culture are embraced by the Spirit when sustaining, healing, redemptive, and liberating. They are transcended by the Spirit when they are not. Moreover, while the Spirit affirms and sustains both maleness and femaleness, Blackness and Whiteness, youth and elders, rich and poor, it transcends all of these even as it is immanent with them. Spirit affirms the diversity of forms which the dust of our bodies take on: male, female, short, tall, Black, White, Brown, Red, Gold, old, young, middle-aged, physically challenged, physically gifted, intellectually gifted, mentally challenged. What is most important are the gifts of the Spirit that the diversity of those who make up the church bring to one another.

As Jarena Lee pointed out more than a century ago, Christ is a whole savior who came to save women and men and not half of a saviour who came to save only the male half of the human race. Therefore, "the woman can preach as well as the man." Moreover, people of color can preach as well as Whites, which was a point of debate in the nineteenth century. Today it means that the physically challenged can preach as well as the physically able. It means that we are called to appreciate the physical, social, economic, cultural, and spiritual differences that exist in the church as the communal embodiment of Spirit. At the same time, we are to appreciate the fact that the Spirit is like ocean waters. It embraces the softest sand along with the hardest rocks. It permeates the air, providing stores of nourishment for those within its farthest reaches. Its fragrance merges with wind to revive and heal the very breath of our lives. It seeps into the crevices of differences and unifies us, embracing and enwombing us all so that we can be birthed again and again into new creation. The living church is always a new creation. Of course this is what the church is ideally. This makes up only a portion of our existential experience. In the fullest scope of our experience the church is a complex mix of living new creation and stagnant, stubborn entrenchment in necrophilic attitudes and practices.

The church is called to live into new creation, whether it does so in every aspect of its practice or not. The Spirit is always with us. Our challenge is to move with it more than against it. In the reality of day to day, year to year, decade to decade, and generation to generation living there are so many mistakes, so many errors of discernment that the church makes. Therefore, as Paul Tillich has observed, the church is not the judge of culture. It is judged with culture because it is part of culture.[18] The church is made up of people. It embodies Spirit but it does not embody Spirit perfectly.

The church, while it embodies Spirit, is a human, cultural institution. The church has a higher calling than to be the final arbiter of right and wrong relationship to God. To claim itself as final judge and arbiter would be to render the church as God. That would be idolatrous. God as Spirit is the final arbiter, which judges even the church. The church must be self-critical and open to criticism. The church is very much like human beings and human institutions generally. It is a complex mix of body and spirit, eternity and finitude, perfection and imperfection. Only if the church understands that it does not possess all the answers to life's questions, but grows into those answers over millennia, can it exist as a living body rather than as a dead or stagnant one.

Given all of the above, what does it mean for the church to be the body of Christ? It is a helpful yet problematic metaphor. On the one hand it is a very powerful metaphor for describing the diversity of peoples and their gifts, which make up the church. On the other hand, the metaphor does not suggest that the church, with all its imperfections, is Christ's self. It is the *body* of Christ. How are we to understand this word "body"? For the ancient Greeks "body" was not merely a physical body. Rather it was that which could be seen. Therefore, one might say that the church as body of Christ is that which is visible of Christ.[19] The church evidences Christ through those acts and words which are consistent with the teachings of Jesus as described in the synoptic Gospels and the Gospel of John. Historically Black women have interpreted these books as proclaiming a message of love, freedom, and equality for all peoples regardless of race or gender. The metaphor of "the body of Christ" is powerful for another reason in our contemporary multicultural world. If we take "body" more literally, we are reminded that Christ's body today is evident in a multitude of colors, shapes, sizes, ages, genders, and physical abilities. Both meanings of "body" are important for Christians today as we seek to realize more fully what it means to act in harmony with God as Spirit as whole persons, physically and spiritually.

Notes

1. Sermonic comments by Rev. Gayle Davis-Culp, Primm Tabernacle A.M.E. Church, Fall 1994.

2. Delores Williams, "Womanist Theology: Black Women's Voices," in Judith Plaskow and Carol Christ, eds., *Weaving the Visions* (New York: Harper & Row, 1989), 185.

3. Ibid.

4. Emilie Townes, *In a Blaze of Glory* (Nashville: Abingdon, 1995), 55–67, 124–25.

5. Ibid., 135ff.

6. Ibid., 130–38.

7. Ibid.

8. Ibid.

9. Ibid., 134.

10. Delores Williams, *Sisters in the Wilderness: The Challenge of Womanist God-Talk* (Maryknoll, N.Y.: Orbis Books, 1993), 204–28.

11. Prathia Hall-Wynn, comments on women in ministry at the Society for the Study of Black Religion, March 1994.

12. Alice Walker, "One Child of One's Own," *In Search of Our Mothers' Gardens* (New York: Harcourt Brace Jovanovich, 1983), 363–69.

13. Reinhold Niebuhr, *Moral Man and Immoral Society* (New York: Scribners, 1932).

14. Anna J. Cooper, "Womanhood a Vital Element in the Regeneration and Progress of a Race," *A Voice from the South*, ed. Mary Helen Washington, Schomburg Library of Nineteenth-Century Black Women Writers (1892; reprint, New York: Oxford University Press, 1988), 16.

15. Ibid., 14–16.

16. Ibid.

17. Ibid.

18. Paul Tillich, *Theology of Culture* (London: Oxford, 1959), 50–51.

19. See Greg Riley, *Resurrection Reconsidered: Thomas and John in Controversy* (Minneapolis: Fortress, 1994), 46–49, for a discussion of Ancient Greek understandings of souls and bodiliness.

Fifteen

Dialogue on CHURCH

Karen

Your discussion of Spirit-Church is a wake-up call to Black churches. You emphasize that while the spiritual happening that many call church on Sunday mornings often provides new personal fuel and a spiritual high with which to get through yet another week, while liberation exists continually in the praises of worshiping voices, it is not enough to rest on one's personal good feelings. This is true, but do you see the positive value in the understanding of "*having* church" — church as a spiritual, active event? Liberating, political action cannot take place without the spiritual empowerment that takes place in a womanist understanding of church as a *happening*. You seem to discount this notion of church, reducing it to its most problematic dimensions. While such problematic dimensions do exist, do you see any positive contributions that African American understandings of "having church" or church as *happening* make to Black spirituality?

KASIMU

Your question is exciting because it aids a fuller discussion of what I would call a *dialectical tension* between the empowering spirituality of "having church," and the mission-type of outreach of the church — be it social justice, evangelism, or healing ministries. The function of spiritual empowerment is what my XODUS work seeks to arouse, and that is outreach. As an active minister of gospel music, I have witnessed the anointing SPIRIT at work in "having church."[1] The problem is that it can produce a personal spiritual "high" so self-absorbing and so self-fulfilling that social outreach gets forgotten. I see an imbalance on the side of personal spiritual empowerment (in African American churches particularly) and seek to find a way toward balancing the dialectic in order for both the personal and social dimensions of faith to be enriched. In fact, we

258

need personal spiritual empowerment in order to be effective agents of social justice.

Karen

Not only does your XODUS vision call for equal treatment of women and men in the church, but you ask the church to consider equality of homosexuals with heterosexuals. Christian womanists who have been particularly outspoken on this issue are Delores Williams, Renee Hill, and Kelly Brown Douglas. Alice Walker solidly affirms sexual preference in her definition of "womanist." However, few theologians and ethicists, Black male or womanist, have brought this issue strongly to the fore. As you suggest, it is an issue that could divide denominational churches, just as they were divided over the history of slavery a century ago. I sometimes wonder why womanists, myself included, are not more forthright about this particular subject. I suspect that for many it is for the same reason that many gays and lesbians hesitate to come out of the closet: fear of losing a job, of being thrown out of church, ostracized in community. Some of my students have noted a "Don't ask, don't tell" policy in Black churches. In conversation you also have observed that whether you agree with it or not, such a policy does seem to exist in Black churches. Do you have a vision for how we could begin to speak more openly about such matters in the Black community at large and in Black churches?

KASIMU

This topic is so damaging to reputations, so controversial, and so divisive that I believe most Christians refuse to talk about it in order to maintain at least the visible semblance of "unity" and "agreement." The loudest voices on this issue are not those of homosexuals seeking entrance and acceptance but of certain Christians who feel that uncritical acceptance of homosexuality in Christ's church is tantamount to crowning the Antichrist on an altar! Courage on this issue comes in fits and starts, and only a kind of revolutionary grace has encouraged me to broach the topic at all. In XODUS JOURNEY I envision Black churches beginning deeper conversation on the issue of homosexuality by first addressing the wider concern (for most) of *the proper expression of our human sexuality*. As we prayerfully address sexuality, rooting our conversations on the *Agape*-principle of forgiveness, love, and humility, we may find that grace comes upon us "in the midst of" our earnest and frank discussions. If we really believe in the "visitation of the Holy Spirit," we may find that Jesus Christ is struggling with us on this very issue, and His answer might surprise all of us!

Karen

What's so interesting to me about the divisiveness of the issue is that it has been there all along. It's as if most of our churches simply placed a rug over a huge crack in the floor we're standing on. But people act as though it's only because we've removed the rug that the crack has come into existence. The truth is, we were hiding from the truth. There has been a division all along that the church needs to address. How do you envision getting people to acknowledge that sexuality in general and homosexuality in particular are not new issues "that threaten to divide the church"? Many people would like to pull the rug back over and pretend no such division has ever existed. This is nothing more than trying to maintain a false peace, in my view.

KASIMU

Yes, to ignore the divisions and pretend that homosexuality does not exist maintains a "false peace," but it is a peace that many would rather maintain than to openly voice disagreement. For XODUS the question is whether liberating and loving churches choose to exist with the disagreements or choose to separate and form new church alliances. The pattern in Protestantism is separation and reformation. The weakness of that pattern, I believe, is that *it never allows us the time necessary to see grace operating despite our differences!*

Karen

You speak from a communitarian understanding of God as liberating and saving Spirit. I am curious about your understanding of the meaning of such a Spirit-led church for "the streetz." You describe XODUS ecclesiology as expanding the walls of the church to the dispossessed, the discounted, the dismissed. While you recognize that there are some large Black urban churches engaged in active ministry to the church just outside its walls, you contend that more need to enter into such ministry. I find myself wondering if perhaps the church should work with its understanding of "blood" to transform itself and the streetz to *re-member* that in Christ Jesus we are all of one Blood. Not only is there no Jew nor

Greek, no Scythian nor Barbarian, no slave nor free, no male nor female, but there is no division between the streetz and the church. Is Jesus Christ in the streetz waiting for the church to join full force in God's ministry of salvation, liberation, and restoration of true community? How can one effectively communicate and realize such a message among traditional churchfolk?

KASIMU

The distance between "the streetz" and the church is not as wide as many of our more self-righteous church-goers think, and this is as Jesus' life ministry portrays. When I look at Jesus I see a person able to successfully negotiate both the "streetz" of his time (prostitutes, tax collectors, "sinners"), and the "church" of his time (the Temple, scribes, Pharisees, etc.). The challenge that is XODUS, at least insofar as GOD has granted me a limited vision, is that *we must follow Jesus.* The words of that old hymn, "Where He leads me I will follow..." are most apt. If we follow Jesus, then the four-walls concept of "church" will break down, and we shall embrace the children of the "streetz" for who they are...OUR CHILDREN. Traditional churchfolk already know this; we just need to insist upon our *connection* with "streetz"-folk rather than our distinctions. I really believe that GOD's SPIRIT operating in the church is stronger than the killing power of "the streetz." We just need to *re-member* that theological tenet, and build from there.

Karen

How would you explain what you mean by "commonalities" to church and street folk? What specific points of common ground do you have in mind?

KASIMU

We share a common human frailty before violence, injustice, and abusiveness which no amount of posturing or symbolism can erase. We are GOD's children, created by GOD. *We build our lives either by working together or in violent competition.* The "streetz" have proclaimed the reality of violent competition, whereas churchfolk (at their best!) proclaim that working together is best. Yet even the most cynical of Rap artists would admit that folk on the "streetz" would rather work peacefully together and live than die fighting. So what one might call the communal logic of life — that we work peacefully together — brings streetz and church toward common ground.

Karen

This is helpful. And yet, at this point, even our language suggests a division or separation between streetz and church. I doubt the reality of this separation. We know that in real life, the street is in the church, transforming blues, jazz, and "soul music" into gospel, for example, or Saturday night dancing into Sunday morning swaying and stepping. Isn't it true that the church has always been in the streets, as you suggest, *and* the streets have been in the church? The distinctions we make are far less real than we pretend they are. There has always been some resistance between the two spheres of action. Each group has always won, with the streetz entering the church in new ways and the church giving new words and expressions to the sounds and rhythms of the streetz. It seems that the latest overly righteous attitude about Rap is just another expression of that tension. I believe that eventually it will be resolved. The question is "how?"

KASIMU

Some Rap deserves critique from the church, whereas other forms may prove liberating. I have already written about a *critical conversation* between church and Rap in *XODUS: An African American Male Journey*. As I was reading your womanist ecclesiology it struck me that you begin your reflections with a concern to show a dialectic between sacred Space and sacred Time. Church, in your view, is not just a holy space or place but is a happening, an event, a Sacred Moment. It seems to me that further conversation needs to take place about what one means by the term "holy." Does "holy" mean a place which has been set aside as more special than other places because it is considered to be "closer" to GOD in some way? Or is a space made "holy" because of the activities we engage in while we inhabit it, such as praying, preaching, singing, healing, or dancing? For instance, the African Independent churches in South Africa, also known as "Zionist churches," all believe that the open sky is the best cathedral and that worshiping in bare feet connects one to the creation fashioned by the Creator. Singing, clapping their hands, and dancing in circles, Zionist worshipers connect their followers to the sacredness of ordinary things like hills, dirt, the air, and the wind in ways that become obscured in traditional church buildings. Do you think that

African American churches could move away from denominationalism to "Having Church" if they moved out of the walled and enclosed spaces most occupy now?

Karen

I believe that all of creation is holy. This can be biblically supported within Christian tradition by Genesis 1, in which God speaks each aspect of creation into existence and sees that it is *good.* The great African Christian forefather Augustine contended that while creation, particularly humankind, was created good it had been corrupted by evil through disobedience to God. However, in its origins all of creation is good. There is no time or space that we can live in in this life, as we know it, that is not sacred or holy. There is holiness everywhere, even in the midst of evil situations. We must ask God to help us reach within to recognize and recover the holiness within ourselves and others. Even with the evil that we must wrestle with I believe that our task is to recognize and recover the holy in everything whether it is our bodies, the earth, or God as Spirit-Itself who is the strength of life. Holiness does not begin with the call to worship and end with the benediction. It does not begin when we reach the sanctuary and end when our feet hit the pavement. Therefore, we can find holiness in the streets, even in the most unexpected places. Likewise, we can find evil where we least expect it, including in the churches.

Every place where there are people good and evil sit, walk, stand, run, and talk side by side. The church ideally is a place where people come to worship God, enjoy fellowship, and work out the problem of good and evil for their everyday lives. In the streets, people also appeal to God in their own ways and struggle with the problem of good and evil. There is no place where God is not present. There is no place where humankind does not engage in the struggle of good and evil. This means that the people in church are not better than the people in the street. Many people in the church are from the street and can have effective street ministries if they resist self-righteousness. Wherever we are, our bodies and minds are holy. But the capacity for evil is there as well. I say evil rather than profanity, because often people known for profanity as far as language is concerned express the greatest holiness of heart in their concrete love of and assistance to others. The problem is whether we choose to express that holiness. How do we choose to treat ourselves and others?

KASIMU

You cite Emilie Townes's call in her book *In a Blaze of Glory* for a responsible and accountable Black church presence in social justice activities. You even go so far as to call this kind of responsible willed compassion "love." How does this compassionate love bring us before GOD and each other in more positive ways than the traditional church practice of love?

Karen

I don't know that I would call it *more* positive, although I would say that we gain more love when we give more love, while also loving ourselves. It is very important for the church to love itself. So I don't fault churches that take great pains to minister to one another within the sphere of a local, regional, or national congregation. But churches also need to recognize the Church Universal, which is beyond congregational, denominational, or even ecumenical boundaries. The Church Universal is invisible. It includes strangers and people from other faith traditions. The Church Universal requires that we expand our love so that it includes the known and the unknown, moving beyond our fears, because perfect love is without fear. We cannot be afraid to love, although it may be very intelligent not to *trust* each person equally. My understanding of Jesus is that even though he loved his enemies he did not trust all of them. Sometimes his love was tough, sometimes tender depending on the situation. Obviously, churches should not appoint drug addicts, for example, to be on the trustee board, but they can be welcomed into fellowship, into the choir, and into a drug rehab program. Most important, Jesus' command to show concrete, nurturing compassion for the hungry, the stranger, the sick, the prisoner in Matthew 25 is too direct to ignore.

KASIMU

You say that the church does not judge culture, but is judged *with* culture, as Paul Tillich once noted. Nonchurch culture is judging itself on issues of wife abuse, child abuse, and treatment of outcasts, immigrants, and homosexuals. Should the church take an oppositional view to the verdict of culture (Christ against culture), support culture (Christ of culture), or attempt to transform culture's dictates (Christ transforming culture)?

Karen

You know this question makes me smile, because I appreciate these three types of culture, which are part of H. Richard Niebuhr's five-part typology. Like Niebuhr, I believe a diversity of responses work together by informing and correcting each other. Yet, also like Niebuhr, I lean strongly toward envisioning Christ as transformer of culture. Christ is not entirely *of* culture nor is Christ entirely *against* it. Culture, which has to do with creaturely creativity — particularly human creativity — is *ambiguous* (to use Paul Tillich's word). We can lean toward forms of creation that are destructive or that are life affirming. On the one hand, I would say, creativity is good because Creativity Itself is its source. On the other hand, it is often evil because we who create cultural institutions like governments, families, schools, even churches are capable of profound sin. The bad gets mixed in with the good. The same nuclear energy that saves some lives from cancer can destroy the planet. The modern medications that destroy common bacteria create superbacteria, new strains resistant to antibiotics. The will to *civilize* — to create structured, ordered societies where there are safe places for children to play and systems for trading goods for survival — is also used to control, manipulate, conquer, and dispossess innocent peoples. Those with controlling power in culture can be greedy, desiring to keep the greatest goods for their small, elite group. Given the ambiguity of human culture, Christ is not entirely *of it* or *against it*. Christ is both of it and against it. This means that Christ wills the transformation of culture, loving it at its best and desiring change of its evil aspects.

Notes

1. *Having Church* is the title of the last album recording of the late, great Rev. James Cleveland and the Southern California Community Choir (Savoy Records SAV 7099 CD, 1990).

Part VI

LAST THINGS

Sixteen _____

Future Now!

XODUS Eschatology

T ALK ABOUT an "End" can always degenerate into fatalist and fantastic speculations on a great cataclysmic finale to the symphony of LIFE as we know it. In such scenarios the End is posited as the culmination of human sinfulness. In this vision of the "End things" (the meaning of the word "eschatology"), a narration of increasing horror and triumph ensues, from the dramatic "Rapture" of all the "true" saints, the worsening catastrophes as vividly portrayed (and literally interpreted) in the Revelation narration of "scrolls" and "seals," and finally the judgment of GOD, the second Coming of Christ as Warrior Lamb, and the New Heaven and Earth victory celebration! Yet eschatology in its most potent theoethical import must always aid us in discerning the "things of GOD" in the NOW. That is why so many Christians throughout the ages have really focused on Jesus' eschatological consciousness, symbolized in the empowering phrase "the Reign of God is with you." If GOD is truly reigning, then the uncertainties, hopes for cosmic revenge, or fear of ultimate catastrophe take on a more relativized importance in our current theological imagination.

At the end of the first millennium there was an increased surge in *apocalyptic eschatological* imagination. Note that by "apocalyptic" I mean that which pertains to a "revelation" or "revealing of hidden things in the future," while the term "eschatological" means that which pertains to a study of the Last or End things. In popular imagination we often understand the two terms to mean the same thing and associate the term "apocalypse" with images of a final violent destruction — Armageddon in scriptural symbolism. At the end of the first millennium Christians were certain that Jesus was returning at the very stroke of the new millennium. It seems that our millennium-ending apocalyptic eschatological frenzy has become an even more widespread phenomenon than at the previous millennium. We feared a terrible nuclear holocaust during the Cold War, painting it as one of the terrible plagues of death foretold in

269

certain verses of the book of Revelation (see especially Rev. 8:7). The air, water, and land under our feet have been so misused and have become so toxic that it would appear that the "third angel" of Wormwood (Rev. 8:10–11) *and* the fourth angel of Darkness (Rev. 8:12) have already blown their angelic trumpets of Divine Judgment. With rumors of super-viruses and outbreaks of horrifying proportions (such as the Ebola virus outbreak in Kitwit, Zaire, in the spring of 1995), it would also seem that we stand at the verge of yet another Revelation torture (Rev. 9:1–6). Various kinds of persons, even those with no connection to an informed and critical theological debate, have found their creative imaginations fueled by the possibility of a terrible END to all of LIFE.

XODUS theo-ethics concretizes one apocalyptic fear, that of Black genocide at the hands of an uncaring Euro-dominated, postindustrialized capitalist global economy which no longer has any need for African bodies. Such a fear cannot be dismissed as a paranoid fancy for those who work to make real the hope of Christ on the city streets. Every day some mother's son, some father's child is shot, maimed, or infected, and at a rate that *appears* to be increasing. Alarms are being sounded even by the most reasonable. At such a time reflecting on our future seems romanticized sentimentality unless we can articulate a vision of the NOW healthy enough to carry us into a future. XODUS theo-ethics responds to such a time by resisting the easy temptation to conform our conceptuality and rhetoric to the "party-line" of doom-and-gloom prognostications. Rather, in line with the revelational nature of the Gospel message, XODUS eschatology offers Revolutionary HOPE as the proper psychospiritual antidote to grim eschatological despair.

XODUS Revolutionary HOPE insists that living into the present with a determination to find concrete ways to embody what is good and healthy for all of Creation is the most important way for LIFE to be affirmed and Death denied. If the affirmation of John 10:10 is correct, that Jesus came to bring LIFE and that more abundantly, then *Abundant LIFE is the primary goal, the telos, of a follower of Jesus.* To follow Jesus, the norm of being a "Christian," ought to be the embodiment of Jesus' promise to bring Abundant LIFE. This Abundant LIFE cannot be realized by intellectual pursuits, material gains, or the accomplishment of social policies, whether conservative, liberal, or radical. Rather, Abundant LIFE is the incarnation of GOD's SPIRIT. As that LIFE was embodied in the life of Jesus of Nazareth in a perfect form so we, though imperfect and sometimes prone to turning away from those things of SPIRIT which could truly be healthy, nevertheless may also embody it.

Realistic appraisals of human beings often emphasize this frailty, finitude, and propensity toward moral failure. As Romans 7:14–25 notes, even those who claim to be "spiritual" recognize that there is a contrary "Law" working within their innermost self which subverts and contradicts their most noble, true, and good moral intentions. Thus our concrete choices often fail to embody that which affirms GOD, the good, and Abundant LIFE. Nevertheless the gift of GOD to us is HOPE, and such HOPE enables morally imperfect human beings to make better, more LIFE-affirming choices than is possible without HOPE. In XODUS I would say that HOPE becomes revolutionary in our lives because we slowly learn to choose and decide in ways that continually reaffirm the goodness of the Creation, the GOD who created it, and the LIFE which animates all that IS.

The problem that XODUS Revolutionary HOPE addresses is the paucity of LIFE in most apocalyptic eschatology. When our eschatological imagination is filled with images of torture, defilement, and loss, we are left only with an impoverished understanding of hope. Such enervated eschatological hope desires a God to come back and set things aright which have been on the long sliding-slope of decline, decay, and corruption. Embracing such a universe is easy for many of the oppressed who are believers because it preserves the goodness of GOD while explaining the apparent lack of power such a Divinity must have in actually transforming the injustices that press in and destroy dreams. XODUS Revolutionary HOPE insists that LIFE is NOW, change begins NOW, and NOW is the time for action to be taken.

This NOW is not impatient but is determined. Such a NOW affirms, in standard academic language, the *realized* aspect of eschatology, namely, that GOD has already broken the powers of injustice which threaten LIFE in the good Cosmos. While there are elements of injustice, lies, and domination which continue to reign in our sociopolitical and economic reality, theirs is not the final word or ultimate agency. The power to give LIFE and take it away is not in the hands of those who pollute the earth, nor in the hands of misguided despots and tyrants, be they gang members or members of the Congress. The power to control the distribution of capital and its goods is insignificant, in the moral and cosmic scheme of things, in comparison to the power of LIFE which is GOD's and GOD's alone. In GOD's NOW we respond to the energy of goodness imprinted in every leaf, rock, tree, raindrop, snowstorm, and earthquake. LIFE is present, and we must attune our moral choices and lifestyles to LIFE's call. The future and the past are enfolded in GOD's NOW; therefore our attention is drawn to the fullness and primacy of the present because it is only in this present moment that we choose.

It is in the NOW that our moral choices and decisions effect any kind of future.

J. Deotis Roberts's *Liberation and Reconciliation* rightly notes that it is only in the *realized eschatology of the present* that most Black Christians find any concrete hope in which to live. Roberts defines realized eschatology as "the manifestation of the will of God in the present — abstractly as social justice and concretely as goods and services to 'humanize' life."[1] James Cone's groundbreaking *Black Theology and Black Power* roundly criticized the corrupting infestation of otherworldliness into the preaching and hopes of Black folk.[2] For Cone the crucial contribution of Black theology to the entire theological enterprise was in its insistence that "genuine biblical faith relates eschatology to history.... It is only because of what God has done and is now doing that we can speak meaningfully of the future."[3] Both Roberts and Cone condemn eschatologies whose emphasis on an afterlife of rewards for suffering reinforces sociopolitical passivity in this present sphere. Yet Roberts is more willing to speak about such theological symbols as "eternal life," "heaven," and "hell" than is Cone. For the early Cone these traditional symbols typifying eschatological imagination subvert concrete sociopolitical praxis. Instead Cone calls on a view of the future as a "means of making him [people] dis-satisfied with the present."[4] Cone embraces a sociopolitical *this-worldly* eschatology as that which goads us out of the status quo and urges us into transformative activities.

XODUS emphasis on the necessary Revolution in psychocultural values and spiritual insights must necessarily embrace a this-worldly eschatology because to do otherwise is to surrender to a spirituality of political quietism. In the 1990s, thus far, we are experiencing a continuation of the sociopolitical doldrums which have afflicted the spirituality of Black churches since the early 1970s. Not able to truly embrace a Black Theology which mediated both legitimate aspirations for economic-political Black Power and the deep resources of SPIRIT-inspired praise and worship traditions as developed since the time of slavery, Black churches have not been able to mount the sustained level of organized resistance to oppression which we mounted in the late 1950s and 1960s. Now, having found that the "taste" of relative social "acceptance" is sweet, many Black churches have opted to continue a SPIRIT-inspired worship experience which does not lead the members to feel any social responsibility whatsoever. In any Black church in the USA on any given Sunday the words are solemnly intoned that we "ought to pray for the young people" who are typified as drug-dealing, sex-crazed, irresponsible, and misdirected! The "young people," however, in the view of this XODUS writer, are not very far off the mark when they see their home churches as more interested in surviving than in helping the community to thrive. Sweet songs about "heaven" as the place where we all want to be (BeBe and CeCe Winans's song) and God's love as "addictive" rather than transforming deepen the social disengagement of Black churches. Although there has not been a full-scale revival of the billowy AFRO hairstyles of the 1960s, perhaps we ought to listen to the challenging words of the late 1960s James Cone when he cried out that Black people did not need an otherworldly eschatology or faith because such a faith anesthetizes us to the pain of oppression rather than awakening us to the possibilities of radical sociopolitical and economic transformation.

Am I being too hard on Black churches? It is true that many of even the smallest of local storefront congregations are attempting to draw young people "away from the sins of the world." I also recognize that Black churches cannot be blamed for four hundred years of economic underdevelopment and discriminatory practices which blocked access to certain privileged jobs. No, it is not the sole responsibility of Black churches to transform the injustices of the USA. White Corporate America *and* White churches must find ways to transform the inhumane mores and value systems of their capitalist members in concert with the host of other peoples (Latino, Asian, and Native) if genuine change is to occur.

Make no mistake about it, XODUS has no grand delusions that Black churches can do all that is necessary to help Black folk! The task of XODUS theology and ethics, however, is to help US find ways to take responsibility for US whether or not THEY are willing to be in solidarity with us. Such a task focuses both criticism and praise on *our* resources, prevents us from degenerating into victimized beggars, and enables a new sense of self-respect to arise from the ashes of both failed pseudo-liberalism on one side and callous neo-conservatism on the other. XODUS brokers no room for pity, only for recognizing the transformative possibilities of the NOW in which, truly, "all things are possible." In understanding the pressing threat of an imprisoned Black manhood and a disheartened Black womanhood we cannot wait for educative strategies to open up Euro-consciousness, we cannot afford the luxury of abstracted dialogues about "race issues," nor can we endure another round of "Blue-Ribbon" commissions to "study the problem" for the umpteenth time! A community which can actually see its End is a desperate community, and that community is US. On the other hand, if the clinging and cringing horror of possible annihilation is the only aspect of our NOW, then we preclude participating in the liberating energies of HOPE. Such a HOPE cannot come from a fixed gaze upon the problem without emptying itself of other considerations. *Rather, HOPE arises from a relationship with the GOD of Scriptures,* the GOD of Israel, Abraham, Sarah, Moses, Zipporah, and Hagar. This GOD is the ONE that we claim to experience through following Jesus the Christ. For the early Cone hope is a practical reality embedded in actual events in this world.[5] HOPE, in XODUS, cannot be tied to the empirical and observable facts of this world, but must arise from the eternal and everlasting reservoirs of SPIRIT which no human being can manufacture.

Roberts understands this aspect of XODUS eschatology, the *quality* of LIFE in all of its fullness and power. His eschatological reflections note that the "eternal life" so often referred to in New Testament Scriptures is an ongoing *experience* of being "with the Lord." Quoting the Pauline reference in Philippians 1:21–23, Roberts notes that believers experience this *timelessness yet duration whether they are physically alive or not.* In XODUS eschatology I would broaden this notion to say that the *experience of GOD's LIFE within us is one of spiritual transport so intense that being "with" GOD and "in" GOD are no longer merely intellectual conceptions.* The element of mysticism is intentional, for one could not speak of SPIRIT-filled existence without the unitive element of mysticism. The "I" remains intact, the self is not "absorbed" but is brought into such a heightened state of contact with the Fullness of LIFE that is GOD that the term "I" no longer means a singular atomized reality. To be "me" in LIFE is to be in Community with the Divine Community/Trinity of SPIRIT/Mother-Father-Son. So the NOW not only is a space of infinite transformative possibilities; it is also the Divinely created SPACE in which autonomous selves become Community with the Divine Community/Trinity.

Reversals

But many that are first will be last, and the last first. (Mark 10:31)

In the final Age Jesus assures His disciples that their leaving everything to follow Him will have the reward of witnessing a Grand Reversal. The rich shall be the ones least likely to be favored in the "age to come," as will those who have clung to their material comforts, privilege, and status. This Reversal of fortune, wherein those previously favored by the value patterns of "the world," will find themselves in "the back of the bus" (to use an old Civil-Rights-based expression). Jesus Himself will exemplify this Reversal as well, no longer the bloodied "lamb of GOD" slain for the "sins of the world" on a criminal's torture-cross. The Second-Coming

Jesus will be a Warrior-Lamb and Horse-Rider wading through the blood of the Armageddon slaughtered millions. Such imagery had a powerful effect on the bruised dignity and torn bodies of African slaves. They composed beautiful spirituals to celebrate what they perceived would be their exalted place next to Jesus in this Final Coming:

> Great day! Great day the righteous marching.
> Great day! God's gonna build up Zion's walls.

They cried out for Jesus to come down and "fix things" for them. For the slaves Jesus was ever-present, taking account of their actions. They prayed that He would come quickly so that they might receive a "crown" for all that they had endured:

> Come down, come down, my Lord, come down,
> My Lord's a-writin' all de time;
> And take me up to wear the crown,
> My Lord's a-writin' all de time.[6]

Reversal is a principle of GOD's disruption of human convention which the Bible cites as far back as GOD favoring the younger son Abel over the elder Cain (Gen. 4). The conventional patriarchal arrangement of fathers granting older sons all of the privileges and wealth of the clan was broken up again in the various twists and turns in the relationship between elder son, Esau, his father Isaac's favorite, and the chosen son, Jacob (who became Israel), favored by his mother, Rebekah (Gen. 27–28). Even Jacob's expectations, however, are disrupted by GOD's agenda when he is tricked into marrying the eldest daughter, Leah, by his crafty uncle Laban (Gen. 29), only to find that after working for *his* choice, Rachel, for another seven years, GOD's favor (indicated by "the opening of the womb" in bearing children) belongs to Leah the unfavored wife! Conventions remain contested in the next generation in the amazing Joseph narrative (Gen. 37–50). The richly detailed account of fraternal jealousy, with his elder brothers selling Joseph into slavery, the sexual intrigue and false accusations of his master Potiphar's wife, Joseph's eventual ascension to power based on his gift of dream discernment, and the complicated chain of events surrounding the famine and reunion of the Israel family stands out as one of the most interesting accounts of GOD's principle of Reversal in the Hebrew Bible.

It is in this aspect of eschatology that XODUS can take up the reigning political symbol of Jesus' preaching, the Kingdom, or Reign, of GOD. The Reign of GOD is both here and NOW, and Not Yet. It *is* in the hearts of believers — albeit in various degrees of intensity. It *is yet to be* in the sociopolitical and economic realms which severely impact the individual lives of Christians. The Reign of God is the final consummate embodiment of GOD, GOD anchored in the vicissitudes of history. Yet one cannot truly examine such a symbol unless one understands that the Reign of GOD touches individuals in the NOW even as it inspires both individuals and groups to work toward a realization of GOD's Reign in sociopolitical and economic structures. It is a consummate Reversal of human political ambitions, self-serving aspirations, and inventive manipulation to attain power. Power, in the Reign of GOD, flows from the source of all powers. Such power is not a neutral tool useful for control and is lethal in the hands of a human tyrant. In GOD's REIGN power is morally Good because GOD *is* POWER in its ultimate sense, and therefore POWER is wielded only in its most healing and mending efficacy.

Can the Reign of GOD occur in the life of those who do not "believe" in Jesus? If GOD is truly GOD, then it is possible, even if we cannot find supporting Christian scriptural references, because the Fullness of LIFE that is GOD's cannot be contained in any one particular doctrine of theism or religion. In the eschaton which XODUS envisions the particularities of religion, dogma, and creed will be left behind in the blazing GLORY and LIFE that is GOD. If the Surprise of GOD is GOD's ability to Reverse our conventional understandings, then perhaps the most surprising Reversal will be when all the followers of Jesus find that heaven is filled with Moslems, Jews, Buddhists, Hindus, and adherents to many other forms of belief which our dogmas insistently refused to include as worthy of such an honor! Likewise, as Matthew 25:31–46, the Sheep and Goats parable, reveals, the Reign of GOD involves far more than adherence to proper doctrines, but is judged on one's practices of compassion to the stranger, prisoner, sick, homeless, and hungry.

Reversal is a prophetic summons meant to jar and subvert the status quo assumptions of an easy salvation that followers of Jesus cling to. Its primary audience is the Christian, not the non-Christian! We ought to be forewarned and careful therefore not to undo the discomforting knot of Judgment which GOD places around our gold-encrusted necks. Eschatology is not a theology for those "at ease in Zion," but awakens all of us to the enormous ethical responsibilities for social justice and political compassion GOD has called us to incarnate. XODUS eschatology embraces Reversal in fear and trembling, recognizing that by embracing such an unrestrainable, irresistible theo-ethical principle, we embrace GOD's right to pass judgment on *all*, even ourselves. Thus none can stand up in self-righteousness, no not one.

XODUS Basepoints for Eschatological Transformation

- *Eschatology must be a relevant and wholistic response to possible futures.*

In a very real way all of the theology and ethics in *My Sister, My Brother* has been eschatological, because all of our individual and joint reflections have arisen as a relevant response to the possibility of an END to a pan-African future. Future will not be a healthy possibility if things continue along the same pathways as they are following right now. The inertia of history precludes a relevant and wholistic response to the many sets of overlapping crises facing Afrikans in relationship to our sociopolitical vitality, economic interdependence, environmental health, and ability to take an active place on the global stage of agency. XODUS eschatology lifts up the quality of *relevance* as an appropriate norm of action, noting that envisioning otherworldly futures which disengage our energies from changing that which can be changed in *this* world must always be condemned as *sinful* spirituality, whether it conforms to traditionally "conservative" or to "liberal" theological tendencies.

In XODUS the need to move beyond convenient categories of socio-political response which shape the current political climate of the United States of America has reached its XO-KAIROTIC MOMENT. By XO-KAIROTIC MOMENT, I mean that there are historic moments in which the JOURNEY which is XODUS comes into full synchronicity with the intention of GOD in the DIVINE revolutionary and transformative INTENT to change human cultural/socio-political and economic structures away from death-dealing practices into LIFE-affirming praxis. These moments in which the *Zeitgeist* (the German term G. W. F. Hegel used to describe the "spirit of the time") also is in conformity with the SPIRIT's intention Paul Tillich called the *Kairos*, that moment in which GOD's transformative event intersected with the *chronos* of human time. Martin Luther King interpreted the Freedom Struggle as a Kairos moment for the United States. Black and Afrikaaner church leaders and theologians joined together in the 1980s to forge a theological document protesting the theologically legitimated injustice of South African apartheid, calling it the *Kairos Document*. In XODUS perception, after the Rebellion/Wake-Up Call/Riot of April 1992 in Los Angeles we are living in the discomforting historic juncture of an XO-KAIROTIC MOMENT. In this XO-KAIROTIC MOMENT the forces of retrenchment, division, and anti-African concern sometimes wear the face of a "Black" Supreme Court Associate Justice whose judicial record follows in goose step the policies of those who never wanted to understand what it meant to grow up "Black" and poor in the United States. It is a Moment in which the forces of concern for concrete change in our social and ecological policies are in retreat nationally, while the local FOLK look on with dismay and disgust. In this XO-KAIROTIC MOMENT the possibilities of genuine multiculturalism and just interaction between the many various cultures and ethnic groups that comprise the USA and the globe have been systematically devalued by the shallow rhetoric of "PC" (political correctness) critique and the political reaffirmation of Euro-male "right to lead" made concrete in the virtually "all White" face of the so-called "Republican revolution" of November 1994.

Those of us who embrace the transformative Revolutionary HOPE of this XO-KAIROTIC MOMENT realize that the END we seek is *wholistic*. We cannot allow the political expediency which uses welfare programs like Aid for Families with Dependent Children as a convenient scapegoat for middle-class frustration with a shrinking economy and lower quality of life. The AFDC comprises less than 3 percent of the national budget, yet so-called "welfare reform" would gut such a program in the name of "budgetary constraints" and "less government," with no sense of the necessary solidarity of concern for all children which a genuinely healthy society must demonstrate. In the awareness that comprises the conflation of XODUS and KAIROS, the people of GOD will demand of ourselves an attitude different from that which gushes out of politicians; we will demand an attitude which reverences all policies which aid the poor and clean up the planet as a vital aspect of GOD's NOW. There will be no future if the poor are discarded because the wrath of GOD will be visited upon those who forget to honor the poor, according to numerous passages from the Hebrew and Christian portions of the Bible. Spouting "family values" without demonstrating a willingness to help "the least of these" results in eternal damnation, according to Matthew 25. Thus XO-KAIROTIC MOMENT consciousness insists that the genuine People of GOD, whatever their particular doctrinal affiliation, must arise and act as agents of GOD's NOW because it is time. We must not allow the forces which have no care for concrete people or the health of the planet to change just policies and laws which lift up concern for the poor and the planet as the proper object of governmental concern. Even if we are a minority within a minority, our voices and our power arise from GOD's NOW and not numbers. Our power arises from the moral rightness and relevancy of our cause and not that we repeat the "popular" opinions of those who have no awareness of the XODUS or of GOD's Kairotic NOW.

- *Eschatology must proclaim the DIVINE "oughts" of healing, participation, and consummation for the entire created order.*

Black males and females cannot participate effectively in the affairs of this world if our sense of self is not healed, and such healing is intimately related to the DIVINE consummation intended for the entire created order. XODUS JOURNEYing emerges from GOD's empowering NOW, that sacred psychocultural SPACE of inner healing and recovery of self. In XODUS eschatology the healing of the poor and the oppressed cannot be divorced from the consummatory inertia of GOD's will for the healing and restitution of the entire creation. Healing is a "mending of the world," or *tikkun olam* in Hebrew. This potent phrase in Hebrew is both a theological tenet and a normative ethical imperative of Jewish Scriptures and moral philosophy.[7] As Scripture proclaims GOD's holy intention to mend that in creation which has been rent asunder by neglect, abuse, and violence, so we who JOURNEY in XODUS join with the DIVINE intention. This Intention is realized in the NOW of GOD by proclaiming healing, participation, and the consummation of the entire created order (nature, humanity, the cosmos) as the essential will of GOD for humanity. This will is announced through a series of ethical imperatives concerning proper relationship of human beings with each other, humanity with the natural environment, and the interaction of the world of SPIRIT with that of "flesh." Healing, participation, and consummation cannot take place without understanding the depth of interaction entailed in the above relationships.

- *Eschatological "consummation" is not a finished event but an ongoing series of choices and decisions arising in GOD's NOW.*

In keeping with the processive imagery of JOURNEY which typifies XODUS, our eschatological reflections note that the consummation of GOD's will in history is not a single cataclysmic event. GOD is always creating new heavens and earths. The END for one aeon always seems to be the birthing ground of a new aeon on grace. There is GLORY, not in the dramatic explosive fire of Armageddon-inspired apocalyptic imagery, but in the processive revealing (Apocalypses) of the NOW as it interacts in XO-KAIROTIC MOMENTUM. Teilhard de Chardin envisaged a cosmic movement toward an "Omega Point" fullness of GOD. The JOURNEY is both the means toward achieving consummation of GLORY and the END in and of itself.

In Evans's language this processive function of eschatology enables us to perceive every social justice accomplishment as penultimate to the ultimate and perfect Reign of God.[8] Evans discerns that this ability to see each social accomplishment as partial, confined by historical ironies, and subverted by human moral failures is *the* key distinction between Christian and secular revolutionaries. As such the processive and perfecting momentum of eschatology prevents Christians from "sacralizing any human social order."[9] Evans understands Christian eschatology as having this *relativizing function* because of the inner-ethical demand for perfection which only the consummation of GOD's Reign on earth (in the future) could satisfy.

Does an XODUS understanding of the processive nature of eschatology agree with Evans? While one certainly resonates with Evans's ability to accurately describe the *traditional* understanding of eschatological processive perfection, his rhetoric does not safeguard against the tendency to put aside, explain away, or just plain succumb to current states of injustice while proclaiming that "everything's gonna be all right" in the "not yet, by-and-by-pie-in-the-sky Kingdom" perfection of GOD. The suffering and abused cannot "wait" until some future "then"; they need an in-breaking Act of GOD in the NOW of eschatological fervor.

Too often such language seeks to refine and accurately distinguish between the all-too-human inadequacies of our grantedly penultimate socioethical accomplishments and the more abstract and absolutely idealized perfection of GOD. Of course GOD's Reign will be spiritually, politically, economically, and psychologically PERFECT! XODUS has no doubt that such is true, but affirming the *theological* truth of such a statement does not affirm the gradual in-breaking manifestations of GOD's GLORY in the NOW. People have needs which ought to be met now, not "then," and the Followers of Jesus err grievously in placing too much emphasis on the abstracted penultimacy of our good actions. For the hungry "penultimate" food in their stomachs satisfies, for the naked "penultimate" clothing covers nakedness, and neither questions whether the "ultimate" food and clothing of GOD's eventual consummate REIGN would satisfy their needs any more completely. In XODUS we agree with Evans that one ought never to sacralize any particular sociopolitical social "order," but naming even the most penultimate in-breaking of GOD's NOW certainly is not sinful either.

Evans goes on to say that the other side of eschatological process reveals that holding on to this ultimate vision of GOD's perfect REIGN prevents our "momentary failures from becoming permanent defeats."[10] He calls this the "vision of hope" which rescues us from being overwhelmed by disappointment. I agree. In XODUS eschatology I would call this *resistance to despair the Power of Revolutionary HOPE*. Revolutionary HOPE provides refreshment to the weary and discouraged Traveler whose strivings for transformation on the contradictory pathways of oppressed life seem to have reached an impasse which could crush courage. To JOURNEY toward GOD's future and envision the consummation of GLORY which is GOD's REIGN does indeed lift those who have fainted and refresh those whose souls have grown parched by the scorching furnace of adversity. Nevertheless, the JOURNEY opens up to our eyes ever new and different understandings of what that "Promised Land" in which GOD REIGNS will be like. When Black Folk began our long march to freedom we thought that the Promised Land looked like freedom from slavery, and a little later social acceptance. Recently we believed that the Promised Land consisted of a truly integrated society in which "genuine intergroup interpersonal power is shared."[11] Our understandings of the "Promised Land" are ever concrete, yet always transforming under the ongoing widening processes of cultural expansion and the march of history. So while we use the ancient Hebrew expression of GOD's consummate promise to the children of Israel, its substantive content constantly evolves as we do.

- *The telos of XODUS eschatology is GOD's "new heaven and new earth."*

Eschatology is telic; it moves toward a goal. Theologically we understand that goal to be the Reign of GOD which concretely manifests the GLORY of GOD in its consummate, unrestrained, and pure perfection. In Revelation 21–22 this goal is described in the ultimate symbols of "a new heaven and a new earth." Yet as was stated in the paragraph above, we fill these symbols of "new heaven" and "new earth" with our particular cultural understandings of what such perfection might entail. In order not to appear to be affirming an unbridled cultural relativism, XODUS conceptuality lifts up the notion that this "new heaven and new earth" will embody the MORE which is GOD's "ultimate" surprise! If we embrace the eschatological consummation as a goal which is really MORE than all we have the power to express, we are better able to understand all of the dazzling imagery of precious stones and jewelry, size, and grandeur which the SEER John uses to describe the "New Jerusalem." Yet the Bible ends with this symbol of a GOD-redeemed CITY, a *Community in which the DIVINE, humanity, the earth, and the heavens are united into a ONEness* beyond all description.

Such a *telos* ought to aid us in the XODUS struggle to hold together the concerns of real flesh-and-blood human beings of Afrikan, Native, and other backgrounds with eco-justice issues. In the New Jerusalem the waters are purified by the "river of the water of life" which flows from GOD (Rev. 22:1). In the New Jerusalem the air is purified by the GLORY of GOD which *is* its light. Likewise, the socioethical norms of healing, participation, and consummation are embodied in the simple imagery of all peoples going in and out of the CITY eternally because "its gates [facing all the compass directions and thus indicating that *all* kinds of peoples are welcomed] will never be shut" (Rev. 21:25).

In the consummation which is this New Jerusalem, the Perfect CITY, Revolutionary HOPE will become reality. No longer will there be any need for a "vision" of what things "might be" because the distinction between the future lure of "what ought to be" and the present "is" will be superseded and sublated into ONE.

In XODUS we can look forward to such an END in faith and gain courage to continue on the JOURNEY. XODUS Travelers cannot allow ourselves the luxury of pausing on such Elysian Fields of theological abstraction for too long. The city Streetz are still crying out "Injustice!" They are still wet with the blood of our young men and stained with the tears of our women. We are not healed. We need GOD's in-breaking NOW, and right now, not "then." Thus the rawness of unfinished, sin-tarnished reality calls us back, and we must re-turn with an Act of GOD's NOW, lest the future be swallowed up and the people perish.

Notes

1. J. Deotis Roberts, *Liberation and Reconciliation*, 2d ed. (Maryknoll, N.Y.: Orbis Books, 1994), 83.

2. James Cone, *Black Theology and Black Power* (Minneapolis: Seabury Press, 1969), 121.

3. Ibid., 126.

4. Ibid.

5. Ibid., 127.

6. Cited in Gayraud Wilmore, *Last Things First* (Philadelphia: Westminster, 1982), 77–78.

7. I am thinking particularly of Emil Fackenheim, *To Mend the World: Foundations of Post-Holocaust Jewish Thought* (Bloomington: Indiana University Press, 1994).

8. James Evans, Jr., *We Have Been Believers* (Minneapolis: Fortress, 1992), 152.

9. Ibid., 152–53.

10. Ibid., 153.

11. Dr. King often used this expression as a way of defining the true meaning of "integration" beyond the social policies which developed around the term.

Seventeen _____

Dust to Dust,
Spirit to Spirit

A Womanist Eschatology

SCHATOLOGICALLY, Jesus' most powerful saying for many Americans is "the Kingdom of God is at hand." Indeed some sense of the Kingdom of God on earth is at the heart of what drew Puritans to the "new world," as they thought of it, in the seventeenth century. America was seen as a kind of promised land with its lush forests and landscape in contrast to the overpopulated cities of Europe. While there were already native peoples living in North America and the land was in no sense empty, there seemed to be room for everyone. The eventual cost to the Native Americans is clear in hindsight, but the Puritans did not consider that their ambivalent understanding of the "Indians" sometimes as friendly, sometimes as "savage," but always as heathens, would contribute to notions of the dispensability and eventual genocide of entire peoples. On the one hand, the notion of America as a kind of promised land where God's Kingdom could be established on earth as in heaven was full of hope and promise for humanity. On the other hand, it was full of false, self-serving hopes and promises that would contribute to justifications for White domination of the land and its laws. Such is the risk involved in efforts to realize God's Kingdom on earth. To whom is the land promised? To whom are freedom and justice promised? Is the land in this world or the next? Whatever our race and ethnicity as Christians these are the questions we must ask. African Americans, whether womanist, XODUS, or neither of these, must not only criticize the errors of our historical oppressors but learn from them.

As I contemplate the concept of the Reign of God, I find it very important to examine both the promises and the dangers of what it means to claim to work in harmony with God to usher in that reign on earth. Visions are both powerful and fragile. They can be insightful or misleading, depending on the vision and how it is interpreted. Whether the Kingdom of God is envisioned in this life or the next, the results of the vision can be helpful or dangerous, depending on the level of discernment, testing, and accountability to others. Apocalyptic visions sometimes turn in on believers in self-fulfilling prophecy by their own hands. David Koresh and Jim Jones, with their apocalyptic leadership into "holy" suicide, most would agree, are examples of leaders who have taken the authority of their personal visions to a fatal extreme.

There are other instances where visions of the Kingdom of God are more profane and violent than they first appear to those who believe in them and feel included in them. Theological visions, for example, that blame the poor for their own poverty, assuming it is a result of sin, are problematic. Racialized notions of slave owners' spiritual superiority to their slaves and the rightfulness of their ownership of people of darker hue are equally problematic. The eschatological vision of James Cone's early writings was not as inclusive in its liberative aim as his later work, which recognizes the necessity of the spiritual and political liberation of an entire community of women and men. Jacquelyn Grant's early work presented a strong challenge to Black male liberation theologians to expand their understanding of liberation to include the sin of sexism and equality for women in church and society as a form of social salvation. Cone subsequently became more inclusive in his theology and charged the Black church and other Black theologians to do the same. J. Deotis Roberts, likewise, has become more inclusive in his later work as have younger Black liberation theologians like Dwight Hopkins and XODUS theologian Garth KASIMU Baker-Fletcher. And yet the work of the churches in this area is far from complete, and barely getting started, as womanist Emilie Townes points out in her book *In a Blaze of Glory*.

For Townes, "the horizon a womanist ethic works toward is a society that respects the rights and humanity of all peoples and nature. . . . It is a society that is uncompromisingly rooted in justice and fueled by people who use their hope to construct and enact meaningful and significant social change."[1] In her book *In a Blaze of Glory,* she fleshes out this understanding of a just society that is respectful of the humanity of all peoples and nature by tying in the ecological problem of environmental racism with the problems of socioeconomic racism.

Heaven and Earth

For Christians the promise of God's Kingdom, or Reign, stands at the center of personal and social salvation. For those who explore the meaning of Christian Scriptures for families, communities, and societies, the promise of God's Kingdom involves more than individual salvation; it involves social salvation. Eschatology — the study of "the last things" or "the fullness of time" — is concerned with the realization of God's Reign on earth as in heaven. "The Kingdom of God is at hand." The Kingdom of God was at the heart of the Christian message for nineteenth-century American reformers across racial lines, reformers committed to realizing salvation in the social sphere as well as the personal sphere. Walter Rauschenbusch, in his *Theology for the Social Gospel*, places it at the center of Christian faith and theology. The significance of Jesus for Rauschenbusch was his role in ushering in the Kingdom of God and transforming not only the world but God's feeling for the world so that God suffered with it. The calling of the church in his view was to follow Jesus' example by preaching a gospel that improved society.[2] Although *A Theology for the Social Gospel* was published in 1917, it was a systematic exposition of ideas and beliefs that had characterized social gospel thought in nineteenth-century and early twentieth-century America.

While Rauschenbusch, Washington Gladden, and Lyman Abbott are among the names most often cited in discussions on social gospel theology, Ronald White points out that there were numerous African American social gospel leaders: Francis Grimké, W. E. B. Du Bois, Ida B. Wells-Barnett, Anna Julia Cooper.[3] James Washington further observes that Black Americans were among the progenitors of social gospel thought and movement.[4] The distinctive contribution they provided the movement was criticism of racism as well as classism. For Anna Cooper and Ida B. Wells-Barnett, equal rights for women were of concern as well. At the heart of such theological thought was an interpretation of the gospel of Jesus as promising not only individual salvation but social salvation — a moral transformation of entire societies.

While the eschatological visions of thinkers like Walter Rauschenbusch, W. E. B. Du Bois, and Anna Cooper were anthropocentric, today theologians must ponder the meaning of the Reign of God not only for humanity but for all of creation. It has to do with the fulfillment of God's vision for the entire cosmos. All of creation is redeemed — delivered from evil, oppressive, and corrupting forces — and brought into healing and wholeness by that which is the strength of life and transforms fear of evil into faith and hope.

Eschatology involves the transformation of society and all creation with it from what it is to what it ought to be according to God's vision for the world. As Psalm 27 and the spiritual "The Lord Is My Light and My

Salvation" indicate, such transformation does not necessarily mean that evildoers are transformed into doers of good. But rather, regardless of the presence of evil in human existence, believers are transformed by the empowering strength of God so that they no longer live in fear. One then has the capacity for the kind of womanist audacity and courage that Alice Walker refers to in *In Search of Our Mothers' Gardens.*[5] Such courage is evidenced in the history of African American women by freedom fighters like Harriet Tubman, Sojourner Truth, members of the Black Women's Club movement of the late nineteenth century, and women's organizations in Black churches. Given such courage there is hope not only for personal transformation in the life of the believer but for social transformation as believers press on with the strength of God for the betterment of society.

Psalm 27 speaks of eschatological hope and promise in God as the strength of life who sustains not only one's self, but the universe. In the end, it is this God that will prevail. For womanists, eschatology does not have to do with the "last things" or "end time" in any far off, abstract, otherworldly sense. Rather, eschatological hope and envisionment have to do with the daily moment-by-moment business of living. The reign of God's strength for life is an ever-present reality. The hereafter is in the here and now. We live into it in our everyday acts. The life that the spiritual refers to is key. That God is the strength of one's life indicates God's presence in human history. Not only is God present, but God's presence is spiritually empowering. God has a saving, strengthening presence in human life and as the light of life provides new vision for transforming the life of all creation from a situation of illness to a situation of wholeness. This also has eschatological ramifications, since God as the strength of life is not only in and with creation, but transcends it and exists beyond history. God as the strength of life is the power of life. Given such power, whom should one fear? Ultimately, that which threatens life is limited in contrast to that which is the source and power of life. That which is the very strength of life transforms fear into faith, salvation, and hope, dreams deferred into real possibilities.

Black women and men can transform present existence by actively remembering and practicing the prophetic, generative wisdom of the ancestors, particularly the greatest of our ancestors: Jesus. Such transformative activity is salvific, communal, and for Christian womanists is based in the God of Jethro, Moses, Zipporah, and Jesus. For womanists, as for so many African American women and men historically, the words "the Kingdom of God is at hand" have profound meaning for how we live our lives on a daily basis in our present existence. The "hereafter" is not so far off. As Anna Julia Cooper put it, it is close enough that we must "live into it."

Womanist theology considers the location of eternity. Is it in those sacred and profane places called heaven and hell in traditional Christian thought? If so, the question of the location of eternity remains unanswered. Where are heaven and hell? Where is the Reign of God? Are there places of salvation and damnation beyond this earth? Black liberation theologians like James Cone and J. Deotis Roberts emphasize that African Americans historically have been concerned about heaven and hell on earth. On the other hand there certainly have been African Americans who ascribed to a "sweet by and by" concept of salvation, as echoed by Celie in Alice Walker's *The Color Purple* and in James Baldwin's *Go Tell It on the Mountain.* These authors present the problem of unhealthy images of a life beyond this present one which encourage the oppressed to accept their oppression. In such worldviews, religion becomes Marx's "opiate" that seduces exploited workers into apathy about their exploitation.

Beyond the concrete symbolizations of heaven and hell in Black liberation and social gospel theologies or the ethereal, utterly transcendent symbolizations of heaven in sweet-by-and-by religious belief, are worldviews based in traditional African and Native American belief systems. In these worldviews the afterlife is transcendent and immanent. It is now and not yet, much as Christians have traditionally described the Reign of God. Not only is it now and not yet; it is past and it is present. The "hereafter" or eternity is not only in the future but in the past. It includes the ancestors and those of the present and future who will be future ancestors. It is indeed a fullness of time in which past, present, and future coexist and are held together. The world of the Spirit is ever present. God is Spirit, the resurrected Jesus is Spirit, the Holy Spirit is Spirit, we human beings are flesh and spirit, and all of creation is matter and spirit. We humans, along with the rest of creation, belong to Spirit itself. We are within it and it is within us. Interrelated with that which is beyond time, we participate in all times and no time in this time from moment to moment. I will say more about this later. First I want to reflect on the understanding of heaven and hell as concrete locations in the thought of Anna Julia Cooper's Black feminist social gospel theology, because it is in keeping with a very strong strand of eschatological understandings in African American history since the nineteenth century. It is older than Black liberation theology and like other Black social gospel theological perspectives of her era forms part of the cultural and religious soil from which it emerges.

Living into Eternity

As I was growing up, the favorite preachment of my grandfather Taylor Baker, Sr., was that "heaven and hell is right here on this earth." He had different ways of coming around to this climactic statement at different times, but that was always the crux of his theological teaching. Sometimes it was a Sunday sermon that sparked this regular statement. Other times it was a Jehovah's Witness who had come by to talk about the last days that fired him up to remind the entire family that heaven and hell were not in some far off place. We were all taught that it is what we do in this life that determines whether we live in heaven or hell. Grandpa Baker is not a preacher or pastor of a church. He is a barber. But anyone who knows anything about neighborhood barbers in Black culture knows they are pretty close to being preachers and ministers in their own right! There are some who actually preach at church on Sundays and preach in shops as barbers during the week. They hear a lot, see a lot, think a lot, and gain quite a bit of wisdom which they pass on. Grandpa was a trustee in the church and involved in the church's leadership. He has had years of experience in church service and work in the community. Like James Cone he is a product of the A.M.E. Church. While he became United Methodist later on in life, it is the independence of the A.M.E. Church, a Black independent church, that he cites as an example of Black spiritual and social empowerment.

Reading the Black liberation theology of James Cone and the Black Christology of Albert Cleage at Harvard, I found that Grandpa Baker was preaching the theology of a multitude of Black Americans. A decade later, by the time I completed my doctoral studies, I learned that certain Black Americans had always believed and taught that heaven and hell are right here on this earth. The teaching I had grown up with on a daily basis and the preachments I still hear when I go back home are rooted in a historical tradition in Black religious thought. Historical figures like Frederick Douglass, Sojourner Truth, Francis Grimké, Anna Julia Cooper, Fannie Lou Hamer, and Martin Luther King, Jr., believed in a God, embodied in Jesus, who ushered in the Reign of God on earth. They envisioned this Reign of God as a Reign of justice, social equality, spiritual and political freedom. James Cone's symbolization of the Reign of God on earth is not at all the fad some of his critics have held it to be. To the contrary, such a concrete understanding of the Reign of God on earth echoes the historical understandings of certain ancestors. Anna Cooper insisted on a concrete understanding of the Reign of God in a poem entitled "The Answer":

> God — is not afar!
> The simple may know:
> The Hereafter is here;
> Eternity is now.
> And myself am Heaven or Hell.[6]

For Cooper, eternity, the hereafter, heaven and hell were not outside of human history and existence. They were present in persons and the moral choices they made. Heaven and hell were actual moral states of existence. Whether one lives into heaven or hell depends on whether one works in harmony with Jesus' gospel message of equality and freedom. For Cooper, this gospel message was like a germ or seed that Jesus the Nazarene planted in the soil of civilization. It is the responsibility of the church to lead humankind into a fuller realization of the gospel within civilization. By "civilization" Cooper had in mind the moral development of humankind in the social sphere, as well as in personal lives. In her view, existence beyond this one is real and "culturable":

> Yes, I believe there is existence beyond our present experience; that that existence is conscious and culturable; and that there is a noble work here and now in helping men [sic] live into it.[7]

We live into the hereafter. We cannot sit idly with folded hands, hoping for entry into a better life. We are not called to say like Walker's Celie before her redemption in *The Color Purple*, "This life soon be over. Heaven last always."[8] Like Cooper and the awakened Celie, we are called to arise from whatever slumber seduces us into inaction and act with God who is on the side of justice.[9] Existence beyond our present experience is not some dream-like state. It is conscious. It is not otherworldly. It is culturable in this life, and we human beings participate in making it a present reality and shaping it. Empowered by the delivering, freeing, healing, and redeeming gospel message of Jesus of Nazareth, we effect the positive possibilities of future existence by our moral actions in the here and now. The promises of heavenly well-being and abundant life require our ethical transformation in the present. The gain from believing in an existence beyond present existence is concrete and social.

Cooper's understanding of the "hereafter" involved development of the here and now by the present generation for the next generation. Far from Lutheran in her eschatological understanding, she argued for faith that works, moving humankind onward and into the hereafter. To help humankind live into the best possibilities for its development "is a noble" work, as she describes it. Such belief, she argued, was central to Jesus' message and ministry:

> Jesus believed in the infinite possibilities of an individual soul. His faith was a triumphant realization of the eternal development of the best in man [sic] — an optimistic vision of the human aptitude for endless expansion and perfectibility. This truth to him placed a sublime valuation on each individual sentiency — a value magnified infinitely by reason of its moral destiny. He could not lay hold of this truth and let pass an opportunity to lift men into nobler living and firmer building. He could not lay hold of this truth and allow his own benevolence to be narrowed and distorted by the trickeries of circumstance or the colorings of prejudices.[10]

Cooper's understanding of Jesus' teachings on salvation emphasizes the perfection of individual human souls and a positive valuation of each "individual sentiency." The destiny of each soul was immortal. Given such positive valuation of the sublimeness of every soul, Jesus refused to participate in color or caste prejudice. He extended the promise of salvation to humankind across circumstances of race, color, class, gender, or nationality. Infinite possibilities for developing the best in men and women were promised to the human race, not exclusively to a White race, Black race, Red race, or Brown race.

While she emphasized the development of individual souls, Cooper was ever the social activist. She placed responsibility for the well-being of the entire society on individuals working together for its betterment. It was the church's role to be a leader in this work, although she was well aware that historically it was full of members who "trampled the gospel" rather than worked toward its fulfillment. In spite of the church's human imperfections it was still the church's calling to work with God in fulfilling God's vision of freedom and equality. The improvement of society was the responsibility of Christ's church — all of those who believed in Jesus' altruism and God's message of freedom embodied in the life, words, and ministry of Jesus. It required working in harmony with God's message of freedom and equality, the germ of the gospel planted in the soil of human culture by Jesus Christ. Jesus, in Cooper's view, was at the forefront of the movement toward human fulfillment. She described Jesus as leading civilization forward the way a mother leads her toddling child:

> The quiet face of the Nazarene is ever seen a little way ahead, never too far to come down to touch the life of the lowest in days the

darkest, yet ever leading onward, still onward, the tottering childish feet of our strangely boastful civilization.[11]

There was not one "idea," "principle of action," or "progressive social force," she argued, "but was already mutely foreshadowed, or directly enjoined in that simple tale of a meek and lowly life."[12] Cooper's representation of Jesus in relation to eschatology speaks to the ministerial empowerment of Black women in two respects. First, her imagery of Jesus is parallel to her imagery of Black womanhood and motherhood. Just as Black mothers are vital elements in the regeneration of a particular race, Jesus is the vital element in the regeneration of civilization universally. In this respect, not only does Cooper sacralize Jesus as the Christ, but she also sacralizes Black women's bodies, hands, and hearts. The fulfillment of God's vision of freedom and equality for humanity is embodied in the work of Black women as far as the particular salvation of Black communities is concerned and in Jesus as far as salvation of the larger human civilization is concerned. Second, it is the life of Jesus, not his death, that is most important for Cooper. Present generations have hope for the future because of the legacy Jesus the Nazarene left in the past. This legacy is still unfolding. It is in the everyday living that Black women and humankind in general ought to place its energies, not in prospects of death. This life is good, valuable, and worth living.[13] Hope is not only in the future. Hope is in the present and in history as each moment lived in faith moves from future time to present time and past time.

The Fullness of Time, the End of Time

As I mentioned above, there are at least three strands of thought among African Americans regarding the intersection of present life with the Reign of God. One strand, represented by Cooper and James Cone, emphasizes a concrete understanding of the Reign of God. Another, criticized by writers like Alice Walker and James Baldwin, points to fulfillment in a life beyond present, concrete existence. Certain traditional African cosmologies, such as Bantu Muntu cosmology or Gullah understandings of West African cosmologies in North America, suggest a both/and understanding of a life beyond present existence as we know it that holds past, present, and future times together within a spiritual reality that is both immanent and transcendent. In Walker's novel *The Color Purple*, the weakness of Celie's early faith in existence beyond her present oppressive condition was that it was thoroughly otherworldly.

She accepted beatings and verbal abuse as her lot in life with the hope and expectation that she would find happiness after she died in a new, heavenly world.

Traditional African spirituality is wholistic in its understanding of time in relation to Spirit. Eternity is in the past, not simply in the future. It is also in the present, since the present becomes the past and the future becomes the present. As Nana Peazant reminds her son Eli in Julie Dash's acclaimed film *Daughters of the Dust*, about a Gullah, African American family in the Georgia/South Carolina Sea Islands, the womb and the ancestors are one. In other words, past, present, and future are one. They are not disconnected from each other. God, who is Spirit, transcends time. Moreover, to the extent that we human beings participate in Spirit, we participate in eternity with God. Ancestors participate in the eternity of God. The dying, the born, and the yet to be are not forgotten or unknown to Spirit. Process theologians like Marjorie Suchocki and John Cobb would say that we continue in the memory of God. Memory extends forward into the future, because everything is on a continuum in process. We continue in the memory of God's "antecedent" or "initial aim." "Memory" is one way of naming God's consciousness, God's feeling or knowing of all that is. This has to do with the eternity or *everlastingness* of God.

Nana Peazant's understanding of womb and ancestors as one is another way of naming such everlastingness in God. Her spirituality moves beyond debates about the location of God's Reign to insist on a both/and perspective. It affirms both concrete and "otherworldly" concepts of the world of the Spirit. The world of the Spirit and the Reign of God as Spirit is everywhere at all times. It transcends time and space, it is in time and space, and it is with time and space.

Dust to Dust, Spirit to Spirit

An adequate eschatology is one that envisions God as empowering Spirit who is the strength of all life in and outside of all time. God as empowering Spirit keeps humankind in harmony with the sacred in our everyday work through which we live into eternity. Its ultimate and eternal aim is the healing and wholeness of creation, not only the known creation but unknown and even future creations. The words of Nana Peazant, matriarchal character in *Daughters of the Dust*, refer to spiritual memory within that is ancient, belonging to ancestors and descendants, present time, future time, and past time:

Those in this grave, like those who're across the sea, they're with us. They're all the same. The ancestors and the womb are one. Call on your ancestors.... Let them guide you.... There's a thought... a recollection... something somebody remembers. We carry these memories inside of us. Do you believe that hundreds and hundreds of Africans brought here on this other side would forget everything they once knew? We don't know where the recollections come from. Sometimes we dream them. But we carry these memories inside of us.... I'm trying to teach you how to touch your own spirit. I'm fighting for my life, Eli, and I'm fighting for yours.[14]

Nana Peazant's words are grounded in an African worldview in which God as Spirit is in all of creation. There is great continuity between past, present, and future. Eternity transcends and coexists with all of these. The ancestors, or "old souls," like the saints of Christian faith, carry wisdom from the past that has meaning for the present and must be remembered to sustain present life.[15] Life continues beyond the temporal world we are all a part of, but this does not mean we can be irresponsible in the here and now. The memories we are called to carry of those who have gone before us remind us of who we are and whose we are. We are children of Dust and Spirit, earth creatures who carry within us the strengthening breath of life, Spirit itself. Those who have lived in the past continue to live in spirit. To touch one's own spirit is to be connected with the past, present, and future. It is to be connected to the creative, life-giving source of all that is. In addressing various crises in the lives of Black women, men, and children today, it is important to consider the ways in which we become disconnected from our own spirits and thereby disconnected from Spirit, the source and womb of life itself. There is a tendency to forget that there is something greater than our individual selves or communities within the very midst of us that can transform fear into hope, ignorance into the light of wisdom and knowledge, weakness into strength, and brokenness into salvation.

For Nana Peazant, spirit is so interrelated with dust that when her daughter Viola says to her, "We're going to be watching from heaven, Nana," she responds: "No! I'm not going to be watching from heaven while there's soil still here for me for planting."[16] On the one hand, Nana Peazant means that her children and grandchildren can stop thinking that she has any intention of dying soon. She believes she will live a long life and although they may be moving from the island of their birth to the mainland, they should not treat her as if she were dead. On the other hand she means that her spirit will always be connected to the land she

claims as her home and theirs. She associates the "old souls," or ancestors, with the land and cosmological elements. The afterlife for her is not
in some far-off place. Spirit is entwined with dust. Dust is a metaphor
for the earth and the entire cosmos, with the many elements that sustain
it. For Nana Peazant heaven is on earth; it is in the very dust she has
depended on for planting and sustenance. It is not separate from the cosmos or present, concrete daily life. Whereas Western Christians appeal
to "the bread of life" and Asian Christians appeal to "the rice of life,"
one might say that Nana Peazant appeals to "the dust of life." Dust is
a metaphor for that which is the sustaining source of life and the most
basic resource for survival.

I remember that after my grandmother died I would sometimes dream
of her bones mingling with the dust, returning to dust, in such a way
that she was one with it. I had ambivalent feelings about this dream because, in my heart of hearts, I tended to separate my understanding of
heaven and earth at that time even if I agreed intellectually with my pa-
ternal grandfather's assessment that "heaven and hell are right here on
this earth." While I had developed an understanding of what such a concept meant for a moral life and Christian social justice, I had not resolved
intellectually or spiritually what it might mean for existence beyond our
present lives. Perhaps this was because of a long background in Christian teachings that understood Jesus as promising heaven and "the Old
Testament" promising a return to dust, Sheol at best. Churches tend to
teach that the Christian promise is superior and somehow separate from
ancient Hebrew understandings. Yet, the concept of "heaven and hell on
earth" seemed more true to me, seemed in accordance with the Lord's
Prayer and its request that God's will be done on earth as in heaven, and
needed fleshing out. How do we make meaning of the saying "heaven
and hell are on earth" in the face of the reality of death, which is inevitable for all people? While it is well and good to focus on living this
life according to life-affirming moral principles in our daily lives with
the expectation that it is what we do in the here and now that determines whatever peace we may experience with God and the universe at
the time of death, what does one make of "heaven" and "hell" in relation
to "afterlife"?

Several years later when I experienced another personal loss, I felt
drawn to a lake for some quiet time and meditation. There are moments
in one's life where one may experience the meaning of life and death very
keenly in a new way. Religious experience sometimes involves a new insight. It may be a shaking of the foundations in which one experiences
conversion and changes one's lifestyle from self-destructive patterns to

life-affirming patterns. Or it may involve an insight that brings peace and a sense of wonder about the magnificence of the empowering, loving nature of God. I have had a few moments where I have experienced insights that give new religious meaning to my understanding of life. This particular moment of insight involved a deepening of faith. I felt a sense of union with God and the universe (in some limited sense) that resolved my ambivalences about life and death enough to give me great peace and comfort. In my journal, I described the experience thusly:

> *I am at a lake. This body of water could be any body of water in the world. It reflects the sky when you look at it from above. It looks clear with brown sandy earth, grey-black rocks, and white pebbles and shells underneath when you wade into it from the shore. When you walk in this water, the sandy soil flies up into the water the way sand and soil fly up into the water just about everywhere....The lake conceals and reveals at the same time, never showing all of itself, but always showing its beauty. I believe the lake reflects the beauty of the ancestors, of the past, the present, and the future. I am remembering my Indian and African ancestors — the dispossessed — at this place. Here, I not only know intellectually, but I feel[17] that my ancestors were in harmony with nature. They did not fight nature. Nor did they try to own it. They loved it. And more than that they respected it — the land, the water, the trees, the fowl, all of creation....All that lives and breathes and has being belongs to God. The land, the water, the sky, the trees, are part of one Great Spirit. Coming to a place like this, and seeing so very, very few Brown or Red people, I long for the people of the land. The European style homes that border the lake's circumference in parceled pieces of land stand out awkwardly as symbols of past conquests. I long for the people who have been raped from this land to return. I sense something of their spirits, alive, singing, blowing, crying, wailing... in the rush and blow of the wind, in the rippling laps of the water, in the loud whispering of the trees, and the calls of the ducks, the cries of the gulls.*
>
> *I believe that no one or nothing that has lived ever truly dies. The ancestors have survived in their descendants in remnants or multitudes. But they also survive in the wind, the trees, the birds, creation itself even in the midst of death. We all belong to one Spirit. Those who oppress long for this belonging, but ownership does not permit belonging....If we are one with Creativity itself, if we choose not to oppress, then the waters, the land, the cosmos, and our fellow creatures will teach us about belonging. The belonging is to those who choose to be as one with Life*

itself. And if we give up the notion of owning some piece of creation that is outside the sphere of our own bodies and minds, we may belong.

The heart of my experience was that I came to a new understanding of "heaven" and "earth." I moved beyond traditional dualistic Western categories of heaven as one place and earth another. In a new experience and expression of my faith I came to truly believe that earth belongs to God who is Spirit and that they are within each other. To return to the dust, to the waters, the winds is also to return to Spirit because Spirit is present in Life. We humans belong to heaven and earth. Spirit and the land do not belong to us. We belong to them. They are our Mothers, our Fathers, the source of our humanness, spirit and body. Over time, as I became introduced to Julie Dash's film and screenplay *Daughters of the Dust* I applied the insights from my lake experience to my queries about Nana Peazant's claim that she would not be in heaven as long as there was dust for planting. Is such a claim antithetical to Christian doctrine? Aren't we supposed to desire union with Spirit rather than earth? Is it idolatrous to seek such union with earth?

Christian womanists, rather than envision heaven and earth as op- positional realities, might reenvision them as within each other. While Nana Peazant eschews a Western notion of heaven as some otherworldly, transcendent, abstracted reality, she does not eschew the notion of an af- terlife or the world of the Spirit. Whereas Nana Peazant uses "dust" as a metaphor for the interrelationship of spiritual and material worlds, Chris- tian womanists might redefine "dust" and "heaven." As African American women and men have done historically, a Christian womanist perspective speaks of the interrelationship of heaven and earth. The word "heaven" is not exclusive of our bodiliness, just as the word "dust" is not exclusive of spirit. God as Spirit embraces body and spirit. "Heaven" is not antitheti- cal to "dust." Neither is "dust" antithetical to "heaven." Heaven is but the realization of the Reign of God as empowering Spirit in all aspects of life, concrete and spiritual. The Reign of God as empowering Spirit re- veals itself in history, in human experience, to people and other creatures with bodies. The Reign of God as Spirit is revealed to embodied spirits. The spirits of the ancestors, those old souls, saints if you will, who have gone on before, leave their marks in our memories and concrete lives.

Heaven is not separate from earth, because heaven is within God and there is no place where God is not present, although we humans are not always present to God in our actions, desires, and attitudes. Because God is always present, there is hope in the universe even in the dreariest, gloomiest, most imprisoning hours of life. There is, as Lucie Campbell wrote, "something within" that cannot be explained. This "something within," as she called it, or "singing something," as Anna Cooper called it, cannot be squelched. It rises up like a flame that cannot be put out to give energy for survival and resistance against evil. This "something within" is Spirit touching human spirit. While evil may inflict itself on peoples in horrendous ways, Spirit in the human heart has the capacity to resurrect us back to life in the midst of physical and psychic death.

We may have many names for God. We may not always agree on who God is or how to describe God. Indeed, what an ambitious task it is to name the unnameable. For this reason, in the Hebrew tradition God is simply called *Ha Shem*, which means "The Name." This name is a name above, beneath, beyond, and within all the great names we can conceive of for God — the very source of our lives and of our power to name. What we know best about this unnameable, unseen God are the ways in which God has functioned, acted, and moved, in our various communities, histories, and individual lives. God as Spirit is the Strength of Life who is the source of courage, power, and salvation. This God has functioned both as a God of survival and of liberation for Black Americans historically. The calling of the people of God, who are a community in communion with Spirit, is to more perfectly embody empowering, liberating, sustaining Spirit to give new life to one another and all of creation.

We are called into the apocalyptic vision of New Creation, a moment-by-moment, day-by-day, generation-by-generation process of earthly and spiritual renewal. The creation of a new heaven and a new earth requires that the people of God, who is Spirit, more fully embody Spirit, which is found in the dust of the earth as well as in the invisible breath of life that is the Gift of Spirit to all of creation. To love Spirit we must, then, more fully love one another and the environment that sustains us physically. This is not an otherworldly, abstract, self-indulgent activity of spiritual self-gratification, which seems to be the goal of certain popular forms of creation-centered mysticism. But rather it involves putting our hands both in the generating dust of the earth that produces food and in the dust that threatens to bury the poor, the hungry, the homeless, the ill, the dying, the mourning, and the weeping, a dust which needs to be removed. By the Spirit, we are called to realize the apocalyptic vision of a new heaven and a new earth by being wise stewards of body, dust, and spirit, employing each in the task of healing and wholeness. The creation of a new heaven and a new earth need not be a violent, destructive, fiery event. If enough people choose to act in harmony with God as Spirit who loves its creation, the creation of a new heaven and a new earth can be a

gradual, life-affirming, reviving, and replenishing process in which God's
original intention for the freedom to live abundantly and for the equality
of the well-being of all is fulfilled.

Notes

1. See Emilie Townes, "Living in the New Jerusalem," in *A Troubling in My Soul*
(Maryknoll, N.Y.: Orbis Books, 1993), 89 and *In a Blaze of Glory.*

2. See Walter Rauschenbusch, *A Theology for the Social Gospel* (New York:
Macmillan, 1917; New York: Abingdon, 1981).

3. Ronald White, *Liberty and Justice for All* (San Francisco: Harper & Row,
1990), xvi–xxiv, 107–13, 118–19, 136–40. The entire text examines Black social gospel leadership and its extended influence in the twentieth century, as evident in the
life of Martin Luther King, Jr. The weakness of the volume is that while it men-
tions women like Ida B. Wells-Barnett, it does not provide very extensive discussion
of her role or the roles of numerous other church women and members of the Black
Women's Club period who played a vital role in addressing sexism *and* racism as social gospel concerns. Yet the book is important in its examination of the social gospel
movement as cross-racial.

4. James Washington, lecture, Harvard University, September–October 1994.

5. Alice Walker, *In Search of Our Mothers' Gardens* (New York: Harcourt Brace
Jovanovich, 1983), xi–xii.

6. "The Answer," Anna Julia Cooper Papers, Box 23–4, courtesy of the
Moorland-Spingarn Research Center, Howard University, Washington, D.C.

7. Anna Julia Cooper, "The Gain from a Belief," in *A Voice from the South*, ed.
Mary Helen Washington, Schomburg Library of Nineteenth-Century Black Women
Writers (1892; reprint, New York: Oxford University Press, 1988), 303.

8. Alice Walker, *The Color Purple* (New York: Harcourt Brace Jovanovich,
1982), 39.

9. See Marcia Riggs, *Arise, Awake, Act: A Womanist Call for Black Liberation*
(Cleveland: Pilgrim Press, 1994), for a discussion of this important motto of the
Black Women's Club movement in America, which serves as the title for her book.

10. Anna Cooper, "The Gain from a Belief," 298.

11. Cooper, "Womanhood a Vital Element in the Regeneration and Progress of a
Race," in *A Voice from the South*, 17–28.

12. Ibid.

13. Karen Baker-Fletcher, *A Singing Something: Womanist Reflections on Anna Julia
Cooper* (New York: Crossroad, 1994), 68–97.

14. Julie Dash, *Daughters of the Dust: The Making of an African American Woman's
Film* (New York: The New Press, 1992), 94–96.

15. Ibid., 97.

16. Ibid., 159.

17. I do not use "feel" here in Rousseau's romantic sense of feeling as a form of
reason. Rather, I have in mind William James's pragmatic and psychological understanding of feeling as a form of reason. For James, we later rationally explicate what
we have already intuitively come to know. I am also influenced by the women's tradition of intuition as a form of knowing, as well as by traditional African concepts of
connectedness to the cosmos and the ancestors.

Eighteen

The "Shout"

AT THE END of a traditional African American sermon there is a call of the SPIRIT which spirals ever higher toward the glory of GOD. This utterance is affectionately known as "the Shout!" Although sometimes it is nothing more than a stylized cultural artifice, a rousing peroration tacked on to the end of a homily meant to signify closure, theologically it is much more. The Shout arises at the intersection of human intentionality and divine creativity. It is the coming together of human words with the divine Nommo, the infusing of Logos-power into the fragile container of human language. When it is genuinely SPIRIT-infused there is a sense of electricity that suffuses the air, a magic and a mystery that is at once indescribable and unforgettable. For us, after much prayer and hard work, it seems fitting to honor our sermonic ancestors in this theological-ethical exercise by ending with a "Shout!"

The Shout is more than the work of the Spirit in the Preacher, who is still usually male — although sometimes female as the Spirit opens hearts and minds to receive leaders in both genders. The Shout is also the work of the Spirit in the hearts of the entire congregation. The Shout is a communal act and event. It is a raising of many different voices in call and response. The Spirit calls to all. Each voice calls to the Spirit and to one another. Each voice responds. The call begins again in a deepening echo, with new, deeper responses. A womanist Shout moves a diversity of people, as good sister and scholar Emilie Townes reminds us, to participate in more of a ring Shout than a sermonic Shout. In the ring Shout each voice has a different story to tell, a different testimony to Shout About. The Shout is *not* just sermonic, an individual act. It is *a communal event of praise and healing, where soul shares with soul God's empowering presence in the lives of the community.* If one person is simply watching another "go off," there is no possibility for communal change. Only if there is agreement on the movement of the Spirit to change and revive hearts, minds, and hands to renew commitments to work that brings wholeness for the *entire* community is the Shout full and authentic. In the best of Shouts, folk renew commitments to work for communal wholeness, for

299

men *and* women, young *and* old, adult *and* child. In the best of shouts, as folk renew commitments to the empowering, healing movement of Spirit, the calls and responses crescendo higher, as high as hearts can soar that day. As souls receive peace about the right things to do and the right ways to be, there comes a deeper listening to the Spirit.

In the end there is Silence. But Silence is Alive with the rhythms and pulses of the SPIRIT who Is and Was and ever Shall Be.

In the end there is GOD, standing with us, caring, uplifting us. GOD is a Shadow and Light, a Shield against the churning conflicts, a Rock that can always withstand the ebb and flow of tidal woes and bliss, the Wings of the Power that is Life.

In the end we have GOD.
In the end we have each other.
There is peace, and we are many-and-one.
In the end we have each other. And love will grow ... *regardless.*
There is a stillness of knowing that surpasses our utterances.
There is a rhythm of the heart that surpasses our dances.
And we know that we are known by the One who IS, WAS, and
    EVER SHALL BE.
We know that we are called to love by the One who dances within
    hearts, earth, rivers, trees.
Our words are for You.
Our hearts are inclined to You.
Our music is the sound of Your resonance echoing.
Face to face we look upward, outward, inward.
We have "come this far by faith, leaning on the Lord."
And still we cry out
with the prophet Habakkuk, "How long, Oh Lord?"
How long? Not very long. For there is a rising Hand that lifts our
    vision beyond these words and ideas.
How long? Not very long. For there is "sweet, sweet Spirit in this
    place, and I know that it's the Spirit of the Lord."
How long? Not too long. For there is a shining in this glory which
    is and was and ever shall be GOD.

KAREN & KASIMU

Index

African American Religious Studies, 43
African religiosity: and ancestors, 44,
    45–46, 84, 90–91, 101–2, 204,
    212–13, 287, 292–93; and blood
    sacrifices, 101; and creation, 86; and
    dust, 170; and eschatology, 287, 291,
    292; and modes of worship, 262; and
    Spirit, 137, 230, 287; and XODUS
    perspectives on God, 43–46. *See also*
    Ma'at
Agape: Martin Luther King, Jr. on,
    52–53; and XODUS theology, 58,
    241–42, 259
Ancestors: and African religiosity, 44,
    45–46, 84, 90–91, 101–2, 204, 212–
    13, 287, 292–93; and Jesus, 89–92;
    and rememory, 155–56; womanist
    perspectives on, 179–81, 186–91,
    216, 219–22, 286, 295–96; XODUS
    perspectives on, 212–14
Anger in XODUS theology, 105
Ankh, 105–6
Anthropology, XODUS, 119–41
Anti-Semitism, 98–99, 167, 255
Aquinas, Thomas, 124, 206
Arise, Awake, Act: A Womanist Call for
    Black Liberation (Riggs), 144–45
Aristotle, 205–6
Arrested Development, 55, 228
Asante, Molefi Kete, 20–21n15
Atonement theory: and African Amer-
    ican churches, 101; blood imagery
    in, 111; and womanism, 75–77; and
    XODUS theology, 102
Augustine, Saint: *The City of God*, 252;
    Confessions, 86, 124; on creation, 263;
    on Spirit, 254
Awakening in XODUS theology,
    128–31

BABAhood, 195–204
Baldwin, James, 287, 291

Beloved (Morrison), 89, 90–91, 155–56,
    163n20, 184
Black Belief (Mitchell), 43
Black-on-Black Violence: The Psycho-
    dynamics of Black Self-Annihilation in
    Service of White Domination (Wilson),
    126–27
Black Theology and Black Power (Cone),
    272
Black Women's Health Book, The, 145,
    146, 165
Blood: in African American Christology,
    100–103; in womanist theology, 111;
    in XODUS theology, 101–2, 104,
    110–11, 260
Book of Khun-Anup, The 207
Brothers and Sisters (Campbell), 139
Brown Douglas, Kelly: on Jesus, 74,
    81–82; and sexual preference, 259;
    on survival, 156, 159; and XODUS
    creativity, 9
Burroughs, Nannie Helen, 154, 159

Campbell, Bebe Moore, 139
Campbell, Lucie, 26, 296–97
Cannon, Katie Geneva: on feminist
    texts, 195; and iconoclastic method-
    ology, 18–19; on survival, 156, 157,
    159; on womanist ethics, 3; and
    XODUS creativity, 9
Childbearing, 173–75, 180, 212
Christ. *See* Jesus
Christ and Culture (Niebuhr), 16
Chuck D, 54–55
Churches, African American: adulthood
    initiation programs in, 174–75; anti-
    Semitism in, 98–99; and environmen-
    talism, 14; imaging God in, 47–49;
    male movement in, 196–97, 199–203,
    209; Spirit in, 12, 33–34, 225–42,
    244–47, 253–56, 258, 261, 299–300;
    and womanism, 243–57, 258–65;

Churches, African American (*continued*): and women's oppression, 74–77, 247–51; women's role in, 154, 196; and XODUS theology, 11–12, 57, 129, 201, 203, 225–42, 258–65, 272–73

City of God, The (Augustine), 252

Classism: and superwoman myth, 144; and womanism, 5–7, 158, 160, 161; and XODUS theology, 8

Cleage, Albert, 96, 288

Coleman, Will, 8, 15, 130

Collins, Patricia Hill: on mothering, 176, 177, 181; and stereotypes of African American women, 143; and XODUS creativity, 9

Color Purple, The (Walker), 37, 193–94: concept of God in, 28, 37, 39, 74, 85, 93n, 243; concept of Jesus in, 73; media depictions of, 1–2, 164, 192, 218; portrayal of men in, 193–94; salvation in, 287, 289, 291–92

Community, African American: extended families in, 177–78, 211–12; gender roles in, 2, 161; resistance to, 138–41; and self-destructive behavior, 127; sin in, 125–26; symbols of, 84; women's building of, 153–54, 182; and XODUS theology, 203–4, 210–11, 225–42

Cone, James: and A.M.E. Church, 288; and Black Christianity, 96, 167; on Black churches, 231–33; eschatology of, 272–74, 284, 287, 288, 291; *For My People*, 130; on God, 56; and Jacquelyn Grant, 25; and racial justice, 8; *Martin & Malcolm & America*, 9; *The Spirituals and the Blues*, 235; symbol theory of, 81

Confessions (St. Augustine), 86, 124

Conjuring Culture (Smith), 107

Cooper, Anna Julia: on community building, 153; eschatology of, 287–91; "The Gain from a Belief," 18; on human embodiment of God, 27, 151, 154, 158, 297; on Jesus, 82–83, 94, 253–54, 290–91; resistance of, 157, 159; and social gospel theology, 285, 287; *A Voice from the South*, 82, 140, 160; on women's liberation, 200–201

Cooper, J. California, 177, 179

Cooper-Lewter, Nicholas, 43, 56

Corporal punishment, 185–86

Cosby, Bill, 192, 214n1

Creation: and womanism, 85–89, 263; and XODUS theology, 99–106, 120

Criminalization. *See* Imprisonment of African Americans

Cross: as symbol, 78–80; in XODUS theology, 79, 104–6. *See also* Atonement theory

Crucifixion: womanist perspectives on, 77–80, 82; XODUS perspectives on, 100–101, 104

Cummings, George, 8, 130, 131

Cut Loose Your Stammering Tongue (Hopkins), 235

Daly, Mary, 39, 197, 221

Dash, Julie: *Daughters of the Dust*, 25, 87, 89–90, 180, 292, 296

Daughters of the Dust: ancestors in, 89–90, 180, 292–94; and dust metaphor, 87; naming God in, 25; view of heaven in, 293–94, 296

Davis, Kortright, 89, 105

Death: African perspectives on, 44–45; dust as metaphor for, 169–70; womanist perspectives on, 67, 294–96; XODUS perspectives on, 110–11

Deontology, 62n12

Dialogical ethics, 15–16

Diop, Cheikh Anta, 142n27

Disabled people, 50–51

Disciples of Christ (Rap music group), 227–28

Diunital thinking, 16–18, 78

Douglass, Frederick, 158, 226, 288

DRS (Dirty Rotten Scoundrels), 55

Du Bois, W. E. B.: Christ imagery of, 78; on intellectual freedom, 158; modes of resistance used by, 138–39; and social gospel theology, 285; *The Souls of Black Folk*, 98; on spiritual striving, 184

Dust: as death metaphor, 169–70; and eschatology, 292–98; Jesus as, 86–87, 91, 113–14

Ebonics, 15

Ecology. *See* Environmentalism

Elaw, Zilpha, 30, 149, 151

Elders, Joycelyn, 1, 153

Emancipation Still Comin' (Kortright), 105

Empower the People (Walker), 11

Environmental racism: and womanism, 5–7, 83–84, 114, 151–52, 154, 158, 160, 161, 179–80, 284; and XODUS theology, 230–31

Environmentalism: and God, 39–40; and Jesus, 88–89, 99–100; and XODUS theology, 13–14, 99–100, 135–37, 141, 204, 230, 278–79, 281–82

Eschatology: womanist, 283–98; XODUS, 269–82

Ethic of risk, 79–80

Evans, James H., Jr.: on apostolicity, 238, 239; on black humanity, 119–20; on church mission, 236; on eschatology, 279–80; on liberation, 229; on spiritual essence of God, 93n16

"Everything Is a Human Being" (Walker), 85

Family (J. C. Cooper), 179

Family values and XODUS theology, 11, 278

Farajaje-Jones, Elias, 8–9

Fatherhood (Cosby), 192

Fatherhood and XODUS theology, 192–214, 218. *See also* Mothering

for colored girls who have considered suicide when the rainbow is enuf (Shange), 25–27, 66

For My People (Cone), 130

"Gain from a Belief, The" (Cooper), 18

Gangs: and martyr norms, 103; and Rap music, 228; and XODUS theology, 120

Generationalism: and womanism, 173–91, 216–22, 251–52; and XODUS theology, 179, 183, 192–214, 216–22, 225. *See also* Ancestors

Gifts of power, womanist perspectives on, 149–61, 205, 206

Gilkes, Cheryl Townsend, 9, 146

God: classical concept of, 148–49; mothering image of, 174; naming of, 27–28, 35, 37–38, 46–49, 65–66, 152, 297; as Spirit, 25–40, 66–67, 74–75, 77, 82, 87, 160, 161, 189, 250, 253, 292, 296–97; systematic theology of, 2; Western concept of, 58–60; womanist perspectives on, 5, 25–40, 64–69, 115–16, 148–50, 155, 189, 220–21, 243–44, 286, 296–97; XODUS perspectives on, 43–62, 64–69, 95, 132, 271, 274–76

Go Tell It on the Mountain (Baldwin), 287

Grant, Jacquelyn: and Black male liberation theologians, 284; and community building, 153; on God, 25, 36, 159; on Jesus, 74, 75–76, 81, 83, 100; on survival, 156; womanist Christology of, 18, 79, 81; and XODUS creativity, 9

Grimké, Francis, 285, 288

Gyn/Ecology (Daly), 197

Hall-Wynn, Prathia, 248

Hamer, Fannie Lou: and concepts of God, 158, 288; as embodiment of Christ, 82; rebellious posture of, 139, 157; regenerative work of, 154

Health of African Americans: and environmental racism, 180; womanist perspectives on, 145–48, 164–66, 250–51, 253; XODUS perspectives on, 165–66, 226

Her Blue Body Everything We Know (Walker), 85

Heterosexism: and womanism, 5–7, 161; and XODUS theology, 8

High John, 140–41

Hill, Renee, 9, 259

Holiness, Womanist perspectives on, 262–63

Homosexuals: and African American churches, 238, 239–40, 259–60; hostility toward, 6–7 hooks, bell: and Kemetic philosophy, 142n; on mothering, 176; *Sisters of the Yam*, 185; and stereotypes of African American women, 143; and XODUS creativity, 9

Hoover, Theressa, 153, 182

Hope: in womanist eschatology, 286, 291; in XODUS eschatology, 270–71, 273–74, 278, 280–82

Hopkins, Dwight: on Black theology, 235; inclusiveness of, 8, 284; on liberating experiences for African Americans, 56, 130–31; on Martin Luther King, Jr. and Malcolm X, 9–10

Humanity: African concepts of, 137; womanist perspectives on, 143–61, 164–70; XODUS perspectives on, 119–41, 164–70

Hurston, Zora Neale, 145, 157, 249

I Asked for Intimacy (Weems), 146

Iconoclasm in XODUS and womanist theology, 18–19, 37

Idowu, E. Bolaji, 45

Immanuel. *See* Jesus

Imprisonment of African Americans: and male movement, 196; and XODUS theology, 119, 121–29, 226

In a Blaze of Glory (Townes), 145–46, 230–31, 264, 284

In Search of Our Mothers' Gardens (Walker), 4–5, 195, 286

Inductive logic, 16

Interracial marriage, 187, 216, 217, 218

Islam: and Rap music, 54–55, 228; and XODUS theology, 168

Jackson, Rebecca Cox, 74, 149, 152, 157

James, George C. M., 142n27

Jesus: and African American Christology, 94–97, 106–7; as dust, 86–87, 91, 113–14; and Godly love, 51–52; mothering image of, 174; as spirit, 31, 80, 83, 87, 114; womanist perspectives on, 73–92, 110–16, 252–57, 264, 265; XODUS perspectives on, 94–108, 110–16, 129, 229, 237, 261, 270, 274–75

Jews: as African peoples, 97–98; J. Deotis Roberts on, 233–34; and XODUS theology, 168

John Henry, 139–40

Jones, Arthur C., 130, 131

Kairos Document, 277

Karenga, Maulana: on African religiosity, 43–45, 62; and *The Book of Khun-Anup*, 207

Karenga, Ron Maulana: and *Kwanzaa*, 129–30

Kaufman, Gordon, 15, 119

Kemet. *See* Ma'at

King, Martin Luther, Jr.: on Agape, 52–53; and concepts of God, 158, 288; and ethic of risk, 79–80; and Kairos, 277; on law, 133; martyrdom of, 103; and Promised Land, 126; rebellious posture of, 139; view of Jesus, 94; and XODUS theology, 9–10, 167, 217, 226

Kuse, W., 45–46

Kwanzaa, 129–30, 188

LA J, 227–28

Language and XODUS theology, 14–15

Law in XODUS theology, 133–34

Lee, Jarena, 149, 151, 238, 255

Lerner, Michael, 98

Lesbians. *See* Homosexuals

Liberation and Reconciliation (Roberts), 234, 272

Liberation theology: and eschatology, 284, 287; and God, 56; and Jesus, 81; and womanism, 84, 88, 249; and XODUS ethics, 10, 131–41, 166–67, 229, 231–33

Living by the Word (Walker), 85, 186, 188

Long, Charles, 61

Los Angeles, riot in, 7–8, 17, 277

Luther, Martin, 124, 240

Lynching and Christ imagery, 78, 80

Ma'at and XODUS theology, 133–35, 166–70, 206–10, 214

Malcolm X: on African American imprisonment, 121–23, 128–29;

rebellious posture of, 139; and X symbolism, 104–5; and XODUS theology, 9–10, 167–68, 217, 226

Martin & Malcolm & America (Cone), 9

Martyr norms, 103, 110

Mary in womanist theology, 82, 111

McClendon, Howard, 232–33

Media: African American stereotypes in, 1–2, 164, 192, 218; and 1992 Los Angeles riot, 8

Meridian (Walker), 188

Millenniums and apocalyptic eschatology, 269–70

Million Man March (1995), 178, 209

Mitchell, Henry, 43, 56

Moral philosophy: and imaging God, 67–69; and XODUS theology, 56–61

Morrison, Toni: on ancestors, 89, 90–91, 155–56; on community building, 153–54; on mothering, 176–77, 181–85

Mothering, womanist perspectives on, 173–80, 220

Native Americans: as African American ancestors, 186–91, 216, 219–20, 295; cosmologies of, 86; eschatology of, 287

Niebuhr, H. Richard: on Christ and culture, 16, 265

Niebuhr, Reinhold: on Agape, 53; on humanity, 132, 253

Ogbannaya, A. Okechukwu, 31, 34, 60

Oswald, Martin, 205

Pan-Africanism: James Cone on, 232; and environmentalism, 14; and psychospiritual character building, 19–20; and XODUS theology, 12–13, 129, 132, 141, 195, 204–5, 229, 235, 241, 277

Parenting. *See* Fatherhood; Mothering

Paris (Rap musician), 54–55, 228

Patriarchy: and African American women, 2, 74, 125, 248; and XODUS

theology, 61, 64–65, 125–26, 195, 199–200, 212, 218, 219, 237, 275

Peazant, Nana. *See Daughters of the Dust*

Possessing the Secret of Joy (Walker), 73–74, 76, 78, 91

Power. *See* Gifts of power

Prisons. *See* Imprisonment of African Americans

Process theology, 92, 149, 161n3, 292

Prophethood of Black Believers, The (Roberts), 233, 234

Public Enemy, 54

Pure Lust (Daly), 197

Queen Latifah, 222

Racism: and God's embodiment in Jesus, 96–97; and superwoman myth, 144–45; and womanism, 5–7, 158, 160, 255; and XODUS theology, 120, 125, 218

Rap music: church criticism in, 227–29, 262; God in, 54–56; lexicon of, 222; nihilism of, 210, 261; and XODUS theology, 167

Rauschenbusch, Walter, 125, 285

Reversal in XODUS eschatology, 274–76

Resistance: as gift of power, 157–61; praying as, 179; in XODUS theology, 130–31, 138–41

Resurrection: and African American Christology, 94–95; womanist perspectives on, 77–80; XODUS perspectives on, 105, 111

Riggs, Marcia, 144–45

Roberts, J. Deotis: on Black churches, 233–35; inclusiveness of, 284; and racial justice, 8; on realized eschatology, 272, 274, 287; *Roots of a Black Future: Family and Church*, 11

Roots of a Black Future: Family and Church (Roberts), 11

Ruether, Rosemary, 87–88

Rukungah, Peter, 137, 154, 161n3

Sambo, 138–39

Sanders, Cheryl, 9, 153

Setiloane, Gabriel, 45–46, 204

Sexism: Jacquelyn Grant on, 81; and parenting, 176; and Rap music, 222; and superwoman myth, 144; and womanism, 5–7, 158, 160, 161, 255; and XODUS theology, 8, 120–21, 124–25, 129

Shange, Ntozake, 25–27, 66

Shoes That Fit Our Feet (Hopkins), 235

Sin: in African American communities, 125–26; theologic definitions of, 124–25; in XODUS theology, 124–26

A Singing Something (Karen Baker-Fletcher), 164, 205

Sister Souljah, 54–55

Sisters in the Wilderness (Williams), 102–3, 152, 248

Sisters of the Yam (hooks), 185

Sixth Sense, 213, 215n

Smith, Theophus, 16, 107

Soul Theology (Mitchell and Cooper-Lewter), 43, 56

Souls of Black Folk, The (Du Bois), 98

Speech (Rap musician), 55–56, 228

Spielberg, Steven, 193–94

Spirit: and African American churches, 12, 33–34, 225–42, 244–47, 253–56, 258, 261, 299–300; and African religiosity, 137, 230, 287; and ecology, 13–14; as embodied in African American women, 82–83, 84, 174; and eschatology, 292–98; God as, 25–40, 66–67, 74–75, 77, 82, 87, 160, 161, 189, 250, 253, 292, 296–97; and humanity, 134; Jesus as, 31, 80, 83, 87, 114; and reason, 92; womanist perspectives on, 25–40, 66–67, 74–75, 77, 82, 86–87, 160, 161, 189, 250, 253, 292, 296–99; womb of, 180–81

Spirituals and the Blues, The (Cone), 235

Stereotypes of African Americans: and black humanity, 119–20, 143–48, 164–65; and Stewart, Maria, 151, 153

Subjection, 202–3, 219

Suchocki, Marjorie, 92, 125, 292

Superman, myth of, 164–65, 199

Superwoman, myth of, 143–48, 161, 164–65, 199, 249

Tar Baby (Morrison), 153–54, 181–83, 185

Their Eyes Were Watching God (Hurston), 249

A Theology for the Social Gospel (Rauschenbusch), 285

Thomas, Clarence, 1, 277–78

Thurman, Howard, 94, 167

Tillich, Paul: on church and culture, 256, 264, 265; on God, 38–39; on Kairos, 277; on sacred symbols, 220

Tough Love, 50–51, 65

Townes, Emilie: on Black churches, 246–47; on confrontation, 153, 159; *In a Blaze of Glory*, 145–46, 230–31, 264, 284; on mothering, 176; on womanist spirituality, 34–35; on women's voices, 151, 162n8, 299

Trinity, 60–61

Truth, Sojourner: and African American birthright, 226; courage of, 286; as embodiment of Jesus, 82, 91; eschatology of, 288; on God, 30, 31–32; on Jesus, 77, 94; rebellious posture of, 139, 157, 159

Tubman, Harriet: and African American birthright, 226; and concepts of God, 158; courage of, 286; as embodiment of Jesus, 82, 91; and Jesus, 94; resistance of, 74, 157

Turner, Nat, 91, 139, 158

Virtue: Aristotle on, 205–6; and XODUS theology, 205–11

Vitalism, 137

Voice from the South, A (A. J. Cooper), 82, 140, 160

Walker, Alice: and ancestors, 186–88; and ecological issues, 158; and eschatology, 287, 289, 291–92; on God, 27, 28, 32, 37, 39, 243; on Jesus, 73–74, 76; on mothering, 177, 181, 249–50; portrayals of men by, 193–94; and Spirit, 33, 85–86,

93n16; on womanism, 3–5, 29, 85, 146, 154, 166, 181, 190, 195, 222, 228–29, 259, 286

Walker, Theodore, 9, 11

Wedding, The (West), 187

Weems, Renita, 146, 177, 183–85

We Have Been Believers (Evans), 119–20

Welch, Sharon, 80

Wells-Barnett, Ida B.: and community building, 153, 154; and concepts of God, 151, 158; resistance of, 157, 159; and social gospel theology, 285

West, Cornel: and George Cummings, 130; father of, 209; inclusiveness of, 9; and Jewish community, 98; and Kemetic philosophy, 142n27

West, Dorothy, 187

White, Evelyn, 145, 146, 165

Wickedary (Daly), 221

Williams, Delores: on atonement theory, 101, 102–3; on Black churches, 241, 248, 259; and Christian womanism, 4; and community building, 153; on God, 25, 31, 152; on Jesus, 74–78, 104; on mothering, 176; on Spirit, 33–34, 82, 245; on survival, 152, 156–58, 159; and XODUS creativity, 9

Wilmore, Gayraud, 8, 56

Wilson, Amos N., 126–27

Womanism: and ancestors, 179–81, 186–91, 216, 219–22, 286, 295–96; and church, 243–57, 258–65; definition of, 3–7, 152–53; and diunital reasoning, 17–18, 78; and environmental racism, 5–7, 83–84, 114, 151–52, 154, 158, 160, 161, 179–80, 284; and eschatology, 283–98; generational aspects of, 173–91, 216–22, 251–52; and God, 5, 25–40, 64–69, 115–16, 148–50, 155, 189, 220–21, 243–44, 286, 296–97; and health of African Americans, 145–48, 164–66, 250–51, 253; and humanity, 143–61, 164–70;

iconoclasm in, 18–19, 37; and Jesus, 73–92, 110–16, 252–57, 264, 265; social-historical context for, 19–20, 32–33; Alice Walker on, 3–5, 29, 146, 154, 166, 181, 190, 195, 222, 228–29, 259, 286

Women, African American: embodiment of Jesus in, 82–83, 84, 100, 112–13, 291; gifts of power of, 149–59; health of, 145–48, 250; and new lexicons, 222; ordination of, 239, 248–49, 299; perceived community role of, 2; and superwoman myth, 143–48, 161, 164–65, 199, 249

XODUS theology: and African American churches, 11–12, 57, 129, 201, 203, 225–42, 258–65, 272–73; and African American communities, 203–4, 210–11, 225–42; blood in, 101–2, 104, 110–11, 260; and combining theology and ethics, 3; definition of, 7–15, 16, 236; and diunital reasoning, 17–18; and environmentalism, 13–14, 99–100, 135–37, 141, 204, 230, 278–79, 281–82; and eschatology, 269–82; generational aspects of, 179, 183, 192–214, 216–22, 225; on God, 43–62, 64–69, 95, 132, 271, 274–76; and health of African Americans, 165–66, 226; on humanity, 119–41, 164–70; iconoclasm in, 18–19; on Jesus, 94–108, 110–16, 129, 229, 237, 261, 270, 274–75; and pan-Africanism, 12–13, 129, 132, 141, 195, 204–5, 229, 235, 241, 277; on patriarchy, 61, 64–65, 125–26, 195, 199–200, 212, 218, 219, 237, 275; social-historical context for, 19–20

XODUS: An African American Male Journey (KASIMU Baker-Fletcher), 10, 104, 216, 262

Young, Josiah, 8, 12, 89